"Beer, it's the best damn drink in the world."

JACK NICHOLSON
AMERICAN ACTOR, WRITER,
FILM DIRECTOR 1937–

WORLD'S BEST BEERS

**One Thousand Craft Brews
from Cask to Glass**

Ben McFarland

STERLING INNOVATION
An imprint of Sterling Publishing Co., Inc.

New York / London
www.sterlingpublishing.com

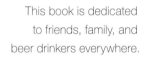
This book is dedicated
to friends, family, and
beer drinkers everywhere.

10 9 8 7 6 5 4 3 2 1

Published by Sterling Publishing Co., Inc.

387 Park Avenue South,
New York, NY 10016

Distributed in Canada
by Sterlling Publishing
c/o Canadian Manda Group,
165 Dufferin Street, Toronto,
Ontario, Canada M6K 3H6

Printed in Singapore

Sterling ISBN 978-1-4027-6694-7

First published in the UK in 2009
by Jacqui Small LLP,
an imprint of Aurum Press

Publisher Jacqui Small

Editorial Direction Joanna Copestick

Managing Editor Lesley Felce

Designer and Art Director Robin Rout

Picture Research Catherine Ball
Mona Mahmoud Melissa Smith

Production Peter Colley

For information about custom editions,
special sales, premium and corporate
purchases, please contact
Sterling Special Sales Department
at 800-805-5489 or
specialsales@sterlingpublishing.com

Contents

"He was a
wise man who
invented beer."

PLATO
PHILOSOPHER
427–347 BC

WORLD'S BEST BEERS
INTRODUCTION

Adventures with Beer

All over the world people have been drinking beer for more than 10,000 years, but never has there been a more wonderful time to be a serious beer lover.

Beer is in the midst of a worldwide renaissance, a global revolution in which both the old and the new are united in the passionate, boundary-pushing pursuit of flavor, taste, and new epicurean experiences.

From Portland to Prague and Munich to Melbourne, talk of great beer is getting louder, and the depth and breadth of choice are getting bigger. Countries that were hitherto bland lands of brewing are now home to thriving beer cultures. Old styles are being revived, and new styles are being discovered, with art, science, and history being magically melded in the mash tun. Brewers are using increasingly esoteric ingredients and borrowing techniques from winemakers, while distillers and gastronomic gurus the world over are waking up to the wonders of beer's fascinating relationship with food.

This book celebrates all of this and more. It shows that beer's history is one of never-ending evolution and reinvention, and embraces beer at its most enthralling. It delves into the history of beer and explores the joys of beer and food, demystifies beer styles and the brewing process, explains how to look after beer, and features a hand picked selection of 1,000 beers from hundreds of breweries in more than 40 countries, each with something very special.

Whether you are a seasoned beer aficionado or an occasional imbiber thirsty to discover more, this entertaining and enlightening tour through the world of beer will provide you with everything you need to know and bring on a thirst, too.

So come, slide yourself onto the barstool of discovery, and raise your glass to beer's wonderful and exciting revolution.

Cheers,

Brewing history

The History of Beer

Beer is the oldest fermented beverage in the world. You can't miss it—it's everywhere. Well, not everywhere exactly. There are parts of the Middle East where, it has to be said, brewing isn't widespread. But therein lies the irony. Mesopotamia, which now forms part of Iraq and a bit of Iran, was where barley was first grown and brewing first started. OK, so people had been consuming a crude, fermented grain-based beverage akin to porridge as far back as 10,000 years ago (and in parts of Africa still do so), but it was the Sumerians, living in Mesopotamia, who first started brewing seriously.

A Sumerian clay tablet dating back to 1800 BC provided not just the earliest "official" record of brewing, but also the oldest recipe in the world. Written as part of a rather catchy hymn to Ninkasi, the Sumerian goddess of brewing, the recipe involves crushing a bready substance with honey and herbs, water, dates, raisins, and spice, squeezing it through a sheet of straw, and leaving it to ferment.

Far from fresh and fizzy, the beer would be still and sludgy, and probably wasn't very tasty. But, back then, beer was for food, not just for fun. Life expectancy was poor, there was waterborne illness and disease all over the place, and drinking beer was a way of keeping healthy.

The Egyptians were keen brewers, too. Ancient Egyptian cities were built around beer. Storing and malting grain was big business, and beer was used as currency—the craftsmen who constructed the pyramids were paid in beer.

Ancient Egyptian paintings and pots are rife with brewing depictions, with images showing brewers as women, not men. Right up until brewing was seized upon as a large-scale commercial venture, it was the exclusive preserve of women. They had long held forth in the home, cooking food, making the beer, and overseeing the collective consumption of beer in primitive society, fulfilling the roles of both bouncer and barmaid.

Religion's Role

But brewing's role transcended the mere provision of sustenance and social supervision. As religion became increasingly interwoven into daily life, beer and those who brewed it took on an emblematic, spiritual dimension. Certain types of beer were reserved exclusively for religious ceremonies, both to honor the dead and reach a heightened state of consciousness, while women were regarded, and revered for, as having a religious relationship with Ninkasi, who blessed their beer vessels by magically turning grain into grog.

While Islam was eventually to blow the froth off the brewing business in Egypt, beer continued to play a religious role in Europe, where monasteries were the first commercial brewing operations. Evidence in the *Domesday Book* of 1086 records other brewing enterprises, but it was the monks who first made real money (and missionary success) from the mash-fork — especially the Benedictine ones.

Monastic brewhouses mushroomed all over medieval Europe, and most were founded near rivers and developed their own maltings. It was the monks who oversaw the widespread introduction of hops in 1000 AD and, 400 years later, it was Bavarian brothers who discovered bottom-fermenting techniques.

The dissolution of the monasteries saw the church's grip on European brewing loosen (although the Trappist ales of Belgium are a living albeit displaced legacy of Benedictine brewing) and, by the early 1800s, beer had shifted from ecclesiastical to industrial hands.

Right: The monks at Maredsous Abbey, a Benedictine monastery in Belgium, have been brewing beer for centuries. The brewery is now part of the Belgian giant Duvel-Moortgat, but their beers live on.

Technical Innovation

Prior to the British Industrial Revolution, breweries were small concerns whose dark beers, brewed solely in the winter, rarely roamed beyond a limited radius of the brewery. But thanks to a number of groundbreaking industrial advancements, all that changed in the 19th century.

By the late 1800s, beer was easier to make, easier to store, easier to drink, and easier to transport across long distances. The advent of the steam engine had given rise to larger-scale production, railways, and industrial refrigeration—first unveiled in the Spaten brewery in Munich during the 1870s—while the French chemist Louis Pasteur had lifted the lid on yeast and given brewers the scientific insight with which to preserve and prolong the life of their beer. Brewers had also developed greater control of the malting process courtesy of the introduction of coke as the core fuel. Up until then, wood had been used, and malt had been dark and smoky, but coke allowed brewers to produce a paler malt.

Pasteurization, refrigeration, and paler malt paved the way for Pilsner—the golden lager that took Europe by storm in the second half of the century. In a world of murky ales, the advent of golden lager was a marketing master stroke, and it still remains, more than 120 years later, the world's most popular beer style.

While mass distribution has consolidated world brewing and opened the door to behemoth brewing businesses, these are anything but dull beer-drinking days. Thanks to a global, grassroots—and in some cases guerrilla—craft-brewing movement, historical recipes are being revived and reinterpreted, the art of the old is being merged with the science of the new and, in their quest for new flavor experiences, brewers are looking both forward and back, as well as to each other, for inspiration, experimentation, and innovation. These are indeed historic times for the cross-fertilization of beer styles and ever more daring brews.

Ingredients Hops

Let's hear a big hand for the hop—making beer beautiful since the ninth century. Before the hop reared its cone-like head, packed with resins and essential oils, brewers had been adding herbs, flowers, and spices, ranging from heather to bog myrtle, to counterbalance the crude sweetness of the malty mash.

The Original Hops

Hops are grown on vines up to 20ft (7m) in height and are a member of the same botanical family as cannabis. An aphrodisiac for men, yet an inducer of sleep for females, hops also cure earache. It was the Roman writer Pliny who, in the sixth century, first referred to hops. He christened them *"Lupus salictarius"*, meaning "wolf plant", due to a creeping fondness for growing wild among willow trees and soil, like a wolf among sheep.

While hops had long been consumed as a remedy for a wide range of ailments, they were not purposely cultivated until the eighth century, and their widespread involvement in brewing did not materialize for another hundred years. The first written account of brewing using hops came from an unlikely source: a German nun called Abbess Hildegard Bingen who, it is claimed, was also the first person to write about the female orgasm.

Initially treated with suspicion by brewers, especially those with vested interests in the trade of other herbs and spices used in brewing, the hop had become a staple on the European brewing scene by the 14th century, and was deliberately introduced to North America during the 1600s. As a dioecious plant, the hop's male and female flowers grow separately. Only the larger female flowers, the "cones", are used in brewing.

Many hail hops as the "grapes of beer" but that is a little misleading. Yes, they're varietal like grapes and provide unique flavors and aromas, just as Cabernet Sauvignon or Riesling do with wine, but unlike grapes they don't provide fermentable sugars during brewing.

What Hops Do

Hops are the spice and seasoning that bring balance to a liquid that would otherwise be sweet and syrupy. Picked in the summer, dried, and used mostly in pellet or fresh flower form, they give beer its bitter zing and delicate, floral aroma. Hops are oily green gargoyles that ward off bacteria and preserve beer. They also help to clear the beer and retain the head.

Alpha acids and hop oils are the flavor compounds that brewers seek to coax from the hop cones. Hops abundant in alpha acids, known as "bittering hops", are added early for bitterness while "finishing hops", heavy in hop oils yet unresponsive when boiled for long periods, are added late in the process to enhance the aroma.

To really emphasize aromatics in their ale, brewers will often throw more finishing hops into the cask, known as "late hopping" which provides extra aromas.

There are hundreds of hop varieties, each one having its own bitterness level and flavor. All hops can be dual-purpose but, like a soccer player, some are better at finishing and some prefer playing at the back. A major part of the brewer's art is to find a blend that works best although, in recent years, brewers have been experimenting with single-hop beers.

The essential oils of the hop can be seen when the cone is gently rubbed in the hands and sniffed. In the hop cone, a resinous yellow powder called "lupulin" holds the wonderful taste sensations that brewers need, their holy grail of flavor. Lupulin flavors are complex, ranging from from aniseed and basil to wet hay, citrus, lemongrass and lychees, tobacco and nutmeg, pine, fresh grass, and juniper.

Hop Alternatives

Doctrine dictates that hops must be used in brewing but as we all know doctrine is the last refuge for the unimaginative, and an increasing number of innovative micro-brewers are turning to alternative plants, herbs, and spices to season their beers. Kaffir lime leaves, juniper, poppy seeds, Muscat grapes, pomegranate, and chili are just some of the ingredients being added by new-wave brewers. And lest we forget, the Belgians have been adding spices and herbs to their beers, especially their wheat beers, for centuries.

International Bittering Units

International bittering units (IBU) is the currency by which bitterness in beer is measured. An IBU rating is a complex calculation that takes the weight of hops, alpha acids, wort, and alcohol into account.

As hops are less prominent in malty beers, IBU ratings tend to be lower (15-30) in, say, brown ales, stouts, and porters and even lower in light "lawnmower" lagers such as Bud Light. In pilsners with a hoppy, snappy character, the IBU rating can be as high as 40; aromatic English ales may hover around the 50 mark, while in heavily-hopped India Pale Ales, especially those brewed in the USA, the IBU can reach three figures and, among lupulin-loving drinkers, be regarded as a badge of honor.

Hip hops

Noble Hops

There are four varieties of noble hop: Hallertau, Zatec (Saaz), Spalt, and Tettnang. Their names are derived from the areas in which they were originally grown. High in hop oils and low in alpha and beta acids, these varieties are hailed for their aroma, rather than their bitterness.

Hallertau (Germany)

With an aroma that is delicate, floral, and slightly fruity, it is traditionally used in lager-type beers: however, it has also been successful in the production of some of the lighter English cask-conditioned ales. It is also grown in the Spalt region.

Tettnang (Germany)

An aroma variety that is grown mainly in the Tettnang cultivation area of the Baden-Bitburg-Rheinpfalz region of Southern Germany. Some growers in the Hallertau region are also now growing this variety. A very fine traditional aroma hop, well established in the European lager-type beers and, increasingly, in traditional lighter English cask ales.

Zatec/Saaz (Czech Republic)

Saaz hops originate from the Czech Republic and are renowned for their high-quality aroma. The variety has developed over many years from hops grown in and around the Zatec (Saazer) area. Regarded as the Rolls-Royce of hops and a key component of Czech pilsners, it is a noble hop, renowned for its spicy, citrus zest that adds bite to the beer.

Spalt (Germany)

Slightly spicy and loved by lagers, Spalt is a classic German noble hop that brings both refined bitterness and uplifting aromas to the party. Lagers love it and so do Pilsners.

Other Hop Varieties

Admiral (UK)

Very good high-alpha hop that will be mainly used as a replacement for the Target hop in extracts and pellets where bitterness value is the main consideration. Not as harsh as Target in terms of quality of bitterness, Admiral has a very pleasant hoppy character.

Amarillo (USA)

A new-ish hop from the United States resplendent in tangerine, grapefruit, and lime flavors. Shares a lot in common with Cascade, Centennial, and Chinook hops.

Bramling Cross (UK)

A hop of considerable character. Its distinctive "American" aroma put many brewers off this variety in its early years, but an increasing number of makers of cask-conditioned beer are calling upon its strong spicy/blackcurrant flavor.

Cascade (USA)

Originating in Oregon in the 1970s, Cascade became synonymous with craft brewing in the United States. An excellent high-alpha variety, Cascade has a unique floral/spicy aroma both in the cone form and in the beer, mainly due to abnormal levels of some of the essential oils. It is very popular due to the unique character it imparts to the finished beer.

Centennial (USA)

An experimental hop variety that is currently under evaluation by UK and US brewers. It has floral qualities that are quite similar to that of Cascade.

Challenger (UK)

Challenger was born in 1972 as a high-yielding dual-purpose variety grown mainly in the English counties of Herefordshire and Worcestershire, although quantities are also grown in Kent and Belgium. An excellent all-round hop with good alpha and aroma properties. As the main copper hop, it provides a refreshing, full-bodied rounded bitterness that makes an excellent platform. As the late addition hop, Challenger can give a very crisp, fruity character.

Chinook (USA)

A high-alpha acid hop, this has a very unusual aroma profile. Released in 1985 and becoming increasingly popular, Chinook has an extremely potent grapefruit character in both the rub of the hop and in the beer. Ideal for one-off and seasonal special brews.

Columbus/Tomahawk (USA)

Generally used as a main copper hop, in the form of extracts and pellets because of the exceedingly generous high-alpha content. Columbus is very aromatic as a late hop, in cask ales, and is big in the USA.

Crystal (USA)

Part of the Hallertau family, Crystal is a craftbrewer's favorite and imparts enormous aromatic qualities to the beer.

First Gold (UK)

Suitable both as a general kettle hop and also for late and dry hopping in all types of beer. First Gold has good aroma and bittering qualities, with a citrus quality that endows a well-balanced bitterness.

Opposite above: At Crannóg Ales, Canada's only certified organic farmhouse microbrewery, hops are grown for the brewing, while the brewing waste provides food for the livestock.

Fuggles (UK)

The delicate, minty, grassy, slightly floral aroma produces a clean, refreshing full-bodied flavor present in many traditional ales. Before the advent of dual-purpose and high-alpha hops, Fuggles were used as the main copper hop and were often complemented by an addition of Golding, to give a full-bodied, rounded flavor for which English ales became famous. Grown predominantly in Herefordshire and Worcestershire, Fuggles was the dominant hop variety in England for more than 70 years, until the development of high-alpha varieties made it less economical for bittering purposes. Probably the most famous traditional English aroma variety, Fuggles are also grown in Slovenia as Styrian Golding and in the United States they are known as as Oregon Fuggles.

Galena (USA)

Galena is an excellent high-alpha hop with balanced bittering potential. The very strong tomcat/blackcurrant aroma characteristics are similar to that of the old Bullion variety, which for many years was used in Guinness. A very strong fruity character and a relative of First Gold.

Goldings (UK)

Goldings is a delicate flower in need of tender, loving care. She doesn't like getting wet or cold, and would probably be bullied at school. Brimming with youthful fruity lemon/orange zest and sweet citrus aromas however, she's a hit in sprightly summer brews. Goldings has been grown in England for more than 100 years and, as with Fuggle, these hops were named after the grower who developed them. A traditional English aroma variety valued for its smooth (almost sweet), delicate, slightly spicy quality, which produces the classic Golding finish. As with Fuggles, it forms the basis of many archetypal English ales. It is a hop now grown in the USA, too.

Green Bullet (New Zealand)

A sleek, smooth hop whose aroma qualities match its excellent bittering power. Popular among Australasian breweries, Green Bullet has been likened to giving a piney/lemon Styrian style of flavor to the beer and an excellent aroma.

Liberty (USA)

Relatively new and grown mostly in the Pacific Northwest, Liberty shares a lot of characteristics with the Hallertau hop. The aroma is mild and clean with a hint of lemon/citrus flavor that gives it an extra edge on the smooth Golding flavor.

Mount Hood (USA)

Introduced in Oregon in the 1980s, Mount Hood is generally perceived as an aroma variety with similar characteristics to the German Hallertau. The aroma is generally pleasant, mild, and grassy. In British-style ales, the flavor comes through as delicate, floral, and slightly herbal.

Northdown (UK)

An excellent all-round hop that sits in the dual-purpose bracket, with good alpha and aroma properties. Very popular used either on its own or in conjunction with an aroma variety. A slightly richer flavor than Challenger, although it is quite similar in many other ways.

Northern Brewer (Germany)

Developed from a cross between a male seedling of Brewers Gold and Canterbury Golding in the 1940s. The English variety Northdown is a direct descendant of Northern Brewer and has very similar brewing characteristics. Used as a dual-purpose variety it has excellent bittering properties and a pleasant aroma.

Nugget (USA)

High in alpha acid and emanating an enormous aroma, Nugget is an extremely bitter American hop with a pungent, heavy herbal aroma.

Pacific Gem (New Zealand)

A high-alpha hop which provides a pleasant aroma, with a useful bitterness level. Very fruity, it brings with it distinct and prized berry fruit aromas.

Perle (Germany)

Perle is generally perceived as an excellent enduring-aroma hop, with characteristics as good as those of Hallertau, but with a higher alpha acid content and better yield. This variety was bred at the Hop Research Institute in Hüll, Germany, and released generally in 1978.

Pioneer (UK)

The Pioneer has proved to be quite unusual, with a very pleasant lemon citrus aroma. Initial brews have proved to be very successful, with extremely distinctive, hoppy characteristics.

Pride of Ringwood (New Zealand)

Often frequenting lip-smacking lagers from Down Under, Pride of Ringwood brings balanced bitterness and gentle hop aroma. At the time of it first release in 1965, Ringwood was the highest alpha-acid hop in the world.

Progress (UK)

Progress was originally introduced as a replacement for Fuggle and has very similar characteristics. Slightly sweeter and with a slightly softer bitterness, it is has excellent potential at both the start and end of the boil. This is a well-bittered British hop that is hailed among darker ales for its distinctive fruity, juicy juniper and spice flavors.

Hops: A brewer's story

Simcoe (USA)

A hybrid American hop, Simcoe has been all the rage in recent years. Although it is primarily a bittering hop, it has a clean, pine-like aroma and a taste with a slight hint of citrus. It is less astringent than other pine-like hops and finds favor in idiosyncratic and unique pale and American ales.

Styrian Goldings (Slovenia)

Although known in Slovenia as the Savinja Golding, this variety is the same as the British Fuggle. It is recorded that hops were introduced into Slovenia from England, and it seems likely that the Fuggle variety was supplied under the misnomer of "Fuggles Goldings" — a practice at one time resorted to because Goldings were deemed to be of superior quality to Fuggles. The variety was fully adopted by Slovenia in 1930. This distinguished variety is well known throughout the world and, although identical to Fuggles in many ways, it does have its own distinctive characteristics. The perfume-like hoppy character that was again used mainly in European lagers works very well in the less malty flavored golden-colored beers.

Target (UK)

An excellent high-alpha variety, Target gives bitterness at a very competitive price. It tends to be too harsh for aroma purposes late in the boil, but has produced good results in the cask.

Willamette (USA)

Willamette is generally perceived as a new yet good-quality aroma hop. The rub of the hops gives an ester/blackcurrant/herbal aroma that is very pleasant, but can be quite strong. Differing results have been achieved with this variety. Some brewers have found it to be a suitable replacement for Fuggle; others have had poor results when using it this way, but have found that it stands up admirably as an aroma variety on its own merits.

Sean Franklin, head brewer at the Rooster's Brewery in Yorkshire, explains why hop aromas are at the forefront of his incredibly aromatic ales.

"Quality" means different things to different people. Judges and beer aficionados want the beer to conform to its style guidelines. Technicians look for clarity — clean flavors without sensory faults. We look for a little more excitement.

We use an aesthetic quality definition. We want clarity of course, but also complexity and intensity in the aromas—pleasant aromas such as fruits, flowers, and spices. On the palate we want balanced "primary tastes" (sweet, sour, bitter, and salt) and the same aromas and complexity in the flavor as we found in the aroma. The beer must have a long aromatic finish.

All this has a rational basis. Any sensory product should engage and hold the taster's attention. Complex pleasant aromas pull the attention of the drinker, and long-lasting pleasant aromas give ten times the pleasure, and therefore worth, of short "finishing" aromas. Quality beers have great sensory value.

Key to what we do are the hops. That doesn't have to be the same for every beer; yeast, malt, and spices can be used in the same way. But hops give scope for a huge spectrum of flavors as they interact with yeast, malts, and the brewing process. Hops we use from around the world can give aromas of tangerine, ginger, orange, grapefruit, passion fruit, lychees, guava, roses, and many other additional flavors.

There are two difficulties to our approach. First, we cut our market in two when we put flavor in the beer—some people will like the flavor, some won't. But we're determined, like many small brewers, to make something worthwhile that adds to the beer-market taste spectrum. The second difficulty is the technical and artful work of getting the right flavors in the beer. Understanding beer as a cooking recipe is the simple way to look at it. But it is perhaps more correct to consider it as a 3D matrix of complex cause and effect. This teaches you that any action you take as a brewer is likely to have an effect on the flavor down the line. Hops vary across the hop yard, from year to year and grower to grower. Malt is the same. Yeasts are alive and are as capricious as children. Timings, quantities, and temperatures take time and knowledge to understand. Finally, knowing how some of the above interact, we paint a canvas of malt flavor on which we lay the hop aromas. Sounds easy, but I've been trying for 20 years (less than most brewers) and am still filled with wonder and achievement when we hit the nail on the head.

So who do we make the beer for? We make it for anyone who might be attracted to the flavor of our beers. To get the most out of our sort of beer, the taster needs to concentrate and test the beer against the criteria above. In short, it must give interest and, above all, enjoyment. Great brewing is an art form, and we feel like lucky apprentice painters.

Other ingredients: Grain, malt, yeast, and water

Grain and Malt

Grain is to beer what the grape is to wine. It's the key element of beer, furnishing it with fuel for fermentation, dictating mouthfeel, flavor, body, and color, and serving as a springboard of sweetness from which hop and yeast can excel.

Rice, rye, wheat, oats, sorghum, maize, and spelt are just some of the grains used by brewers, but, when they talk of malt, they usually mean barley.

Barley is a brewer's best friend. It's the only grain to adhere to the German purity laws—the Reinsheitsgebot. Notoriously robust and resistant to mold, barley grains are low in fat and protein, but awash with easily extractable starch. Unlike other cereals, barley has its own husk, which protects the germinating sprout and acts as a natural filter when the brewer is trying to separate wort from the spent grains. It also gives the beer a malt character that's clean, crisp, and soft.

First used to brew beer, and make bread, by the ancient Egyptians, barley is now grown in more than a hundred countries, predominantly in the northern hemisphere between the latitudes of 45 degrees and 55 degrees.

There are three principal classifications of barley — two, four, and six-row — which take their name from the number of kernel rows at the top of the stem. Four-row barley is unsuitable for brewing while, outside of North America where it's used in light lagers alongside rice and corn, six-row is seldom seen. The majority of brewers turn to two-row barley, rich in starch and low in protein, and mostly grown in Central and Western Europe.

Barley is by no means the sole cereal in beer, and in their pursuit of new flavors, textures, and tastes, brewers are experimenting with other varieties. If a brewer wants an amplified creamy mouthfeel to a stout, or a rustic graininess to a pale ale, then oats or rye is called upon to play a cameo role.

The use of rice or corn is mostly confined to North America and Australasia. These ingredients offer less flavor than other grains and their neutral character is linked with mass-produced yellow fizz. Being such unexciting bearers of taste, they are regarded with suspicion by beer purists; however, they do provide considerable style to some light lagers and pre-Prohibition beers.

Despite the rise in recent years of Weizens and Witbiers, wheat still only accounts for about 2 percent of the malt used in beer. It looks pretty, but is high-maintenance and a nightmare to work with. Awkward with husks that don't self-filtrate, it causes mayhem in the mash tun, clashing with hops and only getting along with wayward yeast.

Malting/Kilning Malt derives its name from the malting process, which involves hoodwinking the grain into thinking that it is spring and therefore time to sprout. Warm weather is replicated by steeping the cereal (be it barley, wheat, or rye) in water until germination begins. In order to fuel germination, enzymes in the grain convert insoluble starch into sugar, and it is these sugars that are the fermentable material used in beer production. To ensure that the grain doesn't steal these sugars for continued germination, it is kilned in order to halt the process. If you taste some crushed malt, the sweetness is apparent. Normal barley tastes dry and starchy.

Kilning is a slow-cooking process which gives the malt different levels of dryness and color. By varying the temperature and length of time the barley spends in the kiln, the maltster can produce a kaleidoscope of flavors and characteristics. Depending on the duration of kilning, malt can vary in color from very light to extremely dark and some malts, such as Crystal, are heated while still moist. This process intensifies the caramelized, nutty flavor.

It is the mix of different-colored malts that decides the color of the resulting beer. Malts can be roughly divided into two camps: base malts and specialty malts. Base malts will make up most, sometimes all, of the grain for a particular beer and will often be blended with other base malts. Specialty malts, by contrast, are used in smaller quantities to add color and flavor to the beer.

The light, bready shortbread characteristics of pale malt and Pilsner malt are often the cornerstones for lagers and ales, respectively. Crystal malt, cured for longer in the kiln, is sweeter and slightly darker with a touch of toffee; the ocher-colored Vienna malt adorns the eponymous lager with its amber hue and toasty taste, while Munich malt, slightly darker and drier, is what gives Munich lagers, bocks, and Oktöberfest beers their caramel and toffee footprint.

Highly kilned malts such as chocolate and black malt, are increasingly used in specialty beers such as imperial stouts and porters. They bless the beer with coffee, chocolate, ash, and bitter character, while malt smoked and cured over smoldering Beechwood is used for Rauchbiers/smoked ales.

Yeast

It may be a smelly fungus that has Latin names of far too many letters, but there is nothing unappealing about yeast.

It is wonderful, enigmatic, enchanting, sensual stuff and, without it, beer would have no alcohol in it and, thus, be less fun to drink. As any brewer knows, it's the single most important ingredient in beer.

Its central role in beer is to munch on sugars, excrete alcohol, and belch out the CO_2 (carbon dioxide) that gives beer its carbonation. On good form, yeast can provide beer with fantastic fruity flavors but it can also fail to deliver.

Yeast is a single cellular organism visible only through a microscope—a luxury not afforded to the Mesopotamians, ancient Egyptians, and beer makers of Babylon. Blissfully oblivious to the wonders of molecular biology, all they knew was that something in the beer, somewhere in the froth and dregs of the wort, was somehow transforming a sugary solution into a liquid that made you happy and healthy. This strange shape-shifting substance was christened "God is Good", for it was mysterious manna from heaven.

While plenty of boffins prodded and poked yeast underneath the microscope during the 17th century, it wasn't until 1857 that Louis Pasteur realized that, far from being a divine gift, fermentation was a natural chemical reaction in which yeast ate, expelled, and multiplied.

Yet it was an Emil Christian Hansen, a novelist and full-time chemist working at the Carlsberg Brewery in Denmark, who discovered how to domesticate wild yeast. Not content with devising a way to isolate a single beer yeast cell and propagate it, he worked out that different yeasts behave and feed more effectively at different temperatures and that, once fermentation reaches a certain alcohol level, the yeast gives up and dies.

There are hundreds of different beer yeast strains but, based loosely on the distinctions highlighted by Hansen, they can be divided into two categories. Top

fermenting yeast, known as ale yeast or Saccharomyces cerevisiae, like eating maltose in a warm temperature 55°–75°F (13°–24°C) and remains buoyant in the fermentation vessel.

Bottom-fermenting yeast, known as lager yeast or Saccharomyces carlsbergensis, excels at lower temperatures 34°–55°F (1°–13°C) and prefers to eat in smaller groups, which means that it floats to the bottom of the fermentation vessel. Beers that rely on the yeast for much of their character tend to be top fermenters, while those that rely on the other main ingredients tend to be bottom fermenters.

Yet what differentiates ale yeast from lager yeast is what they eat. Lager yeast is a polite if dry dinner guest. It will consume everything, won't contribute much, and will remain in the background. Ale yeast, by contrast, is a fussy eater that will refuse to consume the residual sugars and by-products dished out by the wort. It will stamp its opinions on the evening, and its outbursts may clash with other dinner guests—be they malt, water, or hops.

The ale and lager distinction can be misleading, though. When making a stout, a brewer is interested in the harmonious mix of roasted malts and rich mineral character. Even though history says an ale yeast should be used, a lager yeast is better suited as it won't interfere with character the brewer is coaxing out.

Yeast is a living organism that undergoes 13 different stages before fermenting. Brewers must ensure that the temperature, oxygen, and alcohol levels in the mash

Left: Top-fermenting yeast at Anchor Steam Brewery, San Francisco.
Far left: A malting kiln in action at the Fuller's brewing facility in London.

are all to the yeast's liking. Most breweries jealously guard the bespoke yeast strain that defines their beers' character.

Water

Water is a critical component of the brewing process, constituting 95 percent of the ingredients and exerting an immense influence on the overall character of beer.

For every pint of beer made, almost five pints are used in the production process. Without it, the grain couldn't germinate.

Not all water is the same. Once rinsed from a rain cloud, water picks up an acidic edge from gases in the air. On hitting the ground, the rainwater accrues mineral salts and characteristics as it soaks into the soil, permeates porous rocks, and settles on the stone of the water table.

Consequently, the geology of a given geographic area once determined the mineral content, hardness, and softness of the local water—and, before the age of water treatment, the type of beer that could be brewed.

In the Czech Republic town of Pilsen, for example, water is very soft, with barely any mineral salts. As such, the local water here complements the delicate hop and measured malt flavors of the Pilsner style.

By contrast, the mineral-rich, high-alkali waters of Dublin and London lent themselves perfectly to the brewing of porters and stouts, while the water in Burton-on-Trent, harder than a grave-digger's heart and high in minerals and sulfates, gave the town's eponymous ale its dryness and sulfuric aroma, the "Burton Snatch".

Technology developed over the last 50 years or so means that modern breweries can replicate water from anywhere in the world and alter its hardness, softness, and mineral content according to the style of beer being brewed.

How beer is made

There are several key processes in making beer, some of which are changed or varied at certain stages according to the art of the individual brewer.

Above: A brewer at the Schenkerla brewery in Germany perfects the world-famous rauchbier.
Opposite above right: Mikkel Borg Bjergsø of award-winning Danish Brewery Mikkeller rakes out spent grains from the mash tun, before they are sent off to feed cattle.
Opposite below right: High-tech brewing takes place in the Belgian Duvel-Moortgat brewery in Breendonk. Here, white-coated boffins undertake some filtration.

Milling

Once the blend of malts has been carefully chosen, it is put through a mill. The milling process splits the kernel into grist, a granular mixture of husks and fine starchy flour.

Mashing

The grist is then transferred to a vessel called a "mash tun" where it is mixed with hot water (at about 150°F, 65°C), to form the mash, which has the consistency of porridge and a sweet, bready aroma. During this time, the enzymes in the malt are broken down, and soluble sugars are slowly unleashed. Temperature is key, with different sorts of sugars unlocked at different temperatures. Brewers can stick to a single-temperature mashing or play around with heat in order to coax out the desirable sugars. Brewers often step the mash, halting the heat in stages, at specific temperatures—notably 113 degrees, 143.6 degrees and 163.4 degrees Fahrenheit.

After about an hour, the mash has been transformed from porridge into wort—a dark orange, smooth, sweet syrupy solution that contains all the sugars required for fermentation. As it also contains unwanted and useless broken barley husks, the wort is "run off" through a lauter tun (essentially a sieve). While the spent grains are captured, then cast aside, to be sold to local farmers as feed for grateful cattle, the wort that has been separated is sent to the kettle, otherwise known as the "copper".

The initial runnings of the mash are notoriously sweet and ideally suited to making strong beer, as there are more sugars for the yeast to munch on and turn into alcohol. For less potent beers, the mash is often sparged (sprayed with water) to achieve the right level of sugar content. This is often referred to as "brewing degrees" or the "Plato scale" but is not to be confused with ABV (alcohol by volume), which is the measurement of the final strength of the beer itself.

Boiling

Once the copper is filled with wort, containing just the right sugar concentration, it is brought to a bubbling, undulating boil, and this is when the hops are added. As the intense heat will prove too much for delicate hop aromatics and evaporate the aroma compounds, the hops added at the beginning of the boil are used mostly for bitterness and herbal flavors. The high temperatures also sterilize the boil, zapping any unwanted yeast prior to fermentation.

After an hour or so, the wort is brought off the boil and cooled, and further hops are added. "Late hopping" at a lower temperature adorns the beer with floral aromatics. The heat is then turned off and the bitter wort is left to simmer and aerate. This dissolves the oxygen that the yeast likes so much.

Fermentation

Once the spent hops and any congealed malt are strained away, or separated and siphoned off using a whirlpool, the wort plummets in temperature and is pumped into a fermentation vessel, where the yeast, knife and fork in hand, and napkin tucked eagerly under its chin, awaits.

For the first hour or so, the wort lies dormant, and there's little sign of any activity, but, as anyone who has seen *Jaws* will testify, the dead calm always precedes a thrashing feeding frenzy. Before long, the surface has been transformed from mill pond to a seething, foaming mass of liquid bubble wrap that bursts and bloats both wide and high. Things get heated in the eating orgy, but the temperature is controlled using cooling jackets, so that the yeast doesn't expire from the excess.

As with humans, alcohol seldom aids stamina and, after a while, the yeast really needs to sleep. It tends to lose appetite and enthusiasm before it has eaten all the sugars, but this is a good thing because brewers require residual sugars to add finesse to the flavor and bulk to the body.

Conditioning

After all this activity, the beer needs a breather. If it is an ale, it is unlikely to age or mature for more than a month or so, unless it is a strong beer and is being barrel-aged for longer periods, when it will pick up more complex flavors. The age-old tradition of dry-hopping, whereby flower hops are stewed in the ageing beer, adds extra aromas and is being revived by a number of experimental breweries.

Lagers need a longer rest than ale. After a chilly fermentation, lager needs to rest further, rid itself of its rough edges, and get in touch with its delicate flavors. This takes time, and the longer a lager can relax, the better, which is why lagering times are so often a bone of contention among the beer-drinking community.

While loving brewers will let their lagers sleep for a few months, mass-market lagers are rudely awoken from their slumber after just a couple of weeks, dragged out of bed, and sent off to work in the hope that a bit of hastily applied makeup, known as marketing, will disguise any lethargic underperformance.

Filtration

After conditioning, most beers are filtered to sieve out all the yeast and undesirable proteins, and leave it as "bright beer".

Pasteurization and Packaging

To keep the beer fresh and able to last longer in the bottle and the keg, "bright beer" is often pasteurized. It is held at high temperatures (partially boiled) for about 15 minutes to destroy stray bacteria that might infect it once packaged.

In a producer-driven market, uneven flavor undermines the commercial viability of brands and this method is favored among "industrial-brewers".

While pasteurization can be frowned upon for removing flavors so carefully produced, it does not always mean boring beer. Some distinctive beers, well rewed and crafted with integrity and excellent ingredients, are pasteurized.

BEER BASICS

Beer basics Storing, pouring, temperature & bottles

While the storing and maturing process for beer is less complex than that of wine, there are a few basic guidelines that will enable you to store, pour, preserve, and condition your ales, so that you can enjoy them year-round. Some bottle-conditioned beauties need to be set aside for maturation, while others should be kept instantly at hand for when you wish to try them.

Storing

To prevent heat and light contamination, a beer store needs to be dry, dark, and at a consistently cold temperature. Just as with food, lower temperatures help to preserve the beer.

A cellar is therefore ideal if available, but a refrigerator is the next best thing. After all, you can always quickly warm up a beer, but it takes time to chill it back down. A fridge is not suitable for vintage ales, as chilled temperatures will freeze the maturation and ruin the taste.

If you're looking to store and mature over the long term, keep your beer bottles upright. Not only does it ensure that the sediment remains at the base of the bottle, but it also reduces the surface area for potential oxidization.

There are many beer lovers who suggest that, like wine, beer is best laid down but there's little evidence to support this claim. Even if a beer is closed with a cork, there's no real need to put it on its side, as there are very few modern-day beer corks that are prone to shrinkage—especially within the optimum aging period of ten years.

Pouring

The art of pouring a beer is all about a gentle and careful action— a considered process which helps to generate as much anticipation as it does thirst. You should be aiming for a glass of beer that is topped with a foamy head of approximately 1 in (2.5 cm).

Hold the glass at an angle of 45 degrees and aim for the pour to hit a spot about halfway down the side of the glass. The pour should be kept steady and slow, and, as the liquid is about to hit the spot where it's being aimed, the glass should be tilted slowly and carefully towards an upright position.

When done properly, the beer that is poured once the glass has assumed an upright position (about a third of the bottle) should form a lovely "two-fingered" head. If, when drinking a bottle-conditioned beer, you don't want the yeast sediment to float around in the glass, then gently roll it on the bar or a tabletop prior to pouring, as this wraps up the yeast sediment and leaves it behind. All that's left is to take a first, lingering sip, and admire your technique.

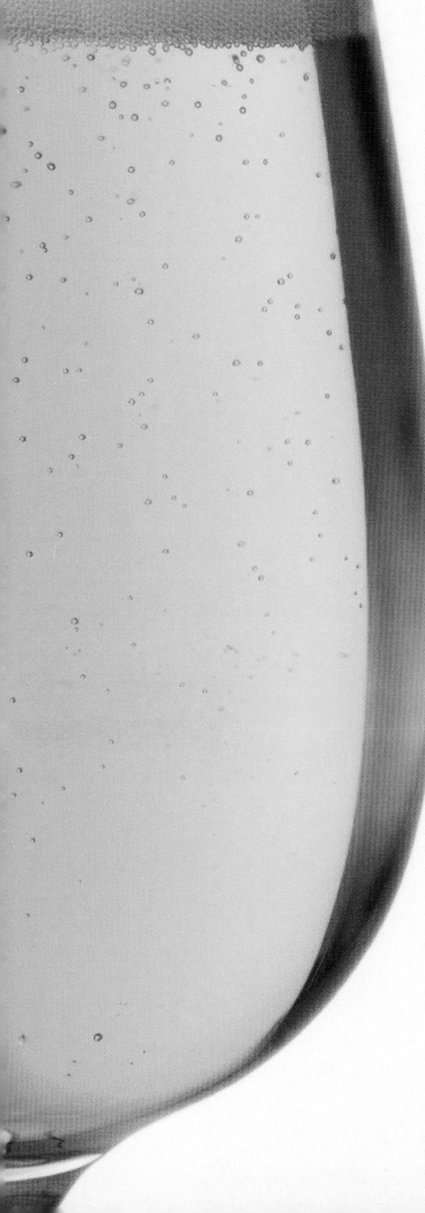

Temperature

The temperature at which you drink a beer can have a huge effect on the flavors that you experience. Cold temperatures enhance refreshment and carbonation, while warmer temperatures will bring out the body of the beer and enhance the aromas and flavors.

As a general rule, the lighter the beer the lower the temperature; Lagers are best served between 39° and 46°F (4° and 8°C), with amber, Oktoberfest, and Märzen varieties veering toward the upper end of the scale. The same goes for wheat beers although, as summer drinks, people often drink them colder.

British beers, contrary to cliché, are not served warm and should not roam above or below 50°-57°F (10°-14°C) —known as "cellar temperature".

This is also the preferred climate for Belgium's golden ales, while darker versions, stouts, and Barley Wines like things when the mercury rises a little higher. If you're not sure of the optimum temperature for your chosen beer, most brewers will suggest a serving temperature on the bottle label.

Bottles

Bottles of beer are not house plants. They don't like light, and they don't like heat. If a beer is exposed to bright light, it will soon become "lightstruck"—a byword for "skunky" and inconsistent. This is particularly rife when beer is stored in green or clear glass bottles, but can also occur when the beer bottle is made from dark glass. That's why many bottle-conditioned beers that improve with age are packaged in boxes.

On the whole, dark glass is better for the natural preservation of beer than light or clear versions. Historically, beer bottles were made from black glass, and early porters were stored in this type of vessel.

As other beer types such as lager, wheat beer, and bitters became more popular, bottle shapes evolved for each type. Bottle fasteners developed from glass stoppers, swing-type closures, and corks to the mass-produced crown cap. These days the crown cap is the most common type of bottle closure, although esoteric ales such as champagne beer and hoppy IPAs, are often topped with a Champagne-style cork

Beer basics Tasting beer

When you join a fine wine club, you are given a thermometer, a foil cutter, a pourer and breather, a bottle stopper, a fancy futuristic corkscrew designed by NASA, and one of those bottle neckerchief items that catches stray drops of wine. When you join a beer club, you get given a cap or maybe, if you're lucky, a T-shirt. In terms of pomp and ceremony, and style in the serve, wine is to beer what royalty is to a redneck.

Beers are seldom stored and stirred from secretive slumber in temperature-controlled cellars; there is no triumphant pull and "pop" of a cork, nor a meticulous decanting into a voluptuous holding vessel. There is no eyes-closed analysis of the aromas, no talk of "letting it breathe", no swirling and sniffing from delicate glassware, and certainly no brewer telling you about the beer and inviting appraisal of the label.

There's none of that. But there should be. As noble a drink with as noble a history, and abundant in just as many complex flavors and aromas, distinctive, full-flavored beer is deserving of just as much reverence as wine.

Beer Evaluation

Sight

We drink with our eyes because the visual sense whets our appetite. When we see a Pilsner cascading from a shiny tap into a glass and surging up into a tight, white head, witness the billowing pour of a creamy, velvet stout, or peer at a an open fire seen through a golden prism of a barley wine, our brain sends our salivating mouth a lip-licking message.

A good beer should be handsome and beautiful, but not all beers look the same; each style has a distinctive appearance. Visual evaluation is best undertaken using white walls and natural light, but where this isn't possible try to find some light, and hold your glass up to it. Kölsch, Pilsners, and lagers should be clear and bright, sparkling with a candle-like flicker; ales and bitters should drop clear, bright, and vivacious; stouts take on an opaque, ebony silky sheen and a thick, creamy white head; while the haze in a wheat beer should be enticing and lively.

The head should be tight, compact, and daring you to drink it. As the beer is drunk, the head should retain its structure and leave layers of lace in its wake right to the bottom of the glass.

Smell

Aroma is an essential attribute of the brewer's art, and there are more than a thousand aromatic compounds in beer that are capable of being discerned. The nose is very clever, and one need only take a swig from the beer while holding it close to realize as much. The nose picks up flavors and sensations that the tongue (restricted to sour, bitter, sweet, and salty) simply can't. Without it, one misses the delicate espresso roast of a stout or a porter, the flowery notes of a pilsner, wheat beer's distinctive bubblegum and cloves bouquet, the vinous port-like perfume exuded by Barley Wine, and the aniseed aromas of a Saison or a Bière de Garde.

Drinking a beer straight from the bottle denies these sensations, so pour it into a glass and, to elevate the aromas, give it a swirl. Then stick your nose in. If your nose is wet then you've either stuck it in too far or you're a dog and you shouldn't, by rights, be able to read this. Instead of taking lots of deep inhalations, mix them up with lots of quick, small sniffs, and let the fabulous, flavorsome fumes fill the nostrils.

Taste

Before you raise your glass to your lips, ensure that your taste buds are in tip-top condition, to embrace the impending sensations. A punch-drunk palate is useless, so avoid smoking, and eating spicy or fatty foods, before tasting. Be sure to rinse the mouth with water, and arm yourself with unsalted wafers or crackers to soak up any unpleasant flavors.

If tasting a range of beers in one session, arrange them in order of intensity of flavor. A big, butch Barley Wine will obliterate the taste-buds and render them oblivious to the delicate nuances of, say, a Pilsner or a Kölsch.

Unlike their wine counterparts, beer tasters don't require a spittoon. The first rule for tasting beer is to swallow and not spit—less to do with greed and more to do with the fact that bitterness receptors are at the back of the throat and tongue.

Take a slow sip of the beer, allowing the liquid to seep into the sensory receptors on your lips (and allowing the aromas to infiltrate the nose again). Take a small yet not insignificant amount of beer into your mouth, and circulate it around the tongue. Aerate the flavors by sucking the beer around the mouth as if you're whistling backward.

Take note of the tingle: sweet sensations should tickle the tip of the tongue, the back borders are where sour and acidic sensations will show themselves, while salty flavors reveal themselves at the front sides of the tongue.

Bitterness is felt at the back of the throat, but also, to a lesser extent, on the entire surface of the tongue, which is why, when a beer is extremely bitter, the mouth puckers up. A good way of detecting the bitterness of a beer and the hop flavors is to eat a bit of foam from the head with a teaspoon. It may look odd, but it's extremely revealing.

Mouthfeel and body are important. Full-bodied beer fills the mouth like an oyster, while thin-bodied beers dissipate on the tongue like a shrimp cracker. Mouthfeel can be thin or thick, smooth or grainy, creamy, leathery, metallic, mousse-like, or cloying and coating.

Does the beer develop and grow in character as you drink it? Are there layers of flavor? Is there a finish that stays longer? Or does it vanish without trace?

Translating taste sensations into words is a notoriously tricky undertaking and may seem a little pompous. But it's incredibly useful to develop a lexicon of flavors, a personal flavor wheel with your own personal terms, similes, and metaphors that work as signposts and reference points. There's no right or wrong, so don't be swayed by others, as they may not be detecting what you're detecting. Descriptors need not make sense nor be "foodie" either—"horse sweat" or "horse blanket" is often referred to when tasting Lambic beers, for instance. Keeping a notebook is one way to remember your beers.

Beer basics Glassware

First of all, regardless of shape or size, glassware should be clean and clear. It should be squeaky clean and free of soapy suds—oily residue destroys the heads on beer and will impede the flavors and aromas.

Historically, beer drinkers have chosen glassware in terms of quantity rather than quality. But now it is time to forget vulgar vessels and to consider a more refined receptacle. You wouldn't slosh a bottle of vintage wine into a pint glass, so why do we do it with a decent beer? What holds true for the grape holds true for the hop; like wine, different beers need different glasses to enhance the taste, bouquet, and balance of the glorious liquid that lies within.

If all you have is a predictable "pint" glass, then break free and bring out the wine glasses. It may seem incongruous to use a stemmed wine glass to taste beer, but they actually suit a number of beer styles. Glasses designed for white wine, or even Champagne flutes, are ideal for light and spritzy beers such as Pilsners, kölsch, and wheat beer. Wine glasses used for red wine, conversely, bring out the best in dark, fuller-

1 Highball. Use for thirst-quenching lagers. 2 Balloon. Use for light, delicately-hopped ales. 3 Dimpled pint glass. Traditional British bitter glass making a retro comeback. 4 Wheat beer glass. 5 Modern-day tulip glass for one-off strong beers. 6 Tulip pint glass. A sexy alternative to conical versions. 7 Goblet. Ideal for complex ales such as Trappist. 8 Snifter. Use for after-dinner ales. 9 Flute glass for champagne beer, Pilsners, golden ales. 10 US pint glass.

bodied beers. Their bulbous shape allows you to warm up the beer, cradle it, and swirl the aromas awake.

Wine has inspired a revolution in beer presentation in recent years. Huge strides have been taken in improving glassware, new shapes have been formed, glasses have been nucleated (etched) to improve head retention, and breweries have gone to great lengths to introduce vessels that ameliorate the aroma, appearance, and flavors in the beer.

For British beers, the pint glass is great for drinking from, but less so for appreciating the taste of beer. Instead, decant it into a goblet or a balloon more readily associated with Belgian ales and Trappist tipples. If a beer is big in body and flavor, be it a Barley Wine, an imperial stout, or an intensely hoppy IPA, then a snifter or brandy balloon makes sense. It eases the impact of overwhelming aromas and holds the flavors in tightly.

Aromas and flavors associated with Pilsners and light lagers need channeling and funneling direct into the nose with a glass that tapers inward at the top, while wheat beers are divided into two camps: Bavarian weissbiers look and taste magnificent from a tall and shapely narrow-waisted flute, designed to create a thick, creamy head. Belgian wheat beers, spicier and more herbal, require a thick, wide-mouthed tumbler that shows off its hazy hue and refreshing complexity. Many serious beer lovers bring back glasses from their beer travels, particularly from countries such as Belgium and Germany.

Eminent glassmakers such as Riedel and Dartington have both released a range of bespoke beer glassware in recent years, while the Boston Beer Company in the United States unveiled a new chapter in glass design with the launch of a glass based on function rather than form.

BEER STYLES

Top five beers by beer style in key regions

Each of the world's key beer regions is best known for a specific range of beer styles. Here are the best beers in each style for those regions.

Britain and Ireland

1 **Pale Ale/Bitter**
Timothy Taylor Landlord

2 **India Pale Ale**
Meantime IPA

3 **Best Bitter**
Harveys Sussex Best Bitter

4 **Barley Wine**
O'Hanlon's Thomas Hardy's Ale

5 **Wood-aged Beer**
Harviestoun Ola Dubh

Belgium

1 **Lambic**
Cantillon Bruocsella Grand Cru
Old Vintage Lambic

2 **Flemish Brown Ale**
Rodenbach Grand Cru

3 **Trappist Ale**
Rochefort 10

4 **Wood-aged beer**
Struise Pannepot Grand Reserva

5 **Trappist Ale/Barley Wine**
Westvleteren Abt 12

Germany

1 **Alt Beer**
Uerige Alt

2 **Doppelbock**
Augustiner Maximator

3 **Doppelbock**
Ayinger Celebrator

4 **Rauchbier/Smoked Beer**
Aecht Schlenkerla Rauchbier

5 **Weissbock**
Schneider Aventinus

Czech Republic

1 **Premium Lager**
Budweiser Budvar

2 **Dark Lager**
Pivovar U Fleků
Flekovský tmavý Ležák

3 **Unfiltered Lager**
Strahov Monastic Brewery
Svatý Norbert Jantar

4 **Pilsner Urquell**
(Kvasnicový)

5 **Pilsner**
Pivovarský Dům Světlý Ležák

Italy

1 **Barley Wine**
Birrificio Baladin Xyauyù

2 **Barley Wine**
Montegioco Draco

3 **Porter**
Birra del Borgo Ke To Reporter

4 **Kriek**
Birrificio Italiano Scires

5 **Sour Red Ale**
Birrificio Panil Barriquée

Scandinavia

1 **Imperial IPA**
Amager Rated XX (Denmark)

2 **Imperial IPA**
Nørrebro North Bridge Extreme
(Denmark)

3 **Espresso Stout**
Mikkeller Beer Geek Breakfast
(Denmark)

4 **Lager**
Nils Oscar God Lager (Sweden)

5 **Sahti**
Nøgne Ø Ut Pa Tu (Norway)

France

1 **Bière de Garde**
La Choulette Bière des Sans Culottes

2 **Bière de Garde**
St. Sylvestre 3 Monts

3 **Bière de Garde**
Brasserie de Theillier La Bavaisienne

4 **Blonde Ale**
Brasserie de Thiriez
Blonde d'Esquelbecq

5 **Wheat Beer**
Pietra Colomba (Corsica)

The Netherlands

1 **Barley Wine**
De Hemel Nieuw Ligt Grand Cru

2 **IPA/Barley Wine**
T'IJ Columbus

3 **Imperial Stout**
De Molen Rasputin

4 **Bock**
De Pauw Bokbier

5 **Pilsner**
Sint Christoffel Christoffel Blonde

USA

1 **Stout**
AleSmith Speedway Stout (California)

2 **Stout**
Brooklyn Chocolate Stout (New York)

3 **Cherry Beer**
New Glarus Wisconsin Belgian Red
(Wisconsin)

4 **Double Imperial IPA**
Russian River Pliny the Elder (California)

5 **IPA**
Victory HopDevil Ale (Pennsylvania)

Canada

1 **Barley Wine**
Alley Kat Olde Deuteronomy

2 **Imperial Stout**
Dieu du Ciel! Péché Mortel

3 **Seasonal Ale**
Les Brasseurs RJ Snoreau

4 **Belgian-style Tripel**
Unibroue A Fin du Monde

5 **Cherry Porter**
Wild Rose Brewery

Australasia

1 **Porter**
Baird Kurofune Porter (Japan)

2 **Vintage Ale**
Coopers Vintage Ale (Australia)

3 **Pale Ale**
Epic Pale Ale (New Zealand)

4 **Espresso Stout**
Hitachino Nest Sweet Stout (Japan)

5 **Barley Wine**
Redoak Special Reserve (Australia)

Vintage ales

Vintage ales are beers that can be cellared, laid down, and left to improve over time, their character becoming more complex over the years. The epitome of the brewer's art, they share more in common with a port or a fine cognac than they do mass-produced bland-tasting beers.

They are ales deliberately crafted to improve in the hands of Old Father Time, served in snifters as an after-dinner drink and best listed on a bar's beer menu under a separate, more discerning section, much like fine or rare wines.

To ward off any negative influences such as oxidization, light strike, and bacteria, vintage ales need to be high in alcohol. We're talking robust Barley Wines, old ales, porters, stouts, and strong Scotch ales here. Lily-livered lagers and bony bitters need not apply.

According to John Keeling, head brewer at Fuller's in London, "A vintage beer should have the strength to last between five and ten years, and they've got to be above seven or eight percent to develop over time."

Heavily hopped beers are a good bet, too, because hops act as a preservative. When drunk young, these astringent beers may induce a painful pucker, but the harsh hop character substantially mellows over time. India Pale Ales and Double India Pale Ales are specific beer styles that will age particularly gracefully.

As vintage ales have not been stabilized by pasteurization or filtration, they tend to be bottle-conditioned (live yeast is added to the beer in the bottle). Over time, the beer carries on fermenting in the bottle and, as the yeast sucks up the residual sugar "Pac-Man-style", the beer's body becomes leaner and the flavor becomes drier and crisper. In addition to its sugar-munching, the added yeast can adorn the beer with some fascinating fruit flavors. Bottle-conditioning, however, is by no means a prerequisite for laying down beer, as some unpasteurized beers have also been known to intensify with age.

Wood-influenced beers are an emerging niche market and are ideal for laying down. Unlike their wine and spirit brethren, brewers traditionally use wood that's fresh, thoroughly cleaned, and designed to have no influence on the beer flavor (other than a slight oxygenated smoothness that's absent when beer is stored in metal casks).

Vintage beer may not deliver the same returns as vintage wine (sadly, an indolent, deaf dog riddled with rickets would fetch more at auction), but the initial outlay comes at a fraction of the cost and risk.

Storing Vintage Ales

Regardless of whether the intention is to make money or merry, it is best to store these beers in a box, out of light, away from heat, and not refrigerated. "One of the joys of vintage beers is that the owner is part of the story," advises John. "If you look after the beer it will improve, if you don't look after it, it won't".

Recommended Vintage Ales

Anchor Christmas Ale (USA)
Brooklyn Black Chocolate Stout (USA)
Cantillon Gueuze (Belgium)
Carnegie Porter (Sweden)
Coopers Vintage Ale (Australia)
Fuller's Brewers Reserve (UK)
Harviestoun Ola Dubh (Scotland)
O'Hanlon's Thomas Hardy's Ale (UK)
Sierra Nevada Celebration Ale (USA)

British-style beers

Crouch Vale Brewers Gold *UK*   **Hale's Ales** Mongoose IPA *USA*   **Dogfish Head** 90 Minute Imperial IPA *USA*

Pale Ale

Pale Ale denotes a broad group of beers including lightly shaded bottom-fermenting beers, from the Belgian classic Orval to the highly hopped Sierra Nevada, from California and the interesting Little Creatures from Australia. But it is Burton-on-Trent in England where, in the early 19th century, pale ales were first brewed, using newfangled pale malt and the notoriously hard, mineral-rich indigenous water that is revered. The huge success of Burton Pale Ales inspired other breweries to follow suit and today there are few British ale-makers that don't produce a pale. Often referred to as golden ale, light ale and, often erroneously, as India Pale Ale (IPA), pale ales tend to be medium-bodied, light copper to golden in color, tremendously refreshing, and offer easy-drinking, with an elegant equilibrium of malt flavors and delicate, floral hop bitterness and aroma. Pale ales are open to flexible interpretations. American varieties are often more bitter, less malt-accented, and closer to traditional British India Pale Ales (IPAs).

India Pale Ale (IPA)

This is the liquid legacy of 18th-century India, where it was always hot and the British expatriates were gasping for a pint. A London brewer, George Hodgson, created India Pale Ale (IPA), a bespoke beer capable of keeping calm around the Cape of Good Hope. It developed its swashbuckling sea legs from ingredients that included plenty of alcohol and copious amounts of hops—both armed with preservative powers to survive the long journey from Burton-on-Trent, England, to Calcutta in India. The style is enjoying a remarkable renaissance in the United States, especially on the West Coast, where an IBU (international bittering units) arms race is ongoing, with many heavily hopped ales enjoying huge popularity. The majority of contemporary British IPAs are merely pale imitations of the original brews.

Double/Imperial India Pale Ale

Beloved of the American craft-brewing scene, Double IPA is an IPA with more hops, more alcohol, more malt, and more unashamed coming-at-you attitude. First brewed by the Blind Pig Brewery in 1994, Double IPAs are brewed with hops, plenty of them, and yet more hops. And then some more hops are added to the brewing process before being finished off with more hops. There's lots of malt in there and plenty of alcohol, but mainly, it's all about the hops.

Adnams Bitter *UK*   **Fuller's** ESB *UK*   Manns Original Brown Ale *UK*

Bitter/Best Bitter

Chances are, if a pub is serving English ale, then it's a bitter. Don't be hoodwinked by the misleading moniker because bitters aren't necessarily bitter in flavor. They earn their alias because they have higher hop character than sweet milds and, more recently, lagers. Bitters are the classic British pub pint, often gold to copper colored with medium bitterness. Ideally served slightly carbonated from a cask, they usually offer a gentle, crisp hop character underlain by a moreish malt and a medium body. Classic bitters hover around or below 4% ABV in strength, while best bitters break free, up to the 4.7% mark. In the United States, where hoppy beer reigns supreme, the term "bitter" is rarely used and "ale" is the generic name most often applied to these traditional-style beers.

Premium/Extra Special Bitter

Extra Special Bitters (ESBs) are bigger, brasher, and more bitter than standard or best bitters, with a characteristic caramel sweetness. With the thirst for bombastic beers growing among ale aficionados, ESB has risen from relative obscurity to gain a newfound prominence in both the United Kingdom and the United States. These brews are often, but not always, graced with crystal malt, Fuggles and Goldings hops, and a higher alcohol content than standard bitters.

Brown Ale

Traditional British beer style steeped in the sepia tint of yesteryear. Once the bread and butter of British breweries, they were sweet, murky-brown beers, low in alcohol—often mixed with mild—and, if you believe the cliché, associated with sooty-faced salt-of-the-earth drinker types. Now very much a sidelined sip, brown ales are drier, nuttier, and stronger, than they once were. When resuscitated by American craft brewers, they tend to be hoppier, too. In Belgium many traditional brown ales remain popular with serious beer connoisseurs.

Springhead Brewery Roaring Meg *UK*

Moorhouse's Black Cat *UK*

Primátor Premium *Czech Republic*

Golden/Blonde Ales

In the 1980s, British ale-accented brewers began giving lager lovers the golden glad-eye in the shape of pale ales which were moderate in hops and juicy in biscuit malt, and which acted as easy-sipping stepping stones across the chasm of misunderstanding that inexplicably divides ales and lagers. Rarely exceeding 5% ABV in strength, golden ales have become a powerful weapon in craft brewing's commercial arsenal, and in recent years they've swept the board at British beer festivals. Often served chilled, these popular beers are referred to in Europe and the US as "blonde ales".

Mild

Marvelously malty, sometimes sweet, low in alcohol yet big in flavor and eminently drinkable, Mild was a mainstay of British pubs until the 1960s. It was first brewed to quench the rapacious thirsts of sweaty-browed farmer types and, later, wet the weary whistles of industrial workers. Now that the main thing that Britain's labour force hits is deadlines or a mouse key, Mild has struggled to survive, and CAMRA (the Campaign for Real Ale) has been lobbying to save it from extinction for some time now, with a month-long Mild Month campaign each May taking place in many UK pubs.

Premium/Mainstream Lager

A catchall term for the most popular beers on the planet. It originates from the German word for storage, and the best brews should be lagered for long periods in cold conditions, where they develop flavor, body, and complexity. Ideally, they should be brewed to an all-malt recipe with a discernible hop bitterness, flavor, and aroma, but sadly the lager world is not an ideal one. Mainstream lagers tend to cut more fermenting corners than a jaywalking seamstress, with many adding cost-saving adjuncts such as rice and flavorings, stunting storage time, and scrimping on genuine ingredients. Look for depth as well as drinkability.

Nils Oscar Barley Wine *Sweden*

O'Hanlon's Thomas Hardy's Ale *UK*

Verhaeghe Duchesse de Bourgogne *Belgium*

Barley Wine/Strong Ale

During the 18th century, England was forever getting into fisticuffs with France and, consequently, drinking wine—the enemy's elixir—was regarded as most unpatriotic. So, in order to challenge "posh" plonk on the tables of the upper class, strong grandiose ales called Barley Wines were devised and often brewed in aristocratic country houses. Ranging from amber to deep copper-garnet in color, they're full-bodied, malty sweet, and/ or hop-heavy, and designed to develop maturity over time. It's a style that is enjoying a renaissance among the global craft-brewing community, especially in the United States and Belgium, where many Barley Wines are brewed to order for the American market.

Old Ale

An English pre-Industrial Revolution ale stored for long periods in unlined wooden tuns that is also known as "stale" beer by drinkers. Barrel-dwelling wild yeast gifted it its tart, lactic sourness that tended to be consumed as the spike in a blended porter. By no means exclusively dark, old ales are middle rather than heavyweight in strength (4%-6.5% ABV) and tend to be brewed with a predominance of malt. Stronger examples include Fuller's Gale's Old Prize Ale (9%) and the classic O'Hanlon's Thomas Hardy's Ale, which, at 11.7%, is Britain's strongest ale.

Wood/Barrel-aged Beer

Once a term associated with English brewers who stored their beer in wooden rather than metal kegs, wood-aged beer means something completely different today. An increasing number of techniques used by wine and whiskey makers are being applied at the cutting edge of New World brewing, with barrels once used to house old sherry, bourbon, Scotch whisky, port, and wine being used to develop a variety of beer styles with maturation. Particularly popular among go-against-the-grain microbrewers in the US, Scandinavia, and the UK.

AleSmith Wee Heavy *USA*   **Meantime** London Porter *UK*   **Wye Valley** Dorothy Goodbody's Wholesome Stout *UK*

Scotch Ales

Caramelized, sweet, and full-bodied beers, made up of masses of malt, and given a lengthy boil with little or no hops. Traditionally, Scotch ales varied in alcohol; their strength was denoted by their taxable value in shillings per cask —a pint of "80 shilling" being more potent and pricey than a pint of "60 shilling". Wee Heavy, meanwhile, tends to be strapping, kilt-lifting beer, between 7% and 11% ABV. While Scotch ales are still available in their homeland, Scottish brewers are more interested in having fun with hops, so some of the more noteworthy Scotch ales are coming out of France, the United States, and Belgium, with the latter being home to some of the strongest versions.

Porter

An opaque18th-century opium of the masses that oiled the wheels of the British Industrial Revolution and is arguably the most important beer style in history. Born in London, it first referred to a blend of three beers (strong ale, pale, and Mild) but soon became a beer in its own right. Thick and strong, incredibly cheap, and with unprecedented consistency, porter spread through working-class London quicker than the Great Fire and was soon a phenomenon both nationwide and as an export to the Baltic states. The emergence of lighter beers and World War One restrictions on making roasted malts accelerated porter's demise, but today, especially in the United States and Scandinavia, the popularity of porter is rising again. Colored blackish or burnished dark brown, porters are medium-bodied dark malt-accented beers. A chocolate and coffee character is common, sweeter than stouts, more drinkable, and with less burnt roast malt notes. Baltic porters are really like porters that are on steroids.

Stout

A drier, darker, fuller-bodied, and some would say stouter descendant of porter. Born in London as "stout porter" and raised in Ireland, it soon lost its surname and became synonymous with a brand founded in 1759 by Arthur Guinness. Having drunk imported porters and stouts from Britain, the Irish brewer decided to brew his own "dry Irish" version using unmalted roasted barley instead of dark malts—producing a more acrid, astringent and thicker interpretation. London stouts, by contrast, were made with 100 percent malt grist including the original brown malt, and with no roast barley. When the British government imposed restrictions on malting and beer strength during World War One, the dry Irish style overtook its British counterpart and, aided by both canny advertising and the missionary zeal of Irish diaspora, it's become the benchmark for stouts.

Bartrams Brewery Egalitarian Stout *UK*

Great Divide Brewing Co. Yeti Imperial Stout *USA*

Imperial Russian Stout/ Foreign Export Stout

Imperial stouts date back to the days when Britain exported dark beers to the Baltic states. They're beers that are big in booze (9% ABV and above), bountiful in body, and filled with full-on fruit flavor and dark malt dryness. Once the chosen tipple of Catherine the Great, imperial stouts now dovetail neatly with the needs of high-octane-ale drinkers in the United States. Foreign Export Stout (FES), meanwhile, has a strong following in Africa and the Caribbean.

Oyster Stout

Given that oysters and stout make such a smashing culinary couple, brewers thought it would be a good idea to bring them together in the barrel. What clever folk they are. The addition of a few oysters gives a bit of briny bitterness and added smoothness to the beer. Not all oyster stouts are brewed with oysters, though. It's all a bit confusing.

Chocolate Stout

Indulgent ales sometimes brewed with extra amounts of chocolate malt and sometimes brewed with actual chunks of chocolate. Expect cocoa, coffee, and, of course, chocolate characteristics. Young's Brewery in the UK and Rogue Brewery in the US both produce great examples.

Oatmeal Stout

A beer style back in fashion after being on the brink of extinction. The addition of oatmeal to the barley grist endows the beer with a smoother, nuttier mouthfeel that goes down with glide in its stride.

Sweet Stout/Milk Stout

Suitable for sweet-toothed drinkers, these stouts are lower in alcohol than conventional stouts, counteracting the dry bitterness of the malt, and to some extent the hops, with the addition of lactose, a sugar found in milk. Yeast deprived of lactose means that the unfermentable sugars supply sweetness and body.

American-style beers

Driven by derring-do and the kind of cheeky chutzpah that leaves Europeans in a state of bewildered awe, the vibrant North American beer scene has blown the doors off conventional beer-style categorization.

At the Great American Beer Festival, the US beer equivalent of the "Oscars", beer is spliced into 75 different categories ranging from "fresh hop ales" and "gluten-free lagers" to "robust porters" and "American-style light lagers".

While the plethora of new styles, hybrids, and twists on tradition only goes to reflect the richness and diversity of what's going on in the States, it would be dreadfully unfair on the world's rainforests to list them all in detail here.

Suffice it to say, American craft brewers tend to—but not always— take conventional European beer styles and make them bigger, brasher, and bolder. The "American-style" prefix often, but not always, denotes an amplification of a beer style's distinguishable characteristics: IPAs are bigger in their bitterness, Double IPAs are even bigger, the spice in Saisons is spiked, fruit beers are fruitier, the alcohol in Barley Wines is increased, and the alluring fruity aromas of wheat beers are enhanced. But, when brewed well, they're no less complex in their flavor, balance, or character.

In the past couple of years, things have gone full circle, with a new wave of English and Belgian brewers aping "American-style" interpretations of their native beer styles, and then exporting them back to the US.

Belgian-style beers

Maredsous 8 Brune *Belgium*   **St. Bernardus** Abt 12 *Belgium*   **Brasserie Dupont** Saison Dupont *Belgium*

Abbey Beers

Abbey-dwelling monks brewed beer in Belgium as early as the 5th century, and it's estimated that Europe has, over time, boasted more than 500 abbey breweries. The beer the monks made served as a benevolent boost to the local community, a healthier alternative to local polluted water and a particularly persuasive piece of religious public relations.

When the French Revolution stuck a secular spanner in the works in 1783, and the monks were stripped of their wealth, influence, and mash-forks, it wasn't until the early 19th century that the monks got into the habit of brewing again.

Inspired by the growing consumer thirst for Trappist beers, abbey beers emerged after World War Two. Today, they can be divided into two categories: The first are commercial concerns bereft of "brotherly" influence, named after fictitious or defunct monasteries, yet modeled on the style of beers associated with Trappist brewing. The second are "monastic visions" realized by commercial brewers on behalf of, and with permission from, religious orders

and institutions who haven't the means to do so themselves (the cloisters receive cash to spend on pious deeds, and the brewery benefits from the halo effect of saintly association).

They can be awesome efforts, as seductive and saintly as Trappist tipples, or they may be bottled iconoclasm, inferior imitations of angelic ales. It would be useful if the level of monkish involvement correlated directly with the quality and integrity of the beer, but it doesn't work like that. Some of the best abbey ales are in fact named after entirely fictitious monastery breweries.

Like Trappist beers, most abbey beers are either Dubbels or Tripels, although many have been making maneuvers into blonde/pale ale territory.

Farmhouse Ales/Saison/ Bière de Garde

The Farmhouse, or Saison, beers of Belgium were and are still best drunk in the summer, after a hard or fun day toiling or frolicking in the field. Back in the days when brewing in the hazy heat of summer was problematic, Saisons were brewed in the spring with lots of preservative hops and spices, laid down until the weather warmed up, and released to slake the thirst of rural workers in Wallonia, the southern French-speaking region of Belgium. They tend to be tart, bitter, and spicy brews with lots of fruit flavor, and are usually well hopped and, more often than not, bottle-conditioned. French interpretations are known as Bière de Garde, or "keeping beers", and traditionally hail from the Pas-de-Calais region of northern France.

Caracole Nostradamus Strong Belgian Ale *Belgium*   **Rodenbach** Grand Cru *Belgium*   **Drie Fonteinen** Oude Geuze *Belgium*

Flemish Brown Ales/Oud Bruin

Brewed predominantly in and around the waterside town of Oudenaarde, on the river Scheldt in East Flanders, "old browns" are all smoothness, sweetness, sourness, and spice, not to mention incredibly refreshing. Oudenaarde's local water profile, low in sodium and high in sodium bicarbonate, gives the beer a complex consistency; its sweet caramel character is born of long boiling times and the use of myriad malts; while the multistrain, top-fermenting yeasts adorn the ale with its lactic acetic character. Extra complexity comes with secondary fermentation that takes place in the bottle.

Flemish Red Ales

A quirky cousin of Flemish brown ales hailing from the other (western) side of Flanders. Like Lambics, Flemish reds are fermented spontaneously using wild yeasts, matured in oak, and are often a blend of young and old. Typified by Rodenbach, they're reddish brown in color, fruity, seductively sour, and hugely refreshing. An enduring Belgian classic.

Lambic Beers

Beer doesn't come much more crazy or blissful than Lambic. Steeped in romance and tradition, Lambic differs from other beer styles in that it is fermented using wild, naturally occurring yeast, rather than strains that are intentionally added.

Once upon a time, this was how all beer was brewed, but now the traditional technique is exclusive to the Payottenland region of Belgium, to the south west of Brussels. Lambics are brewed using at least 30 percent unmalted wheat, and second-hand dilapidated hops are added, more for their preservative powers than for flavor. After a prolonged boil, the wort is left to cool in open, shallow tanks where it patiently waits, arms outstretched, for airborne magical microorganisms to drift through the vents in the brewery roof and leisurely have their wondrous, wicked way.

Once the beer is decanted into wooden casks, the wild yeast (Saccharomyces) fermentation carries on for a fortnight or so until it gets tired. The beer then assumes an acrid, raw character courtesy of microbugs and microcritters in the wood, before Brettanomyces, a magical slow-fermenting yeast, takes control. "Brett" gives lambic beer its "horse-blanket" aroma, sharp citric character, and musty profile, while delivering a deep and quirky complexity to the beer. Lambics that have matured for between 6 and 12 months are regarded as "young" while "old" Lambics have generally been developing in oak for two years or more.

Young lambics are a very lightly carbonated acquired taste—sour, vinegary, dry, mildly mildewed, with tartness and tobacco flavors. Older versions, the nearest beer gets to wine, are armed with added complexity, textured with tannin—there's tartness and a measured cheesy pong. Comparisons with a bone-dry fino sherry are not just highfalutin hyperbole.

Boon Oude Geuze *Belgium*

The Lost Abbey Cuvée de Tomme *USA*

Cantillon Kriek Lambic *Belgium*

Oude Gueuze

Also known as "Brussels Champagne", genuine Oude Gueuze is a unique and quite extraordinary beer made using a blend of old and new Lambic. Elder lambics donate vinous flavor and depth to the beer, while young Lambic brings youthful citric zest and effervescence, courtesy of unfermented sugars.

The art of Gueuze blending is a noble one, as complex and intricate as that practiced by the whiskey- or winemaker. A blender will use nothing but his nose and his taste buds to achieve the right balance before bottling the beer, caged and corked like Champagne, with a batch of sugar to kick-start fermentation. Gueuze is then laid down for as much as three years, during which time it will develop a delightfully dry, sharp character.

Old Gueuze, acidic and shocking at first, is an acquired taste, but perseverance will be rewarded with one of the world's most incredible imbibing experiences. The name is protected by Belgian law, and only Payottenland producers using 100 percent lambic can use it on their bottles.

Oude Kriek

The finest and most authentic form of Kriek (cherry beer) made from steeping cherries in Lambic casks for several months. The tradition of steeping whole cherries in beer, which dates back to a pre-hop era when fruit was used to make the beer more palatable, provides extra sugars for fermentation and terrific tartness. As with Oude Gueuze, the Oude Kriek appellation is protected by Belgian law. Oude Kriek is not, under any circumstances, to be confused with sweet and sickly synthetic cherry beers that cheekily call themselves "krieks".

Fruit Lambic

While cherry and raspberry are the most common fruit macerated in casks of Lambic, an increasing number of brewers are showboating with left-field examples, including apricot, apple, banana, and pineapple. The fruit gives the traditionally, sour, dry, and acidic Lambic beer a wonderfully sweet yet slightly tart edge.

Orval Orval *Belgium*

Westmalle Tripel Trappist *Belgium*

Caracole Troublette **Witbier** *Belgium*

Trappist Beers

Today, the only monastic order that owns its own breweries and brews its own beer is the Cistercian Order of the Strict Observance, also known as the Trappists. Renowned for their rigorous religious obedience, sustained silence, and strict adherence to self-sufficiency, the Trappists have six abbey breweries in Belgium (Westvleteren, Orval, Rochefort, Westmalle, Chimay, and Achel) and one in the Netherlands (La Trappe/De Koningshoeven) and, by law, are the only producers allowed to brew Trappist beer.

Trappist beers, mostly bottle-conditioned, are strong top-fermented beers ranging from pale ale to Quadrupels. They command sacrosanct status among aficionados and, although some accusations of corner-cutting have emerged in recent years, they remain hugely complex ales of colossal character.

Dubbel

If there's a Trappist/abbey ale that's rich, medium-to-full bodied, refermented in the bottle, malty, and dark, with fruit flavors, caramel character, candy sugar sweetness, and mellow alcohol, then you hardly have to be Hercule Poirot to recognize it's a Dubbel or, if you're of French persuasion, a Double.

Tripel

Traditionally the strongest ale offered under the abbey and Trappist banners. Tripels disguise their strength and complexity under a golden-blonde cloak and a fluffy mousse head. Well attenuated with a pale malt character, Tripels are often sweetened with the addition of candy sugar and/or spiced up with light-to-heavy hop bitterness and refermented in the bottle for further flavor.

Witbier

Like weissbier, Belgian witbier made an incredible and unexpected comeback in the 1960s when a milkman named Pierre Celis, almost single-handedly, hauled Hoegaarden back onto its feet and breathed life back into a Belgian classic ale. Known as witbier (wheat beer) in the Flemish tongue and Bière de Blanche in French, it is spicier than its Bavarian brethren, unfiltered, often calls upon coriander and orange peel for added flavor. It tends to be lower in alcohol —hovering around the 4-5% ABV mark.

German-style beers

Uerige Obergarige Hausbrauerei Uerige Alt *Germany*

Rothenbach Brauerei Aufsesser Bock **Bier** *Germany*

Ayinger Celebrator *Germany*

Alt Beers

The drink of Düsseldorf, "Alt" is a top-fermented copper-colored "old ale" that predates lager. It shares similarities with English pale ales and British bitters, but long lagering at low temperatures creates a cleaner, crisper character. Brewed using pale malt, Alts are traditionally fairly fruity, with heavier hop flavors than German lagers. A moderate strength of around 4.8% ABV and a dry finish make them a jolly drinkable group of beers.

Bocks

In the 14th century, these strong, massively malty beers were exclusive to the north German town of Einbeck but, following the town's demise in the Thirty Years War, they were revived in Bavaria and are now brewed all over Germany and beyond, mostly as seasonal beers for both winter and spring.

While pale bocks have increased in popularity recently, most bocks are dark in color, brewed with Vienna and Munich malt, a light dusting of hops, and a long lagering period of around 12-5 weeks. Drinking between 6.3% and 7% ABV, bocks are rich, warming, and full-bodied with a notably long, lingering finish.

The word "bock", a distortion of the "beck" part of Einbeck, translates as "billy goat" and the hairy member of the Bovidae family is often seen on German bock beer labels.

Doppelbock/DoubleBocks

An extra-strong version of bock bier, Doppelbock emerged in the late 18th century as a powerful lager version of old monastic strong beer, brewed by monks as "liquid bread", to tide them over during the fasting period of Lent.

Exceptionally malty, with faint bitterness, Doppelbocks usually check in at around 7% ABV with the stronger versions reaching as much as 13%. Darker, maltier, hoppier, more potent, and often recognized by the "–ator" suffix as in Salvator brewed by Paulaner, Celebrator by Ayinger, and Spaten Optimator.

Kulmbacher Eku 28 *Germany*   **Binding-Brauerei** Schöfferhofer *Germany*   **Schwaben Bräu** Das Schwarze *Germany*

Eisbock

Intense and intoxicating, ice bocks are categorized as some of the world's most potent beers. They achieve their strength from being frozen at the latter stages of maturation. With water freezing before alcohol, the beer loses about a tenth of its water content and, consequently, the beer reaches an ABV of around 10%. A thick, treacle-y winter warmer with a massive malt profile, Eisbock offers big body and plenty of alcohol.

Weisenbock

A strong version of weissbier and Hefeweizen that, unlike the barley-based lager bock beers, ale made with at least 50% wheat malt.

Maibock

While most bocks are dark, malty, and sweet, maibocks are bright, hoppy, and bitter, with a similar strength to Doppelbock (7% ABV and above). Mostly brewed as seasonal ales to be drunk in April and May, Maibocks are a sure sign that spring has sprung.

Dark Lagers

Don't be fooled by the hoodwinking hue; dark lagers go down just as easily as a dizzy, fizzy blonde. They gain their deep copper color from a kaleidoscope of kilned malt, and lager yeast lends a lightness of palate that is absent from ale. The hops, while present, should play second fiddle to the dry bitterness of roasted malt. Dunkels, German dark lagers, are the most impressive examples of the style. In hotter climates such as South America and Asia, where lackluster yellow lagers live, discerning drinkers should reach for dark versions if they can.

Great Lakes Brewing Co. Dortmunder Gold *USA*

Warsteiner Premium Dunkel *Germany*

Paulaner Original Münchner *Germany*

Dortmunder Export

Germany's big, bruising blue-collar beer from Dortmund, once Germany's largest brewing city, is famous for slaking the thirst of coal and steel workers during the 19th century. Strong, robust, and dry, but lacking the flowery overtones that emanate from Pilsner, Dortmunder is a no-nonsense beer brewed for no-nonsense drinkers. With bolshy bitterness and substantial malt sweetness, and strong (5.2% ABV and above) yet hugely refreshing, Dortmunders have, like British Milds and brown ales, waned in popularity with the demise of industrial toil, but a few versions still survive. Go drink them if you think you're tough enough.

Dunkel/Münchner Dunkel

Before the arrival of golden beer, Dunkels dominated Germany's drinking landscape but, as palates have opted for paler beers, it's become a catchall term for all dark beers, bandied about in German beer drinking circles with wild abandon.

As a descriptor, it's used to denote any beer that is dark in color—from the bitter Dunkels of Franconia to the roasty, toasty Dunkels of Munich via the hoppier northern versions. It can also go before other beer styles—such as Dunkel Hefeweizen or Dunkel Bock. When drunk from the swaying steins of Bavaria, authentic Münchner Dunkels are dark brown-colored beers, mellowed with maturation, brimming with rich roasty malt sweetness, and displaying a subdued hop character.

Helles

A pale straw blonde Bavarian lager, also known as "Munich Original Lager", first brewed by the Spaten brewery in March 1894. Helle may translate as "light", but this merely denotes its eye-catching, alluring hue and by no means suggests a dizzy, air-headed blonde. Helles are rich and malt-accented, full-bodied yet delicate, and eminently drinkable with a light hop finish. Often seen swaying in steins in Bavarian beer gardens. Alcohol strength ranges from 4.7%-5.4% ABV.

Harpoon Brewery Harpoon Ale *USA*

Früh Kölsch *Germany*

Augustiner Edelstoff *Germany*

Kellerbier

An unfiltered "cellar beer" with a strong aromatic hop signature, bronzed with plenty of Munich malt, and closely associated with the boutique breweries of Franconia. In their most authentic form, Kellerbiers are unpasteurized with little to no effervescence, served straight from the cask into earthenware mugs. They make terrific apéritif beers and fine summer thirst-slakers. A selection of Kellerbiers is available in bottle and exported widely.

Kölsch

Kölsch looks like a German lager, but it has more in common with blonde British ale. Meaning "from Cologne", Kölsch accounts for more than half of all the beer consumed here. In 1948, the cluster of Kölsch brewers managed to pass a law preventing this extremely pale palatable ale being made anywhere other than in and around Cologne.

Like its darker cousin Altbier, Kölsch gets its fruity flavor from a unique top-fermenting yeast strain. Where it differs from British pale ales is in its use of one type of malt and cold, lager-like, fermentation, plus a lengthy maturation. Kölsch is always served in a straight-sided, narrow, 8 fl oz pint (200 ml) glass called a "stange" that prevents it from getting warm. Extremely subtle and delicate with fruity ale-esque flavors, Kölsch is light in both body and appearance, with subdued maltiness, unobtrusive hoppiness, and plenty of effervescence. While unable to call it Kölsch, craft brewers outside of Cologne ape the style using wheat.

Märzen/Oktoberfest Beers

Back in the Middle Ages, prior to the advent of refrigeration, brewing beer in the summer was difficult due to the infection of airborne bacteria. So, in March, brewers amassed plenty of beer, strong and heavily hopped, to tide them over until fall. Stored in cold-cellared casks, Märzens were full-bodied malt-accented beers, deep amber to copper in color and around 5% or 6% ABV. By October, brewers cleared out their barrels of Märzen in order to make room for new beers. Having lots of beer to finish off was a good excuse for a party, and thus the Oktoberfest was born.

Today, Oktoberfestbier tends to be a paler version of a Märzen, lagered and matured for between three and four months. Technically, genuine Oktoberfest beer can be brewed only within the city limits of Munich, by brewers participating in the annual festival. Confusingly, these beers aren't often drunk there now, as the easier-drinking Helle beers are preferred. Beyond Munich, imitations must be called Oktoberfest-style beer.

Jever Pilsener *Germany*

Sprecher Black Bavarian *USA*

Aecht Schlenkerla Rauchbier *Germany*

Pilsner

The lord of lagers, Pilsner was first brewed in the Bohemian town of Pilsen. Also known as pilsener and pils, it's now brewed all over the world to varying degrees of excellence/tedium. In its most authentic form, Pilsner is a well-structured, full-bodied beer with a shimmering golden hue. Beneath the dense, luxuriant white head, the velvety mouthfeel comes courtesy of the soft water; the all-malt backbone is firm and succulent; and the high hop bitterness, on both the nose and palate, is shaped by Saaz hops. Lagering should be long and loving. German Pilsners tend to be brusquer in their bitterness than others.

Schwarzbier

Schwarzbiers are to lager what stout and porters are to ale, and originate in the south of Germany. Blacker than the Black Hole, Schwarzbier's opaque appearance raises expectations of roasted bitterness, burnt flavors, and top-fermenting fruit flavors, but dashes them with something much milder and Pilsner-like. In this dark beer you'll find measured maltiness, creamy, dark-colored, and full-bodied, with a subdued hop presence, a dry finish, and gentle, centered sweetness.

Smoked Beer/Rauchbier

Smoked beers date back to before the 18th century, when malt used for brewing was dried over wood-fueled fires, giving the beer a deeply smoky character. The advent of clean and crisp coal, which left no flavor trail in the beer, banished smoked beers to the brewing background, and today there is only a handful of breweries producing Rauchbier using the traditional technique.

It's a crazy Märzen-style beer that's very, very smoky. It's like drinking a campfire through a barbecued kipper that's been swimming in lapsang souchong tea. Some people adore it, but others will find it a little too smoky.

While Rauchbier is synonymous with Bamberg, a number of craft breweries in the United Kingdom and the United States are experimenting using smoke and smoked malt. Alaskan Smoked Porter, while not strictly a Rauchbier, is a sublime showcase for the peaty malt.

Delicious as a digestif or teamed with smoked cheeses, barbecued meats, fish, or anything from the barbecue.

Samuel Adams Boston Lager *USA*   Weihenstephaner Hefeweissbier Dunkel *Germany*   Hacker-Pschorr Dunkle Weiss *Germany*

Vienna Red

A maroon malt-driven lager first brewed by the Dreher family in the Austrian capital back in the 1840s, just a year before the arrival of Pilsner. Nutty, slightly sweet, and notable for a refined roast character and lengthy finish, Vienna-style lagers are absent from their eponymous birthplace but are enjoying a revival in Central America, the US and, Scandinavia.

Weissbier/Weizen (wheat beer)

Known in Bavaria as Weizen and elsewhere in Germany as weissbier, this beer was so popular during the 15th century that it sparked a price hike for wheat. The German beer purity law (Reinheitsgebot, see Glossary), when introduced, meant only that breweries owned by the Duke of Bavaria were permitted to brew wheat beer. Its success continued until the emergence of dark, and later golden, lager signaled a dive in sales. But after marketing efforts in the late 1970s wheat beer now makes up 20 percent of German beer output.

  Wheat beers get all their banana and clove-like flavor from the use of a unique yeast strain that brings out the true character of the wheat malt used in the brew. The proportion of wheat also tends to be higher in Germany than it is in Belgium, and German brewers would never throw herbs or spices in to the mix. Most brewers produce two versions: Hefe (with yeast) or Kristal (without yeast). The latter may look clearer, but the former is by far the more flavorsome and popular.

Dunkel-weizen

Complex dark Bavarian wheat beer brewed using a combination of darker wheat and darker barley malt. In addition to the bubblegum, banana, and clove signature synonymous with "white" Weizens, here there is more chocolate flavor, more roast, and more dark fruity tones in the mix.

Esoteric beer styles

Anchor Anchor Steam **Beer** *USA*

Spaten Oktoberfestbier *Germany*

Brasserie de Saverne Kasteel Cru *France*

Steam Beer

An amber-colored rich and creamy all-malt hybrid beer that is fermented with lager yeast at warm temperatures. Bridging the gap between ale and lager, it's also known as "Californian common" and was introduced almost exclusively to the US West Coast in the latter part of the 19th century as a blue-collar beer. It's synonymous with San Francisco where, at its peak, there were more than two dozen steam beer breweries. The style survived Prohibition and big brewery consolidation to spearhead the American craft-brewing revival in the 1970s, thanks to Fritz Maytag's Anchor Brewery. Confusion surrounds the "steam" reference, with even Maytag unsure of its exact meaning, but the most convincing explanation is that "steam" was caused by the addition of a small dose of fermenting beer to the finished product. This "krausening" increased the pressure of carbon dioxide, which needed to be expelled before dispense (see Glossary, page 271).

Seasonal Ales

Prior to the advent of refrigeration and modern brewing techniques, seasonal ales were originally dictated by the seasons. This tradition continues today, with most breweries releasing a series of seasonal beers throughout the year. While some are designed to suit the climate and honor the brewing trends of yesteryear, other seasonal ales are an opportunity for a brewery to showboat and experiment without having to make a long-term commercial commitment. Seasonal ales stick a spoke in the wheels of complacency, prick up the ears of drinkers, and help to keep the creative juices of the head brewer flowing, and are often a brewer's most interesting efforts. Particularly well-received seasonal ales are often promoted to "permanent" beers that are brewed all year around.

Champagne Beer

The notoriously disobedient Champagne yeast baffled brewers for years, but, since the Belgians tamed it a few years ago, champagne beers have emerged to undermine the perception of beer as a poor man's drink.

Proper posh, rightly pricy, and often referred to as Bière de Brut, champagne beers mimic the processes undertaken by Champagne houses, such as lengthy maturation, remuage, dégorgement, and the méthode champenoise. Some champagne beers are even cave-aged in the French region of Champagne. Often caved and corked in bottles more readily associated with sparkling wine, champagne beers tend to be elegantly intoxicating and effervescent, with a touch of acidic dryness on the finish.

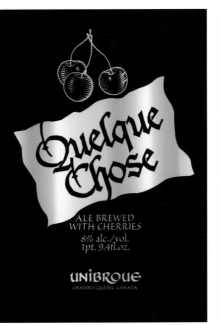

Brooklyn Brewery Black Chocolate Stout *USA*

Unibroue Quelque Chose *Canada*

Finlandia Sahti Strong *Finland*

Chocolate Beer

Yes. Chocolate and beer. Together. United in indulgent harmony. Boffins with spectacles, clipboards, and brains the size of beanbags have discovered that early 18th-century inhabitants of Mexico and Central America drank something resembling chocolate beer, and chocolate malts can often be found working their magic in stouts, porters, and dark ales.

But proper chocolate beers don't just impersonate the taste of chocolate; they actually include chocolate or chocolate essence in the brewing process—often added to the mash as powdered chocolate or in chunks. Chocolate beers tend to be stouts and porters. Meantime and Young's in the United Kingdom and Rogue in the United States produce some of the finest examples.

Fruit Beer

Tread carefully, as fruit beers range from the awe-inspiring to the downright awful. At their best, they are brewed using real fruit extract in either primary or secondary fermentation, and make for fine summer sips and dessert or apéritif beers. At their worst, using adjuncts and sickly syrups, they're daft drinks to be steered clear of.

Spice, Herb, and Seed Beer

Before hops were discovered, brewers balanced out their grain base with all manner of herbs and spices to enliven their beer. Heather, juniper, spruce, sage, poppies, and even nettles are now being called upon by quirky craft brewers in their quest to create ever more individual flavors and aromas.

Sahti

One of the world's oldest beer styles, Sahti is a Finnish farmhouse ale brewed in a rather bizarre fashion. The mash, made up of a variety of grains including rye and barley, is filtered through a bed of juniper twigs, seasoned with juniper berries instead of (and/or in addition to) hops and fermented with baker's yeast, from where it gets its banana undertones. Tasting like a slightly loony love child of a German Hefeweizen or a Belgian Lambic beer, Sahti is heady and hazy, with a resinous aroma of pine needles, mint, and cloves and a tart tingle on the palate. Having traditionally been the exclusive domain of the ambitious home brewer, Sahti brewing has lately been undertaken by ambitious brewers eager to explore esoteric, quasi-extinct ale styles.

A WORLD
OF BEER

A world of beer: featured countries

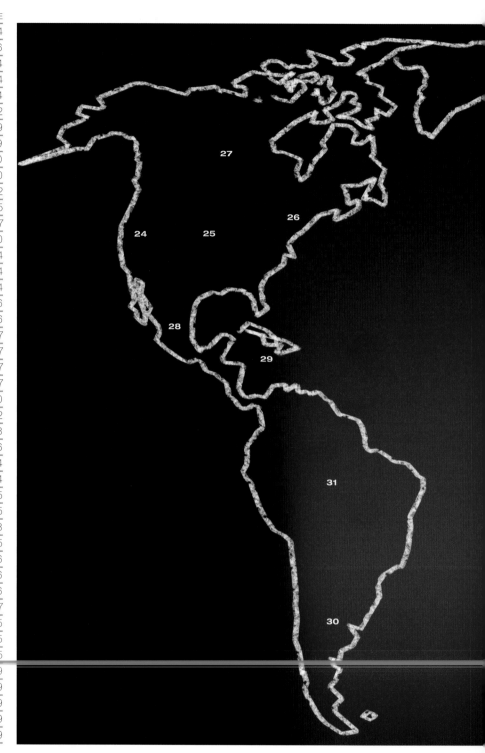

"You can't be a real country unless you have a beer and an airline – it helps if you have some kind of a football team, or some nuclear weapons, but at the very least you need a beer."

FRANK ZAPPA
AMERICAN MUSICIAN, SATIRIST, & SONGWRITER 1940–1993

A world of beer: making the selection

It's a well-worn cliché, but beauty is, indeed, in the eye of the beer holder.

Taste is a subjective sensation, everyone's palate is different, and, even if you were to take a hundred beer drinkers and ask them to compile a list of their favorite top ten beers (never mind a thousand), no two lists would be exactly the same. No bad thing for if we all liked the same ones, life would be dull.

The criteria used for choosing the beers have been, first and foremost, flavor and taste. The worst crime a beer can commit is being forgettable and bland. From the strong, stifling smokiness of a German Rauchbier to the delicate, dry hop finish of a Pilsner, all the beers on the following pages have taste and flavor, and I'd like to think they're all memorable, too.

In terms of both styles and geography, the net has been cast far and wide, from the southern tip of Argentina to the northernmost outpost of Scandinavia; by featuring a dazzling array of beer styles, from American IPAs to Zoigl, I've done my utmost to capture the remarkable diversity of beer.

And what diversity there is. These are blissful beer-drinking days in which we live. It's madness, the sheer amount of lovely beer being brewed out there. Great beer is now a global phenomenon. Deep-rooted beer-drinking nations continue to thrive, while countries such as Denmark, Italy, and the United States, once barren beer terrain, are now fertile lands for beer adventurers.

In terms of ingredients and approach, experimentation and innovation are rife; new styles are being created and traditional styles are being revived, often with a New World–style avant-garde twist; brewers are exploring the past but, with the appliance of modern science, not getting stuck there; beer is rekindling its kinship with food and can currently be found at the forefront of a global gastronomic renaissance. I'd like to think that the beers reflect these vibrant beer-drinking times.

For ease of reference, the thousand beers and the breweries that brew them have been listed under country and ranked in alphabetical order. While the style of the beer is mentioned, it doesn't always tell you everything about the beer so, using a selection of symbols, I've also taken the step of suggesting the ideal occasion on which to drink it, whether it goes well with food, if it's a must-drink classic, and whether it should be quaffed or carefully contemplated.

Tasting ratings

As well as providing brief tasting notes and the odd mention of ingredients, an attempt has been made to capture the history, the tales, and the people behind the beers, because I believe the experience of drinking a beer is always enhanced if you know what shaped it.

While every step has been taken to ensure accuracy, the beer world is spinning at an increasingly rapid pace, and there will inevitably be some beers or breweries that will change names, change hands, be relocated, or close altogether. Apologies in advance for any possible disappointment.

Many of the world's finest beers are brewed by small producers without means of distribution beyond their locale. I haven't deliberately opted for the obscure, but it would be an error to omit some elusive brews because of their rarity.

Symbols used in the "A World of Beer" beer listings correspond to the following definitions:

 CONNOISSEUR CLASSIC Cult or classic beers that are essential drinking for any discerning beer connoisseur.

 SESSION SIP Easy-drinking, refreshing, and thirst-quenching beers that are usually of modest strength.

 SUPER STYLE Beers that exemplify a particular style.

 COOL QUENCHER Refined and refreshing thirst-slakers.

 GOOD WITH FOOD Beers that find favor and flavor with food.

 THINK WHILE YOU DRINK Beers suited to quiet and measured contemplation.

 DARK SIDE Malt-driven dark beers with a touch of sweetness.

 HOP HEAD Big, bitter heavily hopped beers with a high IBU rating.

NEW WORLD An innovative, avant-garde twist on a traditional beer style.

 FRUITY Funky and fruity beers that are both sour and sweet.

A LITTLE UNUSUAL Quirky or unusual beers using esoteric or exotic ingredients.

ONE IS ENOUGH Potent and powerful beers to be drunk responsibly.

The world's top ten beer-drinking cities

1 Bamberg *Germany*

Beer courses through Bamberg's veins; it drifts deep down into its psyche and percolates its past. The town first issued a license to brew beer back in 1122, and in the early 1800s there were 65 breweries for a population of just 20,000. Today, there are 11 traditional breweries and a host of terrific taverns and inns, mostly decked in dark wood, in which to sample Rauchbier, Bamberg's celebrated smoky local beer specialty.

Recommended Beer
Aecht Schlenkerla Rauchbier
The archetypal Rauchbier.

Recommended Bar
Schlenkerla Tavern "The Limping Man" is Bamberg's most famous beer bar (left) where getting totally "Schlenkerlared" is a must for any beer tourist.

Thing to do before Beer O'clock
Visit the Old Town Hall.

2 Bruges *Belgium*

Belgium is blessed with numerous brilliant beer towns, but Bruges gets the nod because it's a devilishly handsome fellow. Known as the "Venice of the North" and one of Europe's most popular weekend destinations, it looks like a magnificent medieval 15th-century film set, with narrow cobbled streets and stepped houses mirrored in the meandering canals. Despite its beauty and impressive architecture, there's not much to see or indeed do apart from drink beer in one of Bruges's myriad bars.

Recommended Beer
Anything and everything Belgian.

Recommended Bar
't Brugs Beertje Legendary bar with more than 300 Belgian beauties on its beer list.

Thing to do before Beer O'clock
Eat chocolate.

Beer culture is part of everyday life in all these cities. Whether you want to discover a seriously hoppy ale in Oregon, sample a traditional pint of bitter in London, or sip a Trappist ale in Belgium, here are the key ale places worth leaving home for.

6 Portland *Oregon, USA*

Portland, in the United States' Pacific Northwest, is home to more than 30 breweries all by itself. Legendary beer writer Michael Jackson once described it as "Munich on the Willamette", as Portland surpasses the German city in terms of the number of breweries. While craft-beer sales account for just below 4 percent of the entire beer market in the United States, in Portland they represent a staggering 45 percent of all beer drunk.

Recommended Beer
BridgePort IPA A Pacific Northwest classic brew.

Recommended Bar
The Horse Brass Pub A beer-supping shrine run by the godfather of Portland's beer scene.

Thing to do before Beer O'clock
Get on a bicycle. Portland is well known as the United States' best cycling city.

7 Prague *Czech Republic*

There are approximately one million people living in Prague, and all of them drink beer. Every single one. Its beer halls and pubs may not have the diversity of, say, Belgian cafés, but the beers they do serve tend to be first-class, and the whole city is steeped in the stuff.

Recommended Beer
Plenz z tanků Unpasteurized Pilsner Urquell "from a tank".

Recommended Bar
U Fleků The world's oldest brewpub, and one of Europe's most famous beer halls. It's a little touristy, but still a must-see for beer boffins.

Thing to do before Beer O'clock
Take a stroll on the ornate Charles Bridge.

3 Munich *Germany*

The south German region of Bavaria is to beer what the Sahara is to sand. There are more than six hundred breweries in Germany's largest state, and its sun-kissed capital Munich reveres the beer with unbridled gusto. The birthplace of lager and the Reinheitsgebot, Munich is home to nine breweries—including Augustiner, Hofbräu, Löwenbräu, and Paulaner—and more than 20 beautiful beer gardens. And that's before you even think of including the annual Oktoberfest.

Recommended Beer
Forschungsbrauerei-Pilsissimus
Not many people know about this Munich Pilsner, so don't tell anyone.

Recommended Bar
Augustiner Keller Tourists go to the Hofbräuhaus. Beer drinkers go here.

Thing to do before Beer O'clock
Go to watch Bayern Munich play.

4 London *England*

London still hails the ale in style, courtesy of an unrivaled dedication to drinking. Handpulls, from which real ale flows, adorn the bar tops of hundreds of terrific traditional pubs in the city, while the number of specialist bars with broadened beer horizons has risen hugely in recent years. Every August, the city plays host to the Great British Beer Festival, where the Campaign for Real Ale showcases the best brews in the land.

Recommended Beer
Fuller's *London Pride*
The fruity flagship pint from London's only independent family brewer.

Recommended Bar
The White Horse A fantastic pub on Parson's Green in Fulham where cask ale rubs shoulders with the best German, American, and Belgian beers.

Thing to do before Beer O'clock
Take a trip on the London Eye.

5 Boston *Massachusetts, USA*

Boston belongs in the top ten for many reasons, not least because it's the hometown of the world's most influential beer drinker: Norm Peterson from 1980s hit TV show Cheers. It's also home to the Boston Beer Company, the largest and most innovative craft brewery in the United States, which often furnishes local bars with one-off specialties. There are hundreds of Boston brewpubs and specialty beer bars, but you can find quality craft beers in every establishment.

Recommended Beer
Harpoon Brewery's *Harpoon Ale*
A wonderful beer from the waterfront.

Recommended Bar
The Publick House As well as offering more than 150 different types of craft beer and more than two dozen on draught rotation, it even cooks its food in beer.

Thing to do before Beer O'clock
See the Boston Symphony Orchestra.

8 San Francisco *California, USA*

San Francisco is the only city that kept the plate of US craft beer spinning through Prohibition and the dark days of the 1970s. Fritz Maytag, who bought the Anchor brewery in 1965, is regarded as the forefather of US microbrewing, while San Francisco has been at the epicenter of the West Coast beer movement and also the larger artisan food and beverage renaissance. The San Francisco Brewers Guild, made up of the city's numerous leading brewpubs, breweries, and beer bars, has cultivated a thriving beer culture.

Recommended Beer
Anchor Steam A must-sip for visitors.

Recommended Bar
Toronado Not just the best beer bar in San Francisco, but maybe the best in the whole of California.

Thing to do before Beer O'clock
Visit Alcatraz.

9 Brussels *Belgium*

While waffles, mussels, chocolate, fries, and sprouts all have their time and place, it's beer for which Brussels is rightly famous. Reverence is rife in the city's vast array of specialist beer bars and restaurants, and each year, in September, Brussels plays host to the huge Belgian Beer Weekend in the Grand Place, where more than 2,000 Belgian beers are showcased. What's more, Lambic is native to Brussels and its surroundings, and Cantillon, a brewery/museum near Bruxelles Midi station, is its spiritual home.

Recommended Beer
Cantillon Gueuze
The Champagne of the people.

Recommended Bar
Delirium Beer Café An imbiber's paradise, with a beer menu of more than 2,000 beers from all around the world.

Thing to do before Beer O'clock
Marvel at the Mannekin Pis.

10 Cologne *Germany*

It might lack the aesthetic alfresco charm of Munich and Kölsch, the local lager style may lack the deep, intensive flavors of Bamberg's Rauchbier or, say, Berlin's Weisse, but there is no German city better equipped to host a first-class pub crawl. (See profile on page 130.)

Recommended Beer
Mühlen Kölsch A cracking Kölsch from a traditional brewery.

Recommended Bar
Früh am Dom Cologne's most famous and popular pub, located next to the Kölner Dom (Cathedral).

Thing to do before Beer O'clock Take a look at the impressive Gothic cathedral, which took more than six hundred years to build and survived World War 2.

The world's top ten designer beers

Greater than the sum of their parts, these key global beers are design classics, amalgamating delicious beer, iconic bottle design, distinctive packaging, unmistakable labels, and devilish good looks.

1 Deus Brut des Flandres *Belgium*

A supremely elegant 75cl Dom Perignon–style bottle with foil, wire, and the all-important pomp-inducing pop of a cork. If the Champagne glass is modelled on Marie Antoinette's décolletage, then you don't have to be Freud, or even know who he is, to realize what the humble beer bottle represents.

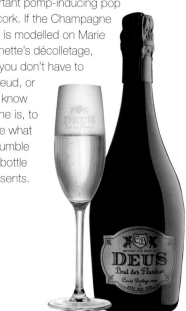

2 Grolsch Swing-Top *Holland*

While many brewers ditched the swing-top bottle after World War Two, Grolsch had the foresight to keep it. A smart move because, now, the Grolsch bottle is the brand. Relatively untouched since 1897, the bottles was streamlined by celebrated designer Koen van Os in 1966. In 1988 the stopper became a short-lived fashion icon when British boy band Bros attached them to their Dr. Martens shoes. Hordes of girls followed the trend and, for six months, the nation's schools were teeming with bottle tops.

6 St. Peter's *UK*

Usually, watching British real ale breweries trying to come up with a cool bottle design is like watching your grandmother trying to make sense of an iPod. But St. Peter's is different. Owner John Murphy, former head of a hugely successful branding company, recognized the dearth of decent design in British beer and went for something rather unique. Modelled on a bottle he'd bought at an antiques market years before, the oval quart receptacle is like an apothecary bottle.

7 Orval *Belgium*

The Orval bottle was created by architect Henry Vaes. He also redesigned the Orval Trappist abbey after it was burnt down during the 1920s. The bowling-pin shape of the bottle, and the grandiose goblet that accompanies it, mimics the base of a conical fermenter and retains the conditioning Brettanomyces yeast within. There's a terrific Art Deco label adorned with a fish and a ring, too, and, lest we forget, the beer is arguably the world's greatest pale ale.

3 Adnams Explorer *UK*

All clean lines and complete with embossing, Adnams' stylish 500ml (18 fl oz) bottle is the lightest beer bottle in the United Kingdom. This means less physical energy expended when drinking and, also, less harm for the planet. Brown in color yet green in outlook, the 500ml (18 fl oz) bottle was reduced in weight by 34 percent to 299g (8¾ oz). This makes an annual saving of 624 tonnes—in terms of annual CO_2 reduction—equal to removing 138 cars from the roads for a whole year.

4 Kwak *Belgium*

Nearly all Belgian beers boast their own bespoke glass, but nothing comes close to Kwak's whacky glass and wooden stand (see page 288). In Napoleonic times, mail coach drivers passing through the hometown of former brewer Pauwel Kwak were forbidden to stop for a pint. So Pauwel designed a receptacle that allowed them to drink while they drove their horses. It was hung on a notched wooden holder on the side of the coach. This unique glass can cover the uninitiated in delicious Dubbel beer.

5 Liefmans Kriek *Belgium*

The Liefmans Kriek corked bottle is wrapped up, all nice and tight, in oversized tissue-paper adorned with cutesy cherry-holding cherubs. The brewery was the first to use tissue paper and, despite being owned these days by the large, mechanized Belgian brewery of Duvel-Moortgaat, the paper is still wrapped around the bottle by hand.

8 Delirium Tremens *Belgium*

Hallucinogenic visions of pink elephants are common symptoms of "delirium tremens"—the confused, agitated state of "trembling madness" that is often brought on by a withdrawal of alcohol. The Huyghe brewery in Belgium has kindly painted a pink elephant and other fantastical animals on the label and the packaging of the bottle so that all your brain has to do is to concentrate on feeling better.

9 Rogue Old Crustacean *USA*

Rogue's head honcho Jack Joyce was once the marketing chief at Nike and helped to broker the brand's deal with slam-dunking star Michael Jordan. So it's no surprise that Rogue's beers are marketed in style. As well as using slick silk-screened bottles, Rogue showcases its XS range of big beers in marvellous matte-black 75cl black ceramic bottles. Classy.

10 Utopias *USA*

When Jim Koch at the Boston Brewing Company embarked on his mission to change pejorative perceptions of beer with this pioneering elixir to rival the world's finest ports and Cognacs, he needed a beer bottle that would justify a $100 price tag. This is it.

A world of beer labels

Beer label art is going through exciting times as contemporary craft brewers realize that well-designed labels can be as important as the beer itself in persuading adventurous beer consumers to buy and try new and daring brews.

FLYING DOG

DOGGIE STYLE CLASSIC PALE ALE

Good ... good beer. —Hunter

MOORHOUSE'S

BREWERS SINCE 1865

BLACK CAT

ABV 3.4%

SUPREME CHAMPION BEER OF BRITAIN WINNER

HANTVERKSBRYGGERIET

JULNARREN

Extra Strong Ale

7,0 %

Västerås

O'HANLON'S BREWING COMPANY LTD

BREWED IN DEVON   DOUBLE CHAMPION

GOLDBLADE™

FULL FLAVOUR TRADITIONAL WHEAT BEER

4.0% ABV

SHMALTZ BREWING COMPANY PRESENTS

L'Chaim!   To Life!

SAN FRANCISCO   NEW YORK

HE'BREW

THE CHOSEN BEER

A Smooth and Distinctive Light Brown Ale

GENESIS ALE

Est. 5757/1996

KSA

"4 Stars...Deserves a large inter-denominational audience!"
- San Diego Union-Tribune

FREEDOM

5% VOL

Crisp

CELEBRATOR

DOPPELBOCK

FINEST BAVARIAN DOUBLE BOCK BEER

Ayinger

Brewery

OTLEY O1
ABV 4.0%
500ML

O

OKELLS

AILE

BREWED IN HARMONY

SMOKED CELTIC PORTER

ALC 4.7% VOL

AILE ... THE MANX CELTIC WORD FOR FIRE

Mc LAREN

- - - - -
VALE ALE
- - - - -
330 ML

'norwegian wood'

from **Haand**Bryggeriet

Little Korkny Ale

DAS SCHWARZE

SCHWABEN BRÄU

SCHWARZBIER
SPEZIALITÄT

Vollwürzig und hopfenherb
zugleich

PRODUCT OF FRANCE

Thiriez
AMBER
french farmhouse ale

1 PT 9.4 FL OZ

32
AUDACE

Gavroche
Fermentation
Haute
SPECIALITE
BIERE SUR LIE
BRASSERIE DE SAINT SYLVESTRE (FLANDRE)
33cl

PILSNER
LAGER

Taste

Augustinerbräu München

MÜNCHNER BIER
MAXIMATOR
SINCE 1328 AD

DARK BEER · BREWED & BOTTLED IN MUNICH, GERMANY
BY AUGUSTINER BREWERY ALC. 7.4% BY VOL. 12 fl oz 355 ml

ELiXir
baladin

Imperial Stout
brewed with
Ryan Bros. Coffee Beans

SPEEDWAY
STOUT

AWARD WINNING
AleSmith
BREWING COMPANY

12.6% Alcohol by Volume

BREWED & BOTTLED BY
BRASSERIE DE LA SENNE · BRUSSELS, BELGIUM

STOUTERiK
THE BRUSSELS STOUT

WWW.BRASSERIEDELASENNE.BE

HAND CRAFTED BELGIAN STOUT REFERMENTED IN THE BOTTLE
PRODUCT OF BELGIUM IMPORTED BY SHELTON BROTHERS, BELCHERTOWN MA 1 PT 9.4 FL OZ

Sv.NORBERT

SPECIAL BEER
Medium bodied · medium
bitter · all · malt
AMBER BEER
made by Klášterní pivovar Strahov

YSPRID
Y
DDRAIG

6.5%
ABV   6.5%
                           ABV

THE
BRECONSHIRE
BREWERY

8,5%

WILLY
BROUWERIJ · DE PRAEL

sciros ®

RRA ACIDA ALLE CILIEGE DI VIGNOLA
5% VOL. D'ALCOL – 75 CL - LOTTO N. 060601

Since 1872
Brewery Náchod, Czech Republic

QUALITY

PRIMATOR ®
ENGLISH PALE ALE

A WORLD OF BEER
BRITAIN & IRELAND

Britain & Ireland

Britain and Ireland have been generous beer benefactors. They've furnished the world with most of its ale—be it bitter, porter, India pale ale, Mild, Scotch ale, or stout.

Beer-drinking culture has been cultivated in the pub, where it's become synonymous with cask-conditioned beer. Neither warm nor flat as clichéd misconception would have one believe, "real ale" is a gently carbonated, living celestial liquor that, at its best, has few rivals in the world of beer.

In the 1960s, when the march of chilled keg ales and lagers threatened to trample cask ale into oblivion, the courageous Campaign for Real Ale (CAMRA) came to its rescue. While it's still widely available, cask ale is very much a niche product nowadays, with the vast majority of beer sold in the United Kingdom & Ireland being mainstream, mass-produced lagers owned by global brewing giants run by accountants.

That's not to say that the British pint glass is half-empty however. Mainstream beer may be being sold cheaper than water, and markets and beer sales may be at their lowest since the 1930s, but those drinkers who crave quality not quantity have rarely had it so good.

Having suffered at the neglectful hands of the big breweries for so long, cask ale is now being championed by breweries that care about it and look after it. Regional brewers such as Fuller's, Marston's, and Greene King have taken huge strides in improving the consistency and image of cask ale, and the sector has a newfound glint in its eye, a spring in its step, and plenty of reasons to be hopeful for the future.

Thanks to a growing interest in local produce and a tax break for small brewers introduced in 2002, Britain's craft-brewing movement is in fine fettle, too, with more than 500 microbreweries now making magic with their mash-forks. According to SIBA (the Society of Independent Brewers), Britain's local brewing industry is the only segment of the UK beer market that's in growth and, regardless of where you are in the United Kingdom, you're never more than 10 miles away from a microbrewery.

While cask ale remains at the crux of much of what the craft beer community does, it's not just "ordinary bitter" any more. In terms of innovation, the likes of Brewdog, Thornbridge, Harviestoun, and Meantime rival anything being brewed in North America and mainland Europe.

Thanks are due to the thriving dynamic businesses that understand cask ale and have picked up the slack left by big brewers too busy fighting over market share to bother with cask ale. These new beer champions deserve recognition as torch bearers of the "small is beautiful" mantra, as they continue to provide inspiring brews for an ever-growing group of discerning pub goers.

Above: Fuller's in Chiswick, London, is one of only two major breweries still active within the greater London area, the other being Meantime in Greenwich.
Above Center: A traditional street-corner pub in Britain is often an important part of the local community.
Right: Bungs being banged into casks of real ale, sealing in the liquid gold for later enjoyment.

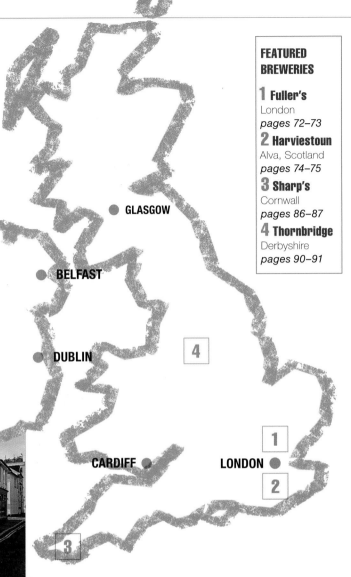

FEATURED BREWERIES

1 Fuller's
London
pages 72–73
2 Harviestoun
Alva, Scotland
pages 74–75
3 Sharp's
Cornwall
pages 86–87
4 Thornbridge
Derbyshire
pages 90–91

GLASGOW

BELFAST

DUBLIN

4

CARDIFF   LONDON

1

2

3

Acorn Brewery
Barnsley, South Yorkshire
www.acornbrewery.net

Barnsley Bitter 3.8%

In 2003 Acorn rose from the ashes of the dear-departed Barnsley Brewery that dated back to the 1850s. Using the same yeast strain as its predecessor and on a ten-barrel brewery, former Barnsley employee Dave Hughes brews a trio of traditional Yorkshire beers, including this award-winning, full-bodied biscuity bitter that wraps plums around your gums.

Adnams Brewery
Southwold, Suffolk
www.adnams.co.uk

Adnams Bitter 3.7%

Since 1872 the warming aroma of Maris Otter malt has wafted from Adnams' Sole Bay Brewery in the coastal town of Southwold, traveling over the jumbled assortment of whitewashed cottages, past the lighthouse, the picture-postcard pier, and out to sea. Its flagship bitter, showcasing the resinous charms of the hop, is a crisp, floral, and superbly balanced beer brewed using three quintessentially English hops.

Adnams Explorer *Blonde Ale* 5.5%

Ideal for luring lager loyalists across to the joys of ale. Grapefruit and zesty citrus flavors spring forth from this light, refreshing blonde beer in which dwells a blend of American hops.

Arkell's Brewery
Swindon, Wiltshire
www.arkells.com

Kingsdown Ale *Bitter* 5%

The Wiltshire town of Swindon has two claims to fame: roundabouts and the family-owned Arkell's brewery, which dates back to 1843. Arkell's is the better one. A fruity, full-bodied strong bitter brewed from the same mash as Arkell's flagship 3B bitter, it owes its crisp finish to the use of Goldings and Progress hops.

Badger (Hall & Woodhouse Brewery)
Blandford St. Mary, Dorset
www.hall-woodhouse.co.uk

Stinger *Organic Esoteric Ale* 4%

Dynamic Dorset-based brewer whose beers boasts a fervent following. Traditionalists may lean toward the delicious, golden Tanglefoot or hop-driven Badger Best, but this tingle-tastic organic ale is brewed with nettles picked from the garden of celebrity chef Hugh Fearnley-Whittingstall. It layers grassy, herbal, and lychee notes over the citrus character of Admiral and Golding hops.

Ballard's Brewery
Nyewood, Hampshire
www.ballardsbrewery.org.uk

Nyewood Gold 5%

A gorgeous golden ale with a fantastic floral hop character, very drinkable given its strength. Named after Nye, an ancient term for the group of pheasants that live near the small, award-winning brewery.

Barngates Brewery
Ambleside, Lake District
www.barngatesbrewery.co.uk

Cracker Ale *Bitter* 3.9%

In 1997 Barngates began brewing exclusively for the Drunken Duck pub, legendary among Lake District's fell walkers. Having expanded the brewery, it now brews for pubs all over the Lake District. Named after the pub's late dog, Cracker is a copper-colored, tangy, and refreshing brew.

Bartrams Brewery
Bury St. Edmunds, Suffolk
www.bartramsbrewery.co.uk

Comrade Bill Bartrams Egalitarian Anti Imperialist Soviet Stout 6.9%

A Russian Imperial Stout that's not really made, as the bottle boasts, with the "blood of the bourgeoisie, the sweat of the proletariat, and the tears of the capitalists", but brimming with indulgent chocolate and coffee notes, burnt barley, and a peppery palate-coating prickle. If you can't pronounce its name, you've probably had too many. This is a velvet-flavored revelation.

Batemans Brewery
Wainfleet, Lincolnshire
www.bateman.co.uk

Batemans XXXB *Bitter* 4.8%

Set in stunning scenery beneath an imposing windmill and steeped in heritage dating back to 1874, Batemans has remained steadfast in purveying "good honest ales", of which this classic auburn-colored bitter, all citrus and shortbread, is typical.

Salem Porter 4.7%

Golding and Liberty hops, pale malts, crystal malts, and roasted barley are all flung into the cauldron and stirred with a magic mash-fork to conjure up this bewitching black-as-midnight porter. Roasty, toasty, and a sweep of bitterness at the back.

Bath Ales
Warmley, Bristol
www.bathales.com

Gem Bitter 4.3%

An exciting, erudite array of ales has seen the stock of this superb steam-powered microbrewery, located between Bath and Bristol, rise above and beyond its West Country heartland. Gem is the jewel in its crown and dovetails a succulent malty mouthfeel with a touch of smoke, toffee, and a Goldings-plated finish that is hard to resist.

Wild Hare Pale Ale 5%

Lively yet dry pale ale brewed with wheat, organic English hops, and pale malt. Clean, crisp citrus character, deliciously dry, and extremely drinkable to boot.

Belhaven Brewery
Dunbar, East Lothian, Scotland
www.belhaven.co.uk

80/- *Bitter* 4.2%

A russet-red classic Scottish shilling ale once described by an Austrian emperor as "the Burgundy of Scotland". Massively malty, dried fruits, and a touch of bitterness courtesy of Scotland's biggest and oldest regional brewer, now owned by the British brewer Greene King.

Black Sheep Brewery
Masham, North Yorkshire
www.blacksheepbrewery.com

 Black Sheep Ale Pale Ale 4.4%

Like the five generations of Theakstons before him, Black Sheep founder Paul Theakston ran the famous brewery that bears the same name. Yet, in 1992, following an acrimonious takeover and a family feud, he set up the aptly named Masham rival a few doors down. The best-selling bottled ale boasts a stiff Maris Otter backbone—adorning it with a smidgeon of seaweed on the nose and a mighty mouthfeel, a generous helping of aromatic Goldings hops, and a parched spicy finish.

Riggwelter *Strong Bitter* 5.7%

There's nothing wooly about this esoteric ale from the Dales. A Riggwelter is a sheep that's rolled over and is unable to get up—a quandary in which drinkers over enamoured with this complex ale may find themselves. Nutty, toffee-ish, a touch of aniseed, and with the merest hint of overripe bananas, it's deceptively drinkable. A wolf in sheep's clothing, perhaps?

Brains
Cardiff, Wales
www.sabrain.com

Brains Dark *Mild* 3.5%

As Welsh as rarebit and red dragons, Brains is Wales's largest and most famous brewer, renowned for quenching industrial thirsts since 1882. A marvelously malty Mild that mixes molasses with milk chocolate and mellow mocha notes. A light, lip-smacking bitterness delivers drinkability.

Brakspear Brewing Company
Witney, Oxfordshire
www.brakspear-brewing.co.uk

Brakspear Bitter 3.4%

Brakspear was orphaned, in 2002, from the ornate Oxfordshire town of Henley-on-Thames. The picturesque riverbank-side brewery site is now a hotel chain specializing in wine. Wychwood Brewery rescued Brakspear beers and retained the famous Double Drop fermentation system. For a modest-strength session bitter, this glorious gulp owes its extraordinary fruit character to the staggered "drop" technique, in which the beer is fermented in one tank for 12 to 24 hours, then dropped down into another tank for a second fermentation.

Brakspear Triple Strong Ale 7.2%

A triple-hopped triple-fermented bottled beer—twice during the brewing process and once more in the bottle—broadening Brakspear drinkers' horizons with a Belgian slant. Ideal digestif beer or cheese accompaniment; strong caramel notes and hints of rum and molasses.

Breconshire Brewery
Brecon, Powys, Wales
www.Breconshirebrewery.com

 Brecon County Ale
Bitter 3.7%

To a bucolic backdrop of the Brecon Beacons, Justin "Buster" Grant is one of a number of innovative microbrewers putting the ale into Wales. Traditional, light copper-colored bitter brewed with whole flower hops. Refreshing, delicate, and slightly spicy.

Spirit of the Dragon (Ysprid y Ddraig) *Oak-aged Ale* 5.5%

To create this elusive oak-aged seasonal beer, Justin takes an ale from Breconshire's core range and sends it to sleep in Scotch barrels for two to three months, where it adopts a touch of Gaelic spirit, rich fruit, vanilla, and a mightily smooth mouthfeel.

Brewdog
Fraserburgh, Scotland
www.brewdog.com

 **Hop Rocker**
Lager 5.5%

Inspired by the audacious antics of the American craft-beer scene, the young duo of James Watt and Martin Dickie founded Brewdog in March 2007 and tore up the rulebook of British brewing like a frenzied schoolboy experimenting with mind-altering substances and substantial risk-taking. This is a loudmouthed lager that talks up the hop character.

 Paradox Smokehead *Oak-aged Imperial Stout* 10%

A rich, strapping slightly sweeter Scottish stout that develops in complexity by maturing in a variety of Scotch whisky casks (Islay, Speyside, and grain). Smokehead, an intensely peaty Scotch, adds smoke, a touch of seaweed, iodine and vanilla to the beer.

"Give my people plenty of beer, good beer and cheap beer, and you will have no revolution among them."

QUEEN VICTORIA
BRITISH MONARCH, 1819–1901

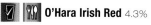

Burton Bridge Brewery
Burton-on-Trent, Staffordshire
www.burtonbridgebrewery.co.uk

Empire IPA 7.5%

A celebrated brewpub in the town of Burton-on-Trent, the spiritual home of British brewing and the engine room of the IPA boom years. It's hoppy, and it knows it; clap your hands…, especially for the fruity, orange aroma from the late addition of Styrian hops.

Butcombe Brewery
Bristol, Avon
www.butcombe.com

Butcombe Bitter 4%

Whetting the appetite of the West Country since 1978, this all-English ale has been a three-times finalist at the Great British Beer Festival. A tasty bridesmaid with a superb floral bouquet.

Cairngorm Brewing
Aviemore, Scotland
www.cairngormbrewery.com

Trade Winds *Spiced/Herb Beer* 4.3%

CAMRA's Champion Specialty Beer of Britain in 2004, 2005, and 2006 mixes elderflower together with Perle hops and a weighty dose of wheat. Delicate, floral, and smooth.

Camerons Brewery
Hartlepool, County Durham
www.cameronsbrewery.co.uk

Monkey Stout 4.4%

Legend has it that, during the Napoleonic wars, a French ship was sunk off the coast of Hartlepool and a monkey, dressed in a French sailor's uniform, was washed up onto shore. Mistaken for a Frenchman, he was interrogated, put on trial, denied of bananas, and sentenced to death by hanging. Raise this rich and roasty dark stout in memory of the poor fellow.

Carlow Brewing Company
Carlow, Country Carlow, Ireland
www.carlowbrewing.com

O'Hara Irish Red 4.3%

Small craft brewery set up in 1998. In recent decades, Irish Reds have been more popular in Mediterranean markets than in their homeland. Fruity and aromatic, sprinkled with notes of coffee, and with a hop bitterness and sizable mouth-feel, owing to plenty of roasted barley.

O'Hara Irish Stout 4.3%

Carlow specializes in Celtic beer styles from yesteryear and is located about 80 Kilometres (50 miles) from Dublin in the Barrow Valley region, which was once Ireland's hop-growing heartland. This splendid brew won the Gold Medal at the Millennium Brewing Industry Awards for its dark black, dry, and marvelously mineral-y Irish stout.

Castle Rock Brewery
Nottingham, Nottinghamshire
www.castlerockbrewery.com

Harvest Pale 3.8%

A zealous purveyor and promoter of traditional real ale, Castle Rock was set up by former CAMRA (Campaign for Real Ale) chairman Chris Holmes in 1977 and now has more than 20 dedicated cask-friendly pubs and bars. Golden aromatic ale, gently embittered with American hops, belies its modest strength with big, quenching citrus flavors.

Chiltern Brewery
Terrick, Buckinghamshire
www.chilternbrewery.co.uk

Chiltern Ale *British Bitter* 3.7%

An early pioneer of the recent microbrewing revival, Chiltern was the first new brewery in Buckinghamshire for more than a century when it opened its doors in 1980. As well as this classic English ale and other beers, Chiltern makes hop cologne, pickled onions in hopped vinegar, beer cheese, mash-tun marmalade, and even beer shampoo.

Coach House Brewing Company
Warrington, Cheshire
www.coach-house-brewing.co.uk

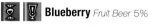

Blueberry *Fruit Beer* 5%

It can't be easy shoehorning a blueberry muffin into a bottle, but the chaps from Coach House seemed to have managed it. A fruity ale whose sweetness is delivered from the malt. One of many esoteric ales from a brewery set up by three former Greenall Whitley employees when the famous Warrington brewery closed in the 1990s.

Coniston Brewery

Coniston, Lake District
www.conistonbrewery.com

⭐ 🍺 🍸 **Bluebird Bitter** 3.6%

Challenger, the sole hop in this awesome award-winning bitter, delivers flavors of marmalade, lemon jelly, oranges, and peppery spice. Named after the speedboat used by Donald Campbell in his ill-fated 1967 attempt to break the world water-speed record on Coniston.

🍴 **Old Man Ale** *Amber Ale* 4.2%

A deep ruby-colored full-bodied ale that certainly doesn't dodder about. Abounding in water from the mineral-rich Lakeland fells and warm, vinous fruit flavors topped and tailed with Curaçao and grapefruit — courtesy of Challenger and Mt Hood hops.

Cotleigh Brewery

Wiveliscombe, Somerset
www.cotleighbrewery.com

🍺 🍸 **Tawny Owl Premium Bitter** 3.8%

Since 1979 this wonderful West Country brewery has moved its home more often than an indecisive nomad. But its traditional ales, all named after birds, have remained unwaveringly flavorsome. This head-turning tawny-colored bitter, which floats on a breeze of biscuit-malt and measured bitterness, is just one of them.

Cotswold Brewery Company

Foscot, Oxfordshire
www.cotswoldbrewingcompany.co.uk

🍸 **Cotswold Premium Lager** 5%

A floral, firm, and deliciously dry lip-smacking lager laced with Liberty Hops. Having shipped out of the rat race in 2005, Rick and Emma Keane shipped over an American brewery in 2005 and now furnish local punters and pubs with a trio of lagers and a classy, weighty beer.

Cottage Brewery

Castle Cary, Somerset

🍴 🍸 **Norman Conquest Strong Ale** 7%

This strong ale, from a seriously small-scale Somerset brewery, is named after the Anglo-French tussle of 1066. It's a cordial entente of dark, vinous fruit, a rich malt mouthfeel, and a long, convivial finish. Very good.

Crouch Vale Brewery

South Woodham Ferrers, Essex
www.crouch-vale.co.uk

🌿 **Amarillo Golden Ale** 5%

This recently expanded Essex brewer casts its net further than most when it comes to discovering new hop varieties, showcasing Amarillo in all its lightly spicy, herbal glory.

🍺 🍸 **Brewer's Gold Golden Ale** 4%

This pale, aromatic golden ale won CAMRA's (Campaign for Real Ale) Champion Beer of Britain in 2005 and 2006 with its floral charms. Soft, delicately bitter, and a sensational summer sup.

Daleside Brewery

Harrogate, Yorkshire
www.dalesidebrewery.co.uk

🍸 **Morocco Ale** *Spiced Ale* 5.5%

Dark, strong, and delightfully spicy, this unusual winter warmer is brewed to a 16th-century recipe. Piquant, peppery, and perfect with kebabs, it even has its own definition in the Oxford English Dictionary.

Dark Star Brewery

Haywards Heath, West Sussex
www.darkstarbrewing.co.uk

🍴 🍷 **Espresso** *Stout* 4.2%

Dark Star was born in 1994 in a pub in Brighton but, as word of its beers spread, it moved to a farm in rural Sussex. The dedicated beer-blogging community of ratebeer.com has since voted its hoppy ales the best in Britain. This jet-black stout is full of beans, quite literally. Freshly ground espresso beans are added to the copper just after the boil.

🍺 🍸 **Hophead Bitter** 3.8%

A pale golden, velvet-gloved hop-hitter that punches well above its weight. Strong floral aroma and elderflower notes, very quaffable, and clean on the finish. Ideal if you like to drink beer beside the seaside.

Darwin Brewery

Sunderland, Tyne & Wear
www.darwinbrewery.com

🌿 **Rolling Hitch** *India Pale Ale* 5.2%

A British interpretation of an American take on a British beer that was drunk in India. This whole IPA thing can be a little confusing, but all you need to know is that this excellent IPA, brewed by a laboratory in Sunderland using American Amarillo hops, tastes tremendous.

Everards Brewery

Narborough, Leicestershire
www.everards.co.uk

 Tiger *Best Bitter* 4.2%

This delightful dry-hopped traditional bitter bops you on the nose with a "Burton Snatch" aroma and lays orange-zesty East Kent Golding hops and nutty malt on the palate. Having returned to its Leicestershire roots in 1979, following more than 80 years' brewing in Burton-on-Trent, this forward-thinking family brewery also designed the Cyclops tasting note method used by CAMRA (Campaign for Real Ale).

Exmoor Brewery

Wiveliscombe, Somerset
www.exmoorales.co.uk

 **Exmoor Gold** *Golden Ale* 4.5%

Somerset's most sizable brewery picked up the brewing baton dropped by the defunct Hancock brewery. After winning the Champion Beer of Britain in 1980 with only its 13th brew of Exmoor Ale, it realized that people "drink with their eyes" and launched what is regarded as the first sparkling single-malt golden ale. Floral, soft, fluffy malt mouthfeel and radically refreshing.

Freedom Brewing

Abbots Bromley, Staffordshire
www.freedombeer.com

 Freedom Pilsner 5%

Once the tipple of fashionable London types and brewed in Soho during the 1990s, Freedom retired to a country farm in 2005 a few years ago, where it brews lager in line with the German purity laws. A rare microbrewed British lager, it's sweeter than Czech Pilsner, but boasts lip-smacking grassy, flowery hops.

Freeminer

Cinderford, Gloucestershire
www.website.lineonenet/~freeminer.brewery

 Bumblebee *Honey Beer* 4.6%

The first British beer to have a Fairtrade label pinned to its chest, this sweet-scented ale is the bee's knees. Robust, golden, and holding up heaps of hops, its honeyed tones come courtesy of Fairtrade producers in Chile and is one of several super sips from a much-lauded micro. Also look out for Deep Shaft Stout and Trafalgar.

Fuller's

see Brewery Profile pages 72–73
Chiswick, London

Brewer's Reserve
Oak-aged Vintage Ale
7.7%

Take Fuller's 1845, Golden Pride Barley Wine and ESB Export, blend together and place in 30-year-old Scotch whisky casks to mature for more than 500 days. Take it out of the barrel at 10% ABV, add fresh ESB to reduce to 7.7%, and package it in a limited-edition boxed 500ml bottle. A beautifully complex bottle-conditioned oak-aged ale, this is brimming with all the wonders of Scotch and wood. A stand-up hop character mellowed by malt leads to rich, tangy marmalade flavors, subtle vanilla notes from the oak, and a fantastic flourish of Scotch on the finish. This is a vintage ale you dare not miss.

Chiswick Bitter *Best Bitter* 3.5%

A brewer's beer that can be drunk all day. Tweaked in 2007, Chiswick Bitter has retained its fabulous quaffable quality, but with added bite. In terms of complexity and depth of fruity flavor, it drinks well above its modest strength as a satisfying session ale.

ESB Extra Special Bitter 5.5%

A legendary London liquid layered with tangerine hop flavors, full-bodied malt character, touches of toffee and plums, and a lengthy, lingering fade of a finish. Widely available in a grandiose 500ml bottle, this tastes extra special on cask hand-pump.

Gale's Prize Old Ale *Vintage Ale* 9%

Tart, vinous, and stacked with frisson-inducing fruit flavors, Prize Old Ale was brewed in Hampshire by Gale's, and then, for the first time in 2007, matured for 18 months at the Fuller's Griffin brewery in London. A massive fruit aroma and a sharp, puckering port-like finish mellow with every sip. A rare British version of an acidic beer which was once called "stale ale". This is what British beer tasted like in 1850.

Vintage Ale (2005) *Barley Wine* 8.5%

The Fuller, Smith & Turner brewery is the largest in London, fashioning fine ales by the river in Chiswick since 1845. Each year, Fuller's releases a bottle-conditioned vintage ale with a difference. Golden Pride barley wine is always its foundation and inspiration, but each year there's always a twist in the brewing tale, whether that be a different variety of malt or hop. This is a beautifully balanced bottle-conditioned ale—the jewel in the Fuller's crown and an annual treat to look out for.

Greene King

Bury St Edmunds, Suffolk
www.greeneking.co.uk

XX Mild 3%

Black and crystal malts meet Northdown hops in a dark, nutty, chocolate beer from this Super-regional brewer that's been brewing in Bury St. Edmunds since 1799. It is now a major UK brewery.

Old Crafty Hen *Vintage Ale* 6.5%

A classy, and indeed crafty, coming-together of its Old Speckled Hen and Old 5X beers, blended and aged for two years in oak casks. The result? A Belgian-style fruity, fig-like fermented fusion of flavors that weaves wood, a wealth of complexity, and weighty caramel and toffee character. Complex and contemplative.

Old Speckled Hen *Bitter* 5.2%

This archetypal English bitter is Greene King's flagship beer and the United Kingdom's number-one bottled ale. Big spicy malt flavors, fruity sweetness, and a smattering of citrus are its keynotes. Now that Greene King has, to the despair of traditionalists, gobbled up smaller breweries like a peckish Pac-Man, this beer is available throughout much of the UK.

Strong Suffolk *Vintage Ale* 6%

A mellow, harmonious mix of two beers: Old 5X, brewed to 12% ABV, is matured for at least two years in 100-barrel oak vats and blended with a mahogany-hued full-bodied ale. Fruitcake, vanilla, and fall fruits, are the flavors that flourish here.

Hambleton Ales

Melmerby, North Yorkshire
www.Hambletonales.co.uk

Nightmare Stout 5%

Brewery on the banks of the river Swale set up in 1991 by Nick Stafford, a leading light in the craft-brewing movement. This former CAMRA (Campaign for Real Ale) Champion Winter Beer of Britain is a dark, dreamy, and luxurious liquid with a creamy, full-bodied mouthfeel. It tastes even richer when drunk slightly warm.

Harveys

Lewes, West Sussex
www.harveys.org.uk

Imperial Russian Stout 9%

Of all the beers that Harveys makes this is the most unashamedly decadent. Bottle-conditioned and brewed using a thick mix of specialty malt and spicy hops, it's peppery, roasty, and slightly sour, with a soothing sweet mouthfeel.

Sussex Best Bitter 4%

Lewes, the quaint Sussex town in which Harveys resides, is known for three things: a spectacular Bonfire Night procession, with witches and lovely beer. The Victorian-tower brewery, founded in 1790, looms large above the Lewes skyline and is known as the "Lewes Cathedral". Miles Jenner, head brewer since 1986, is loyal to local producers in his sourcing of ingredients, while the beers rarely roam beyond Sussex and its surrounding counties. This is a superb, perfectly poised session beer that won CAMRA's Champion Best Bitter award in both 2004 and 2006.

Harviestoun

see Brewery Profile pages 74–75
Alva, Scotland
www.harviestoun-brewery.co.uk

Bitter & Twisted *Blonde Beer* 4.2%

The mantelpiece at Harviestoun's brewery sags under the weight of beer awards—many of which have been pinned to the chest of this zesty, refreshing light ale full of pear-drop, candy, lemon, and grapefruit flavors.

Ola Dubh *Oak-aged Ale* 8%

This gloriously gloopy collaboration between Harviestoun and Highland Park Scotch whisky distillery looks like the viscous liquid usually seen on sorry-looking oil-spill seabirds. A porter-like old ale matured in casks that have previously housed Highland Park's 30-year-old Scotch. Big but not brutal, it oozes chocolate, espresso, and vanilla pod.

Schiehallion *Cask-conditioned Lager* 4.8%

Named after a nearby mountain, this rare example of a cask-conditioned lager is a balletic balance of sturdy biscuit malt and snappy citrus hop. Flowery, yet with a big barley backbone.

FULLER'S

The Griffin Brewery, Chiswick, London

www.fullers.co.uk

London was once an unrivalled brewing metropolis, its pubs and breweries the envy of the world. It was the engine room of a swaggering British Empire and it was beer that generously greased that empire's cogs of commerce and industry.

Behemoth brewers such as Whitbread, Watney, Ind Coope, Trumans, and Charrington smudged London's smog-smeared skyline with their bellowing brick stacks; numerous smaller, simpler ventures wetted the whistles of a rapidly growing population; and, at its brewing peak, the city was home to more than 160 breweries.

Today, there are two—just two breweries for 15 million people. London gave birth to, Porter, India Pale Ale, and Stout, yet now has fewer breweries than the county of Suffolk. When Young's abandoned the wonderful Ram Brewery in Wandsworth back in 2006, and went to live in a bigger house in the Bedford suburbs, the only living legacy of London's brewing heyday that remained was Fuller, Smith & Turner.

But what a legacy it is—dating back more than 350 years to the days of Oliver Cromwell. Flanked by the river Thames on one side and one of London's main arteries on the other, Fuller's has been wafting sweet malt aromas across the chimneypots of west London since 1845.

Strictly, there's been a brewery on the Fuller's site since 1654, when it was home to the Griffin Brewery, but it wasn't until 1829—when John Fuller provided financial assistance for the Griffin's owners—that the Fuller family first became involved.

By 1841, the original owners had moved on, and John found himself at the helm of a brewery without a brewer. His son John Bird Fuller came on board, recruited Henry Smith and his brother-in-law John Turner (who had been head brewer at Ind & Smith in South London), and Fuller Smith & Turner was founded in 1845 and still remains on the same premises.

More than 150 years later, Fuller's is still an independent family brewer and one of the UK's leading regional players, with more than 360 pubs and, in London Pride, the number- one selling premium bitter in the United Kingdom.

Like Young's, its long-term London rival across the river, Fuller's beer holds up a mirror to its surroundings. Before it moved to Bedford, Young's beer was "pwopa sarf L'ahn"—a loudmouthed, unpredictable pint that ducked 'n dived, and dropped its consonants. In contrast, Fuller's vintage ale speaks with the buffed vowels of London's leafy middle-class mild west. It is more refined, consistent, and floral. Were Fuller's London Pride to spot consonants on the floor, it would pick'em up, dust 'em down, and return them with a doff of the cap.

Right: Fuller's produce a fine stable of beers to suit everyone's palate, from the classic London Pride bitter, Discovery blonde, and London porter, to vintage oak-aged brews and the historical Gale's vintage ale.
Far right: Award-winning head brewer John Keeling has been creating beer alchemy at Fuller's for more than 25 years.

AWARD-WINNING BEERS

Well mannered and extremely well made, Fuller's beers have won CAMRA's coveted Champion Beer of Britain not once, not twice, but thrice. The fabulously fruity and tangy London Pride, the beer on which Fuller's success has been built, scooped gold in 1979, a year after ESB, its rich mahogany-colored spicy strong bitter, did the same. Served in an angled brandy balloon, London Pride has pepper and grassy hop notes from Challenger, Goldings, Target and Northdown that are gently laid down on a bed of pale ale and Crystal malt.

In 1989 CAMRA pinned its cherished gong to the chest of Chiswick Bitter, an immensely aromatic "brewer's beer", dry-hopped with mellow bitter Goldings and with a depth of flavor that reaches well beyond its modest 3.5% ABV.

Honey Dew, an organic blonde ale infused with honey, and Discovery, a blonde beer launched in 2005, are superb summer- slurping missionaries capable of converting even the most ardent lager loyalist.

Key Beers

Fuller's Brewer's Reserve *Oak-aged Ale* 7.7%

Fuller's Chiswick Bitter 3.5%

Fuller's Discovery *Blonde Ale* 4.5%

Fuller's ESB *Extra Special Bitter* 5.9%

Fuller's Gale's Prize Old Ale 9.0%

Fuller's Organic Honey Dew *Golden Ale* 5%

Fuller's London Pride *Bitter* 4.7%

Fuller's Vintage Ale 8.5%

Fuller's ESB 5.9%

CONNOISSEUR BREWS

The popularity and profitability of Fuller's core ales afford head brewer John Keeling the freedom to experiment with Fuller's "Fine Ales" which are more concerned with connoisseurs than commercial success. John, a learned and likable Lancastrian, has been at Fuller's for more than 25 years and, recently aided by ex-Young's brewer Derek Prentice, has been responsible for introducing some quite outstanding elixirs.

In 2007, after years of grappling with the United Kingdom's archaic tax attitude towards ageing beer in Scotch barrels, Keeling unveiled Brewer's Reserve, a blend of Fuller's 1845, its Golden Pride Barley Wine, and ESB Export, aged in 30 year-old oak Scotch whisky casks for more than 500 days.

Taking it out of the barrel at 10% ABV, John adds fresh ESB to reduce it to 7.7% and packages the brew in a limited-edition, boxed, 500ml bottle that's individually numbered. "We tried many different recipes, ageing different beers in whisky casks, but the one we selected has really surpassed all expectations. It has the Fuller's blend of hoppy bitterness and rich, tangy marmalade flavors, along with subtle vanilla notes from the oak and a wonderful hint of the whisky."

Another bottle-conditioned connoisseur collectable is Vintage Ale, an annual release that always has Golden Pride Barley Wine at its foundation and as its inspiration. Each year, John gives the beer a twist in the brewing tale, be it a different variety of malt or a change of hop, the idea being that one can then behold the influence that time has on the flavor, aroma and appearance of the beers. Yeast, John explains, has the biggest impact on the flavor of the beer. "We only use the Fuller's yeast," he declares. "Having two types of yeast is like having a wife and a mistress. Never introduce one to the other!" He recommends ale aficionados buy two bottles: one to drink now and one to lie down for ageing. "When you bottle a beer it can be a very traumatic experience for the beer and it takes time to settle down," he said. "Don't store it in a garage as it's too hot. Store it in its box so it's not exposed to light and keep it in a room with a neutral temperature."

In 2005, when Fuller's bought the struggling Hampshire Gale's brewery, John was fortunate to inherit Gale's Prize Old Ale—the closest British beer gets to a Belgian Lambic.

"It's an acquired taste and something to be gently sipped, but if you were drinking beer in the 1850s it would have tasted very much like this," says John.

HARVIESTOUN BREWERY

Alva, Scotland
www.harviestoun-brewery.co.uk

It's funny, the obsession Brits have with lager and ale. Beery battle lines have been drawn.

It all started when the former had the audacity to blow the froth from the latter's pint in the 1970s. More a matter of lifestyle than beer style, it means that you're either on one side or you're the other, and it's rare the twain shall meet. Beer's version of the Mods and the Rockers, if you like.

It's an obsession peculiar to the Brits and a fairly daft one given that yeast is regarded as the core distinction. Lagers are brewed using bottom-fermenting yeast and ales with top-fermenting yeast. That's the only difference. Except, of course, that it's not. In fact, there's no difference at all, really. So, let's all have a group hug, shall we?

"Yeast doesn't know what's up or down or where to go, it just does what it does—eats sugars and releases CO_2 and alcohol," said Stuart Cail, head brewer at Harviestoun. "Top- and bottom-fermenting yeast is not the important thing, it's more the type of fermentation receptacle used and where you add the yeast. Lager yeast just happens to work better at lower temperatures."

Whether it's Schiehallion, its dry and fruity cask-conditioned lager conditioned at low temperatures, or the viscous and velvety Scotch barrel-aged Ola Dubh ale, Harviestoun uses the same lager yeast to brew all its core beers. "We originally used a lager and an ale yeast, but the latter was prone to infection, so we brewed the ale using the lager yeast, and it worked just as well—if not better."

It may be a novel approach, but novel approaches are what Harviestoun does very well. Ken Brooker, a former Ford car worker from Dagenham in South London, went against the grain, quite literally, when he jump-started Scotland's craft-brewing scene in 1984. In a land of stoic, malty beers, where the national tooth is sweeter than a puppy in a tutu, Brooker

Right: Deep, dark, and interesting, Harviestoun's Old Engine Oil is a luscious mix of chocolate notes and port flavors, making it a perfect after-dinner beer.
Far right: Inviting packaging that apes vintage port bottles declares the oak-aged credentials of Ola Dubh, a connoisseur classic that benefits from further ageing in a beer "cellar".

abandoned automobiles for ales and began brewing highly aromatic hippy hoppy beers within the thick stone walls of a farm in Dollar, a rural town between Edinburgh and Glasgow at the toes of the Hillfoots.

Dollar is derived from "Doillier", the Scots-Gaelic word for "dark and gloomy", and one well equipped to describe Old Engine Oil, Harviestoun's darkest, most distinctive drop and a departure from its flowery stablemates. It's an ebony, opaque after-dinner ale that'll work bolts loose and coat one's cogs of consciousness in a silky, soporific sheen. A high-temperature mash, curtailed early to ensure the inferior "heads and tails" are left behind, segues roast barley with oatmeal and pale malt for a gloopy, globular mouthfeel that oozes dark chocolate tones and port flavors. A healthy dose of hops, the earthy Fuggles and tobacco-tinged Kent Goldings, steers it away from a stout, toward an old ale with spice and licorices.

While Old Engine Oil lubricated talk among beer connoisseurs, it's the delightful, delicately hoppy Bitter & Twisted that's driven Harviestoun's growth over the years. There's a biscuity backbone of pale malt, with wisps of wheat to fluff up the head, and a kaleidoscopic coming-together of peppery Challenger, Hallertau Hersbrucker, and, for the aroma, the Celeia variety of Styrian Golding from Slovenia.

"We only use whole hop flowers," said Stuart, "it makes a huge difference to our beers. They wouldn't be the same if you used oils or pellets. It's like a Michelin-star chef using freeze-dried herbs and spices in lieu of fresh ones."

Bitter & Twisted represents approximately 60 percent of Harviestoun's 7,500-barrel annual output; it was named Champion Beer of Scotland in 1999, went on to be crowned the overall Champion Beer of Britain four years, later and demand for its aromatic charms both necessitated and paid for a 2004 move to a bigger 60-barrel ex-St. Austell brewery down the road from Dollar and a long way from the bucket that Brooker began brewing with in 1984.

In 2006, with more than 20 years on the clock, he handed the keys over to the Caledonian Brewery, which revved up the marketing, the packaging, and the distribution, but dared not tinker with the talent. When Caledonian was bought up by Scottish & Newcastle and subsequently Heineken, Harviestoun regained its independence via a management buyout, before unleashing Ola Dubh, a beer born out of Old Engine Oil yet reared in Scottish single-malt whisky casks.

In the world's first official collaboration between a brewery and a world-renowned Scotch whisky distiller, Harviestoun joined forces with Highland Park in Orkney, one of only five Scotch whisky producers that still use traditional methods of malting and peating, to produce a trio of barrel-aged beers aged in casks that had previously housed either Highland Park 12-, 16-, or 30-year-old.

Pronounced "O-la doo" and meaning "black oil", Ola Dubh is an awe-inspiring, extraordinarily elegant ale that, unlike some barrel-aged beers, isn't one-dimensionally wooden or whisky-ish. While added complexity comes with age, a voluptuous, viscous vortex of vanilla, peat, port, and spicy chocolate adorns all three expressions. Served in snifters a sliver below room temperature, they're incredible alongside game or lamb, or an ample cheeseboard, and simply sublime with a particularly brûléed crème brûlée. The first batch of Ola Dubh, available in slickly packaged numbered and boxed bottles, was snatched up by the oh-so eager North American market to much acclaim. But, with a ten-year contract secured with Highland Park, Harviestoun aims to oil the wheels of distribution elsewhere.

Key Beers

Harviestoun's Bitter & Twisted *Blonde Ale* 4.2%

Harviestoun's Ola Dubh *Oak-aged Ale* 8%

Harviestoun's Old Engine Oil *Dark Beer* 6%

Harviestoun's Schiehallion *Cask-conditioned Lager* 4.8%

Hawkshead Brewery

Staveley, Cumbria
www.hawksheadbrewery.co.uk

 Hawkshead Bitter 3.7%

This is a pale, effortlessly drinkable ale with a bitter back end courtesy of hops from Slovenia. Comes furnished with a mellow Maris Otter body.

Lakeland Gold Premium Bitter 4.4%

Veteran BBC foreign correspondent Alex Brodie worked in some of the world's most hazardous trouble spots before swapping the microphone for the mash-fork in 2002 and opening the Hawkshead Brewery in the heart of the Lake District. Highly aromatic, hoppy ales are the Hawkshead way. Brusque, bitter, and brewed with both English (First Gold) and American (Cascade) hops, Lakeland Gold goes brilliantly with smoked cheese and also with fish curry.

Highgate Brewery

Walsall, West Midlands
www.highgatebrewery.com

Dark Mild 3.6%

Highgate has been driving drinkers wild with its Mild since 1898 and has retained much of the Victorian brewery equipment to this day. Melodious malt flavors, a fruity aroma, and a piquant palate soothed by chocolate and Camp coffee.

Highland Brewery

Orkney, Scotland
www.highlandbrewingcompany.com

 Scapa Special *Pale Ale* 4.2%

In 2008 former aerospace engineer Rob Hill set up Highland Brewery, after cutting his brewing teeth at the Moorhouse's Brewery in Lancashire. From an old Orkney creamery, Rob brews an impressive mild, and this delicate pale ale made with Maris Otter pale ale malt and a blend of four spicy, grassy hops. Champion Beer of Scotland 2008.

Hilden Brewery

Lisburn, Co. Antrim, Northern Ireland
www.hildenbrewery.co.uk

 Molly's Chocolate Stout 4.2%

In 2006 Northern Ireland's oldest independent brewery celebrated its 25th year of real reverence. Its star Anglo-Irish ale is a rich, coffee-capped dark stout brewed with malted oats, chocolate barley, and Northdown and First Gold hops. Each year, owners Seamus and Ann Scullion host a beer festival with more *"craic"* than a natural fault line.

Hobsons Brewery

Cleobury Mortimer, Shropshire
www.hobsons-brewery.co.uk

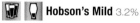 **Hobson's Mild** 3.2%

A much revered micro that's grown in stature since it began brewing in 1993. Supremely nutty and hoppy, Hobson's Mild usurped golden ales from the top of the Champion Beer of Britain podium in 2007.

Hog's Back Brewing

Tongham, Surrey
www.hogsback.co.uk

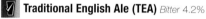 **Traditional English Ale (TEA)** *Bitter* 4.2%

A well-built, burly brunette bitter that spikes the malt flavors ahead of a restrained hop bitterness. This well-crafted flagship ale with a long dry finish, a classic best bitter, is the biggest-selling brew from a much-admired micro that opened in the summer of 1992. And in 2007 it won CAMRA's prestigious Champion Beer of Britain award.

Holden's Brewery

Dudley, West Midlands
www.holdensbrewery.co.uk

Holden's Golden Glow
Golden Ale 4.4%

Aromatic, award-winning golden ale from a family-owned Black Country brewery whose brewing heritage dates back to 1915. A deliciously dainty drop that boasts subtle but fragrant hop aromas.

Joseph Holt

Manchester
www.joseph-holt.com

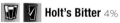 **Holt's Bitter** 4%

Big, brawny, and bitter, with heady hop aromas, spice and pepper on the tongue, and a bone-dry delay on the finish.

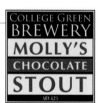 **Mild** 3.2%

This Mancunian Mild is one of the more traditional tipples from a brewery that's been in the Holt family hands since 1849. On the palate, malt flavors sweeter than a last-minute goal in a European Soccer Cup Final are lengthened by an impressive finish.

Hook Norton

Hook Norton, Oxfordshire
www.hooknortonbrewery.co.uk

 Hook Norton Bitter *Best Bitter* 3.6%

A glorious session ale that brings light hop bitterness and juicy malt drinkability together in an uplifting manner. Very difficult to have just one.

★ **Old Hooky** *Premium Bitter* 4.6%

Creviced away in the Cotswolds, Hook Norton is the only steam-powered brewery in Britain and a classic example of a Victorian tower brewery. The clunking, wheezing 25 horsepower steam engine has been helping to produce traditional British beers since 1849, when it was started by farmer and maltster John Harris. It is still family-run.

Hop Back

Salisbury, Wiltshire
www.hopback.co.uk

★ **Summer Lightning** *Golden Ale* 5%

A classic, hugely popular golden ale capable of converting even the most lazy Luddite lager drinkers. Sprightly summer thirst-quencher brewed exclusively with East Kent Golding hops, a burnished gold color, lively citrus aroma, and a touch of tropical fruit mellowed out by a light floral hop finish.

Innis & Gunn

Edinburgh, Scotland
www.innisandgunn.com

 **Innis & Gunn** *Oak-aged Beer* 6.6%

A liquid love child of Scottish distilling and brewing, this ale is matured in a whisky cask for a minimum of 30 days, nosed after 25 days by a master blender, and further matured in a marrying tun for 47 days. The 77-day process results in an outrageously smooth beer that is lightly oaked with vanilla and toffee notes and more than a hint of Scotch.

Jennings

Cockermouth, Cumbria
www.jenningsbrewery.co.uk

Sneck Lifter *Premium Bitter* 5.1%

Many feared for the future of Jennings when it was purchased by Marston's, but the new owners updated the brewery, there since 1828, and spread word of its brews. Cockle-warming, robust, red ale brewed with mineral-rich Lakeland water; nutty, rich, and toffee-ish with a bit of burnt roast on the finish. A "sneck" is the local term for a door latch.

JW Lees

Manchester, Greater Manchester
www.jwlees.co.uk

 **Moonraker** *Strong Ale* 7.5%

Opens with a sweet, chocolate aroma; nutty and spicy flavors follow on the tongue. Viscous texture, maple syrup, and a swirl of dry, herbal notes on the slightly minty finish.

★ **Vintage Harvest Ale** *Barley Wine* 11.5%

Since 1828 six generations of the Lees family have been making mash-fork magic in the "People's Republic of Mancunia". This fabulously complex strong ale, ideal for laying down in the cellar, is a classic quaff and makes a far better cheese companion than port. Brewed every fall and smartly packaged in 275ml bottles, it combines rich and bulbous Maris Otter malt with piquant Goldings hops.

Kelham Island

Sheffield, South Yorkshire
www.kelhambrewery.co.uk

★ **Pale Rider** *Pale Ale* 5.2%

Kelham Island has sustained the city's rich brewing heritage by crafting splendid small-batch beers in a brewery that has close associations with the famous Fat Cat pub. This is a strong, North American hop-inspired pale ale that, with its medium-bodied, fragrant, grapefruit charms, was CAMRA's 2004 Champion Beer of Britain.

Kinsale Brewing Company

Kinsale, Co. Cork, Ireland
www.kinsalebrewing.com

Kinsale Irish Lager 4.3%

Small, no-nonsense brewery located in the pretty town of Kinsale in County Cork on the west coast of Ireland. It was founded in 2001 on the site of an old brewery. Its bestselling beer is this light-bodied thirst-slaker that, thankfully, is bottled with a cap. You know what they say: "You can take an Irish lager out of Cork, but you can't…"

Little Valley Brewing

Hebden Bridge, West Yorkshire
www.littlevalleybrewery.co.uk

 **Hebden's Wheat** *Wheat Beer* 4.5%

Up-and-coming Soil Association-certified organic brewery. Young, Dutch brewer Wim van der Spek brings ethical awareness to bear on traditional European ales, here with a wonderfully bracing, spicy and fruity coriander-tinged wheat beer.

Mackeson's (Anheuser-Busch InBev)
Bedfordshire
www.ab-inbev.com

 **Mackeson's** *Stout* 3%

A legendary liquid that once graced British pubs up and down the country, but is now difficult to find. Synonymous with its advertising slogan "It looks good, tastes good and, by golly, it does you good," Mackeson's is sweeter than a puppy in a dress, but with an interesting dried-out bitterness on the finish, layered with tones of coffee, nuts and bittersweet chocolate in between.

Marston's Beer Company
Burton-on-Trent, Staffordshire
www.marstonsbeercompany.co.uk

Duchy Original Organic Ale *Bitter* 5%
www.Duchyoriginals.com

Here, the Prince of Wales doesn't just grow vegetables; he brews beer, too. Sort of. A quintessentially British organic ale brewed on behalf of Duchy Originals; a charitable organization set up by Charlie to champion local sustainable food, and drink and regenerate the countryside.

Manns Original *Brown Ale* 2.8%

A sweet, smooth sepia-tinted sip of yesteryear, this brown ale was widely used in the past as a mixer to improve ale of dubious quality. Sadly, it's no longer a Manns world—where mustaches, monocles, and manners made the the man—but the beer has remained, and has even flirted with the London cocktail scene as a cult classic and cultured Coca-Cola substitute.

Marston's Pedigree *Premium Bitter* 4.5%

Britain's largest ale brewer based in Burton-on-Trent, the historical and spiritual home of British brewing. Hailing the ale since 1834, Marston's is famous for its classic oak-cask Burton Union System which enhances, retains, and refines the yeast character in the beer. The Union-fermented Pedigree, the best-selling ale in the country, is a cult and complex classic renowned for its flourishing fruit flavors, delicate dryness, mineral-rich water profile, and sulfur nose known as the "Burton Snatch".

Old Empire *India Pale Ale* 5.7%

IPA was once the engine room of Burton brewing, and this highly hoppy, copper-toned lip-smacker is a fantastic faithful, albeit more mellow, re-creation of the swashbuckling beer of yesteryear.

McMullen
Hertford, Hertfordshire
www.mcmullens.co.uk

McMullen's AK Bitter 3.7%

Hertfordshire's oldest independent brewery has, after a few tumultuous years of late when closure beckoned, got back to its brewing best, and the 180-year-old AK is still a fruity, herby, easy-drinking drop.

Meantime
see Brewery Profile pages 80–81
Greenwich, London
www.meantimebrewing.com

Coffee Beer 6%

A thinking man's espresso martini brewed with Araba Bourbon coffee beans from the Abahuzamugambi Bakawa Cooperative in Rwanda. The caffeine content in each bottle is the equivalent of a cup of coffee. Voluptuous and velvety, it'll open your eyes and keep them open. Best drunk chilled.

London Porter 6.5%

Fans of full-bodied, bottle-conditioned mouth-pleasers will fall hard for this jet-black, smoky and devilishly smooth porter whose recipe, featuring no fewer than seven malt varieties and a flourish of Fuggles hops, dates back to the 1850s.

Meantime IPA 7.5%

Munich-schooled brewer Alastair Hook has drawn on London's India Pale Ale legacy and crafted a rich, resinous reproduction full of spicy hop oils and aroma, tones of tobacco and marmalade, a sweet moreish malt body, and warm alcohol "burn." This is a genuine IPA.

Meantime Raspberry Grand Cru *Raspberry Beer* 5%

Fruit flavors thrust forth on the nose and tongue. Banana and clove from the yeast and bittersweet tang from the raspberry influence. Dry enough as an apéritif, but also for dessert, alongside dark chocolate.

Mighty Oak Brewery
Maldon, Essex
www.mightyoakbrewery.co.uk

Oscar Wilde
Mild 3.7%

Fruity and dry, much like its notorious namesake—who famously proclaimed that "work is the curse of the drinking classes." Accented with coffee, blueberry, and chocolate, this marvelous Mild has been at the forefront of the style's revival and goes down a treat.

Milton Brewery

Cambridge, Cambridgeshire
www.miltonbrewery.co.uk

 **Marcus Aurelius Roman Imperial Stout** 7.5%

Petit yet prolific craft brewery that owns pubs in London and Peterborough and whose bountiful beers pick up awards with consummate ease. This superb vanilla-veneered stout is strapping yet silky.

Moorhouse's Brewery

Burnley, Lancashire
www.moorhouses.co.uk

Black Cat Mild 3.4%

This legendary Lancashire brewery has been producing life-enhancing liquids since 1865. A classic ruby-colored northern Mild that shoehorns chocolate, raisins, and a dry finish has been CAMRA's Champion Beer of Britain.

Mordue Brewery

North Shields, Tyne & Wear
www.morduebrewery.com

Workie Ticket Best Bitter 4.5%

Mordue's beers once slaked the thirst of 19th-century Newcastle, but closed in 1879. Dormant until 1995, the name was revived by Garry and Matthew Farson and now lends itself to some superb ale, of which this barnstorming, balanced bitter is the most well known. 1997 CAMRA Champion Beer of Britain.

"Few things are more pleasant than a village graced with a good church, a good priest and a good pub."

JOHN HILLABY
ENGLISH WRITER AND WALKER . 1917–1996

Oakham Ales

Woodston, Cambridgeshire
www.oakhamales.com

JHB (Jeffrey Hudson Bitter) 3.8%

Ace Peterborough-based micro that threw its hat, more likely a Stetson than a Bowler, into the craft brewing ring in 1993. This British bitter is gloriously drinkable, multi-garlanded, and gilded with American hops and a cheek-drawing, citrus character.

White Dwarf Wheat Beer 5%

It may not be big but it's certainly clever. Juicy fruity esters whipped into shape by crisp, grapefruit-leaning hops, with a terrifically tight finish.

Oakleaf Brewery Company

Gosport, Hampshire
www.oakleafbrewing.co.uk

Hole Hearted Bitter 4.7%

Great grapefruit and plenty of it, this northwest American-style ale from the southwest of England is brewed with 100 percent Cascade hops. Floral, zesty, and refreshing, it is one of several smashing beers from a family-run brewery that came on line back in 2000.

O'Hanlon's

Whimple, Devon
www.ohanlonsbeer.com

Goldblade Wheat Beer 4%

A wonderful wheat beer that has bready notes and fiercely fruity and estery aroma, with a brisk bite at the back.

Port Stout 4.5%

Born in London in 1995 to an eponymous pub, O'Hanlon's brewery fled the Big Smoke in 2000 and now cuts quite a dash in Devon with some superb esoteric ales. A beer inspired by the Irish corpse-reviving tradition of adding a splash of port to one's stout. A velvety smooth beer with a finish that owes its sweetness to the two bottles of Ferreira port that are thrown into every brewer's barrel.

Thomas Hardy's Ale Barley Wine 11.7%

Many regard this as the world's best Barley Wine, formerly brewed by the late Eldridge Pope brewery. How to describe it? Well, Thomas Hardy gave it a rather eloquent try in his book *Trumpet Major*. "It was of the most beautiful color than the eye of an artist in beer could desire; full in body yet brisk as a volcano; piquant, yet without a twang; luminous as an autumn sunset; free from streakiness of taste but, finally, rather heady." It is Britain's strongest ale, too, so beware.

THE MEANTIME BREWING COMPANY LIMITED

The Greenwich Brewery, London SE7 8RX

www.meantimebrewing.com

In the "traditional" world of British brewing, cask-conditioned ale is assumed to be as constant as the moon.

Meantime Brewing, however, is not your usual traditional British brewery. Unwilling to wait in line with the cask ale breweries whose commercial "cojones" are firmly in the frosty, ever-tightening hands of the United Kingdom's omnipotent pub companies, Meantime has broken rank by cold-shouldering "cask-conditioned" beer and broadening its horizons beyond the classic constraint of hand-pull.

Alastair Hook, Meantime's outspoken brewer and founder, is a man on a mission, a fairly lonely and ambitious mission, to flush out bland beer from the minds of the masses with flavorsome avant-garde elixirs that salute tradition, but are by no means shackled by it.

Although Alastair learned the brewing basics at Heriot-Watt University in Edinburgh in 1989, it was his postgraduate years at Weihenstephan in Munich and the Kaltenberg Brewery that, along with the infectious entrepreneurial zeal he'd encountered while living in the United States, shaped Meantime's mantra: "to put before the consumer the most exciting flavors to be found in beer that we are able to create, with the wit and technology at our disposal."

"I went to Germany because I wanted some brewing reverence in my life," recalls Alastair. "People there have respect for beer; it's a country where brew masters are as important as lawyers in every town and where they don't tax their sins. It made me decide that I wanted to be a brewer, and I was determined to bring these values back to England."

Right: Brewer and founder of Meantime, Alastair Hook, is a man on a mission to banish bland beer from the supermarket shelves.

Far right: Distinctive labels and packaging are helping Meantime 's position at the forefront of pioneering UK breweries whose beers are receiving worldwide, award-winning attention.

Alastair set up the brewery back in 1999, in an unprepossessing industrial estate near the Millennium Dome in South London, and began brewing Continental bottom-fermented beers for some of London's most prestigious style bars, whose owners were fed up with fobbing off moribund mainstream swill to drinkers that knew better.

In 2002 a deal to brew boutique beers for a major supermarket boosted the coffers and allowed Meantime to expand its breadth of beer styles. Meantime's beers are all brewed in small batches using natural ingredients, with no additional additives, and are unpasteurized ("It may kill the bugs, but it also kills all the flavor"). Its range now numbers more than a dozen brews and includes a Helles, a Kölsch, a chocolate beer, a raspberry beer, and the wide-eyed wonder that is Meantime's coffee beer, brewed using Certified beans from the Abahuzamugambi Bakawa Cooperative in Rwanda.

While Alastair admits a lack of cask ale is a blind spot, Meantime can never be accused of snubbing British brewing traditions. In 2005 Alastair breathed life back into an 18th-century India Pale Ale, first brewed down the river Thames in Bow by George Hodgson. "Short of putting it in wooden casks and flinging it round Cape Horn on a boat, we couldn't get it any closer," says Alastair.

"It was London where IPA was born, and it was the success of Hodgson that inspired the Burton-on-Trent brewers to follow suit. It's Britain's most authentic IPA."

Further dusting down of brewing tomes resulted in the resurrection of a wonderfully chewy and unadulterated London porter, made with seven different malts. "The idea was to replicate the beer that once made London the brewing capital of the world and the kind of beer that you would have drunk down the pub back then."

Corked and caged in ornate 70cl champagne bottles, the IPA and the porter were initially and exclusively earmarked for export to the United States where real IPAs are appreciated. "American brewing is an inspiration, it's like acid house, and it's no surprise that our beers are appreciated so much over there. The American brewers are incredibly innovative, and they're teaching us arrogant, conceited Brits a lesson."

Thankfully, the ripples made by the American craft-brewing scene are now lapping the United Kingdom's shores, and both IPA and porter are getting the domestic acclaim they deserve. They're sublime beers with one foot in the past and the other in the future yet, unlike other, often overly wacky, beers that try to straddle the two, Meantime's beers maintain their balance.

It's not the only defibrillating jolt Meantime has delivered to the heart of London brewing's past. In 2007, Alastair took time out from mischievously poking a mash-fork into the sides of bland British brewing to excavate, restore, and resume brewing at the old Royal Naval College in Greenwich, one of London's oldest brewing sites dating back to 1717.

From a pilot brewhouse on the former site of the Royal Hospital brewery, where seafarers' sickness was allayed with daily rations of beer, Alastair administers an antidote to beer drinking lives suffering from a lack of flavor.

One of these is a replica of a London porter, first produced in the 1750s by the hospital brewery, using water from the original well and the *Brettanomyces* yeasts and *Lactobacillus* and *Pediococcus* bacteria that, back in the early 18th century, would have resided in the wooden tuns that stored the beer.

"It's sour, rich, acidic, acrid, and smoky, and not many people like it, but I do it anyway, as I think it's an important thing to do and it's what you'd expect from a thoroughly modern London company," says Alastair. "It's a hedonistic indulgence with no boundaries with regards to processes, ingredients, or time. It's my retirement home if you like, and a place where I do what I want for the sake of beer."

"We've taken what history has to offer and we're taking everything that cutting-edge technology has to offer and we're condensing it into modern London living," he says. "Our philosophy is to look at the ingredients in beer and discover the ways to best express them. We understand the microbiology, we understand the science, but we also appreciate the art, the style, and the significance of the past."

"What we're doing is taking the world beer order, grabbing it by its feet, turning it upside down, giving it a shake, and watching all the grubby coins fall out."

Key Beers

Meantime Chocolate Beer 6.5%

Meantime Coffee Beer 6%

Meantime Helles Bier 4.4%

Meantime India Pale Ale 7.5%

Meantime London Porter 6.5%

Okell & Son

Douglas, Isle of Man
www.okells.co.uk

Mac Lir *Wheat Beer* 4.4%

Named after Manannán Mac Lir, Celtic god of the sea, this wheat beer is brewed with summer wheat and six, yes six, different varieties of hops: one from New Zealand, two from the Czech Republic, two from the United States, and one from Britain. A distinct aroma of vanilla gives an initial burst of sweetness, complemented by a subtle banana flavor. A hint of lemon is followed by a complex dry finish.

Okells Aile Smoked Celtic Porter 4.8%

The Isle of Man's most significant brewer began life in 1850, moved into a state-of-the-art steam brewery in 1874, and updated only in 1994, where it conjures up ales that are both classic and quirky. Seductively smoky and complex, with hints of licorice and Irish coffee, this peculiarly drinkable dark porter is certainly the latter. Brewed, like all Okell ales, to the Manx Brewers Act, which forbids the use of any ingredient other than malt, water, yeast, and hops.

Old Chimneys Brewery

Market Weston, Suffolk
www.oldchimneysbrewery.com

Good King Henry Special Reserve *Imperial Stout* 11%

Brilliant bottle-conditioned beer, matured in cask, is what former Greene King brewer Alan Thomson hangs his hat on. Oak-aged for six months and left in the bottle for two years in commemoration of the brewery's tenth anniversary, this hard-to-find version of Good King Henry is steeped in dark malt, vanilla, almonds, and a hearty dose of hops for preservation. If you can't find this special edition, Good King Henry is a robust, ruby-hued revelation.

Orkney Brewery

Quoyloo, Orkney, Scotland
www.sinclairbreweries.co.uk

Dark Island *Premium Bitter* 4.6%

Twice Champion Beer of Scotland, this bitter bestows melodious mocha and molasses in the mouth, sharpened at the back of the throat by First Gold and Goldings hop bitterness. Its fruity finish clamors for the cheese board.

Red MacGregor *Strong Ale* 5%

An awesome, intensely ecologically aware brewery nestled in the far north of Scotland. This convivial, cozy ruby beer, with toffee and plum flavors and a touch of lychee, is magical with a red meat roast.

Otley Brewing Company

Pontypridd, South Wales
www.otleybrewing.co.uk

O1 *Pale Ale* 4%

Wonderful Welsh brews packaged so that they're as pleasing on the eye as they are on the palate. Light, hoppy pale ale, grassy and herbal with a light linger of lemon.

O'Garden *Wheat Beer* 4.8%

Cheekily named seasonal wheat beer that's spicier, more fruity, and with bigger banana notes than its Belgian "namesake" (Hoegaarden).

Otter Brewery

Luppitt, Devon
www.otterbrewery.com

Otter Ale Bitter 4.5%

A Devon-sent classic British bitter, all bittersweet and balanced from a small southwestern outfit with a loyal following in both the US and the UK.

Palmers Brewery

Bridport, Dorset
www.palmersbrewery.com

Tally Ho *Premium Bitter* 5.5%

Housed under the same thatched roof for more than two centuries, Palmers is one of the longest-running family-owned microbreweries in Britain. The russet-flecked head of this tangy, tobacco-tinged ale has been caught up in the facial fluff of many a cask connoisseur.

Pitfield Brewery

North Weld, Essex
www.pitfieldbeershop.co.uk

Pitfield 1837 *India Pale Ale* 7%

After nearly 20 years of brewing boutique beers in the back room of a liquor store, Pitfield swapped London's East End for Essex in 1997, yet continues to eke out edgy, ecologically sound ales worthy of their dedicated following. Its silky Shoreditch Stout is particularly sought after and so, too, is this resinous, unashamedly acerbic IPA, brewed with Northdown and Golding hops.

Porterhouse Brewing Company
Dublin, Co. Dublin, Ireland
www.porterhousebrewco.com

 **Oyster Stout** 4.8%

Hugely successful chain of brewpubs, with outlets in both London and Dublin, who proudly shun the ubiquitous Guinness in favor of their own silky stouts. This award-winning beer is smooth and viscous, with a lovely, minerally metallic mouthfeel. Galena, Nugget, and East Kent Goldings hops are all present, too.

Purity Brewing Company
Great Alne, Warwickshire
www.puritybrewing.com

 Mad Goose Premium Bitter 5%

Named after one of the gaggle of geese that ferociously patrols the brewery. Whether it's mad as in angry or mad as in mentally ill is unclear, but either way this beer is crazily good. Bittered with Hallertau hops and furnished with an American hop aroma, it's a zesty, full-bodied beer with a wheat-inspired smoothness in the mouth.

 Pure Ubu Bitter 4.5%

Purity has gently rattled the cage of conventional cask-ale brewing since opening in 2005 and brewing shrewdly marketed, cleverly packaged real ales that are as friendly to the environment as they are to one's taste buds. This cracking quaffable ale, which calls upon Cascade and Challenger hops for flavor, with an afterglow of Maris Otter, is jolly splendid. Drink it and enjoy.

Purple Moose Brewery
Porthmadog, Wales
www.purplemoose.co.uk

 Dark Side of the Moose Old Ale/Mild 4.5%

A delicious, fruity dark ale from this diminutive yet discerning brewery born out of Lawrence Washington's homebrew hobby. Sweet and roasty.

RCH Brewery
West Hewish, Somerset
www.rchbrewery.co.uk

 **Pitchfork** Best Bitter 4.3%

Now housed in a former cider mill, RCH was born in the Royal Clarence Hotel in Burnham-upon-Sea in the early 1980s, before moving to a bigger brewery in 1993. Word of its top award-winning tipples has spread, courtesy of a successful wholesale arm, especially this pale gold grapefruit-gilded gulp that won Champion Best Bitter in 1998.

Rebellion Brewing Company
Marlow, Buckinghamshire
www.rebellionbeer.co.uk

 Rebellion IPA Bitter 3.7%

Buckinghamshire-based brewer set up in 1993 by two schoolmates with inherited equipment from the neighboring Courage Brewery. It now distributes beers to more than 200 local pubs—and a hotel in Switzerland. Not strictly an IPA, but it's clear to see why this sweet, plummish pint is so popular.

Ringwood Brewery
Ringwood, Hampshire
www.ringwoodbrewery.co.uk

 **Old Thumper** Premium Bitter 5.6%

Hints of tang, spicy twang, pear-drop candy, and smoky dryness are all here in Ringwood's flag-bearing beer. Founded in 1978 by pioneering craft brewer Peter Austin, Ringwood was passed on to Marston's Beer Company in 2007, but remains steadfast in its commitment to classic cask quaff. 1988 Champion Beer of Britain.

Robinson's
Stockport, Greater Manchester
www.frederic-robinson.com

 **Old Tom** Strong Ale 8.5%

A truly epic ale from one of Britain's best-loved breweries that's been in Robinson family hands since 1865. A luxurious oxblood-colored ale that's swirled in chocolate, dark cherry, and licorice, with a touch of spicy after-dinner mint on the finish. Comes in a funky-looking embossed bottle, too.

Rooster's Brewery

Knaresborough, North Yorkshire
www.roosters.co.uk

 **Yankee**
Pale Ale 4.3%

Head brewer Sean Franklin was once an oenophile. He studied in Bordeaux and worked in Burgundy, but, on returning to England, was cured by ale enlightenment in the shape of a pint of Timothy Taylor Landlord. Hops and their heady aromas are what Rooster's crows about, and Sean conducts inspiring "tastings" of his awesome aromatic ales using just one's sense of smell. Yankee, a melange of Cascade hops and soft Yorkshire water, is floral and citrus, and changes ever so slightly depending on the hop vintage. There are roses, lychees, and more tropical notes in there, too.

 YPA (Yorkshire Pale Ale) 4.3%

An outrageously aromatic medal winner at both the 2006 and 2008 World Beer Cups. Brewed with Styrian Golding hops and Golden Promise barley, it's feverishly fruity with peaches, pears, red apple, and kiwi fruit all popping up on the palate.

St. Austell

St. Austell, Cornwall
www.staustellbrewery.co.uk

Proper Job *India Pale Ale* 5.5%

Proper Job, inspired by Bridgeport IPA in Seattle, is a piney, hugely palatable IPA brewed with American Willamette, Chinook, and Cascade hops.

Tribute *Best Bitter* 4.2%

Around since 1851 and forever in the hands of the Hicks family, St. Austell has enjoyed a remarkable renaissance, thanks in part to the arrival of head brewer Roger Ryman in 1999. Roger Ryman improved St. Austell stalwart brews such as HSD and Tinners, before creating Tribute, a bonny bronze bitter with a beautiful bittersweet balance.

"Ale, man, ale's the stuff to drink
for fellows whom it hurts to think."

A. E. HOUSMAN
ENGLISH POET 1859–1936

St. Peter's Brewery

Bungay, Suffolk
www.stpetersbrewery.co.uk

 **Honey Porter** 4.5%

Don't be fooled by this drop's dark demeanor, for beneath the opaque appearance lies a light, coffee-coated sweet beer that's delicious with ice cream.

 **Organic Ale** *Bitter* 4.5%

Soil Association-certified bitter, sweet scented and full of citrus character, from a prolific purveyor of classic and quirky ales housed in a terrific 13th-century country hall complete with its own natural water borehole. While renowned for its apothecary-style 18th-century oval bottle, its ales can also be discovered on draft at London's famous Jerusalem Tavern pub in Clerkenwell.

Saltaire Brewery

Shipley, West Yorkshire
www.saltairebrewery.co.uk

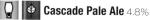 **Cascade Pale Ale** 4.8%

A buccaneering 20-barrel brewery set up in 2005 within the Victorian vestiges of a building once used to power the city's trams, Saltaire shares the name of the neighboring World Heritage site that's spearheaded Bradford's recent regeneration. The range of bottled and cask ales runs a gamut of styles, and twists thereof, but it's this American-influenced pale ale that competition judges like the most.

Samuel Smith

Tadcaster, North Yorkshire
no web address

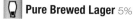 **Pure Brewed Lager** 5%

This is one of the best British-brewed lagers, a deliciously dainty all-malt drop. Golden-hued with a hop bitterness that snaps at the heels of juicy malt.

Yorkshire Stingo *Wood-aged Beer* 8%

Notoriously media-shy and secretive, fiercely independent and family-owned, Samuel Smith is Yorkshire's oldest brewery (1758). It owns several grandiose Victorian gin palaces in London, where prices are the lowest in the capital, while, back at the brewery, its ales are still fermented in traditional Yorkshire Squares (slate fermenting vessels) and often delivered in wooden casks. This ink-black beauty of a beer is aged for more than a year in oak casks, some of which date back more than a century. It is awash with raisin, Christmas pudding, molasses, and oak flavors that intensify in the bottle.

Sharp's
Rock, Cornwall *see Brewery Profile pages 86–87*
www.sharpsbrewery.co.uk

 **Atlantic IPA**
India Pale Ale 4.8%

This superb, highly eco Cornish craft brewer is one of the UK's most dynamic purveyors of exciting ales. Atlantic IPA is laid-back and lavished with citrus, hop, and light cotton candy notes. Profit from this pint, which is sold online, too, goes to the Lifeboat charity.

 Doom Bar *Bitter 4%*

Doom Bar is one of Sharp's leading lights and named after an infamous nearby sandbank. It is clean, fruity, and bittersweet, and a highly recommended dinner companion. Excellent with oily fish and seafood in cream sauces or pies, and also goes very well with a succulent steak. It is one of the fastest-growing beer brands in the United Kingdom.

Shepherd Neame
Faversham, Kent
www.shepherdneame.co.uk

Master Brew
Bitter 3.7%

The oldest brewer in Britain (founded in 1698) and in Neame family hands since 1864, Shepherd Neame brews traditional British ales in the hop-growing heartland of Kent. The brewery is a charming, historic labyrinth of low wooden beams, cobbled walkways, and walls bearing the scars from horse-drawn drays. A low-gravity ale with remarkable complexity and drinkability, Master Brew is balanced, burly, and big on Kentish hops. Lupulin lovers should also look out for the seasonal single-hop variety beers. Shepherd Neame's best-known beer is Kent's top-selling ale and is available by cask and by bottle.

 Spitfire *Bitter 4.7%*

Since the addition of a pilot brewery in 2006, Shepherd Neame has also been experimenting with more esoteric ales such as scallop stouts and Californian IPAs, but it's this dry, aromatic classic English ale, named after the fighter plane that scoured the skies in World War Two, that's the jewel in Shepherd Neame's crown.

Skinner's Brewery
Truro, Cornwall
www.skinnersbrewery.com

 Betty Stogs *Best Bitter 4%*

Steve and Sarah Skinner kick-started this quirky Cornish outfit in 1997, before expanding into a bigger brewery in 2003 on the back of a loyal local following and several awards. Of its radical and gnarly ales, Betty Stogs is arguably the best known and the winner of the 2008 Champion Best Bitter of Britain. Super smooth, lightly hopped sipping ale brewed with Cornish barley and wheat.

Springhead Brewery
Newark, Nottinghamshire
www.springhead.co.uk

Roaring Meg *Blonde Ale 5.5%*

An inspired ale-producer that delivers a wide range of beers with names connected to the English Civil War theme. Roaring Meg, a huge cannon used by both the Royalists and the Roundheads, is a robust blonde that'll blow your turrets off with its ease of drinking and distinctive lemon hop aromas.

Taddington Brewery
Blackwell, Derbyshire
No web address

Moravka
Premium Lager 4.4%

Rare indeed to find a British brewery producing Czech lagers, but Taddington, one of the highest breweries in the United Kingdom, has been doing just that since 2007. Unpasteurized—and unfiltered if you're lucky enough to get near the brewery—it celebrates the grassy Saaz hop with no small amount of skill and brings bready notes and a fruity flavor to the fore as well. This is a great British lager—and that is not a sentence you read very often.

SHARP'S BREWERY

Rock, Cornwall

www.sharpsbrewery.co.uk

The world is full of unlikely comebacks: Elvis … Lazarus … Frank Sinatra … and Cornwall, which was once, like its location, on the way to nowhere. Yes, it is barren and beautiful, and, yes, it has stunning coastlines, but scratch beneath the idyllic veneer and you'll discover the UK's poorest county.

During the 1990s, tourism, tin, and fish trawling, the trades upon which Cornwall has historically relied, were enduring tumultuous times with the last tin mine shutting in 1998, ending 4,000 years of Cornish quarrying, hotels and tourist boards struggling to shed the county's quaint "bucket and spade" image, and the fishing industry floundering under the weight of European catch quotas.

But, in 2001, the opening of the $200m (£130m) Eden Project, a thinking man's greenhouse and visitor attraction, breathed so much life back into the county that now it's considered cool. Cornwall rediscovered its manufacturing mojo in the shape of whirring wind farms, there's a blossoming art scene, tourism is riding high on a wave of surfing popularity, and the county has distanced itself from clichéd cream teas and pasties by becoming a food lovers' paradise, brimming with first-class restaurants and award-winning producers. It has even changed the name of the north coast A road from the A39 to the Atlantic Highway, and given it a Web site.

Cornwall's craft-brewing scene has mirrored the county's gentrification, and the Cornish flag is being fervently flown on the national stage by two terrific breweries; St. Austell, under the stewardship of brewer Roger Ryman, has turned from a rather tired traditional brewery into one of the United Kingdom's most thriving regional players, while Sharp's, based in Rock (the "St. Tropez of the UK") has grown rapidly to become the largest brewer of cask ale in the Southwest.

Sharp's rise to prominence has been fast. It was founded as recently as 1994. Former silversmith Bill Sharp had been creating ale alchemy as a home brewer, before commercially brewing quaffable ales on a ten-barrel system for local pubs.

By 2002 demand was outstripping supply, the brewery was upgraded to 50 barrels, and Bill, more a mash-fork than a money man, sold the business to a pair of ale-loving entrepreneurs who had made their money in the food business.

Stuart Howe, a young London-born brewing graduate of Heriot-Watt University, Edinburgh, was installed as head brewer, having cut his teeth at McMullen and Brakspear. With brains in the brewery and bucks in the boardroom, Sharp's abandoned its standing as a mere micro and ram-raided its way into the realm of major regional brewer.

It's been spearheaded by Doom Bar, a tangy session ale named after the infamous sandbank at the mouth of the local Camel Estuary, which is both easy to drink and, crucially for pub landlords, simple to handle. Unlike the vast majority of cask ales, Doom Bar leaves the brewery almost fully conditioned and steals a march on its regional rivals by dropping bright quickly and consistently. "The most frustrating aspect of brewing cask ales is that, as a brewer, you lose control of your product as soon as it leaves the brewery," says Stuart. "We want to give landlords a beer that's almost completely conditioned, with all the hard work done and with the flavors already there.
We mash all-malt grist at a low temperature, which gives the beer a drier, less cloying malt texture and sweetness."

Representing 70 percent of Sharp's sales, Doom Bar has forged a strong presence in London through some canny

marketing and sponsorship of the famous Oxford v Cambridge University Boat Race. It's also exported as far afield as Japan, Scandinavia, and Canada.

There are nine other ales in the Sharp's locker. Stuart keeps it classic with Cornish Coaster, a bittersweet fruity British bitter, the exceptionally well-balanced Sharp's Own, and Sharp's Special, a deliciously dry strong ale bedecked in dark fruit and light roast flavors.

Among his more adventurous, esoteric ales is the left-field liquid Four, a rounded and really rather robust, Barley Wine that charms cheese with a pungent resinous piny hop rub, sweet jam on the nose, and fat-fighting alcohol.

"B", a bottle-conditioned strong pale ale, is brimming with Bobek, a rarely spotted young Slovenian hop renowned for its awesome aromatics, while Sharp's Massive Ale, brewed using candy sugars and Northdown and Perle hops, is conditioned over the course of a year and is resplendent with flavors of rum, tobacco, rich caramel, and rasping warm alcohol.

Stuart insists on whole hops for all his beers. "I'd never use anything else but whole flower hops," remarks Stuart. "I don't think you can do the same things with oils, pellets, or compounds, and I've never seen any evidence to prove otherwise. There are brewers that make amazing beers with pellets, but I cannot abide their character in my beers." In order to induce the herbal, aromatic hop character, Stuart adds the vast majority of them (85–90%) late to the boil, before setting the yeast to work in open fermentation tanks. "They've got to be open, as we don't think you can get traditional ale flavors from conical fermenters," adds Stuart.

While many of his British craft-brewing peers look to the United States for inspiration, Stuart is guided by Belgian brewing traditions, especially for Gentle Jane, a Lambic-leaning mixed-yeast sour ale. Bottle-conditioned with *Brettanomyces* injected into the bottle using a syringe, its barnyard bouquet gives way to a palate of hard candy, honey, and sharp grapefruit. Another Belgian-style beer is Chalky's Bite, a Saison ale brewed following a challenge from chef Rick Stein.

Key Beers

Sharp's Atlantic IPA 4.8%
Sharp's Chalky's Bite *Saison Ale* 6.8%
Sharp's Cornish Coaster *Bitter* 3.6%
Sharp's Doom Bar *Bitter* 4%

Top left: Sharp's Doom Bar has gone from new brew to representing 70% of the brewery's output in just a few years.
Left: Profits from Atlantic IPA go to the Royal National Lifeboat Institution, who are active on the dramatic Cornish coastline.
Above: Stuart Howe, Sharp's Brewer, insists on using only whole hop flowers in the brewing process.

Teignworthy Brewery

Newton Abbot, Devon
www.teignworthybrewery.com

 Reel Ale *Bitter* 4%

This Victorian tower brewery, in the town of Newton Abbot on the banks of the river Teign, delivers four core ales and a number of seasonal editions. It's easy to get hooked on Reel Ale; nicely nuanced notes—both bitter and sweet—and a brusque back end.

Theakston Brewery

Masham, North Yorkshire
www.theakstons.co.uk

 **Old Peculier** *Premium Bitter* 5.5%

This is the beer that, they claim, made the town of Masham famous. Theakston's classic calling card is a dark purple, palate-pleasing proponent of all that's fruity and full-bodied.

Theakston Best *Best Bitter* 3.8%

Having swapped hands more times than an Internet-surfing ambidextrous adolescent, the brewery is thankfully back in the Theakston family fold, where it began in 1827. This quintessentially British session bitter, beset with Fuggles and Goldings hops for bitterness and aroma respectively, is back to its magnificent best.

Thornbridge Brewery

see Brewery Profile pages 90–91
Ashford-in-the-Water, Derbyshire
www.thornbridgebrewery.com

Jaipur IPA *India Pale Ale* 5.9%

From a stonemason's workshop set within the grounds of a seriously grandiose Jacobean hall and overlooking the Peak District, Thornbridge brews wonderful beer to the mantra of "a contemporary take on traditional thinking". This fruity, honey-tinged, and delightfully hoppy IPA doffs its bowler hat in America's direction.

St. Petersburg *Imperial Russian Stout* 7.7%

An impressive, intensely ink-black beer delivering a full-bodied blend of chocolate, roast, polished plum notes, and attitudinal hop character—all perked up with a dry double espresso finish.

Thornbridge Bracia *Dark Ale* 9%

Chestnut honey, seven malt varieties (Maris Otter, Brown, Munich, Dark Crystal, Black, Chocolate, Peated), roasted barley, and a quintet of hops (Target, Pioneer, Hallertäu Northern Brewer, and Sorachi Ace) collude to craft a enchanting ale brimming with chestnut honey, cappuccino, white chocolate, dark fruits, and vibrant fresh peel. It gives a rich, silky mouthfeel, with notes of coffee, chocolate, licorice, and hazelnuts, too.

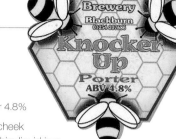

Three B's Brewery

Feniscowles, Lancashire
www.threebsbrewery.co.uk

Knocker Up *Porter* 4.8%

More than just a tongue-in-cheek name, this luxurious Lancashire liquid is a bellowing bottle-conditioned beer from a boutique Blackburn microbrewery. When the label described it as a "porter beer of supreme character with exotic ebony texture and a deep, rich palate of roast barley and chocolate malt", it wasn't lying.

Thwaites Brewery

Blackburn, Lancashire
www.thwaites.co.uk

Wainwright *Golden Ale* 4.1%

A canny, soft-toned golden ale, spicy and fruity, named after the fell-walking writer Alfred Wainwright and brewed by a behemoth of the northwest brewing scene. Thwaites is the seventh-largest beer maker in the land and boasts a family-run history that dates back more than two centuries. Its modern brewhouse has retained open fermentation vessels and still keeps traditional dray-pulling shire horses.

Timothy Taylor

Keighley, West Yorkshire
www.timothy-taylor.co.uk

Golden Best *Mild* 3.5%

Timothy Taylor, established in 1858, does more than just Landlord; its Dark Mild, strong Ram Tam dark ale, and Best Bitter are all outstanding and so, too, is this smooth, golden mild—a deliciously drinkable departure from the usual style and a rare, refreshing example of a Pennine Mild.

Landlord *Pale Ale/Bitter* 4.3%

One of the world's finest beers, Landlord is a masterpiece, an incessant award-winner, and, what's more, Madonna's favorite pint. Brewed, like all Taylor beers, entirely with a Golden Promise malt more readily associated with Scotch whisky, and soft water that runs off the Pennine hills, it's full of zing and tang, shifting effortlessly between rosemary-pine hop character and mouth-filling malt. Genius in a glass. Little wonder the chap on the label is smiling.

Titanic Brewery
Stoke-on-Trent, Staffordshire
www.titanicbrewery.co.uk

Captain Smith's *Bitter* 5.2%

When owners Keith and Dave Bott aren't championing the cause of British craft brewers, they're brewing a range of ales that, like their notoriously porous namesake, go down extremely easily. A ruby ale bulked with hearty, herbaceous hops buttressed by caramel and toffee.

Titanic Stout 4.5%

Darkly seductive stout with dashes of port, chocolate, pepper, plums, hazelnuts, and coffee. A touch of smoke and a dry roasted finish. Sales of the 2004 Champion Bottled Beer of Britain were buoyed when it was used in a recipe for ice cream by a TV chef.

Traditional Scottish Ales
Throsk, Scotland
www.traditionalscottishales.co.uk

Lomond Gold *Blonde Ale* 5%

A pilsner-esque organic copper-gold ale showcasing lemongrass, lychee, and grapefruit flavors from a burgeoning brewery that was created after the Bridge of Allan brewery closed its doors in 2005.

Traquair House Brewery
Innerleithen, Scotland
www.traquair.co.uk

 Jacobite Ale
Strong Ale/Barley Wine 8%

A sensational strong ale seasoned with coriander to enhance its heavy hop character. Voluptuous, rich, and vinous, with a touch of spicy chocolate.

Traquair House Ale *Scotch Ale* 7.2%

A brooding, boozy, and beguiling blend of wood notes, figs, plums, and mulled wine brewed in the grounds of Traquair House, a stunning Scottish castle that teeters on the English border. Now the oldest inhabited house in Scotland, it was brewing beer as early as 1566, but was revived from a long slumber by Peter Maxwell Stuart, 20th Laird of Traquair, in 1965. Under the stewardship of his daughter Catherine, its beers are still fermented in oak and exported all over the world.

Triple FFF Brewing Company
Alton, Hampshire
www.triplefff.com

Alton's Pride *Bitter* 3.8%

Triple FFF has been going for only just over a decade, but what a success it's been, winning many awards. The beers, including a Mild and a best bitter, are all structured on a Maris Otter backbone. This, the 2008 Champion Beer of Britain, is a great brusque, brunette bitter mellowed by mouth-warming malt.

Gilbert White *Smoked Ale* 6%

The brewery unearthed a recipe written by the eponymous 18th-century ecologist, who also happened to be a keen brewer, to create this seductive, smoky golden ale.

Ventnor Brewery
Ventnor, Isle of Wight
www.ventnorblog.com

Sand Rock *Smoked Ale* 5.6%

In 1996 Ventnor rose from the ashes of the Burts Brewery and now oversees an array of awesome ales, including a sexy Oyster Stout and the funky, fruity Anti-Freeze. This smoked ale, a ruby-hued and refreshingly restrained Rauchbier, uses malt that's been smoked in Scotland over smoldering peat. Great with smoked cheese, meats, and fish—or when chilled, chargrilled food from the barbecue.

Wadworth Brewery
Devizes, Wiltshire
www.wadworth.co.uk

Wadworth 6X Bitter 4.3%

Rewarding, friendly, and moreish, 6X appeals to those yearning bittersweet malt 'n' hop balance in their bitter. With its Victorian tower brewery with open coppers, shire horses, bespoke sign-painter, and a rare working cooperage, Wadworth really has been left to its own Devizes since moving into its Northgate Brewery in 1885.

THORNBRIDGE BREWERY

Ashford-in-the-Water, Derbyshire

www.thornbridgebrewery.co.uk

Back in the olden days, British landed gentry often had a brewery within the grounds of their country mansions. Drinking one's own beer was as much an expected titled privilege as shooting animals and employing poor people. But as the landed gentry has dwindled, so too has this brewing convention.

Above top: Award-winning Thornbridge operates out of a workshop in the grounds of an impressive Jacobean manor in the Peak District.

Above: Bracia is an enchanting addition to the brewery's roster, a rich, roasty dark ale with chestnuts, honey, seven malts, and five hops.

Bottom left, left to right: Kelly Ryan, Matthew Clark, Stefano Cossi, and David Pickering of Thornbridge Brewery.

But in 2005, in a corner of rural Derbyshire and within the grounds of a grandiose Jacobean Manor, the tradition was rekindled in the shape of the Thornbridge Brewery—set in seriously stunning scenery amid manicured lawns, stone walls, a magnificent lake with uplifting views across the Peak District, and, of course, the imposing Thornbridge Hall itself.

What not so long ago was a crumbling stately home has been gradually restored to its former glory by Emma and Jim Harrison, a married couple whose affection for the grand edifice dated back to when they visited the hall as children. Within the vast Jacobean vestiges, they've installed a glamorous ballroom, music hall, a marble-clad kitchen, a boardroom, an underground bar, and a swimming pool.

But it was Dave Wickett, a friend and owner of Sheffield's excellent Kelham Island Brewery, who suggested opening a brewery in their back "garden". In 2004 Jim invested in a secondhand ten-barrel brewing system and installed it in a derelict stonemason's shop yards from the stately home. He'd brewed beer in his mom's airing cupboard when he was younger, but he was certainly no brewer, and so he turned to Stefano Cossi, a 26-year-old food scientist from Udine in Northern Italy.

Stefano was joined by New Zealand brewer Kelly Ryan soon after, and a combination of Kiwi creativity and Italian flair saw Thornbridge scoop more than 75 awards in its first three years.

Approximately half of those awards (including Gold Medal Strong Bitter at the Great British Beer Festival 2008) have been accorded to Jaipur IPA, an authentically hoppy India Pale Ale that showcases the holy trinity of strength (5.9% ABV), drinkability, and balance and is Thornbridge's biggest seller.

As well as Jaipur, Thornbridge's core range includes Kipling (5.2% ABV), a South Pacific Pale Ale brewed using Nelson Sauvin hops from New Zealand; Lord Marples, a classic rich and malty bitter; and Wild Swan, a modest 3.5% ABV beer swathed in spice and citrus hop aromas.

Key Beers

Thornbridge Bracia *Dark Ale* 9%

Thornbridge Halcyon *Imperial India Pale Ale* 7.7%

Thornbridge Jaipur IPA 5.9%

Thornbridge Kipling *South Pacific Pale Ale* 5.2%

Thornbridge *St. Petersburg Imperial Russian Stout* 7.7%

In the space of just four years, soaring demand outstripped the capability of Thornbridge's original brewery, yet plans to expand the brewery within the stately grounds were prevented by pen-pushing planning people.

So, in 2009, Thornbridge was forced to move into a state-of-the-art brewery in nearby Bakewell. Despite the move, its unwavering commitment to the unusual, innovative elixirs that first thrust Thornbridge into the limelight has remained resolute, and the old brewhouse is now used as a pilot brewery in which more left-field liquids are fashioned.

Now with a four-strong team of young, dynamic brewers and without the weight of history that shackles so many British ale brewers, Thornbridge courageously ventures into areas of experimentation and innovation where others dare not tread. And it's by no means a new phenomenon.

In 2005 it was one of the first British microbreweries to dabble in the dark, woody art of barrel-aging. Its super satin-smooth St. Petersburg Imperial Russian Stout was put to sleep for 300 days in Scotch whisky barrels sourced from several distilleries, including Caol Ila and Macallan.

More recently, in 2007, Thornbridge teamed up with Garrett Oliver from New York's Brooklyn Brewery and brewed "Alliance", a big British-Brooklyn Barley Wine. It was then matured for more than 18 months before being refermented in bottles, using Champagne yeast to create a unique three-bottle collection: an unoaked Alliance Strong Ale and two versions finished in Spanish oak Pedro Ximénez sherry casks and American oak Madeira casks.

Another ale to embody the Thornbridge mantra of "Innovation … Passion . . . Knowledge" was SuJU, a rustic brown ale brewed in conjunction with Italian brewers Agostino Arioli and Maurizio Folli from Birrificio Italiano, using smoked malt and juniper berries in the brew.

And the innovation hasn't stopped there. Bracia, first introduced toward the end of 2008, is an avant-garde interpretation of an Ancient Roman ale laced with bitter Italian chestnut honey, while Halcyon, a 7.7% Imperial IPA, is "wet-hopped" using hops picked the same day and released as a vintage every year using a different hop variety.

Even seasonal beers are given a tickle with the feather of creativity. Much like a chef, Stefano doesn't choose the recipe or ingredients until he knows what herbs, spices, and fruit are in season within the grounds of Thornbridge Hall. Just like the olden days of sustainable living.

West Berkshire Brewery

Yattendon, Berkshire
www.wbbrew.co.uk

Magg's Magnificent Mild
3.8%

With incredible flavor for such subdued strength, this Mild whips up a whirlwind of spicy chocolate, courtesy of the toasted malt and a heightened hop presence, dark fruit, port, and mocha flavors. Magnificent indeed.

Old Father Thames *Best Bitter* 3.4%

Set up in 1995 by David and Helen Maggs, the secret of this magnificent microbrewery is as well kept as its tremendous, low-gravity traditional ales "of exceptional character". First housed in former brickworks and now in an old, expanded bakery, the brewery brews to bottle and cask using Berkshire-sourced malt and hops. Don't be put off by the label, a scary-looking dude with a beard and a bowler-style hat, as this beautiful British beer is your friend. In fact, after a couple more of this easy-drinking brew, he's often your best friend.

West Brewing

Glasgow, Scotland
www.westbeer.com

St. Mungo *Keller Beer* 4.9%

A cracking Keller beer, displaying esters and fruit with a firm finish, and named after the city's patron saint. West Brewing is also a Glaswegian-cum-Germanic brewpub and restaurant whose beers are brewed in accordance with the Reinheitsgebot purity law.

Westerham Brewery

Edenbridge, Kent
www.westerhambrewery.co.uk

William Wilberforce Freedom Ale
Golden Ale 4.3%

A golden wonder launched for Fairtrade Fortnight 2007 and to commemorate the 200th anniversary of the Abolition of the Slave Trade Act on March 25, 1807. This is a deep golden ale with a mellow bitterness, a long hoppy finish, and a sweet crystal-malt-inspired biscuit base sweetened by Certified Demerara sugar. Every bottle sold helps raise money to abolish modern-day slavery.

Whim Ales

Hartington, Derbyshire
www.broughtonales.co.uk

Dr. Johnson's Definitive Ale *Mild/Strong Ale* 5%

The dark red cloak of this silky yet muscle-clad Mild is lined with tones of toffee apple, brown bread, mown grass, and hickory. Bottled by Broughton Ales, Whim's sister brewery in Biggar, Scotland.

White Shield Brewery

Burton-on-Trent, Staffordshire
www.worthingtons-whiteshield.com

1869 Ratcliffe Ale
Vintage Ale Unknown % ABV

In 2007 a quite extraordinary selection of vintage bottled beers was unearthed from the dusty vaults of the brewery. Originally crafted to celebrate royal marriages, births, and visits to the spiritual home of brewing, the mercifully small-batch bottled ales were recorked, rewaxed, and released to a select few. This is quite possibly the oldest drinkable beer in the world. The appearance is akin to balsamic vinegar and laces like a speeding shoestore assistant. The aroma, meanwhile, is sweet and complex and conjures up Amontillado sherry. When rolled around the mouth, it shouts out random flavors such as smoked kippers, roast coffee, fall fruit, molasses, and Tabasco. All in all a quite remarkable drinking experience.

Worthington's White Shield *India Pale Ale* 5.6%

A legendary beer that is making the biggest, and most unexpected, comeback since Bobby Ewing stepped out of the shower in *Dallas*. One of the five bottle-conditioned beers that was around in 1971, WWS courted extinction before drinkers were reawoken to its estery effervescence, superb balance, gentle bitterness, and thick-cut marmalade and apricot flavors.

Whitstable Brewery

Whitstable, Kent
www.whitstablebrewery.info

Oyster Stout 4.5%

Velvet-textured, indulgently smooth yet strong stout from a small-batch boutique outfit serving up superb brews to the arty denizens of Whitstable, a Kent coastal town that is thoroughly fashionable. Sublime with oysters.

Wickwar Brewery
Wickwar, Gloucestershire
www.wickwarbrewing.co.uk

Station Porter 6.1%

Originally holed up in the cooperage of the Arnold Perrett Brewery, Wickwar moved lock, stock, and many barrels to the main brewhouse in 2004, where it continues to craft quality Cotswold quaff—both in bottle and cask. Potent, pitch-black porter overflowing with boozy notes of chocolate, raisins, dark fruit, and licorices that loiter until late.

William Bros
Kelliebank, Scotland
www.fraoch.com

Fraoch *Spice Ale/Sahti* 5%

In 1992 Bruce and Scott Williams, two brothers who had previously worked in the Scotch business, blew the dust from Scottish brewing tomes and went about recreating 18th-century ales that eschewed hops in favor of other preserving ingredients. Here, fresh heather flowers add spice, pine, mint, and smoke to a light golden ale. A Scottish Sahti, if you will.

Kelpie *Spice Ale* 4.4%

Seaweed beds were once the place where Scottish farmers grew their cereal crops, and the barley produced there provided remarkable flavors for the ale they brewed. Williams Brothers adds Bladderwrack seaweed to the mash tun, along with organic barley—giving rise to an intriguing ale and a seabreeze aroma.

Woodforde's Brewery
Woodbastwick, Norfolk
www.woodfordes.co.uk

Norfolk Nog *Old Ale* 4.6%

A cheeky, chewy brew full of fruity gusto, warm alcohol, and figs and prunes. 1992 CAMRA Supreme Champion Beer of Britain.

Wherry *Bitter* 3.8%

This awesome, award-winning ale is hard to resist for a repeat visit once tasted. One of a bunch of brilliant beers from a brewery named after Parson Woodforde, an 18th-century Norfolk clergyman and beer-drinking epicurean. 1996 CAMRA Supreme Champion Beer of Britain.

Wychwood Brewery
Witney, Oxfordshire
www.wychwood.co.uk

Hobgoblin *Premium Bitter* 5.2%

Brawny brunette bottled ale from Oxfordshire stacked in toffee, caramel, and plum flavors. The bottle is adorned with the drawing of a menacing elf-like figure, his gnarled claw grasping a pint of ruby-colored beer, and the advertising slogan: "What's the matter, lager boy? Afraid you may taste something?" Don't be afraid; it's extremely good.

Wye Valley
Stoke Lacy, Herefordshire
www.wyevalleybrewery.co.uk

Dorothy Goodbody's Wholesome Stout 4.6%

By golly, we love Dorothy. A dose of flaked barley adds silky smoothness to a gloriously dark, shapely body that's filled out, in all the right places, with crystal and chocolate malts, and Northdown hops. If you like this classic bottle-conditioned beauty, then you should also try her 'sisters'.

Young's Brewery
Bedford, Bedfordshire
www.wellsandyoungs.co.uk

Special London Ale *Strong Pale Ale* 6.4%

In 2006 after two hundred years of brewing in South London and amid much outrage from the capital's ale drinkers, Young's sold its charming, charismatic, and slightly chaotic Ram Brewery to property developers. The tangy, malty whiff which had pervaded working-class Wandsworth since 1581 was replaced by the sterile scent of new money, and the beers were moved to Bedfordshire, where many believe they've lost their astringent, almost sour, signature. Special London Ale, however, has retained its sulfurous, South London attitude shaped by the Kentish Goldings and Fuggles hops that characterized much of the Ram Brewery's spicy, peppery beers. An extra dose of Golding and Target adds depth and dryness.

Anno 1871

Duvel

Goudblond speciaalbier van hoge gisting. In België gebrouwen volgens oorspronkelijke receptuur, met hergisting op fles. Bière spéciale blonde de haute fermentation. Brassée en Belgique selon la recette originale et refermentée en bouteille.

Duvel

A WORLD OF BEER
EUROPE

Belgium

Small but brew-tiful, Belgium more than belies its pint-sized dimensions when it comes to beer. In terms of diversity, innovative brewing methods, and sheer reverence, no other country comes close.

The Belgians are the punks of brewing—anarchic advocates of esoteric ales who, unlike their straitlaced neighbors in Germany, refuse to be strait-jacketed by purity laws and think nothing of throwing all manner of herbs, fruit, and spices into their beer. While all other European countries have been conquered by crisp, easy-drinking Pilsners, Belgium's brewing borders haven't been broached, and dedication to diversity and creativity has remained steadfast.

Belgium boasts more indigenous beer styles than any other nation in the world, ranging from abbey and Trappist ales

Above: The Benedictine order of monks from Maredsous have handed over their brewing to Duvel Moortgat, who brew and market the beer but share the profits with the monks.

Above right: Cherries are added to traditional barrel-aged Lambic beers and left to mature for a further three months while they macerate and add further flavor to this most anarchic of beers.

and wild Lambic beers, to sour Flemish reds and farmhouse Saisons. Flanders, to the north, lays claim to a greater variety of styles and is home to Duvel and Westmalle, while Wallonia, in the south, brews spicy, herby beer that reflects the region's rustic rural charm.

Wherever you are in Belgium, beer is served with an unrivaled level of pomp and ceremony. Of the 30,000-plus cafés and bars serving beer in Belgium, you'd be hard-pressed to discover one that doesn't serve beer the way it should—in the right glass and at the right temperature.

Sadly, it's all a bit of a smokescreen. Belgians are drinking less beer than they used to, and Belgium's beer scene is in the tightening grip of big brewers. In order to compete both domestically and abroad, some of Belgium's most famous breweries have been accused of cutting corners and dumbing-down their legendary beers, sacrificing flavor for finance.

Yet Belgium still remains a hotbed of heavenly beer. As well as having its classic brewing dynasties, Belgian brewing now has a new craft-brewing generation. Unshackled by tradition, the likes of De Dolle and Struise are brewing authentic beers that embody Belgium's anarchic approach.

ANTWERP

2

1

BRUSSELS ● ● LIEGE

W A L L O N I A

A R D E N N E S

FEATURED BREWERIES

1 Cantillon
Brussels
pages 100–101

2 Duvel
Breendonk
pages 106–107

Left: Maredsous, an abbey ale that was once brewed by monks in the Namur province of Belgium, is now brewed and distributed by Duvel-Moortgat on the monks' behalf.

Abbaye des Rocs
Montignies-sur-Roc, Hainaut
www.abbaye-des-rocs.com

 **Abbaye des Rocs Brune**
Abbey Ale 9%

A dainty Walloon brewery that has grown from a tiny, tumbledown outfit in 1979 into one of Belgium's most impressive modern breweries. Its brewing processes draw on a dazzling array of spices, grains, and malts. The sweet yet subtle smell and tones of toffee apple and prunes found in this deep rich ruby-red, double-fermented warmer come courtesy of seven different malts, spices led by licorices, a trio of European hops, and no added sugar.

 Blanche des Honnelles Witbier *Wheat Beer* 6%

Named after the river that once supplied the brewing water, this dry beer pulls back the reins on the spice and the full-on fruit. Beneath the light golden veneer there are hints of oranges and lemons, boiled candy, and a touch of chartreuse. It feels as if it's doing you good.

Achel
Hamont-Achel, Limburg
www.achelsekluis.org

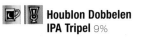 **Achel 5 Blond** *Blonde Ale* 5%

Unlike most Trappist beers, which feel as though they could put hair back on a thinning pate, this herbaceous, nutty golden ale is modest in strength. You will taste pink grapefruit, pear, and a touch of cream soda.

 Achel Extra Bruin *Trappist Ale* 9.5%

Belgium's latest, and increasingly audacious, Trappist brewery, based at the St. Benedictus Abbey, is one of only six breweries officially allowed to use the term "Trappist ale". It began commercial brewing again only in 1999, to raise much needed funds for the abbey.

Achouffe
Brussels
www.achouffe.be

Houblon Dobbelen IPA Tripel 9%

An imperial, highly aggressive India Pale Ale that wears its radioactive resins, stewed bitterness, and deep orange marmalade notes on its dark and golden sleeve.

McChouffe *Scotch Ale* 8.5%

McChouffe, also known as the "Scotch of the Ardennes", is a strong, spicy Scottish ale brewed using an array of kilned malts and more than a handful of hops. Refermented in the bottle.

Affligem
Opwijk, Flemish Brabant
www.afflligembeer.be

 **Affligem Tripel** 8.5%

There is evidence of Affligem beers being brewed as far back as the 16th century. The monastery once owned hop gardens in both Belgium and Kent, England, but is now under the corporate wing of Heineken. Despite this, the ale's sophistication has not been sacrificed. This terrific Tripel leads with an awesome orange aroma, its body bolstered by peppery fruit sweetness before dropping away as dry and Scotch-warm.

Het Anker
Mechelen, Antwerp
www.hetanker.be

⭐ ✓ ☕ **Gouden Carolus**
Classic Brown Ale 8.5%

The "Anchor", founded in the 14th century, is one of Belgium's oldest breweries. "Golden Charlie" named after a coin and first brewed in the 1960s, is a brandy-colored beer, made with pale and dark malt, brimming with nutmeg, spice, Curaçao, peppery Belgian hops, lively fruity yeast, and much alcohol.

Augrenoise
Casteau, Hainaut
www.augrenoise.com

🍺 🍸 **Augrenoise Blonde** 6.5%

Seductively sweet on both the palate and in the finish, with pear-drop candy, cloves, and a very faint hop-dry finish. Overseen by the head brewer of Orval, Augrenoise ales are brewed in rudimentary dairy equipment on a site shared with a home for disabled people.

Bavik
Bavikhove, West Flanders
www.bavik.be

⭐ ☕ 🍺 **Petrus Aged Pale** 7.3%

Since 1894 this brewery has been in the hands of the De Brabanderes, a Flemish farming family. It's been blazing a trail in the United States with its oak-aged pale ale that, until recently, was brewed solely as an ingredient in Bavik's sour brown ales. Aged in huge oak barrels, this hazy yellow ale belies its appearance with massively complex—and slightly unhinged—character. Sherry-like musk, cider apple and woody notes, astringent acidity, and a finish that oscillates between dry and sweet. Unusual but appealing.

Brasserie La Binchoise
Binche, Hainaut
www.belgoobeer.com

🍺 **Belgoo Luppo** *Blonde Ale* 5.5%

Shrewdly packaged and refermented in funky-looking turtleneck bottles, Belgoo beers are new kids on Belgium's brewing block. This crisp dry-hopped blonde ale bathes the back of the throat in bitterness.

✓ 🍺 **Belgoo Magus** *Blonde Ale* 6.6%

"Artisanal" ale made with a quartet of barley and wheat grains and more than a hint of spice. A gateway Belgian ale with a good glug factor.

Brasserie de Blaugies
Dour, Hainaut
www.brasseriedeblaugies.com

☕ 🍺 ✓ **La Moneuse**
Amber Ale 8%

An anarchic amber ale that flips between tartness and subtle sweetness like a moody toddler. One of many beers to look out for from a clever craft brewery that, over the past 20 years or so, has carved itself a revered reputation for its eclectic yet often excellent ales.

Brasserie du Bocq
Purnode, Namur
www.bocq.be

✓ 🍺 **Blanche de Namur Witbier** 4.5%

Founded in 1858 by farmer Martin Belot, Du Bocq is a big family-owned niche player that has retained craft-brewing traditions, yet thinks nothing of sharing its space with other breweries looking for a contract brewer. Its Blanche de Namur is a wheat-led whirlwind of spice, sweetness, and fruit.

🍺 ☕ 🍺 **Triple Moine** *Tripel* 7.3%

A subtly spiced, brusquely bitter, and resinous Tripel that's well placed to lure in skeptical lager lovers. Be careful, though, it's heady stuff, owing to its high alcohol content.

Boon
Lembeek, Payottenland (Flemish Brabant)
www.boon.be

 **Oude Geuze Mariage Parfait** *Gueuze* 8%

In 1977, when Lambics were really not popular, Franck Boon purchased De Vits and brought the brewery back from the brink. This "perfect marriage" Gueuze offers a fine fusion of fizzy fruit, a pungent hop character, and the trademark *Brettanomyces* "horse-blanket" aroma calling card that is pure Gueuze.

Oude Kriek Boon 6.5%

If you've yet to test your palate with Kriek, this traditional tart version of the style, brimming with cherries, may be a bit much. But if fruit, bone-dry acidity, and face-contorting sharpness are your things, then this *Brettanomyces*-based beauty is one to reach for.

Bosteels
Buggenhout, East Flanders
www.bestbelgianspecialbeers.be

Deus Brut des Flandres *Champagne Beer* 11.5%

Powerfully perfumed and alluringly effervescent, this is a tasty beer in a smart-looking Dom Pérignon style bottle. After the brewing process at Bosteels using Champagne yeast, it trundles over to the Champagne region of France, where it's laid down in caves for a year of indulgent maturation and the remuage process. An ideal wedding beer.

Pauwel Kwak *Amber Ale* 8%

The elaborate glass and wooden "stirrup cup" in which Kwak is served can often steal the thunder of the luscious liquid inside. Made from a triumvirate of malts and candy sugar, it is mellow, marshmallow-sweet, and kissed with caramel and toffee on the tail.

Tripel Karmeliet *Abbey Beer* 8%

A classic golden Tripel beer from a grandiose, smartly furnished tower brewery in the middle of the Ghent–Antwerp–Brussels triangle. Drunk from an ornate engraved glass, it's got a big head—and so it should. It's gorgeous. Brewed with a mix of oats, wheat, and barley (both raw and malted for all three), a smattering of Styrian hops, and spices.

Brootcoorens
Erquelinnes, Hainaut
www.brasserie-brootcoorens-erquelinnes.be

Angelus Blonde 7%

When home brewer Alain Brootcoorens went full-time in 2000, local lovers of alternative Wallonian ales were soon in for a treat. Strawberry-blonde-colored ale with firm bitterness yet fragrant, reminiscent of potpourri and just as dry. Rather elusive.

Cantillon
See Brewery Profile pages 100–101
Brussels
www.cantillon.be

Cantillon Bruocsella Grand Cru Old Vintage Lambic
5%

Set within a moldy shed in a run-down part of Brussels that is conveniently close to the Eurostar train terminal, Cantillon brews fiercely authentic and magical Lambic beers. This marvelously musty and mildewed three-year-old sherry-like ale is not really for learners, but rather for learned Lambic lovers.

Cantillon Vigneronne Grape Lambic 6%

OK, so the grain and the grape don't get on, but, as anyone in a stormy relationship knows, bitter rows can often lead to mind-blowing make-ups and, well, this is it in a bottle. A weirdly wonderful wine Lambic in which muscat grapes are steeped.

Cantillon Kriek Lambic 5%

Copious amounts of cherries are packed into the bung hole of wooden casks to produce this deliciously dry, rosy-cheeked Lambic that is as tart as it is sweet. An ideal apéritif beer.

Caracole
Falmignoul, Namur
www.brasserie-caracole.be

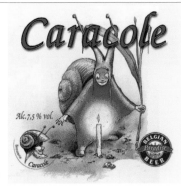

Ambrée Amber Ale 8%

In the tiny village of Falmignoul, François Tonglet and fellow home brewer Jean-Pierre Debras produce quirky-packaged idiosyncratic Wallonian ales in a brewery that's less state of the art and more falling apart. Soothing, smooth amber ale, crammed with caramel and a flicker of fiery chili.

Nostradamus Strong Brown Ale 9.5%

Caracole's strongest brew made with five different malts is a delectable, fruity brown ale furnished with figs, prune, and sweet caramel flavors.

Troublette Witbier 5%

It may have a snail on the label, but there's nothing sluggish about this zesty, moderately spiced wit. Deliciously dry and very drinkable.

CANTILLON BREWERY

56 rue Gheude Straat, Brussels

www.cantillon.be

For those familiar with modern beer, first impressions of Cantillon's left-field liquids can daunt and dumbfound. To the uninitiated, they may seem overly enigmatic, sweeping your anticipations of sweetness and sparkle away with sensations that are very different from anything you have tasted before.

CANTILLON

Grand Cru Bruocsella
1996

Don't be downhearted if you don't "get" them at first, or indeed second, sip, as debut drinkers seldom do. But, like an epic album or a novel whose true magic and complexity dwells deep beneath its initially impenetrable surface, Lambics reward patient perseverance in ways that no other beer style can.

CANTILLON

Kriek 100% Lambic

If you're going to learn to love lambic, and you really should, then there's no better aphrodisiac than a visit to Cantillon, a brewery-cum-working museum just a short walk from Brussels' Eurostar terminal, yet a million miles away from any other brewery you'll visit.

Cantillon has lived here since 1900, in knowing, unapologetic denial of scientific progress—a shoddy, disorganized shrine where preconceived notions of brewing and beer, like shoes at a temple, are best left outside.

Opposite far right: Schaarbeek cherries are added to Lambic after three years of barrel aging, then left to macerate for a further few months, during which time the beer dissolves the fruit.

It's a terrific, tumbledown time warp; big, frothing oak barrels line its crumbling walls and soar high into the musty rafters, rank fumes fill the nostrils, while sacks of grains and crates crammed with cherries are heaped atop bags of moldy hops; pipes drip, hoses trip, and decrepit 19th-century copper vessels and wooden tuns clunk, churn, and creak, to create a beer whose main characteristic is that of horse sweat.

It's the absolute antithesis to modern "push-the-button" breweries that, programmed like a Stepford wife with OCD, control infection by keeping surfaces spotless, sterile, and cleaner than a nun's conscience.

Freeing Cantillon of its fêted filth would rip the heart out of its beers. Disturb the dirt and the dust, and you disturb the delicate natural eco system that has shaped the beers for more than a century.

Unlike other breweries that source their specific yeast from a laboratory, leashing it tight like an obedient, docile dog, Cantillon's head brewer Jean Van Roy relies on wild, unpredictable naturally occurring airborne yeast and bacteria to romp about the place like a flock of cheeky chimpanzees.

Before white-coated boffins with spectacles, clipboards, pipettes, and brains the size of Luxembourg discovered pasteurization in 1860, all beer was made using spontaneous fermentation but, due to trends and increasingly tentative taste buds, Cantillon is one of very few breweries left where the wild things still roam.

The Cooling Room, high up in the brewery rafters, is where the anarchic alchemy takes place; as it's here where, on a whim and a waft, the undomesticated yeast and bacteria weave their inoculating magic. During winter, when the conditions are cold enough (32°–41°F/0°–5°C), around 1980 gallons (7500 liters) of sterile wort is poured into a seamless, extremely shallow red copper, to ensure maximum exposure.

Once the ideal temperature is reached using vents in the roof, more than 80 different types of wild yeast, wee beasties, and bacteria wage war on the wort.

Natural brewing yeasts (such as *Brettanomyces*) are like an airborne infantry. Their mission is to clear the wort of sugar and oxygen, excrete a flavor, alcohol, and CO_2, and flatten the pH level in preparation for the bacteria, foot soldiers if you will, to march in and sweep up whatever remains in the arid, acidic, and worty wasteland bereft of sugar and oxygen.

When the beer is decanted into oak or chestnut barrels, frenzied fermentation continues for three or four days, sending foam billowing from the bunghole all over the barrels. When the wild yeast wanes, slow fermentation in the barrel begins and Lambic is born, staying put for one to three years. Unlike wine growers, Lambic brewers do not refill their 105-gallon barrels to make up for evaporation. After three years of barrel aging, some 20 percent of the liquid is claimed as the "angel's share".

It's brewing at its rawest, brewing with all the science and technology taken out, where there's no chilling or refrigeration, no knobs or dials, and no interference by Jean. "People call me the master brewer, but I'm not a master of the brew, as I don't really have any control over the beer, from the infection to the bottling, we have no control over time," he says. "It's probably the most natural beer in the world."

Jean uses old hops, shorn of their aroma and flavor, to preserve the beer in casks that in a previous life housed French wine, port, and sherry. "We work with old hops because we don't need the bitterness," he said, "but we need the hop's preservative powers."

Jean monitors each cask, periodically tasting the contents of each to determine how long it should sleep for. The younger Lambic is slender, spritzy, and softer on the palate; older Lambic is firmer, more complex, and tongue-twistingly sour. But no two casks are the same, and the tall task facing Jean each spring is to blend the Lambic and achieve harmony. "With natural infection, we've never produced exactly the same beer, and it's for that reason it's such a joy to produce," he says. "You're forever in pursuit of perfection."

"Before you taste lambic, you need to cast all conceptions of beer from your mind," adds Jean. "It's totally flat, very acidic, and is more comparable to a wine than a beer".

"Lambic is a white wine, while Gueuze is a Champagne," adds Jean. Using "méthode champenoise", he blends one-, two-, and three-year old lambic and the mixture of old and

new sparks a second, wondrous fermentation in the bottle. The young beer supplies natural sugars for bottle fermentation, while the old beer contributes to bouquet and finesse. Under proper storage conditions, fermentation in the bottle will continue for years.

And then there are Cantillon's phenomenal fruit Lambics. Once the lambic has left, the barrels are cleaned and crammed with fruit—whole Schaarbeek cherries (Kriek), French apricots (Fou'foune), raspberries (Rose de Gambrinus), Italian muscat grapes (Cantillon Geuze Vigneronne), and Bordeaux Merlot grapes (Saint-Lamvinus).

Using 10.5 ounces (300 grams) of fruit for every 1 liter of beer, maceration takes at least three months, during which time the beer dissolves the fruit (even the pips) and displaces its flavors, color, and sugars. Then, one-third of young Lambic—which supplies sugar for fermentation—is added, and the beer, fruity yet still acutely acidic, is bottled and corked.

Unlike all other Cantillon beers, whose mash consists of two-thirds malted barley and one-third unmalted wheat, the mellow and dry Iris is an all-pale malt brew hopped with fresh Hallertau, both in the boil and for dry-hopping. It's dry, mellow, hoppy, and the likeliest to lure one into a Lambic love affair.

Key Beers

Cantillon Grand Cru Bruocsella *Lambic* 5%
Cantillon Vigneronne *Grape Lambic* 6%
Cantillon Kriek Lambic *Fruit Lambic* 5%

Chimay

Baileux, Hainaut
www.chimay.be

 Chimay Cinq Cents
Trappist Golden Ale 8%

A drier, hoppier beer than the Bleue (see entry below), Cinq Cents was introduced in the 1960s. Gloriously golden in color, with vanilla and almonds on the nose, a voluptuous body full of orange blossom and apricot, resinous tones, and pine on the finish.

 Chimay Grande Réserve Bleue *Trappist Abbey Ale* 9%

Within connoisseur circles, Chimay has come under fire for perceived cutting of corners. But the world's best-known Trappist brewery with the biggest sales is still home to some first-class ales. Chimay Bleue, or Grande Réserve, in a 25.4 fl oz (75cl) bottle, is a deep mahogany-colored classic whose spicy, amazingly aromatic, portlike complexity intensifies in the bottle. Best laid down for some time and then drunk a couple of years after brewing, ideally with blue cheese.

Cnudde

Eine-Oudenaarde, East Flanders
No web address

Cnudde Bruin *Brown Ale* 4.7%

Hard to get hold of and a rare example of an East Flanders specialty, this unusual acidic and slightly sour aged brown ale is available in only a handful of bars around the eponymous brewery that dates back to the end of World War One. Worth seeking out.

Contreras

Gavere, East Flanders
www.contreras.be

Tonneke *Amber Ale* 4.8%

Contreras has been brewing in East Flanders for close to 200 years, since its creation in 1818, but it's only recently that marketing has become a consideration. Plain brown bottles with no labels, distinguishable only by their caps, have been replaced by all-together more interesting affairs, and the beer has been enhanced, too. An appetizing, slightly effervescent amber ale is available from the barrel locally and is distributed in bottles farther afield. It is bittersweet in flavor, with a soft mouthfeel.

De Cam

Gooik, Flemish Brabant
www.decam.be

 **De Cam Oude Geuze** 6.5%

Karel Goddeau is the guy for Gueuze from Gooik. But the fresh-faced Karel doesn't brew beer, he blends it. In 1997, he resuscitated the age-old tradition of buying-in Lambics from elsewhere and merging them together in a utopian union. He now produces some of the finest, most fiercely traditional Lambic beers in Belgium. The corked and caged Oude Geuze is a hazy yellow, thirst-slaking mishmash of tart ripe fruit—melon, pineapple, and dried apricots—all of which are underpinned by the unmistakable presence of "horse blanket" and musty wood.

 **De Cam Oude Kriek** *Cherry Lambic* 6.5%

Using antique barrels that once housed Pilsner Urquell from the Czech Republic, De Cam steeps cherries complete with their pits for a fuller, more rounded almond flavor. Not as tart as other cherry Lambics, De Cam still has a fizzing sharpness. It is softly sour, with many tannins, and a dry, vinous mouthfeel, instills a strong desire to have another one.

De Dolle Brouwers

Esen, West Flanders
www.dedollebrouwers.be

 **De Dolle Extra Export Stout** 9%

Head brewer and former artist Kris Herteleer has painted this after-dinner ale blacker than Darth Vader's shiny helmet. With nods to the Irish and British stouts of yore, and the new wave of black beers being brewed in the United States, there is bittersweet chocolate, astringent ground coffee, and a flurry of burnt toffee on the finish. Hugely popular in the United States.

De Dolle Stille Nacht *Barley Wine* 12%

Highly innovative, slightly subversive, and at the forefront of Belgium's new wave of craft brewing, the "mad" brewers are not mad at all. They know exactly what they're doing: brewing some very special, often brilliant bottle-conditioned beers. This dark orange, outrageously complex barley wine, is brewed for Christmas. It's stewed in pale malt, Nugget hops, and candy sugar. Bittersweet, it has an enormous depth of flavor, with melodic notes of caramel and sugared grapefruit. Seriously strong but subtle, it's not just for Christmas, and is best laid down to mature and intensify.

Oerbier *Strong Brown Ale* 9%

Meaning "beer from the original source", this terrific twist on the local bruin beer was the liquid that launched the De Dolle brewery. A yeast akin to that being used by Rodenbach, three kinds of fresh Belgian hop flowers, and half a dozen malts produce a strong, sharp-tasting brown ale that veers into Lambic land, before making a last-minute turn for Belgian/Scotch ale country.

De Koninck
Antwerp, Antwerp
www.dekoninck.be

 **De Koninck** *Flemish Ale* 5%

An iconic brewery that ticks the boxes of family ownership, brewing integrity, and clever marketing. A fine example of a Flemish pale ale, its flagship beer is a beautifully balanced melange of pale malts, fruity esters, and peppery hops. Best served in a *bolleke* glass.

De Ranke
Dottignies, Hainaut
www.deranke.be

 XX Bitter 6.2%

You'd be forgiven for thinking this intensely hoppy ale hails from the northwest of the United States and not Belgium, but De Ranke is renowned for doing things a little differently. Brewers Nino Bacelle and Guido Devos brew bombastic beers with balance, and boast a dedicated cult following both at home and abroad. Resinous, herbaceous, and with an IBU of 65, it's proper hoppy, folks.

Guldenberg *Tripel* 8.5%

It's a Tripel, but not as the Belgians know it. A hoppy, fantastically fragrant blonde that drinks dangerously well for its strength.

Drie Fonteinen
Beersel, Payottenland (Flemish Brabant)
www.3fonteinen.be

 **Faro Lambic** 5%

A more approachable but no less impressive Lambic, that's available on tap at the fantastic Drie Fonteinen restaurant next door to the brewery. It's sweeter and less tart than some of the other lambics, with lemongrass and lychees, melon and a background of acidic grapefruit. This is Lambic's version of a single malt whisky with a splash of water.

Oude Geuze 6%

Regarded as the godfather of Gueuze, all hail the spritzy lemon and grapefruit flavors, the teeth-chattering tartness, the Stilton-esque aroma, the bone-dry finish, and the masterful blending. A classic.

Oude Kriek 6%

If you're a lambic lover, this is not just Payottenland—it's the Promised Land. The De Belder family have been crafting classics using outside lambics since 1953. Brothers Armand and Guido branched out into brewing their own kriek in 1999. The result provides a sublime sip, a huge frisson of fruit on the nose, archetypal dry and cidery lambic notes, and a sharp, biting bitter finish. Incredible.

Dubuisson
Pipaix-Leuze, Hainaut
www.br-dubuisson.com

 **Scaldis (Bush Ambrée)**
Barley Wine 12%

A family-owned farm brewery since 1769. The Dubuisson family dropped the farming side of the business in the 1930s and now ploughs a flavorsome furrow in the field of big and rather brilliant beers. This elegant amber-hued Belgian take on an English barley wine is the most well known and rightly rated. It is dry and hoppy, with a slightly sweet and rustic Armagnac feel on the finish. Also known as Bush Ambrée.

Bush Prestige
Wood-aged Beer/Vintage Ale 13%

An incredibly elusive oak-aged version of the Ambrée, an upstanding 25.4 fl oz (75cl) bottle of greatness with vanilla, apricots, wood, brandy snaps, and a bitter, tannic finish. If you see it, buy it. Then drink it, slowly, and enjoy the sensation.

Brasserie Dupont
Tourpes, Hainaut
www.brasserie-dupont.com

Avec les Bons Voeux
Barley Wine 9.5%

This unusual Christmas ale is fruity, slightly oily, and leathery, with some citric sharpness and no small amount of kinetic spice sensations jumping on the tongue.

Moinette Blonde
Blonde Ale 8.5%

Bucolic farmyard brewer celebrated for its sensational saisons and, more recently, organic ales. Moinette, Dupont's biggest Belgian seller, is subtly spiced with an underlying snappy hop bitterness.

 **Saison Dupont**
6.5%

A legendary hazy-golden liquid hailed by many as the world's best saison. A piquant, peppery hop bitterness is rounded out by green apple, sugared-grapefruit, and an unyielding yeast character. One not to miss on your beer travels.

Duvel-Moortgat

See Brewery Profile pages 106–107
Breendonk-Purs, Antwerp
www.duvel.be/www.maredsous.be

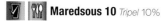 **Duvel** *Abbey Ale* 8.5%

Iconic bottle-conditioned blonde abbey ale first brewed in 1923. Its shimmering lemon coloring and mischievous drinkability make for a devilish disguise. It's satin smooth, strong and fruity, with heady herbal hop aromas and a gorgeous white head. Delicious with seafood.

Maredsous 8 Brune *Brown Ale* 8%

Luxuriant dark abbey ale with caramel on the nose and burnt toffee, dark chocolate, and ripe plums on the palate.

Maredsous 10 *Tripel* 10%

A terrific Tripel with a seductive sparkle in its eye. Sour and sweet do battle on a bitter grapefruit background.

Vedett Extra White *Witbier* 4.7%

A delicious, refreshing and surprisingly crisp "wit", punctuated with coriander and orange peel milled at the brewery. Launched in 2008 after Duvel-Moortgat ended its relationship with Steendonk beer, it is unfiltered, bottle-conditioned, and squeezed into a funky bottle.

Ellezelloise

Ellezelles, Hainaut
www.brasserie-ellezelloise.be

Hercule *Stout* 9%

Forward-thinking farmhouse brewery dating from 1993 named its Hercule Stout after Agatha Christie's detective (who hailed from Ellezelles). A slick, velvet-jacketed stout, as black as night, that is spicy, astringent, and very dry.

Saisis *Wheat Beer* 6.2%

This wheat beer has a hardened citrus hop character, with notes of coriander, pine needles, and Curaçao. Eschewing the use of spices and supplementary sugars, the brewery coaxes magic from just the malt, hops, and distinctive yeast to craft five first-class beers in total, matured in German oak casks. The name is pronounced "el-zel-was".

Fantome

Soy, Luxembourg
www.fantome.be

Fantome Saison 8.0%

Left-field brewer Dany Prignon polarizes opinion among Belgian beer boffins. Few, however, have doubts about this soothing Saison. A grainy, biscuit base spruced up by pear drops, gooseberries, and tart fruit.

Geants

Irchonwelz, Hainaut
No web address

 **Gouyasse Triple** 9%

This "Goliath" of a beer has a sizable footprint of piny hops, sweet shortbread, and a dessert wine finish. Very impressive.

Saison Voisin 5%

A more hoppy, fruity, and less spicy take on a Saison, the Voisin is generously fruity with a biscuit-rich maltiness, a smattering of sweetness, and a balanced bitterness on the finish.

 **Urchon Brown Ale** 7.5%

At the turn of the millennium, Pierre Delcoigne and his wife cobbled together a new brewery from a trio of defunct breweries and began crafting beers with quality ingredients, integrity, and a loyal nod to tradition. This dark copper ale has an inquisitive-looking hedgehog on the label; a caramel and toffee apple tingly effervescence on the tongue; and a bitter, cheek-contracting finish.

Girardin

Sint-Ulriks-Kapelle, Senne Valley
www.specialitybeer.com

 **Girardin Kriek** 5%

A big cherry bouquet, slightly dry with a sweeter signature. Sharpness soothed by full-on fruit and a gentle almond character. Best drunk as an apéritif, a dessert beer, or with succulent duck.

Girardin Oude Gueuze 1882 5%

The jewel in the crown of Belgium's biggest Lambic and Gueuze specialist. A tremendous, tartaric, keenly citrus-scented, and musky masterpiece that epitomizes the inexplicable art of Lambic blending. A balmy balance of lemongrass, grapefruit, wine vinegar, ripening pear, honeysuckle, orange zest, and much more.

Glazen Toren

Erpe-Mere, East Flanders
www.glazentoren.be

 **Jan de Lichte** *Witbier* 7%

Journalist-turned-brewmaster Jef Van den Steen has earned himself a reputation for innovative ales since he began brewing out of a garage next to his house back in 2004. A mouth-filling, weighty wheat beer endowed with spice and cedar flavors, a dry backbone of bitterness, and a crisp, sharp finish.

Hanssens

Dworp, Payottenland (Flemish Brabant)
www.proximedia.com/web/hanssens.html

 Artisanaal Oude Kriek 5.8%

A blender not a brewer, Hanssens is justly heralded for its left-field Lambic liquids. Don't be fooled by the farmyard fragrance. This top-quality oude kriek is a dry mix of tart red fruit, marzipan, and cream soda.

Hopperd

Westmeerbeek, Antwerp
No web address

 **Kameleon** *Tripel* 8.5%

An up-and-coming brewery specializing in eccentric eco-warrior ales and fronted by a former student from the brewing schools of Ghent. Packaged in a bottle adorned with a cartoon chameleon, the beer pours golden and clear, while estery wheat-beer-like aromas waft forth, dry herbal hops form in the mouth, and a spicy finish is Saison-like.

Huyghe

Melle, East Flanders
www.delirium.be

 Artevelde Grand Cru *Pale Ale* 7.4%

Devilishly deceptive in strength, this pale ale is a dark copper color with an alluring lathered head. Satsuma-scent on the nose, syrupy raisins and apricot on the palate, balanced by a ballast of bitterness.

Delirium Tremens *Tripel* 8.5%

Best-known beer from a remarkably prolific brewery armed with a scatter-gun approach to beer launches that, while often profitable, can sometimes misfire. "Trembling Madness" is famous for the pink elephant logo and its gray ceramic bottle. A spicy, sweet Tripel that has an impressive mainstream following.

Mongozo Banana Beer *Fruit Beer* 4.8%

If you like bananas, then you'll like this beer. Brightly packaged and brewed using certified bananas. A subtle and complex ale? No, but it's big on bananas, that's for sure.

Mongozo Coconut Beer *Fruit Beer* 3.5%

Ignore the initial and rather concerning aroma akin to sun tan lotion; the flavors—which can only be described as coconut—are nowhere near as prominent. It's best used as an ingredient in spicy jerk chicken.

Brasserie de Jandrain-Jandrenouille

Jandrain-Jandrenouille,
Wallonian Brabant
No web address

 **IV Saison** 6.5%

Old and new come together in this archetypal Saison beer from one of the youngest breweries in Belgium, created in 2007. Unfiltered and unpasteurized, with a spicy hop signature, this is the nearest the Belgians get to a US West Coast hop-monster.

Kerkom

Kerkom-Sint-Truiden, Limburg
www.brouwerijkerkom.be

 **Adelardus** *Tripel* 7%

Top-class tripel, named after a do-gooder local abbot, is seasoned with "sweet gale", a ten-strong mixture of herbs and spices from the region. Ideally drunk on draft in the incredibly cozy and welcoming café next to the brewery.

Bink Blond *Blonde Ale* 5.5%

The stock of this modest-sized microbrewery-cum-machinery museum in South Limburg has risen ever since Marc Limet and Marina Siongers took over in 1999, but its history dates back to 1878. Bink Blonde, meaning "blond guy", is a lightly tanned, perfumed pale ale propped up by some serious hells-a-poppin' hops, Californian style.

Leffe (Anheuser-Busch/InBev)

Leuven, Flemish Brabant
www.leffe.com

 **Leffe Radieuse**
Abbey Ale 8.2%

While Leffe's popularity may have bred mumbling contempt among connoisseurs, the bean counters at InBev have not dulled the shine of this gateway abbey ale bedecked in spicy clove character, black currant, and roast chestnuts.

DUVEL BREWERY

Breendonkdorp 58, 2870 Breendonk-Puurs, Belgium

www.duvel.be

If the devil does come in many guises, then Duvel must be one of the most delicious versions.

Less painful than listening to heavy metal music backward and a lot tidier than sacrificing a goat, drinking this classic Belgian ale, with its billowing white beehive head and floral-fruity finesse, is the thinking drinker's kind of satanic worship.

Pronounced "Doov'l" with the emphasis on the first syllable, it was first introduced in 1923 by the Moortgat brewery, which, back in 1871, had been started by Jan-Leonard Moortgat and his wife Maria De Block in the small Belgian town of Breendonk.

It was Jan-Leonard's son Albert who first brewed the beer. It was baptized Victory Ale to commemorate the end of World War One, but when local shoemaker Van De Wouwer first tasted the beer he declared: "Nen echten Duvel" meaning "a true devil" and thus the beer was renamed.

Initially, the beer was indeed a Prince of Darkness, brewed with browner and blacker malt, and inspired by the Scottish ales that were all the rage in Belgium during the 1920s.

By the 1960s, though, golden Pilsners and blonde beers were tickling the fancy of Belgian drinkers, and in 1970 the Moortgaat brewery replaced the dark devil drink with a paler version brewed using extremely lightly colored Pilsner-style malt, but still with the elevated 8.2% ABV.

The new Duvel not only gave light-colored beer drinkers the golden glad-eye, but also reinforced its reputation as "a true Devil". Strong beers had, hitherto, been synonymous with darker beers, but Moortgat pioneered top-fermenting brews that were pale, potent, and pleasurable to drink. Like a wolf in sheep's clothing, it's a devilish deception that still dupes drinkers, catching them unawares.

Several Belgian brewers have aped the approach, even going as far as to adopt Beelzebub's various pseudonyms, but none has been able to replicate or improve upon Duvel's light-bodied mixture of poise and power, achieved through Moortgat's bespoke floral-fruity "Scottish" yeast, the spicy presence of Saaz and Styrian Golding, and its unique system

Above: Duvel-Moortgat has invested 12 million euros in a new state-of-the-art brewhouse in Breendonk, where the celebrated Duvel is brewed alongside other acquisitions, including Maredsous abbey ales and the newcomer Vedett Extra White.

Right: Despite a generous amount of high-tech brewing equipment, the enormous brewery still calls upon the sensory skills of expert tasters to check the final beer.

of fermentation and conditioning at various temperatures.

While Duvel represents the bulk of the brewery's sales, with 65 percent of production exported, it's by no means the only string to its bow. In the past decade or so, Duvel-Moortgat has emerged as a major regional player on both the national and international stage. In 2003, it bought the Ommegang Brewery in the United States, having invested in the Bernard brewery in the Czech Republic back in 2001; in 2006 and closer to home, it snapped up fellow Belgian brewer Achouffe, whose Ardennes ale commands a devoted following.

The brewery's wallet took a further walloping when it invested 12 million euros in a new brewhouse that opened in 2008, and where production of Duvel and its sibling beers is expected to triple over the next 10 to 15 years.

In the same year, Duvel-Moortgat made its first foray into fruit beer, when it stepped in to save the legendary Liefmans brewery from financial ruin, and has gone to great lengths to ease concerns that Liefmans' upstanding brewing methods would be compromised.

Vedett is the trendy, attitudinal teenager in the family, is sipped in all the right style bars, and is advertised on concrete-mixing trucks. Launched in 1945, it's a light, well-hopped lager softened with the use of rice and packaged in the same bottle as Duvel. Vedett Extra White, a 4.7% ABV wheat beer made with coriander and orange peel, was launched in 2008.

Duvel-Moortgat's commitment to quality led the Benedictine abbey of Maredsous in 1963 to entrust the brewery with its trio of bottle-conditioned abbey beers. Still brewed under the supervision of the Maredsous monks and recently spruced up with a modern look, the Maredsous range includes a blond (6% ABV), a brown (8% ABV), and a Tripel (10% ABV).

Key Beers

Duvel Abbey Ale 8.5%

Maredsous Blond 6%**, Brown** 8%**, and Tripel** 10%

Vedett Extra White Witbier 4.7%

Pouring a glass of Duvel

Even in a nation that revels in the reverence of the pour and the appearance of beer, the decanting of Duvel from stout and shapely bottle to open-lipped tulip glass is something to behold.

The nucleated Duvel glass, first introduced in 1962, must be clean and dry, and at no time during the pour should it be allowed to touch the bottle.

Tilt the glass at 45 degrees, and pour until the golden liquid just touches the Duvel lettering etched on the side of the glass.

Next, slowly tilt the glass back so that it's upright, and stop pouring when the froth reaches a level about ½ inch (1 cm) from the rim of the glass.

In order to scoop up the flavorsome yeast, give the bottle a circular twirl so that the remaining liquid swishes around the bottle. Use this remaining liquid to top up the beer.

Marvel at the tornado-like swirl created by the letter D that's etched into the bottom of the glass.

Drink. Slowly. And enjoy.

Leroy
Boezinge, West Flanders
No web address

 Christmas Leroy *Scotch Ale* 5.5%

Murky, dark, and complex bottle-conditioned Scotch ale with rich roasted malts, fruitcake flavor, spicy chocolate bitterness, orange peel, and a fading fruit finish.

Sasbrau Dortmunder 6%

That Leroy lives under the radar of most Belgian beer boffins may have something to do with its leaning toward lagers rather than just ales. This Dortmunder, a style rarely seen in Belgium, sips subtly sweet with a muted bitterness. A great lager.

Liefmans
Oudenaarde, East Flanders
www.liefmans.be

Liefmans Gluhkriek *Fruit Beer* 6%

This mulled fruit beer is similar to Liefmans Kriek but with added sugar and an extra dose of aromatic spices. Heated up to 158°F (70°C), it oozes cloves, cinnamon, and a rich cherry aroma. A good drink for Thanksgiving, Christmas Day, or other seasonal winter gatherings.

Liefmans Goudenband *Brown Ale* 8%

An archetypal Oude Bruin (old brown ale) that leapt from local to world fame when its strength was increased and its signature sourness subdued. Full-bodied and rich, it has thankfully retained a high level of tart complexity and a rich, roast malt flavor.

Liefmans Kriekbier *Cherry Beer* 6%

Since the late 17th century, Liefmans has been a landmark on the Belgian brewing map and renowned for its variations on brown ale, whether it's blended, aged, fruity, or sour. The bottled kriekbier, individually hand-wrapped in tissue paper, uses Goudenband as its foundation. A copious amount of cherries is steeped in long, low maturation tanks to produce a sensationally fruity, sweet, and sour sipping beer that has enough dryness to be served as an apéritif.

"Buy a man a beer and he wastes an hour. Teach a man to brew and he wastes a lifetime."

ANONYMOUS

Malheur
Buggenhout, East Flanders
www.malheur.be

Malheur 6 *Blonde Ale* 6%

A fragrant, floral, and spicy bottle-conditioned ale brewed using a trio of flowered hops and a mix of specialty malts. Aimed squarely at everyday appreciation, its faintly acidic, bitter finish entices you to opt for one more.

Malheur Bière Brut *Champagne Beer* 11%

A superior champagne beer from a brewery brought back to life in 1997 after nearly 60 years of hibernation. At the forefront when it comes to marketing and creative, cultured brewing, Malheur uncorked the concept of champagne beers with this brisk and balanced bubbly beauty, based on its Malheur 10 ale. Champagne yeast is called upon for secondary fermentation, the beer indulges in *remuage* and *dégorgement* and, when decanted from a Champagne bottle, delivers a lemon-hued feast of fruit, a crisp bitter bite, and a wine-like alcohol warmth. For weddings, it's an ideal "I do" brew and is significantly more affordable than Champagne.

Malheur Dark Brut Noir *Champage Brown Ale* 12%

This dark brown ale, adorned with the Malheur "superhero" logo, is difficult to define. Is it a beer? Is it a Champagne? No, it's a champagne beer that differs from its bubbly brethren by being aged in young, specially charred American casks to give a nutty and fruity flavor.

Mort Subite (De Keersmaeker)
Kobbegem, Payottenland (Flemish Brabant)
www.alkenmaes.be

Mort Subite Oude Kriek 6.5%

Much-lauded and magnificently measured cherry lambic that drifts between sweet and sour. Brewed using bespoke cherries specifically produced for the beer by the brewery formerly known as De Keersmaeker and named after the "Sudden Death" café in Brussels. The brewery is now owned by Alken-Maes, but the beers have, so far, remained unscathed by the corporate claw of a larger brewery. If anything, they've improved.

Musketiers

Ursel
No web address

 **Troubadour Obscura** *Stout* 8.5%

A strapping sweet stout that resembles an Irish coffee in both looks and aroma. Mouth-filling and stacked with layers of mocha, roast chestnuts, and dark caramel, it is the brainchild of the four "musketeers", a clever quartet of engineer-cum-eager home brewers who ply their hobby at the Proef brewery and export to an admiring American audience.

Orval

Villers-devant-Orval, Luxembourg
www.orval.be

 Orval *Trappist Ale* 6.2%

Beer doesn't get much better than this. In a superb and picturesque setting, the good monks of Orval have been performing ale alchemy since 1931. Founded in 1132, the Orval abbey was nailed by Napoleon and only fully rebuilt in 1926, but five years later, with the builder's bills dropping on the doormat, the monks began making beer. Unlike other Trappist breweries, it makes only one beer—but what a beautiful, intensely aromatic, and uniquely intricate beer it is. Brewed with bespoke specialist malt, the beer is dry-hopped with intensely aromatic whole Hallertau and Styrian Goldings hops and lagered in a long and languid fashion. Prior to its induction into the iconic bowling-pin bottle, and to add magic to magnificence, it is tapped with the *Brettanomyces* wand of secondary fermentation. The greatest pale ale on the planet and worthy of its saintly standing among beer buffs.

Palm

Steenhuffel, Flemish Brabant
www.palmbreweries.com

 **Palm Speciale** *Pale Ale* 5%

Palm is an enigmatic beer-maker that teeters on the tightrope of pleasing both the connoisseur and the common man. With more launches than NASA, it sometimes disappoints, courtesy of some crass commercial ale; however, the 18th-century brewery is also renowned for producing some gems. Palm Speciale, grand old golden Belgian ale with a touch of blood orange tang, is the best selling beer of the bunch.

Proef

Lochristi, East Flanders
www.proefbrouwerij.com

 **Bloemenbier** *Spice Beer* 7%

Bloemen marvelous. Huge honey tones, a fantastic floral aroma, and a sweet finish that sidesteps sickly in style. A delicious dessert beer.

 **Boerken** *Strong Ale* 9.5%

A hedonistically hoppy golden ale full of deep fruit flavor, alcoholic ardor, and a spicy send-off. All grounded on a good, wholesome grainy core and stored in a stylish bottle.

 **Vicaris** 8.8%

Black-as-black and brimming with dates, prunes, "beetroot sweetness," and burnt toast. Given its sinkable strength, it is deceptively dangerous and just a little decadent.

 Zoetzuur *Flemish Red Ale* 7%

Proef offers advice, equipment, and brewing expertise to orphaned ale producers from all over Belgium, executing their instructions with deadly accuracy. Zoetzuur, a copper-colored face-contorting beer, is a particularly sour Flemish red, dry and rather delicious.

Rochefort

Rochefort, Namur
www.trappistes-rochefort.com

 Rochefort 8 *Trappist Ale* 9.2%

The residents of the abbey, which dates back to 1230 and began brewing in 1899, are allowed one bottle of beer a day, but rarely reach for it except on days of celebration. It is hard to know how they resist this fino sherry nose and full-bodied fruitcake character, silky treacle texture, and dry, cider-apple finish.

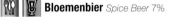 **Rochefort 10** *Trappist Ale* 11.3%

A must-drink beer from the notoriously introverted monks at the Abbaye Notre-Dame de Saint-Remy, who produce cultured, complex tawny Trappist ales that light up beer lovers' faces the world over. A burnished bottle-conditioned burgundy-colored beer made up of two hops, two malts, two yeasts, and plenty of monk-led magic. Lay a bottle down in the knowledge that the portlike body will bulge, that the chocolate, figgy pudding, and pine flavors will intensify, and that, on drinking, all will be well with the world.

Rodenbach

Roeselare, West Flanders

www.rodenbach.be

Rodenbach Foederbier

Flemish Brown Ale 6%

Rodenbach is all about the wood. After the first and secondary fermentation in stainless-steel tanks, the beer is decanted into close to 300 enormous oak barrels known as "foeders". Weighing 18 tons when full and dating back 150 years, each foeder endows the beer with a particular flavor and acidic character. The skill of the Rodenbach brewers is to achieve consistency and perfection through blending. Foederbier, the canvas on which all other Rodenbach beers are painted, is a balance of beer sourced from three to five foeders, with an average age of two years' maturation. Amber and oaky with a bone-dry Riesling acidity, its tremendous tartness is a rite of passage for any ambitious beer drinker. Difficult to drink and difficult to find, this is one of the very few Holy Grail ales.

Rodenbach Grand Cru *Flemish Brown Ale 6%*

The Rodenbach family was a significant presence in 19th-century Flanders. They began brewing in 1820, and their phenomenal, sour Flemish oak-aged red ales, now owned by Palm, are rightly rated as brewing grand masters. Rodenbach ales source their outstanding fruit aromas and distinct, refined tartness and sharp tannin from wood aging, a mixed yeast culture, and the hallowed art of aged beer blending. This is genius in a bottle.

La Rulles

Rulles-Habay, Luxembourg

www.larulles.be

La Rulles Blonde *7%*

When Gregory Verhelst opened his brewery in 2000, this hoppy, strapping, and tasty blonde

caused ripples among locals. Several years later, La Rulles is riding the crest of Belgian new-wave brewing courtesy of esoteric ales admired both in Belgium and the United States. The labels are great, too.

La Rulles Tripel *8.4%*

This is the macho Jean-Claude Van Damme of boutique Belgian beer: a strapping, bronze muscular Belgian Tripel with an American hop accent. Dried apricots, tropical fruit, and spice, with a sweet malt finish.

Saint Bernardus

Watou, West Flanders

www.sintbernardus.be

St. Bernardus Abt 12 *Barley Wine 10.5%*

Set up immediately after World War Two, this cheese dairy turned Flemish brewery contract-brewed St Sixtus ales until introducing its own quartet of beers in the 1990s, including this complex, dark tawny barley wine full of chocolate, raisin, almonds, and fruit character.

St. Bernardus Prior 8 *Dubbel 8%*

Styrian hops and lengthy, languid lagering lend this full-bodied, deep purple Dubbel its depth and drinkability. No wonder the monk on the bottle label is smiling.

Saint Feuillien

Le Roeulx, Hainaut

www.st-feuillien.com

St. Feuillien Brune *Brown Ale 7.5%*

Apart from an 11-year break that ended in 1988, the Friart family has been brewing beer on this site since 1873. In recent years, expansion and ambitious export plans have seen some of the brewing output shared with the Du Bocq and Affligem breweries. Many connoisseurs claim the under-license liquids lack the sweet toffee complexity, full-bodied fig flavor and warming alcohol at the end of the original brew. So purists may want to confine themselves to the big bottles that hail from Le Roeulx itself.

St. Feuillien Triple *8.5%*

Despite its extensive distribution, this piquant, aromatic ale, full of fruit and citrus spice, has stayed in the leading pack of the best Tripels in the world of beer. Again, the brewed-at-source 1.5 liter bottles are preferable, and are improved when laid down and left to develop to their own delicious devices.

Saint-Monon

Ambly, Luxembourg

www.saintmonon.be

La Saint-Monon Brune

Dubbel 7.5%

Award-winning Dubbel from a Wallonian microbrewery set up in 1996. Dark brown color, roasty malt spine, fall fruit aroma, seriously spicy, and a finish whose sourness flirts with a Flanders brown ale.

Brasserie de la Senne
Brussels
www.brasseriedelasenne.be

 Stouterik Stout 4.5%

Iconoclastic brewers Bernard Leboucq and Yvan De Baets have kicked away the crutch of conformity on which so many other Belgian brewers lean. Having outgrown their previous home, they hired space at the De Ranke brewery but, at the time of writing, are poised to sprout a brewery in Brussels, where they'll continue to eschew the spice obsession and embrace a wide gamut of international beer styles. This stout is big and black, silky sweet, and slightly scorched, tainted with tobacco, licorices, raw grassy hop character, and earthy aromas.

Taras Boulba Pale Ale 4.5%

If you thought Belgian beer was all about power and strength, then try this lovely pear-colored, heartily hopped pale ale. A deliciously dry departure from all the big high-alcohol content Belgian brain-fuddlers.

Zinnebir Bitter 6%

A slightly Anglo-centric ale named after "Zinneke"—a pejorative term for stray dogs and those of mixed Flemish/French parentage associated with the poorer parts of Brussels. Slightly pungent, with a biscuit sweetness and a crisp, dry hop finish. Nothing quite like it in Belgium.

Silenrieux
Silenrieux, Namur
http://users.belgacom.net/brasserie-silenrieux.be/

Joseph *Blonde Ale* 6%

A Wallonian barn turned brewery renowned for eco-ales and the use of esoteric grains. Joseph, a rich golden-colored ale with Flemish sour undertones, get its sweetness from buckwheat.

Silly
Silly, Hainaut
www.silly-beer.com

Scotch Silly *Scotch Ale* 8%

Once known as the Meynsbrugen brewery, Silly dates back to 1850. With the original family name a bit of a mouthful and the village name a marketer's dream, it was no surprise when the Silly label was taken up. The yeasty, spicy brews with lots of fruit flavor are well hopped and bottle-conditioned. Scotch Silly was launched in 1920 and named after Payne, a big-drinking Scottish soldier who was stationed in Silly during World War One. Toffee, vanilla, banana, chocolate, and caramel are all present in this marvelously smooth beer.

Slaghmuylder
Ninove, East Flanders
www.slaghmuylder.be

Slaghmuylder Passbier *Lager* 6%

More Bavarian than Belgian, this is a clean, crisp, and crazily drinkable seasonal lager with zesty, herbal hops sprung from a bready malt base. It puts the mainstream nonsense to shame.

Witkap Stimulo *Blonde Ale* 6%

First brewed under the auspices of former owner and Westmalle brewer Henrik Verlinden, this voluptuous blonde ale is brewed by a slightly enigmatic Flemish family brewery that, despite 150 years of brewing heritage, has kept the brilliance of its brewing recipes under its beret.

Smisje
Mater, East Flanders
www.smisje.be

Smisje Calva Reserva *Barley Wine* 12%

Based in Bruges for ten years, brewer Johan Brandt finally shifted his innovative American-leaning beers to Oudenaarde in 2008. Aimed squarely at the US market, his bombastic brews are triple-fermented with Champagne, port, and ale yeast, and aged for 11 months in Calvados casks. This Barley Wine is a combination of explosive esters, tart woody notes, and brandy-snap body that is hard to classify.

Smisje Dubbel 9%

This Dubbel employs the humble date with inspiring results. A molasses-like treat, blackish brown in color, with a wispy white head, that doesn't so much drink as chew, like a partially liquidized rich fruit cake. And if that's not enough, the bottle label features a cartoon of two cross-eyed dogs dressed as monks, to complete the experience.

Strubbe
Ichtegem, West Flanders
www.brouwerij-strubbe.be

Strubbe Pils *Pilsner* 5%

When Norbert Strubbe took hold of the brewery reins in 2008, he was the seventh generation of his family to do so. Founded in 1830, it specialized initially in modest-strength beers and, more recently, it has provided shelter for local ales orphaned by breweries that have closed. The Strubbe Pils is crisp, medium-bodied, and deftly hopped, with a glorious mousse head.

Vlaskop *Wheat Beer* 5.5%

Energetic, enigmatic wheat beer that takes a sour slant on the traditional and nicely balanced mix of coriander, orange, and lemon. Citrus and spice tones, with a long, dry finish.

Struise

West Flanders

www.struise.noordhoek.com/eng

 Aardmonnik

Flemish Red Ale

8%

The "sturdy" brewers —Carlo, Peter, Phil, and Urbain—don't possess a brewhouse of their own. They borrow space and equipment from other breweries, mostly at the Deca Brewery in Woesten-Vleterenfind, to shape beers that many maintain are world classics in the making (Ratebeer.com, the international beer Web site, voted them the world's best "brewery"). A bit too brash and avant-garde for Belgium, their modern interpretations of classic world beer styles, many of them aged, have earned them enormous admiration around the globe and online. Like all Struise ales, Aardmonnik (Earthmonk) is tricky to track down, but is well worth the search. Black cherry-colored, with a wine-like body, sublime tart cherry-tinged sourness, and a delightfully dry delayed finish.

Black Albert *Imperial Stout* 13%

Without the fiscal concerns that come with running a brewery, De Struise has the freedom to create small-batch bespoke brews. This sublime Royal Belgian stout, illusory in its alcoholic strength, has immense character and was brewed specifically for the Ebenezer pub in Maine, USA. It has a dark chocolate, coffee-like fragrance; fresh mocha and kilned barley tones in the mouth, underpinned by dried apricots and prunes; and a robust hop accent at the end.

Pannepot Grand Reserva *Wood-aged Ale* 10%

An oak-aged version of Pannepot, this is Struise's spearhead beer, full of spice and dried fruit flavors, and a modern twist on a late 19th-century Flemish fisherman's ale. Matured in wine barrels for 14 months and then Calvados casks for 10, it's a refined yet rich rampage of oaky tannins, prunes, vanilla, fennel, sour cherry, and a firm bite of bitterness on the back end. Simply stunning.

Val de Sambre

Gozée, Hainaut

www.valdesambre.be

Abbey d'Aulde Triple Brune *Brown Ale* 8%

The Brasserie du Val de Sambre has returned the beers of the long-standing Abbey d'Aulne to their original spiritual home, a grandiose Cistercian abbey that last brewed in 1850. Nestled in the beautiful countryside of the western Hainaut province, the revived brewery uses recipes dating back to 1555. This burly brown ale, swathed in warm spice flavors, is perhaps their finest.

Van Den Bossche

Sint-Lievens-Esse, East Flanders

www.brouwerijvandenbossche.be

Buffalo *Stout* 6.5%

This opaque, astringent ale straddles a stout, a dark Dunkel, and sour ale in style. It celebrated its 100th birthday in 2007 and is mocha-tinged and toffee-ish, with a touch of roast malt. Easy to sip, Buffalo is the beer on which this family-owned brewery, a blend of tradition and technology, has been built.

Van Eecke

Watou, West Flanders

www.brouwerijvaneecke.tk

Hommelbier *Blonde Ale* 7.5%

Van Eecke's most celebrated ale translates as "hop beer" and has a fine floral presence. Bottle-conditioned, dryhopped, and buttressed by a trio of malt varieties, this popular golden-hued brew has a heightened citrusy-spicy hop character, comprising maple syrup, ripe pears, and a dry, hoppy finish.

Kapittel Abt *Barley Wine* 10%

Van Eecke has been family-owned since the 1840s. Working in partnership with the neighboring Leroy brewery, it produces a fine and flavorsome line of weighty ales that improve with age. The Kapittel range is revered among aficionados, not least this copper-toned, parched Barley Wine, with roast coffee and alcohol on the palate and a mouth-puckering finish.

Van Honsebrouck

Ingelmunster, West Flanders

www.vanhonsebrouck.be

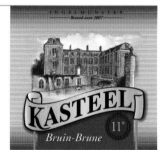

Kasteelbier Bruin

Flemish Brown Ale 11%

A plush, dark plum-colored "castle beer" brewed in the tourist-friendly Ingelmunster Castle and matured in its cellars since 1989. Hopped twice with Kent Goldings and mellowed by dark malts, the double-fermentation process fluffs up the fruitcake body and brandy aroma.

St. Louis Fond Tradition *Gueuze* 5%

Van Honsebrouck is not based in Lambic Land, where this type of beer is traditionally produced, but that didn't stop it experimenting with the style in 1968. The decision may have gone down very badly with the brewing purists, but while the wrangles continue to be waged there's no doubting the tart, bittersweet beauty of this blended beer.

Van Steenberge
Ertvelde, East Flanders
www.vansteenberge.com

 **Gulden Draak** *Barley Wine* 10.5%

Dating back to the 19th century, this impressive entrepreneurial family-owned brewery has willingly embraced modern technology. Its Gulden Draak (Golden Dragon) Barley Wine/dark Tripel is housed in an iconic white bottle, and is a chewy, toffee-tainted dark tripel-style brew, with a sweet medicinal body spruced by herbaceous hop flavors. Delicious but strong.

 Piraat *Golden Ale* 10.5%

Floral Flemish golden ale that owes its spark and spice to Saaz hops. Dry, assertive, and appetizing, with a touch of brandy butter.

Vapeur
Pipaix-Leuze, Hainaut
www.vapeur.com

 **Saison de Pipaix** *Farmhouse Ale* 6%

A fabulous example of a farmhouse ale from a steam-powered brewery brought back to life by two teachers in 1985. The brewery produces traditional Wallonian Saison beer that was first brewed in 1785. Dry, gently hopped, and mashed until a little acidic, the result is a spicy and sharp blend of black pepper, ginger, sweet orange peel, Curaçao, and star anise.

Verhaeghe
Vichte, West Flanders
www.specialitybeer.com/breweries.html

 Duchesse de Bourgogne
Wood-aged Ale 6.2%

In this Burgundy-colored blend of new and old, beer laid down in oak barrels for 18 months is married with eight-month-old ale before being bottled and, preferably, laid down again in a cellar to develop further. Spicy and sweet, Duchesse has a red, glowing allure.

Verhaeghe Echt Kriekenbier *Cherry Beer* 6.8%

Almond-tasting ale made with real cherries merged with the Vichtenaar. A chocolate and cherry character conjures a Black Forest gâteau.

Vichtenaar *Flemish Brown Ale* 5.1%

Around since 1880 as a family-owned brewery, Verhaeghe tightened up the brewery and added some marketing magic a few years ago. Ales aged in oak is what this brewery does best, and this archetypal Oud Bruin (brown ale) has earned a strong following, with its sharply spiked sweetness and cinnamon-slanted mulled wine flavors.

Westmalle
Malle, Antwerp
www.trappistwestmalle.be

 **Westmalle Dubbel Trappist**
Dubbel 7.5%

Westmalle is the largest of the Trappist breweries, dating back to 1836. This quality, dark and fruity classic, with a portlike appearance, has flavors that include raisins, bitter chocolate, and burnt toast, plus a peppery prickle and a finish of almond liqueur.

 **Westmalle Tripel Trappist**
Tripel 9.5%

A tremendous Trappist tripel from the long-established Abbey of Westmalle, one of the seven revered Trappist breweries. Its color approaches that of olive oil, while the bittersweet taste bops you on the palate, then follows up with jabs of herbal elixirs, grainy malt, macadamia nut, and an almost minty pine finish. This is truly an unmissable connoisseur classic.

Westvleteren
Westvleteren, West Flanders
http://www.sintsixtus.be

 Westvleteren Abt 12
Trappist Barley Wine 10.2%

Westvleteren is the tiniest and most secretive of Trappist brewers, producing only 132,000 gallons (5,000 hectoliters) of beer every year. The scarcity of its beers, packaged in plain label-free bottles, may have inflated their perceived excellence, but even so they're hugely impressive ales. None more so than this deliciously decadent Barley Wine that delivers a potent aroma; soothing dark rum character, chocolate-covered raisins, leather, and heather on the palate; and an astonishing finish of port and petits fours.

Westvleteren Blonde *Trappist Pale Ale* 5.8%

First released by the Sint Sixtus abbey in 2000. Beneath its green cap, there's an enchanting, golden-colored cornucopia of resinous, heady yet remarkably refined and defined hop flavors. A marvelous bit of magic that is quite incredible with cheese.

"If you ever reach total enlightenment while drinking beer, I bet it makes beer shoot out of your nose."

JACK HANDEY, AMERICAN COMEDIAN, 1949-

Germany

Many claim that Germany is the greatest beer nation on the planet, and you'd have to be a brave fellow, or a Brit or a Belgian, to argue otherwise.

Germany's contribution to beer, brewing, and beer-drinking culture cannot be overestimated. In the 16th century, it introduced a semblance of order and standards to European brewing with the introduction of the Reinheitsgebot, which stipulated that beer should be brewed using only malted barley and wheat, yeast, hops, and water. Germany, or more precisely Bavaria, is also responsible for the advent of both bottom-fermenting lager and mechanical refrigeration.

Today, there are more than 1500 breweries in Germany, and each German drinks an average of 35 gallons (132 liters) of beer a year. The nation's beer culture is deeply entwined in its social and religious fabric. Beer plays a role, either leading or cameo, in nearly all of the nation's festivals, and brewers mark the passing of the seasons with a change of beer style.

Unlike its European neighbors, Germany has remained relatively unscathed by the insidious creep of global consolidation and international mergers. Many attribute this to the fact that, historically, the Reinheitsgebot has prevented foreign imports from gaining a foothold. But even after the purity law was revoked in the 1980s as a "restraint of trade", brews from abroad have had little appeal among a German drinking public who are fiercely loyal to their local beer style.

There are very few ubiquitous beer brands in Germany. In Bavaria, where there are more than 650 different breweries, people drink Bavarian beers such as weissbier and Dunkels; in Cologne you're served Kölsch without asking, and the same happens with Alt in Düsseldorf. Franconia is synonymous with Krausener and Keller biers; Bamberg is where the smoky Rauchbier resides, Dortmund keeps blue-collar beer drinkers refreshed in the industrial north with bottom-fermented Dortmunder; Berlin has its challenging Berliner-Weisse beer style, and Munich is famous for its Oktoberfest beer, consumed in huge quantities by many thousands of people at the biggest beer festival in the world.

Above top: Waldhaus brewery in Baden-Württemberg in the Black Forest area of Germany has been brewing since 1833.
Above: Beer has long been associated with quenching the thirst of farm workers. This poster was created for the Drei Kronen brewery in Memmelsdorf.

FEATURED PROFILES

1 Erdinger
Erding *pages 120–121*

2 Kölsch
Cologne *pages 130–131*

BERLIN ●

DORTMUND ●
● DÜSSELDORF
2 ● COLOGNE

● BAMBERG

B A V A R I A

1

● MUNICH

Above: The bierkeller is a long-established tradition in Germany. This line drawing comes from the archives of the celebrated and perennially popular Schlenkerla in Bamberg, Bavaria.

Allgäuer Brauhaus
Leuterschach, Bayern, Bavaria
www.allgaeuer-brauhaus.de

Cambonator *Doppelbock 7.2%*

Before being move to Leuterschach in 2005, Allgäuer had been brewing in Kempten, near the Swiss–Austrian border, since 1394. The recipe for this delightfully dark double bock dates back to 1707 and proudly flexes its malty muscle. Treacly, touched with a fragrant hop aroma and a finish that leaves little doubt of its alcoholic prowess.

Altenmünster Jubel Bier
Oktoberfest/Märzen 5.5%

When Allgäuer snapped up the Kronenbrauerei Altenmuster in 2003, it inherited a number of classic historic beers, including this superb swing-topped Dunkel. Beautiful dark brown hue, a fluffy head, strong notes of chewy caramel and brown bread, licorice, and a dry, clove-like finish.

Andechser
Upper Bavaria
www.andechs.de

Andechser Doppelbock *7.1%*

Chocolate raisins, prunes, bitter coffee beans, and a peppery twang all feature in this archetypal maroon-colored triple-decocted Doppelbock from a monastic brewery located at the foot of the "Holy Mountain", south of Munich. Benedictine monks have been brewing here since 1455, yet they are anything but cloistered in their modern brewing techniques.

Andechser Hell *Helles 4.8%*
A sensational gorgeously golden sip, delicate and dry with a heightened hop presence on the finish.

Hausbrauerei Altstadthof
Nuremburg, Bavaria
www.altstadthof.de

Altstadthof Schwarzbier *4.8%*

A Nuremburg brewpub, bakery, and distillery that's been riding the new wave of German micro-brewing since 1984. Techniques and equipment of yore are used to produce half a dozen unfiltered beers ranging from a terrific Helles to this mauve-tinted black lager underpinned by roasted coffee crème brûlée flavors.

Augustiner
Munich, Bavaria

 Edelstoff *Oktoberfest/Märzen* 5.6%

Founded in 1328 by Augustine monks, Augustiner is Munich's oldest brewery, one of the "big six" Oktoberfest breweries and still in German hands. It also owns one of the city's biggest, and most boisterous, beer halls and has never dabbled in the vulgar black art of advertising, preferring instead to let its eight beers (five permanent and three seasonal) do the talking. A golden Helles-Pils hybrid, Edelstoff has an easy balance of sweet malt and citrus hops, with a clipped finish.

Maximator *Doppelbock* 7.5%

A lush, rich, and colossal dark copper-colored Doppelbock, with a superb nuanced sweetness, rated by many as a world-beater. A classic Bavarian Doppelbock.

Ayinger
Munich, Bavaria

Altbairisch Dunkel 5%

On the outskirts of Munich in the tiny town of Aying, beer has been brewed since 1878, the year the town was founded by Johann Liebhard. The beers are more traditional and forceful than most other beers brewed in Bavaria, hence this sweet, fruity Dunkel, laced with espresso and licorice overtones.

Celebrator *Doppelbock* 7.2%

In 1999, the brewery moved to a state-of-the-art site, draped in ivy, from where one in ten beers is exported to either Europe or the United States. Several of its beers are often serial World Beer Cup medal winners. This silky-smooth, deep, darkly rich doppelbock, with a complex Christmas cake character, boasts smoky tones and a substantial Stateside following.

Bayerischer Bahnhof
Leipzig, Saxony

Original Leipziger Gose 4.6%

Gose, Germany's answer to the Lambic beers of Belgium, originated in the East German town of Goslar as far back as 1000 AD yet later, in the mid 18th century, became linked to Leipzig. By the 1960s, Gose was gone thanks to the rise of lagers and dwindling Eastern bloc interest. In 2000, Thomas Schneider (no relation to the wheat-beer brewing family) revived Gose at the Bayerischer Bahnhof, a large brewpub housed in a disused train station. A tart, quirky top-fermenting wheat beer brewed using salt, coriander, and lactic acid added to the boil.

Berliner Bürgerbräu
Berlin

Maibock 6.8%

The big Bürgerbräu brewery has been here, on the bucolic shore of the Muggel See in East Berlin, since 1869. Revamped after German re-unification, it remains a superb spot for sipping a strong, lip-smacking springtime beer brimming with butterscotch and herbaceous floral hops, not to mention a clipped, refreshing finish.

Bernauer Schwarzbier 5.2%

Sweet but not sickly; soft and fruity. Whips up a fabulous frothy head beneath which a deep purple/maroon-colored lager, with lengthy lacing and uncharacteristically high hop presence, lurks. Smooth, light caramel malt body and effortless drinkability. A superb Schwarzbier.

Berliner Kindl-Schultheiss-Brauerei
Berlin

Kindl Weisse *Berliner Weisse* 3%

Berlin beer doesn't come much more unique or authentic than Berliner Weisse, the German capital's quirky, tart, sour, highly effervescent, and modestly alcoholic take on a top-fermented wheat beer. The addition of fruit and woodruff syrups is popular, yet frowned upon by purists. Thankfully, for now, Kindl's version has survived rampant consolidation and change of brewery ownership. Tart yet wonderfully refreshing, like a bone-dry sherry.

Binding-Brauerei
Frankfurt

Schöfferhofer Hefeweizen 5%

Well-balanced, refreshing, hazy, amber wheat beer from an enormous Frankfurt brewery better known for its popular non-alcoholic Clausthaler brands. Bready notes, lychee, and ripe banana, with a spicy nutmeg finish. Now owned by the huge Radeberger group of breweries.

Bitburger
Bitburg, Rhineland-Palatinate
www.bitburger.de

 **Bitburger Premium Pils** *Pilsner* 4.8%

One of Germany's biggest breweries that is still family-owned, Bitburger was founded in 1817 and was the first pioneering purveyor of Pilsner back in 1883. Aided initially by the reach of the railways and later by its iconic "Bitte Ein Bit" (A Bit, Please) advertising slogan, Bitburger Premium Pils has become one of Germany's most popular beers. Yet size hasn't sacrificed style, and it remains a gloriously golden accord of soft, sweet malt and brusque, lingering hop bitterness.

Privatbrauerei Bolten
Korschenbroich, North Rhine-Westphalia
www.bolten-brauerei.de

Ur-Alt Bier *Altbier* 4.8%

While not as widely distributed as Diebels, nor as well-known, Bolten's "original" Altbier is the grand daddy (and granddaddy) of the beer style, having been first brewed back in 1266. Brewed 15 miles outside Düsseldorf, it glows a deep red with a slight, subdued sparkle. Sweet and malty with a touch of vanilla on the nose, there are spice and astringent bitterness to follow and an acute alcoholic accented end. However, It's the mellow, melodic malt that calls the tune.

Landbier 5.4%

An unfiltered, light-colored, crisp, and drinkable beer that, were it not for those Cologne-based sticklers for tradition and German law, should be called a Kölsch. Lemon, grapefruit, and a touch of chamomile.

Diebels
Issum, North Rhine-Westphalia
www.diebels.de

Diebels Alt *Altbier* 4.9%

Like a particularly friendly and diligent Darth Vader, Diebels has been fighting the fight for the dark side against a wave of blonde upstarts for quite some time now. Diebels is the biggest brewer of Altbier in the world and, until InBev-Anheuser Busch opened its wallet in 2001, had been family-owned since 1878. Peaking in the 1960s when Diebels was selling more than 5,300,000 gallons a year, this seriously smooth, chocolate-biscuity Altbier is brewed with a double-decoction mash, perle and Hallertau hops, and dark, caramelish malt.

Dom
Cologne, North Rhine-Westphalia
www.dom-koelsch.de

Dom Kölsch 4.8%

The "cathedral" Kölsch is a particularly fragrant, floral, and fresh example of the Kölsch style. It's best drunk in its very own bustling beer halls, where it's served by men in blue aprons, often with impressive facial hair. Clean, crisp, and clipped in its hoppy finish. See pages 130–131 for a profile of Kölsch beers from Cologne.

Drei Kronen Memmelsdorf
Bamberg, Bavaria
www.drei-kronen-memmelsdorf.de

Stöffla *Rauchbier/Kellerbier* 4.5%

Highly, and rightly, rated hybrid beer dovetailing the smoky smoothness of a Rauchbier with the robust, unpasteurized aromatic hop signature of a Kellerbier. Brewed by a brewery-cum-fancy hotel, located just a few miles outside Bamberg, that was founded in 1457.

Brauhaus Einbecker
Einbeck, Lower Saxony
www.einbecker-brauhaus.de

Ur-Bock Dunkel *Bock* 6.5%

Classic and original, this ocher-brown beer is to bock beer what Pilsner Urquell is to Pils. It was first brewed back in 1378 and purportedly boasts the 15th-century Protestant door vandal Martin Luther as one of its biggest fans. Originally designed to withstand long journeys across Germany, the malt is massive and the hop is huge. A world classic beer, this is the king pin of all the Bocks.

Erdinger

Erding, Bavaria   *See Brewery Profile pages 120-121*
www.erdinger.com

 Erdinger Urweisse *Weissbier* 5.6%

Released in 2008 as an authentic replica of the wheat beers that were drunk back in the day. This is more robust, fruitier and spicier, and brewed with more muscular malt than the world-famous Erdinger beer. Raises the bar for the weissbier aficionados.

 Erdinger Weissbier *Hefeweizen* 5.2%

Easier on the eye and the palate than its wheat beer rivals, Erdinger's globe-trotting flagship boasts zesty fruit freshness courtesy of secondary fermentation in the bottle/keg. Beautifully balanced with a lip-smack of bitterness on the finish. Very refreshing and excellent with fish, salad, and, of course, pretzels.

Erdinger Weissbier Dunkel
Dunkelweizen 5.3%

Caramel, prunes, banana, cookies, and brown bread: Just some of the flavors emanating from this fullbodied, hearty yet drinkable dark wheat beer brewed with kilned wheat and barley malt.

Brauerei Ferdinand Schumacher

Düsseldorf, North Rhine-Westphalia
www.brauerei-schumacher.de

Schumacher Alt *Altbier* 4.6%

A dark-tanned, especially fruity Altbier mellowed out with masses of malt and perked up with piney hops at the finish. Slightly smoky, too. Comes courtesy of Düsseldorf's oldest brewery, dating back to 1838.

Flensburger

Flensburg
www.flens.co.uk

 Kellerbier 4.8%

Flensburger is not just a Pils-plopper. Almost 120 years after a quintet of locals created the brewery in 1888, it released an unfiltered, environmentally friendly Kellerbier that does great things for both the planet and the palate. Grassy, pine-like aromas and sweet caramel notes are the key flavors here.

Pilsner 4.8%

In the 1960s, when the vast majority of German breweries trashed their swing top bottle in favor of capped versions, Flensburger remained loyal to the trademark "plop" design and, consequently, their nicely poised Pilsner stood out among its golden rivals. One of the most popular Pilsners in Germany today.

Forschungs Brauerei

Munich, Bavaria
www.forschungsbrauerei.de

Forschungs-Pilsissimus 5.2%

Scarcely heard of amid the noise made by the big Bavarian breweries is this traditional tinkering brewpub and beer garden founded in the 1920s as an experimental brewery for local breweries. Now a well-kept secret among beer boffins and closed during the winter months, it brews two beers, only one of which is a heavenly and hoppy Helles-cum-Pilsner. A must if you're in Munich.

Früh

Cologne, North Rhine-Westphalia
www.frueh.de

 **Früh Kölsch** 4.8%

Opposite the striking cathedral, the enormous Früh am Dom is Cologne's most famous and most frequently visited brewpub. Downstairs is where the serious drinking seems to be going on. Saying Früh is fruity is not merely indulgent alliteration; it really is. Enjoy the taste of a fruity, crisp hoppiness and a smooth, malty mouthfeel.

Furstlich Fürstenbergische

Donaueschingen, Schwarzwald
www.fuerstenberg.de

 **Fürstenberg Hefeweizen Dunkel**
Dunkelweizen 5.3%

Malty, aromatic, and fruity dark wheat beer that attains its silky smooth mouthfeel from the Black Forest water. Spice, chocolate-coated strawberries, and banana-caramel.

 Fürstenberg Premium Pilsner 4.8%

The brewery, one of the largest in southwest Germany, dates back to the 13th century, when Count Heinrich I was granted the feudal right to brew by King Rudolf von Habsburg. Crisp, snappy Pilsner with big bitterness. This beer is even better than a Black Forest gâteau.

Gaffel

Cologne, North Rhine-Westphalia
www.gaffel-haus.de

Gaffel Kölsch 4.8%

A floral, aromatic, hop-led Kölsch, ideally drunk outside the traditional Gaffel-Haus tavern in Cologne, tucked behind the train station on Alter Markt, one of the city's cutest squares. Also available in bottles.

Göller

Zeil am Main, Lower Franconia
www.brauerei-goeller.de

⭐ 🍺 🍴 **Göller Kellerbier** 4.9%

The Franconian town of Zeil am Main, 15 miles north of Bamberg, is renowned as much for its wine as its beer, and is home to a picturesque brewery and restaurant with a lovely beer garden. Bought by the Göller family in 1908, it specializes in traditional swing-topped German beer styles, of which this cloudy, amber-colored cellar beer is a hop-laden highlight.

⭐ ☕ 🍺 **Göller Rauchbier** 5.2%

Göller's take on Bamberg's specialty beer is lighter, less smoky, slightly sweeter, and easier to drink than more famous interpretations such as Schlenkerla. It's good with food and especially great with smoked cheese, smoked meats, and chargrilled dishes.

Guttman

Titting, Bavaria
www.brauerei-gutmann.de

🍺 🍴 **Guttman Weizenbock** 7.2%

Family-owned Bavarian wheat beer specialist founded in 1707. Amber-colored Weizen that turbo-boosts the bubblegum, banana candy, and pear-drop flavors. Superb season with stealth-like strength.

Hacker-Pschorr

Munich, Bavaria
www.hacker-pschorr.de

⭐ 🍺 **Hacker-Pschorr Animator**
Doppelbock 8.1%

Sensational, seriously strong, and slightly syrupy. Spicy with soothing alcohol like a thinking man's mulled wine, there are dark rum molasses, toffee, caramel, and raisins, too. Signs off with plenty of sweet malt and alcohol.

⭐ 🍺 **Hacker-Pschorr Oktoberfest-Märzen** 5.8%

The Hacker brewery, founded in 1417, earned its double-barreled title in 1793 when Joseph Pschorr married Therese Hacker and took over her family business. In the 1970s, it joined forces with fellow Munich brewer Paulaner, before being taken under the wing of Heineken. Hacker-Pschorr's 16-strong range of beers is now brewed at the Paulaner brewery. Archetypal strong, copper-colored, full-bodied Munich Märzen with a marvelous festive mince pie finish from one of the original Oktoberfest brewers.

Hirsch Brauerei Honer

Wurmlingen, Bavaria
www.hirschbrauerei.de

🍺 🍺 **Hirsch Hefe-Weisse** *Hefeweizen* 5.2%

Major regional brewery, dating back to the 1780s, that blends 18th-century old with the shiniest of new brewing technology on a site to the east of the Black Forest in southwest Germany. Stand-out beers include an awesome aromatic Zwicklbier and this cloudy, clove-tastic conglomeration of spice, tropical fruit aromas, and a flourish of vanilla on the finish.

Hoepfner

Karlsruhe, Baden-Württtenberg
www.hoepfner.de

🍺 🍺 **Hoepfner Pilsner** 4.8%

A hundred years after a priest began brewing in 1798, Hoepfner moved into a new, rather fancy fortress in the eastern part of Karlsruhe, a vibrant university town in the southern part of the Rhine. It's a charming spot to sip, or indeed sink, this terse, totally ace golden lager that calls upon the aromatic armory of four hop varieties. Given that the Hoepfner family name originates from 'hop farmer', the full-on fragrance is a fitting one.

🍴 🍾 **Hoepfner Porter** 4.9%

Unlike other German breweries of its age and more akin to an American micro, Hoepfner veers off-piste when it comes to traditional beer styles and boasts its own maltings. In 1998, this spectacular black beer from the edge of the Black Forest was reintroduced. Ink-black in color, with a singed treacle sweetness and a smidgen of smoke. It's a rare German take on an old, classic English style—Vorsprung durch Technik as they say round these parts.

Hofbräuhaus

Munich, Bavaria
www.hofbrau-muenchen.de

⭐ 🍺 **Hofbräu München Maibock** 7.2%

The Hofbräu brewery, its origins dating back to 1589, is synonymous with the Hofbräuhaus—the most famous pub in the world and not just because it was here, in 1920, that Adolf Hitler announced the 25 theses of the National Socialist German Workers' Party. Regardless of the day of the year, the state-owned Hofbräuhaus is a thigh-slapping, whip-cracking, pretzel-munching, stein-swaying, feet-stomping, oompah-playing, sausage-stuffing shrine to golden lager-driven good times. While the Helles holds forth as Hofbräu's world-famous beer, the best time to don your lederhosen is in the last week of April, when the first barrel of Maibock is tapped. Its Munich's oldest bock, dating back to 1614, it is strong yet medium-bodied, citrus-scented, with a bright, zesty vibrancy on the palate. All together now... "oans, zwoa, g'suffa".

ERDINGER

Franz Brombach Strasse, Erding, Bavaria

www.erdinger.com

In the 1960s, when Pierre Celis was earnestly breathing life back into Belgian witbier in the small town of Hoegaarden, the Erdinger brewery was planning similar revival techniques with weissbier in an increasingly wheat-intolerant Germany. The 1960s may have been the decade of free love, but weissbier hadn't been getting so much as a cheeky wink beyond Bavaria, the flour power in brewing having long since shifted from wheat ales to barley-baesd German lagers.

Yet, like a horny hippie looking for carnal enlightenment, Erdinger came out swinging and dared to play away from those who had loved it so long, some would say too long. In an unprecedented move for a traditional Bavarian brewer, Erdinger embarked on a national advertising mission designed to change clichéd perceptions of weissbier as a drink drunk solely by doddery death-dodgers.

Instead, it championed weissbier as the real beer of Bavaria, where many Germans spent their holidays, and the beer became synonymous with the region's laid-back, sun-kissed lifestyle. In a further attempt to charm German beer drinkers, Erdinger also tweaked the tipple itself—the full-on fruit flavors were softened, the beer took on a less intimidating hue, and drinkability was enhanced.

Thankfully for both brewer and beer style, Erdinger's audacity proved to be a shot in the arm rather than the foot, and sales subsequently soared. Erdinger expanded beyond its Bavarian borders into southwestern, western, and northern Germany and, between 1970 and 1977, the annual beer output rose from 2,166,210 gallons (82,000 hectoliters) to 5,943,871 gallons (225,000 hectoliters). Such was the meteoric growth of both Erdinger and weissbier in general that, in 1983, Erdinger was forced to abandon the original 1886 brewhouse (now a terrific traditional tavern) in the center of Erding and move to the suburbs for more space.

The new brewery, an admirable coming together of tradition and Teutonic efficiency, is now the biggest wheat beer brewery in the world and brews almost 50 million gallons of wheat beer

every year. It is responsible, in no small part, for growing wheat beer's share of Bavarian brewing to 30 percent (after World War Two it was just 3 percent).

Bespoke wheat and barley grown by local farmers, water sourced from a 75-foot well beneath the brewery, and hops (Perle, Tettnang, and Hallertau) sourced from Germany's Hallertau region are united in strict accordance to the Bavarian Purity law of 1516, the Reinheitsgebot.

Its approach to fermentation is where Erdinger differs from its wheat-beer rivals. Primary fermentation occurs in shallow, rather than towering, tanks less than 9 feet high, while secondary fermentation in the bottle/keg comes courtesy of lager yeast rather than the traditional top-fermenting yeast. Why? The brewery claims that it prolongs shelf-life and improves consistency which, with Erdinger Weissbier exported to more than 70 countries, can only be a good thing.

In addition to the flagship Hefeweizen, containing between 50 and 60 percent wheat, Erdinger's second bestselling beer is Erdinger Alkoholfrei, a low-alcohol (0.5%) beer blessed with the isotonic power to slake the thirst of Germany's multitude of Lycra-clad sports folk.

When the mercury rises, as it does in Bavaria, the filtered Erdinger Kristall (5.3%) is one to reach for, while in the winter months the Erdinger "Schneeweise" Winterbier is a more complex, cockle-warming companion, brewed using the first malts from the summer harvest and matured for longer. Its spicy, clove-like flavors can be experienced each year from November to February.

Erdinger's Dunkelweizen is stronger, darker, and more full-bodied than other Bavarian brunettes, thanks to the use of both kilned wheat and barley malt. Erdinger Pikantus, a typical dark bock beer and the strongest of the Erdinger brood, gets its potent peppery sweetness by using a higher amount of wort and a more languid, lingering maturation.

In early 2008, Erdinger resurrected the pre-1970 weissbier in the shape of Erdinger Urweisse (5.2%), a hazy orange-hued, old-style wheat beer that doffs a cap to the Bavarian wheat beers of yesteryear. Adorned with a fuller body, more spice, bombastic banana, and warming caramel than its globetrotting stablemate, it's one for true wheat-beer enthusiasts.

And then there's Festweisse. Every year, the tidy town of Erding, all cobblestoned and chocolate-box charm, has its doors blown off when Erdinger hosts its annual Erdinger "Herbfest" in one of its traditional beer gardens.

Smaller and less touristy than the enormous Oktoberfest in Munich, the Herbfest is a six-day, stein-swaying, rollercoaster-riding, lederhosen-slapping, pork- and pretzel-munching, Bavarian ballyhoo brimming with boisterousness, conviviality, and, of course, lots of lovely weissbier.

Key Beers

Erdinger Kristall 5.3%
Erdinger Urweisse 5.6%
Erdinger Weissbier 5.2%
Erdinger Weissbier Dunkel 5.3%

Opposite above right: Erdinger Dunkelweizen is a stronger, darker version of the more ubiquitous Bavarian wheat beers, made with a combination of kilned wheat and barley malt.

Above: The Festweisse is Erdinger's annual Herbfest, a six-day beer festival.

Left: Together with its gloriously appealing and distinctive signature glass, Erdinger weissbier is distributed throughout the world, to at least 70 countries, including the United Kingdom and the United States.

Holsten

Hamburg
www.holsten.de

Moravia Pils *Pilsner* 4.8%

An archetypal German Pilsner that is light,
delicate, and flint-dry, with a brisk hop signature.
Brewed by a mainstream mover and shaker
synonymous with a lesser lager. It is often difficult to find so, if and when
you do, drink it and enjoy.

Hummel

Memmelsdorf-Merkendorf, Bamberg, Bavaria
www.brauerei-hummel.de

Raucherator Doppelbock *Rauchbier/Doppelbock* 8.1%

It sounds like a medieval torture mechanism and, as with all Rauchbiers,
there's no smoke without ire among some beer drinkers. But, for fans of
peat and streaky bacon flavors, this potent and peaty liquid is well worth
the short bus ride out of Bamberg.

Hütt

Baunatal
www.huett.de

Schwarzes Gold *Dark Lager* 4.9%

A family-owned north German brewery,
brewery tap, and restaurant dating back to
the middle of the 18th century. A story goes that, in 1813, the brewer's
daughter, Dorothea Viehmann, befriended the brothers Grimm (Jacob
and Wilhelm) and passed on to them tall stories and fairy tales she'd
been told by travelers who had visited the tavern. That, however, may
not be true. First, most of the Grimm stories improve with the telling
and, secondly, they've lied about Schwarzes Gold. It's not gold; it's dark
maroon, heartily hopped with sweet shortbread notes.

Privatbrauerei Iserlohn

Obergrune, North Rhine-Westphalia
www.iserlohner.de

Iserlohner 1899 4.9%

Iserlohn, situated on the northernmost border
of the Sauerland in the North Rhine -Westphalia
region of Germany, is the capital of German ice
hockey. After a hard day of giving a flying puck far too much attention
and smashing an opposing player's face in with a stick, this warming,
dark, extremely nutty Dunkel, named after this big brewery's date of
birth, does just the trick.

Jever

Jever, Lower Saxony
www.jever.de

Jever Pilsener 5%

Not just the occupier of the biggest building
in the coastal town of Jever, Friesland, but
also one of Germany's leading purveyors of Pilsner, Jever has had a
tumultuous history since being formed in 1848, but now finds itself in
the safe hands of corporate cash. Pilsners don't come much more
Germanic than this, heaving in biting hop flavors, floral aromas, and
underscored with a faint, almost obsolete malt base. Best served chilled.

Kaltenberg

Kaltenberg, Bavaria
www.kaltenberg.de

Konig Ludwig Dunkel 5.1%

The Wittelsbach royal family, which ruled Bavaria from the 12th century
until World War One, loved their beer. They helped establish the beer
purity law, the Reinheitsgebot, in 1516; founded the Hofbräuhaus; and
invented the Munich Oktoberfest. In 1976, descendant Prince Luitpold,
the great-grandson of Ludwig III, took over Kaltenberg and, from within
the walls of his castle, has blazed a trail with a distinctive, dry-hopped
dark lager. The delicious Dunkel is dark brown, extremely drinkable,
triple-decocted for a fuller mouthfeel, and decked in dark malt, mocha
coffee, and dried fruit flavors.

Konig Ludwig Weissbier Hell 5.5%

A well-regarded, hugely popular golden wheat beer which displays
a haze of yeasty goodness. Well-balanced bitterness with malty
overtones, an apple-like aroma, and an archetypal banana skin sign-off.
Hugely refreshing and ideally consumed in July, when the castle plays
host to a medieval tournament featuring jousting, jesters, drinking,
gluttony, music, drinking, falconry, drinking, some more jousting, and
then some drinking again.

Karg

Murnau, Bavaria
www.brauerei-karg.de

Karg Dunkels Hefe-Weisbier
Dunkelweizen 5.2%

A 50-year-old weissbier specialist based at the
base of the Bavarian Alps and the shores of the
Staffelsee, 25 miles from Munich. The brewery and
restaurant tap are beloved of wheat beer drinkers, who talk
of this mahogany-colored dunkelweizen in hushed and rather excited
tones. Akin to putting banana-caramel pie in a blender, the huge yeast
presence gives it the look of a lackluster Lava Lamp.

Ketterer

Homberg, Bavaria
www.kettererbier.de

Schützen-Bock 7.5%

Deep in the woods of the Black Forest, close to the town of Hornberg, lies a modest, recently modernized family-owned microbrewery famed for its esoteric, eclectic ales. The most remarkable being this opaque, barrel-aged, blackish-brown stout with sweet chocolate on the nose, rich red wine notes (Château Musar) with a little roast bitterness, and a vanilla finish.

Klosterbräu

Bamberg, Bavaria
www.klosterbraeu.de

Klosterbräu Schwarzla *Dark Lager* 4.9%

Melodious matte-black beer from the oldest brewery in Bamberg, founded in 1533 and once owned by the prince bishops who ruled the region. One for the sweet-toothed sipper, it conjures up talk of chocolate raisins, coffee, and aniseed on the finish.

Klosterbrauerei Ettal

Ettal, Bavaria
www.klosterbrauerei-ettal.de

Ettaler Kloster Curator
Doppelbock 9%

Founded in 1333, Ettal is one of very few genuine monastic breweries remaining in Germany today. Still overseen by members of the Benedictine order, the brewery shares billing with a distillery and distributes both locally and to the United States. A delightful doppelbock, with flavors of Christmas cake drenched in dark navy rum. Molasses and maraschino cherries with a dry roast finish.

Ettaler Kloster Dunkel 5%

Complex, reddish brown Dunkel brewed with Vienna, Pilsner, and Munich malt. Dead dry with distinct estery fruit notes, there are cocoa-powder, bitter chocolate, and a dry roasted nut finish.

Kneitinger

Regensburg, Bavaria
www.kneitinger.de

Kneitinger Bock 6.4%

Kneitinger, as the rather inquisitive-looking goat on its bottle label suggests, is renowned for a quite brilliant seasonal bock, rich, dark, and chocolatey. Attached to the brewery is a Michelin Guide restaurant where terrific dumplings, sauerkraut, and other Bavarian specialties are best digested using the brewery's very own bock-based schnapps. Every year, the first cask of bock is tapped on the first Thursday in October. An important date for many dedicated bock lovers.

Kneitinger Dunkel 5.2%

Regensburg, located at the most northerly point of the Danube, boasts a marvelous Old Town, with labyrinthine streets and UNESCO World Heritage status. Kneitinger, one of five breweries in Regensburg, began brewing here in 1530 and is run by a charitable foundation. The brewery's Dunkel is nutty, sweet, bready, and smooth.

Köstritzer Schwarzbierbrauerei

Bad Krostritz, Thuringen
www.koestritzer.de

Köstritzer Schwarzbier 4.8%

Köstritzer is to German Schwarzbier what Michael Jordan is to slam-dunking. Dating back to 1543, it has been a steadfast champion of rich, dark beers, first as a healthy drink, then as a delicious and different one, throughout Communist rule. Spiked with chocolate, roasted nut and coffee flavors, this balanced bitter black cherry-colored beer claims to be Goethe's favorite and, now owned by Bitburger, represents more than half of all the Schwarzbier in Germany. From a marketing perspective, Kostritzer Schwarzbier is often regarded as Germany's version of Guinness.

Krostitzer

Krostitz, Bavaria
www.ur-krostitzer.de

Schwarzes *Schwarzbier* 4.9%

Sizable regional owned by the omnipotent Oetker group, Krostitzer's dark lager is very often confused with the market-leading Köstritzer beer. No bad thing if one does, for this slightly smoky Schwarzbier is equally as impressive, with a melodic malty mix of bitter chocolate, prunes, and black pepper.

Kulmbacher

Kulmbach, Bamberg, Bavaria
www.kulmbacher.de

 **Eku 28 Strong Lager** *Eisbock* 11%

In the past two decades, Kulmbacher has munched its way through Franconia, gobbling up other breweries, to become the region's biggest brewery. When it acquired the EKU brewery, it inherited this—one of the strongest lagers in the world. First brewed in the 1950s according to the purity law, Reinheitsgebot, it stacks the mash with masses of malt and, before throwing it in, lets the yeast know it has nine months of cold fermentation to work its way through the sugar. Citrusy, estery, and acutely alcoholic, Eku 28 has vied with Samichlaus in the quest to become the world's strongest continually brewed lager.

Kulmbacher Eisbock 9.2%

Not to be confused with insipid American "ice" beers, this classic lager was the original Eisbock first brewed by the Reichelbrau brewery, which, in 1996, was bought up by Kulmbacher. Legend has it that a barrel of bockbier, accidentally left in the old Reichelbrau brewery yard midwinter, froze and snapped open. When the ice was chipped away, a denser, more intense, more clean-cut and, with less dilution, far stronger beer was discovered.

Monschof Kapuziner Schwarze Hefeweizen 5.4%

Take the juicy, fruity, and yeasty wheat tang of a Bavarian Hefeweizen, blend it with the deep, dark cocoa bitterness and roasted malt flavor of a black lager and, hey presto, you've got yourself an ace, rather unusual unfiltered hybrid.

Lowenbräu

Munich, Bavaria
www.loewenbraeu.de

Lowenbräu Oktoberfest *Märzen beer* 6.1%

With a brewing history dating back to 1383, "Lion's Beer" is now a roaring success on both the national and international brewing stage. In the 19th century, it was the first Munich beer maker to embrace expansion, advertising, and overseas contract brewing. One of Munich's six Oktoberfest breweries, it makes a ten-strong range of beers in the north of the city with Teutonic efficiency. A well-balanced blonde beer best brewed at source, when the nutty biscuit malt character and upfront bitterness shine bright and bubbly. Now owned by Anheuser-Busch InBev.

Lowenbräu-Buttenheim

Buttenheim, Bavaria
www.loewenbraeu-buttenheim.de

Lowen-Bräu Ungespundetes Lagerbier *Kellerbier* 4.8%

Buttenheim, a market town in Bamberg, has two claims to fame. The first is that jean guru Levi Strauss was born here. The second, and more important, is beer—lots of lovely beer. Not to be mixed up with its mainstream Munich namesake, Lowenbräu is the smaller of the two Buttenheim breweries (see St. Georgen on page 127) and was established in 1880. Distribution rarely roams beyond 35 miles outside Buttenheim, but its beer gardens and restaurant make for charming spots to sip this tasty, tangy unfiltered lager.

Mahr's Bräu

Bamberg, Bavaria
www.mahrs.de

Der Weisse Bock
7.2%

For many, Mahr's 17th-century brewery tap in Bamberg is the best place in the world to drink beer. Unparalleled in its comfy coziness during the winter, Mahr also has a Chestnut tree-lined beer garden —a solar-powered, stein-swaying shrine to cheery summertime swigging of seriously sublime small-batch beers. Originally brewed by the abbey's monks for Lent, this decadent dark wheat beer conjures up chocolate-covered poached pears. It's criminally quaffable and, if you're not careful, the surreptitious strength will sneak up on you like a crafty ninja and steal your legs.

Mahrs Bräu Ungespundet Hefetrüb *Kellerbier* 5.2%

A twist on the Zwickelbier and Kellerbier beer styles, Ungespundet means "unbunged" and refers to the way in which the beer eschews closed conditions in favor of being left exposed to the elements. The result, after eight weeks of lagering, is less a effervescent, more acidic, and hugely refreshing bottom-fermented beer full of tart green apple flavors and quenching notes of citrus.

Mahrs Weiss Bräu *Weissbier* 5.2%

Wonderful yeast-inspired wheat beer that defies its modest strength with a cornucopia of fruit flavors: lychee, kiwi fruit, banana, vanilla, and a sweet caramel base. Hazy on the eye, zesty on the nose, and tingle-tastic on the tongue.

Maisel
Bayreuth, Bavaria
www.maisel.com

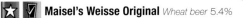

⭐ 🍺 **Maisel's Weisse Original** *Wheat beer* 5.4%

A Bavarian brewery renowned for its wonderful wheat beers. The old brewing site, dating back to 1887, was turned into a chin-scratching brewery in the 1970s, when the brewery expanded into bigger premises capable of meeting the heightened demand of the weisse renaissance. Darker and fruitier than most Bavarian wheat ales, Maisel is toffee, cookie, and banana; like a blended banana-caramel poured into a glass.

Maisel's
Bamberg, Bavaria
www.maisel-bamberg.com

🍴 **Maisel Eine Bamberg** 4.9%

This big Bamberg brewhouse dates from 1894 and is worth a visit. In addition to some marvelous seasonal beers and some particularly well-made Pilsner-style brews, it works wonders with wheat, both in darker, Dunkel guise and here, in its lighter, more spitzy and citrusy form.

Braurei Malzmuhle
Cologne, North Rhine-Westphalia
www.muehlenkoelsch.de

🍺 🥛 **Mühlen Kölsch** 4.8%

A cracking Kölsch from one of Cologne's most traditional brewhouses situated in the city's Haymarket area. Adorned with wood paneling and pork-knuckle guzzling locals, it's a vibrant and lively shrine to sophisticated sipping. Very delicate, mellow in malt, and with measured hop content, it has an ever-so-slightly sweet, fruity finish.

Kommunalbräuhaus Neuhaus
Oberflatz
www.zoiglbier.de

⭐ 🍺 **Zoigl Beer** 5.2%

The Oberpfälz Wald (Palatinate Forest) region, near the border with the Czech Republic, is home to the old-fashioned Zoigl beer style. It's a funky farmhouse lager that's similar to Kellerbier, but with the musty barnyard flavors more readily associated with wild yeast beers. It undergoes short primary fermentation and lagers for about three weeks at around 7°-8° C before being released to "Zoigl houses" in only five towns in the region: Eslarn, Falkenberg, Neuhaus, and Mitterteich. Brewmasters hang a brewer's star, known as a Zoigl, outside their house when the beer is ready.

Päffgen
Cologne, North Rhine-Westphalia
www.paeffgen-koelsch.de

🍺 🥛 **Päffgen Kölsch** 4.8%

Down-to-earth Kölsch that's spicy and a little more estery than its Cologne counterparts. Pockmarked with musty, slightly lactic, woody notes from the barrel and a bitter bite at the back.

Paulaner
Munich, Bavaria
www.paulaner.com

⭐ 🍺 🥛 **Hefe-weizen** 5.5%

Having made its name in the field of barley-driven lagers and bocks, Paulaner now cuts a particularly seductive swathe in the wondrous world of Bavarian wheat beer. Regarded in Bavaria as the "working man's" weisse, it's a zippy, zealously fruity, and refreshing amber ale with a wispy white head and lovely lacing. It looks as good as it tastes, eagerly ticking all the boxes of bubble gum, banana, and grapefruit. Superb in the summer with salads, corn on the cob, and grilled chicken and fish. Or, if you're in Munich, greasy pork knuckle, red cabbage, and, of course, pretzels.

⭐ 🥛 **Original Münchner** *Munich Lager* 5.5%

It's the world's biggest-selling Munich lager, and some would argue the finest. Unlike its Bohemian rival Pilsner, there's continuing conjecture and confusion as to which Munich brewery original pioneered the city's Helles lager. What is certain, however, is that Paulaner has always been hot when it comes to refrigeration and, in the early 20th century, hailed the Helles more than most. Toffee-apple aroma, buttery cookies on the palate, with a cinnamon send-off.

⭐ 🍺 🍴 🥛 **Salvator Doppelbock** 7.5%

When friars from the Order of Saint Francis of Paula arrived in Munich from Italy in 1627, they brewed the first-ever strong beer, designed to tide them over through Lent. The "liquid bread" beer was so good that they sent it off to Rome for papal blessing, for fear that they may be accused of over indulgence during a period of abstention. Luckily, the long, hot journey completely ruined the beer and the pope, unimpressed and unaware of the beer's true glory, confirmed it bad enough to drink by way of penance and mortification. If you've been a really bad person—and you really have—then don a hair shirt and seek solace in the forgiving, amber-colored bosom of this legendary liquid. Majestically malty, nutty with a deliciously dry finish.

Peters Bräuhaus

Cologne, North Rhine-Westphalia
www.peters-koelsch.info

 Peters Kölsch 4.8%

An eminently easy-drinking Kölsch. Pale straw in color, full and creamy in the mouth, and citrus hop bitterness that jumps out of nowhere. Available in bottles, but best swigged from small glasses in the ornate yet rather rowdy brewhouse in Cologne.

Pinkus Muller

Münster, North Rhine-Westphalia
www.pinkus.de

Pinkus Münstersch Alt
Altbier 5.1%

Born a tiny brewery and bakery in 1816, Pinkus emerged more recently as a pioneering proponent of bio-brewing and claims to be the world's first certified organic brewery. This golden Alt interpretation is lighter, fruitier, and more vinous than those associated with Düsseldorf. Pinkus's "Altbier Bowl" is a legendary Alt-based fruit punch concocted every spring and summer.

Pinkus Pils *Pilsner* 5.2%

Under the impressive auspice of the Muller family, Pinkus has outlived more than a hundred breweries in Münster, a university town in the nation's north and known as the "other" Altbier town. Pinkus has grown into a big, bustling brewery tap where students drink this flowery, fragrant pilsner—nearer to Bohemia than Bavaria in style—in quantities that make it seem as if they don't have to get up in the morning.

"Give me a woman who loves beer and I will conquer the world."

KAISER WILHELM
GERMAN EMPEROR 1859–1941

Radeberger

Radeburg, Saxony
www.radeberger.de

Radeberger Pilsner 4.8%

Radeberger, based in Saxony, became the first brewery in Germany to brew Pilsner in its traditional manner back in 1872, the year of the brewery's creation. Once appointed as the official supplier to the courts by Otto Von Bismarck, Radeberger is now owned by the omnipotent Oetker Group, and this fluffy-headed golden lager, brisk in bitterness and mellow in malt, is ubiquitous in its homeland. But its popularity has by no means bred contempt among proponents of proper Pilsner, who rate it as its best when drunk unfiltered from the brewery tap in Radeburg.

Reissdorf

Cologne, North Rhine-Westphalia
www.reissdorf.de

 **Reissdorf Kölsch** 4.8%

Fluffy and soft on the palate with sweet touches of vanilla, aniseed, and fresh pine bitterness, it's served in its brewhouse direct from mini wooden casks hauled up from the cellar via a dumb waiter. Formed in 1894 and still family-run, Reissdorf was bombed seven times during World War Two but recovered to become Germany's best-selling Kölsch.

Rostocker

Rostock, Mecklenburg-Vorpommern
www.rostocker.de

 Bock Hell 6.9%

A big-bodied bitter bock that veers into Double IPA/Barley Wine territory. Treacle, toffee, dried apricots, and butterscotch all drop in to say hello.

Pilsner 4.9%

Formed In 1878 by two engineers, Rostocker thrived until the beginning of World War Two, when equipment was shifted to the Soviet Union and the brewery was nationalized. Today, under the private ownership of Oetker, it's this forceful golden pilsner—which pulls no punches in terms of bitterness —that's the town's default drop.

Rothaus
Rothaus, Baden Württemberg
www.rothaus.de

☑ 🍴 **Rothaus Hefeweizen** 5.4%

Nestled in the hills of the Black Forest and at 300 feet above sea level, Rothaus is Germany's highest brewery and, it claims, draws upon seven mountain springs to produce its trio of beers. A fiercely fruity, effervescent wheat beer complete with all the cloves, coriander, and bubble gum notes you'd expect.

🍺 **Rothaus Pils Tannen Zapfle** Pilsner 5.1%

Rothaus was founded by an abbot in 1791 and Baden state-owned for more than two hundred years. It's thrived in recent years, thanks to the cult and completely unexpected runaway success of Tannen Zapfle, meaning "little pine cones." The traditional beer is packaged in a quirky 33cl bottle with 30-year-old label adorned with a picture of a blonde girl whose name is a play on words meaning "beer makes you stronger".It has developed a fanatical following among young bar goers, who rave about its signature smoothness, dry quality, and retro packaging.

Rothenbach Brauerei
Aufsess
www.aufsesser.de

 Aufsesser Bock Bier 6.5%

A rich, malty, and dry Bavarian bock that pours from a swing-top bottle and is brewed by a family-owned brewpub located on the "Beer Road" in Franconian Switzerland. Its hometown, Aufsess, currently holds the Guinness world record for the most breweries per capita —a population of 1,500 boasts four brewhouses.

St. Georgen
Buttenheim, Franconia, Bavaria
www.kellerbier.de

☑ 🍺 **Keller Bier** 4.9%

Word of this tangy Kellerbier has broadened well beyond the small Franconian village of Buttenheim, to the other side of the Atlantic. The St. Georgen Brewery, situated to the south of Bamberg, has been in the same family since 1624 and it still ignores the advent of refrigeration by continuing to age its beer in durable unbunged oak casks placed deep down in chilly, dark rock caverns on the village outskirts.

🍺 **St. Georgen Pils** Pilsner 4.9%

Medium-bodied perfumed Pilsner; grainy maltiness with substantial hop character in the balance. A slight medicinal bitterness on the finish.

Saalfeld
Saalfeld, Thuringia
www.brauhaus-saalfeld.de

🍺 **Ur-Saalfelder Grottenpils** Pilsner 4.8%

Big and bitter thirst-buster that is rarely seen beyond the borders of Thuringia in eastern Germany. The brewery, founded in 1892, has embraced modern brewing practices with gusto.

Schlenkerla
Bamberg, Bavaria
www.schlenkerla.de

⭐ ☕ 🍺 **Aecht Schlenkerla Rauchbier**
5.2%

The archetypal "genuine" Rauchbier from a boutique, family-owned Bamburg brewery begun in 1405. So smoky it's like drinking a beechwood campfire through a barbecued kipper that's been swimming in Lapsang souchong tea all its life. It is to German beer what Laphroaig is to Scotch whisky and divides opinion in much the same way as dinner-table talk of the death penalty.

Schlossbrauerei Herrngiersdorf
Herrngiersdorf, Bavaria
www.schlossbrauerei-herrngiersdorf.de

🍺 **Trausnitz Pils** Pilsner 5.2%

A perfumed Pilsner defined with lovely biscuit malt and pine forest aroma at its crux brewed in Bavaria. The castle after which it is named, situated nearby, was home to the Wittelsbach dynasty and was built in 1204. This petit microbrewery, however, is even older, having being formed in 1131 which makes it, as far as anyone can tell, the oldest independent brewery in the world.

Schlüssel
Düsseldorf
www.zumschluessel.de

⭐ ☑ **Schlüssel Alt** Altbier 5%

Altbier experiences don't come much more authentic than this. The "Zum Schlüssel" brewery and tap has resided in the old town of Düsseldorf since 1850 and was inherited by the Gatzweilers, a brewing family since the 14th century. Destroyed during World War Two, rebuilt in 1950, and smartened up in 1990; its brewery tap is Altbier utopia, with original Schlüssel served in glasses straight from the barrel.

Schneider Weisse
Kelheim, Bavaria
www.schneider-weisse.de

 **Schneider Aventinus**
Weissbock 8.2%

A truly outstanding ale fully deserving of its
world-classic reputation and first brewed by
Georg Schneider in 1907 as a reaction to the
rise of barley-based doppelbocks. It takes the
spicy, banana-scented fruit salad notes from
the yeast and the chocolate, dark rum, and fig
flavors of the dark malt, and deftly unites them
in a slightly acidic, effervescent embrace. A wondrous wheat beer.

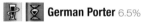 **Brooklyner-Schneider Hopfen-Weisse**
Weissbock IPA 8.2%

Hard to get hold of yet hailed in hallowed terms on both sides of the
Atlantic, this pale weissbock is a joint creation between head brewer
Hans-Peter Drexler and Garrett Oliver of the Brooklyn Brewery. Devoutly
dry-hopped using Hallertauer Saphir, grown on vines close to Kelheim.
Hoppy and zesty, it deftly bestrides an American IPA at its most
balanced and wheat beers at their most fruity and aromatic.

Schneider Weisse *Weissbier 5.5%*

A fabulous, fruity, and fragrant flag-bearer for the Bavarian style,
Schneider Weisse is to wheat beer what Muhammad Ali was to fast-
talking and fisticuffs. While other brewers have blown hot and cold with
regards to wheat beer, the Schneider family has been proudly brewing
nothing else since 1855, when Georg Schneider I began brewing in
Munich on behalf of the Royal Court. In 1872, when wheat beer was
waning, he bought his own brewery and the rights to brew wheat beer
from King Ludwig II. In 1927 the family moved to a traditional wheat-
beer brewhouse in Kelheim where it still resides. This weissbier's
signature burst of bubble gum, bananas, and cloves has often been
imitated, but in my opinion, never improved upon.

Private Landbrauerei Schönram
Schönram
www.brauerei-schoenram.de

Schönramer Pils *Pilsner 5.4%*

Brewmaster Eric Toft, the man currently working the
mash-fork magic at this 18th-century brewhouse,
doesn't hail from Bavaria, but from Wyoming in the
United States and he's continued the Schönram legacy
of brewing seriously smooth and swiggable beers. Using
a bespoke variety of barley, and hops for their aromatic
rather than bittering powers, the Pils is regarded by
many as Germany's finest. A brainy blonde lager with a
zesty lemon aroma, glorious grainy undertones, and a
tingly, tight finish. Delicious.

Schwaben Brauerei
Stuttgart, Baden Württenberg
www.ds-ag.de

 **Das Schwarze**
Schwarzbier 4.9%

A sensational Schwarzbier from
the Schwaben brewery in Stuttgart.
Black and a little bit briny, with
caramel, molasses, herbal hop notes,
and aniseed at the end.

Schwerter
Meissner, Hesse
www.schwerter-brauerei.de

German Porter 6.5%

The picturesque town of Meissen, in the Saxon
Elbe valley, is great if you're a fan of porcelain
because it's home to the world-renowned Meissener
Porzellan factory. It's even better if you're a fan of
porter because Schwerter, a brewery first mentioned
in the 15th century, makes a glorious German
interpretation of the industrial black English ale.
Sharp, roasty and—at 6.5% ABV—stouter than its
British brethren. While it may be authentic to do so,
try to avoid operating heavy machinery after drinking
this particular tipple.

Sion Bräuhaus
Cologne, North Rhine-Westphalia
www.brauhaus-sion.de

 **Sion Kölsch** 4.8%

Sion's brewhouse, a cozy drinking den with old
beer taps bedecking the walls and stain-glassed
windows, has lived in the shadow of Cologne
cathedral since 1318. Its creamy Kölsch, cut short
with a bitter finish, makes for a fine, floral friend to
watch people with.

Spaten-Franziskaner
Munich, Bavaria
www.spatenbraeu.de

 Franziskaner *Wheat Beer* 5%

Records suggest that there was a Spaten brewery in Munich as far back as 1397 (known as Spaeth), but it wasn't until the beginning of the 19th century, under ownership of the Sedlmayrs—arguably Munich's most prestigious brewing family that Spaten came into its own. In 1858 Josef Sedlmayr acquired a Franciscan abbey brewery, and the two breweries—one driven by barley, the other by wheat—were brought together after World War One. A very wheaty, buttery banana-scented beer that, under the ownership of the mighty brewery company that is now referred to as Anheuser-Busch InBev, has gone global.

Spaten Oktoberfestbier
Oktoberfest/Märzen 5.9%

Peerless in its pursuit of brewing excellence, Spaten was the first to use refrigeration and steam engines in the brewing process, the first to export its beers by airplane, and one of the earliest advocates of light-colored lagers. Its spade logo, assumed in 1884, was a groundbreaking marketing move, too. When its Oktoberfest lager was launched in the 1870s, it was a lot darker than it is now, but the muted malt sweetness and smooth, rounded body have been retained. Ideally drunk under a big tent in the company of pretzels, sausages, ladies in Dirndls—in other words the biggest beer festival in the world.

Spezial
Bamberg, Bavaria
www.brauerei-spezial.de

Lagerbier 4.6%

Spezial is the oldest Rauchbier brewery in Bamberg, and its smoked beers are brewed using grain from its own maltings and smoked on site using beechwood logs. Considerably less smoky than Schlenkerla, this is a touch sweeter and more refreshing, with grassy undertones.

Märzen Rauchbier 5.3%

Despite the presence of 70 percent smoked malt, the smoke flavors are gently wafted away by a fruity yeast character and hop bitterness. The subdued smokiness and comparable complexity will suit those beer drinkers who find other Rauchbiers a bit too much.

Spitalbraurei
Regensburg, Bavaria
www.spitalbrauerei.de

Spital Pils *Pilsner* 5.5%

Founded in 1266, it's the oldest brewery in Regensburg and was once a hospital brewery, where patients were given beer as a soporific nightcap. Spital's philanthropy remains, with profits from beer sales funding the adjacent retirement home. Charitable deeds don't come much more enjoyable than sipping this perfumed Pilsner in the brewery's gorgeous beer garden, in view of the Danube and cathedral.

Tucher Braeu Furth
Bavaria
www.tucher.de

 **Tucher Bajuvator Doppelbock** 7.2%

Tucher christened its coppers back in 1672, making it one of the world's most constantly active breweries. Its chief calling card is this mellow, malty mouth-filler. Now owned by the Radeberger Group, it's a definite must-try for doppelbock devotees.

Bergbrauerei Ulrich Zimmerman
Berg, North Rhine-Westphalia
www.bergbier.de

Ulrichsbier *Vienna Lager* 5%

It's been more than 250 years since the Zimmerman family took control of this boutique brewery, it continues to innovate with ingredients, extended lagering times, and alternative interpretations of German beer styles. Hazelnuts, caramel, apple, and sweet cream-soda flavors spring forth.

KÖLSCH

Cologne is a wonderful city, but you wouldn't want to kiss it—even if you're wearing beer goggles.

What once stood regal on the Rhine was reduced to rubble in World War Two, when Allied air forces unleashed the notorious "night of a thousand bombs". The only reminder of the city's handsome past is the magnificent cathedral which, having taken more than 600 years to build, was in no mood to buckle under the mainly British bombardment. But even the Cathedral's undoubted Gothic splendor can't disguise the fact that Cologne has definitely fallen out of the ugly tree and hit every branch on the way down.

A lack of aesthetic charm is one of the reasons why Cologne lags behind other cities in most people's pecking order of great German beer-drinking destinations. Munich, all leafy sun-kissed beer gardens and impressive architecture, and Bamberg, a town whose Baroque beauty has earned it UNESCO World Heritage status, are much easier on the eye.

Another reason that Cologne is overlooked by beer boffins is its local specialty—Kölschbier. Kölschbier, the most fragrant and delicate of beer styles, tends not to be worn as a badge of honor among hardcore, in-the-know imbibers—too accessible to be regarded as unique and too clean, crisp, and quaffable to be considered a classic among connoisseurs.

At the dinner party of German beer styles, Kölsch is the "dizzy blonde" stereotype that clears the plates and knows its place, while the "real men"—the smoky rauchbier of Bamberg, Dusseldorf's Alt, and Berlin's stupendously sour weissbier—retire to the lounge to smoke cigars and take part in the kind of man talk to which Kölsch is not invited.

That is, of course, nonsense. I'd rather spend a weekend in Cologne drinking Kölschbier than suffocating amid Bamberg's acrid smoke beers or swelling and sweltering with steins in Munich. Beer snobs may disagree, often via the medium of indignant spluttering, but they're wrong.

Drinking Kölsch in Cologne is beer tourism at its best. Brewed like blonde ale yet conditioned like a lager, Kölsch was introduced at the beginning of the 20th century by Cologne's brewing community, who were concerned by the meteoric rise of Pilsner—with which it shares some similarities.

Shimmering a brilliant gold and softer than a mattress stuffed with sheep, it boasts both the parch-slaying powers of a light Pilsner yet the fruity roundedness and dryness of a top fermenting beer—but with an immaculate aftertaste shorn of yeasty awkwardness. The hop bitterness is provided by Hallertau and Tettnang, mellowed by small amounts of wheat.

Brisk and convivial, it embodies the city's terrific beer-drinking culture. Kölsch is more than just a beer style; it's the local dialect and a philosophy—a relaxed way of being, a shoulder-shrugging acceptance that *"Hatte noch immer jot jejange"* (It will be all right in the end).

Cologne's informal approach to elbow-bending is more unisex and egalitarian than any other German city, with everyone, regardless of gender or class, quaffing the Kölsch. Karl Marx was right when he famously remarked that Cologne was ill equipped to join his revolution because the bosses frequented the same pubs as their workers.

But it's this all-embracing attitude that makes Cologne the perfect place for a pub crawl. The breweries are mostly small taverns and brewpubs, all clustered within walking distance of each other, while the beers are served in a small, narrow, and session-friendly 7 fl oz glass called a *stange*.

Cologne's Kölsch bars are governed by Kobes, dry-witted waiters clad in blue aprons, who are both rude yet welcoming, and tear about their traditional wood-clad taverns, *alu-kranz* (trays) in hand, plunking Kölsch on tables before you've asked for it. And the beer, often decanted straight from the barrel, will keep coming until you leave your glass half full or place a beer mat over the top. It's marvelous.

One word of warning, don't, under any circumstances, mention the beer from Düsseldorf.

Above: Sion Kölsch is served at its eponymous Bräuhaus, a basic but welcoming place, where the walls are furnished with old beer taps and wooden barrels.

Opposite left and bottom right: Crisp, creamy, and refreshing, Gaffel can be found at the Gaffel-Haus, close to the Alter Markt in Cologne. Alfresco tables are the perfect spot to sit and people watch.

Where to Find Kölsch

Gaffel-Haus
www.gaffel-haus.de

Old, affable Kölsch tavern at the back of the Alter Markt. Creamy yet crisp Kölsch best sunk while sitting at the alfresco tables during the summer months.

Peters Bräuhaus
www.peters-brauhaus.de

Hops hang from wooden chandeliers in this big stained-glass-clad tavern that's home to more hustle and bustle than most other bars.

Sion
www.brauhaus-sion.de

Sion speaks with a hoppier accent than most. A basic, busy drinking den with old beer taps on the wall and wooden barrels on the bar. Outside drinking and a big dining area.

Früh am Dom
www.frueh.de

Vast and very popular, this is the daddy of Kölsch taverns, located at the base of the cathedral. Spread across three floors and littered with tiny alcoves—the serious drinking seems to be done downstairs.

Päffgen
www.paeffgen-koelsch.de

A lively and grandiose beer hall decked out with chandeliers, etched glass, and black wooden beams. Beer, laced with interesting spice and fruit tones, is served straight from the barrel.

Malzmuhle
www.muehlen-koelsch.de

A terrific, staunchly traditional brewpub near the Heumarkt, serving its soft, creamy Mühlen Kölsch. Bill Clinton once drank here, but didn't inhale.

Unertl Brewery
Haag, Bavaria
www.unertl.de

 **Unertl Weissbier** 4.8%

The rather grandiose-sounding Alois III is the latest member of the Unertl family to run things at this medium-sized Bavarian wheat-beer brewery. Traditional weissbier that stays steadfastly between the tracks of tangy fruit, citrus, and cloves. Not to be confused with the Unertl brewery in Muhldorf, although, as they also produce great wheat beers, it wouldn't be a disastrous error.

Unions Brewery
Munich, Bavaria
www.unionsbrau.de

Dunkel 5%

First established as a conglomerate of minor Munich breweries, Unions brewpub was shut down in the 1920s only to be reopened in 1991 in the highfalutin' area known as Hiadenhausen. Often overlooked in favor of its more sizeable city rivals, it's a brilliant beer venue renowned for its helles. But we liked its dunkel. It's great. Drink it.

Veltins
Meschede, North Rhine-Westphalia
www.veltins.de

Veltins Pilsner 4.8%

Like lager? You'll love this. A classic, clean, and crisp well-constructed Pilsner from northern Germany. Steadfastly autonomous, the family-owned brewery is a major player on the home front and has the clout and capacity to commit beyond Germany's borders.

Waldhaus
Waldhaus, Baden-Württemberg
www.veltins.de

Waldhaus Diplom Pils *Pilsner* 4.9%

Waldhaus, buried deep in the bottom of the Black Forest, has been brewing since 1833. Its Pilsner, like all its beers, is acutely aromatic, hails the hop with unashamed enthusiasm, and is lagered long and languid for maximum mouthfeel and yeast-flavor yield. The unfiltered lager, at 5.6%, is jolly special too.

Warsteiner
Warstein, North Rhine-Westphalia
www.warsteiner.de

Warsteiner Premium Dunkel 4.9%

While everyone in Germany is familiar with Warsteiner's clean, crisp flagship lager, there is no reason to miss the warming allure of its mahogany brown Dunkel, which is lesser known. Coffee, nuts, bitter chocolate, a little licorice, and vanilla are all present in this complex ale. Seek it out if you can.

Weihenstephaner
Freising, Bavaria
www.weihenstephaner.de

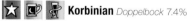

Hefe-Weiss 5.4%

The brewery has withstood all manner of religious and political tumult, not to mention secularization in 1803, to become an esteemed center of brewing education without rival. In 1852, Weihenstephan was affiliated with the university, and it's been responsible for some of the world's most accomplished master brewers. Not many, however, will be able to better this heavenly unfiltered wheat beer, with its big bready base, banana, toffee, and tropical fruit.

Hefeweissbier Dunkel 5.3%

Despite a history that's nearly a thousand years old, Weihenstephan's state-owned brewery is at the diamond-cutting edge of technology. It sources Hallertau hops, Bavarian malt, and soft local water for its beers, and still matures them for 30 days in cellars 45 feet underneath the monastery garden. On the nose its slightly toasty, with chocolate and banana notes; there are nuts and cloves on the palate and a fruity finish.

Korbinian *Doppelbock* 7.4%

The legendary brewery at Weihenstephan is the oldest in the world. Situated on a hill in the Bavarian town of Freising, the brewery site has been home to a monastery since 725, and there are records showing a hop garden here since 768. While it was likely that the "Holy Stephen" Benedictine monks brewed previously, it was 1040 when Weihenstephan was granted a license to brew officially. Korbinian is a deliciously dark brown double bock that's nutty, full of dark fruit, and with a pronounced but not overly malt signature.

Weltenburger Kloster

Bavaria
www.weltenburger.de

 **Urtyp Hell** *Helles* 4.9%

A hell from brewing heaven. Weltenburger is the oldest abbey brewery in the world and arguably the most picturesque, too. Founded in 1050 by a couple of monks named Agilus and Eustasius, it's perched on a bucolic bend on the river Danube next to the Weltenburger castle, in the shadow of huge white cliffs and chestnut trees. A sublime spot to sip on this pale, luscious medium-bodied lager brewed with Hallertau hops and lagered 120 feet beneath the brewery. Only the beers labeled "Weltenburger Kloster" are brewed here. Following a flood at the brewery in 2005, other Weltenburger beers are now made at the Bischofshof brewery in neighboring Regensburg instead.

Würzburger

Würzburg, Bavaria
www.wuerzburger-hofbraeu.de

Hofbräu Schwarzbier 4.8%

Dark lager that bleeds black into deep maroon. A cacao aroma followed by roasted chestnuts, molasses, and a hint of cream soda on the palate. When chilled, it matches marvelously with pretty much anything you care to cook on the barbecue, especially meat and fish.

 Hofbräu Sympator *Doppelbock* 7.9%

The surrounding countryside may have more vineyards than it does barley fields, but Würzburg hails the grain as much as the grape. Würzburger is housed in a 19th-century town-center site with a brewing history dating back to 1643. It's a boozy, breast-beating seasonal beer big on fruit cake flavors, tobacco, and Cognac on the nose, and a toffee-tinged finish.

Brauerei Zehendner

Mönchsambach, Bavaria
www.brauerei-zehendner.de

Mönchsambacher Lagerbier 5.5%

On the label there's a cheeky-looking monk giving a knowing, and rather smug, wink. It's little wonder he's looking so happy with himself, for this unfiltered lager is simply phenomenal. Brewed by a dinky little farmhouse brewery in a tiny, rustic town 15 miles outside Bamberg, it is gently sweet, grainy, and perfectly poised, with plenty of citrusy hops and fruity esters. Terrific.

Zum Uerige Hausbrauerei

Düsseldorf, North Rhine-Westphalia
www.uerige.de

Uerige Alt *Altbier* 4.5%

Zum Uerige is the pre-eminent Düsseldorf brewpub. It serves a classic Altbier, and in the opinion of many, the finest. Very aromatic, bright, and coppery, and bursting with both malt and hops in the bouquet, this very assertive beer would be too bitter for some were it not for the rich, dark malt platform to offset the hops. Smooth, deep and savory, the hops linger forever, a constant reminder of what is to come. The label proudly refers to its beer as *"dat leckere Dröppke"*, the delicious drop. The brewpub is nestled in the heart of the Altstadt and is the quintessential Altbier experience.

Ueriges Weizen 4.5%

Thumbing its nose at its Bavarian brethren, Ueriges proved that the hard-working north can do wheat beers as well as the sun-kissed south when it released this Weizen in 1995. Brewed using the same yeast as its other ales, it can't compare with Schneider or Erdinger in terms of spice or fruit, but it's more floral, cleaner, and crisper in its hop bitter finish. Highly refreshing.

Czech Republic

The Czech word for beer is *Pivo*. Not knowing that in the Czech Republic is akin to not knowing the Eskimo word for "Brrrrrrrrr".

Since it was annexed from wine-supping Slovakia, the Czech Republic can lay claim to being the greatest beer-drinking nation in the world, as the Czechs drink more beer than any other nation. Every citizen, on average, polishes off a staggering 92½ gallons a year, and it's easy to see why.

Czech beer can call upon not only a rich brewing heritage, but also a wealth of natural brewing resources. The world's most sought-after hop variety, the spicy Saaz, is grown in the northwest region of Žatec, while the barley hailing from the Hana plateau along the river Moravia affords Czech beer with its signature malty smoothness. And then there's the natural water, softer than anywhere else in Europe.

All these indigenous ingredients dovetailed together to magnificent effect in the autumn of 1842 when, in the brewing town of Pilsen, the first golden lager was born in a watershed moment that changed the face of beer forever. As well as inventing the first Pilsner, the Czech Republic was also brewing Budweiser beers in the town of České Budějovice long before the American Anheuser family began producing its "king" beer.

While Communist rule stifled growth and investment in Czech breweries, it also inadvertently froze traditional, time-honored brewing techniques in aspic and spared smaller breweries from the clutches of corporate conglomeration.

When the 1989 Velvet Revolution laid out a red carpet for foreign investors, a number of the Czech Republic breweries were bought by outsiders, dusted down, and dragged into the 21st century. Thankfully, more often than not, outside interference has not led to a dumbing-down in terms of quality and authenticity in the brewing process.

The Czech government, which was still the owner of Budweiser Budvar at the time of writing, still remains a major player in a market shared with SAB Miller and Anheuser-Busch InBev. This trio has a tightening grip on the nation's pubs and bars but, if you know where to look and know where to go, then you're sure to find some fantastic and fascinating pivos in the Czech Republic.

Right: A rare picture of an empty Prague pub. It surely must have been taken before opening time.

Above: The Klášterní Strahov Monastic Brewpub in Prague is near to the castle on the site of the 12th-century Strahov monastery.

Opposite center: The Czechs drink more beer per capita than any other nation in the world, and Staropramen, brewed in the city since 1869, is now one of their major international brands, owned by Anheuser-Busch InBev.

Right: The Klášterní Brewpub in Prague is home to some great beers.

Bernard

Humpolec, Vysočina
www.bernard.cz

Dark *Dark Lager* 5.1%

When in 1991 a trio of investors led by Stanislav Bernard breathed life back into a 16th-century brewery, he lent his name to a smashing selection of full-flavored unpasteurized beers. Five types of succulent malt, all sourced from the brewery's own maltings, conspire to create a slighty spicy and superbly smooth ebony-hued lager that is remarkably refreshing and delicious.

Celebration (Sváteční Ležák) *Lager* 5.1%

A fruity, estery bottle-conditioned beer with plenty of unfiltered hoppy finesse which, since Duvel-Moortgat bought a 50 percent stake in the brewery, has accumulated a strong following on the export market.

Březňák

Velké Březno, Ústí Nad Labem
www.breznak.cz

Březňák světly výcepní 14 ° 6.5%

Extensive and extravagant lagering times and open fermentation are what the Březňák brewery, one of the few to have a female brewer, is known for. This glorious golden lager gets its gloop and acute alcohol accent from four months of ageing.

FEATURED BREWERY

1 Pilsner Urquell
Pilsen *pages 140–141*

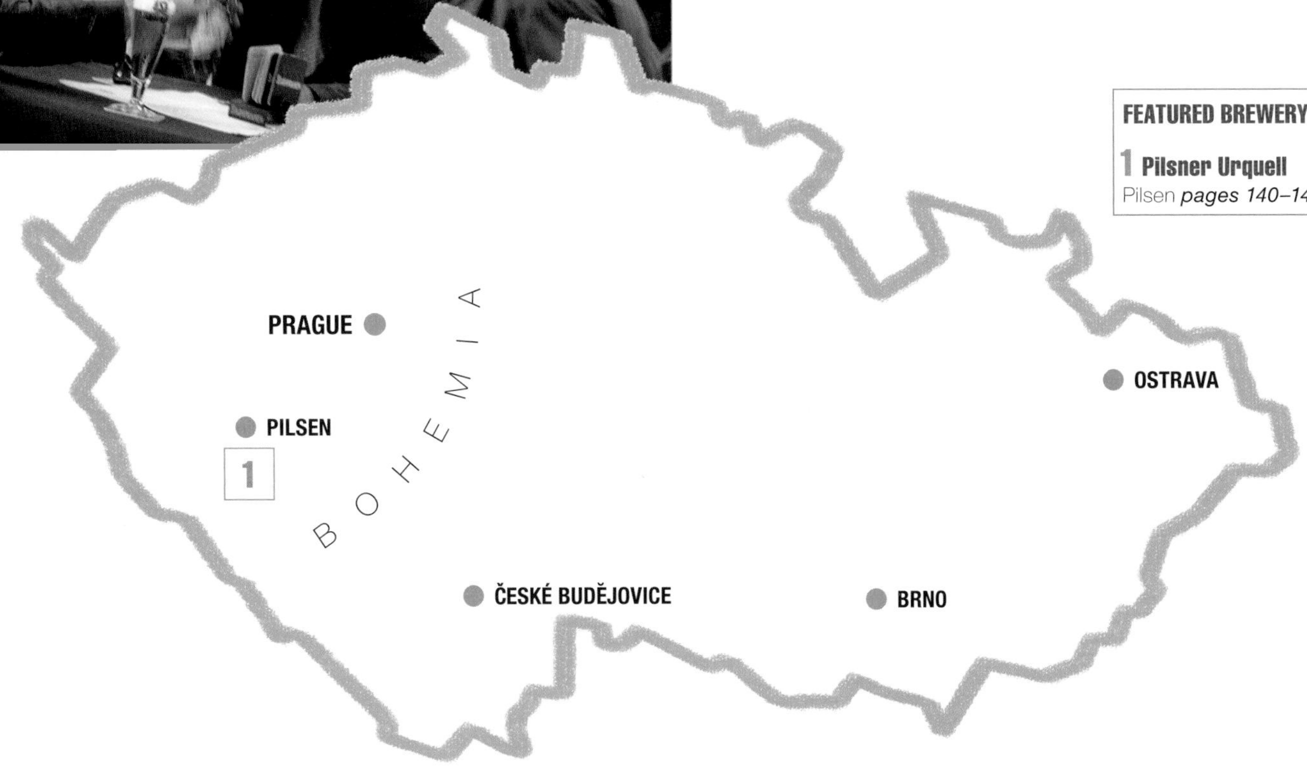

PRAGUE ●

OSTRAVA ●

PILSEN ●

BOHEMIA

1

● ČESKÉ BUDĚJOVICE

● BRNO

BUDWEISER BUDVAR

Historically, the town of České Budějovice is as significant a beer town as Pilsen, Munich, and Burton-on-Trent. In the 15th century, it was home to 44 breweries and the Royal Court brewery of Bohemia. Its beers were known as Budweisers and, due to the royal connection, as the "beer of kings".

Alas, like Pilsen, České Budějovice neglected to trademark the name of its flagship beer, and in 1845 American brewer Anheuser-Busch was able to choose Budweiser as the name of its new, bland-tasting yellow lager.

Twenty years later, the Budějovice Brewery was founded, began brewing Budvar and exporting it under the name Budweiser Budvar. This miffed those in Missouri and, more than a hundred years later and nearly as many lawsuits, the two breweries are still arguing over the Budweiser brand name.

Even though Anheuser-Busch can claim its beer preceded Budvar's beginning by two decades, the Czechs cite geographical significance and the fact that Budweiser beer had been exported by Samson, the other surviving brewery in České Budějovice, long before the Americans adopted exactly the same beer name.

Differing legal decisions have meant that both beers have had to adopt pseudonyms in countries that have ruled against them (Budvar is known as Czechvar in the United States). The situation is further complicated by ongoing speculation that a cash-strapped Czech government may soon be forced to sell the state-owned brewery, with the most likely buyer being, of course, Anheuser-Busch InBev.

Budweiser Budvar
České Budějovice, South Bohemia
www.original-budweiser.cz

 Bud Super Strong *Strong Lager* 7.6%

Aged for more than six months, this may have plenty of boozy brawn and muscular malt, but not at the expense of complex flavor. Light treacle, apricot, cinnamon, and a touch of toffee.

Dark Lager 4.7%

A dark brunette lager launched in 1994 and brewed using Munich, Crystal, and roasted malt. Coffee and chocolate character, with a touch of chicory and spice on the finish.

Kroužkovaný Ležák *Lager* 5%

Rarely encountered outside the Czech Republic, this golden kräusened lager delivers a fuller flavor and heightened hop character, thanks to the addition of yeast before bottling —affording a softer, less sparkling mouthfeel.

Premium Lager 5%

Cynics may suggest that the Czech brewery has benefited from exposure as the underdog in a global "David versus Goliath" battle but that would be an injustice to one of the world's great beers. Clever-clogs lawyers may be able to argue that Anheuser-Busch's beer was first, but there's no courtroom on the planet that can say it is better. Fermented in open vessels and cold-conditioned for three months, Budvar sets succulent biscuity malt off against a flourish of floral Žatec (Saaz) hop. Beautifully balanced.

Pivovar Černá Hora
Černá Hora, South Moravia
www.pivovarch.cz

1530 *Specialty Lager* 6.3%

The village of Černá Hora (Black Mountain) is renowned for two things: skiing and this well-respected brewery, which has been frozen in time since October 28th, 1530. Bottled golden beer launched in 2006 to celebrate the brewery's creation and, lagered longer than other Black Mountain beers, reaches its peak after three months cold conditioning.

Moravské sklepní nefiltrované *Unfiltered Lager* 4%

This hazy, hoppy unfiltered golden lager, which drinks deeper and more complex than the alcohol content would have you think, is the beer to reach for at the brewery's annual, and increasingly notorious, beer-fest.

Chodovar
Chodovar Plana, Pilsen
www.chodovar.cz

 Chodovar President 5%

The family-owned Chodovar brewery dates back to 1573 and is renowned for its labyrinth of rock cellars. In recent years, it champion beer's health-giving properties with its famous beer spa, where one's mind, body, and soul are enhanced with brewing yeast, hops, and herbs. The brewery also lends its name to beer shampoo and beer cosmetics, but the beer will make you feel and, if you drink enough, look better, too. A golden, grandiose lager that intertwines a Southern Bohemian malt signature with a Pilsner-esque hop character.

Herold
Březnice, Central Bohemia
www.heroldbeer.com

Bohemian Black Lager
Schwarzbier 5.3%

Schwarzbier in style, lagered for ten weeks, and brewed using a quartet of dark malts. Dark mahogany brown verging on black, shaped by a sturdy malt backbone. Creamy vanilla, bitter chocolate, and a long, cedary, dry smoky finish.

Traditional Czech lager 4.1%

A crisp and clean "working person's workhorse Czech lager" from a 16th-century castle brewery, located 40 miles south of Prague. Following the Velvet Revolution, its beer flourished under a new Herold name and ownership of the Research Institute of Malt and Brewing. In 1998, it was bought by American investors who have retained the traditional brewing techniques such as the hand turning of its own malt and the use of Saaz hops and well water from the park on the estate.

Jihlava Brewery
Ježek, Vysočina
www.pivovar-jihlava.cz

Jihlavský Grand 8.1%

The heavily-hopped, honey-colored, muscular malt-accented jewel in the crown of a thoroughly modernized brewery that, back in the 16th century, graced the beer glasses of Austrian royalty.

Strahov Monastic Brewery
Prague
www.klasterni-pivovar.cz

Svatý Norbert jantar *Unfiltered Lager* 5.2%

A Prague brewpub in prime position near to the castle on the site of the Strahov Monastery founded in 1140. The brewery was closed in 1907 but revived in 2000 as a modern brewpub, and is now doing a nice bit of monk-y business courtesy of some rather impressive unfiltered lagers and sought-after seasonals.

Svatý Norbert tmavý *Unfiltered Dark Lager* 5.5%

A brown-to-black beer with Munich roots, yet drier and more bitter than a Bavarian dark beer. Attenuated with whole malts and heaps of hops, it comes up with caramel, honey, and toffee-apple tones. At the brewpub, it's best drunk with the beef fillets, goose liver, and bacon.

Kout na Šumavě
Kout na Šumavě, Pilsen
http://koutske.pivni.info/

Světlý Ležák *Pilsner* 5%

What many Czech beer cognoscenti regard to be the most impressive and underrated Pilsner in the country and thus the world. Soft and spritzy with fruity yeast, a boundary-breaking bitterness, and a voluptuous, velvety malt mouthfeel. Find it if you can. Drink it. And then drink some more. A golden gift from the gods.

Tmavý Super Speciál *Dark Lager* 9%

Much to the delight of right-drinking beer lovers, Kout burst back into life in 2006 after nearly 20 years of hibernation, and this delicious, deeply drinkable dark lager is both super and special.

Royal Brewery Krušovice
Krušovice, Central Bohemia
www.pivo-krusovice.cz

Imperial *Premium Lager* 5.5%

Krušovice beers have brewed at the Imperial Brewery, 30 miles west of Prague, since 1517. In 1583 the brewery was bought by the Holy Roman Emperor Rudolf II, yet now it's under the control of the Oetker Brewing Group and has become the fifth largest brewery in the Czech Republic. This is a full-bodied, bitter hoppy lager whose popularity hasn't weakened its allure.

Krušovice Dark *Dark Lager* 3.8%

The Czech Republic's biggest-selling dark beer. Dark lager with mild hop bitterness, sweet caramel, and a hint of blackberry, reminiscent of a British Mild. Ambitious drinkers can indulge in the tradition of layering Krušovice Dark on top of the Imperial.

Pivovarský Dvůr Lipan

Dražíč, South Bohemia
www.pivovarlipan.cz

 **Světlé pivo** *Lager* 5.3%

If you're ever down in the South Bohemian town of Dražíč, then beat a path to the door of this brilliant brewpub and distillery offering bed and breakfast, big portions, a bevy of fruit brandies, and—best of all—lots of lovely yeast-laden beer. Sparkling and soft, figgy on the nose, butter and bread on the palate, and sweet on the finish.

 Tmavé pivo *Dark Lager* 5.3%

Murky maroon copper-topped dark lager that positively prances prunes and plums on the palate.

Pivovar Litovel

Litovel, Olomouc
www.litovel.cz

Kvasnicové pivo *Yeast Beer* 4.8%

A big brewery that belies its sizable stature in the shape of some impressive, finely tuned beers, of which this yeast beer, zapped with a flourish of Saaz hops and a big barley base, is arguably the finest.

Lobkowicz

Vysoký Chlumec
www.lobkowicz.cz

Lobkowicz Baron
Dark Lager 4.7%

While other small breweries have disappeared, Lobkowicz has thrived by remaining steadfast in its commitment to open fermentation, lengthy lagering below the brewhouse, and the use of its own water and environmentally friendly malt. The darker grains come to play here, providing flavor that is earthy and nutty, with a smoldering sweetness.

Lobkowicz Princ *Lager* 4%

The aristocratic Lobkowicz family who, it says here, are a pretty big deal in Bohemia, regained control of the brewery in 1992, having first brought it back into family hands in 1474. A classic Czech lager that drinks deeper than its modest strength suggests. Hoppy, clean, and crisp.

Nová Paka

Nová Paka, Hradec Králové
www.novopackepivo.cz

 Hemp Valley Beer *Pilsner* 4.5%

While Nová Paka has avoided the temptation to replace fiercely traditional brewing methods with the cost-saving measures adopted by some of its peers, it's not shy to veer off-piste with integrity. Brewed with Swiss hemp, this sweet and heady herbal Pilsner celebrates the close kinship between cannabis and the hop.

Kumburák *Lager* 5%

A wonderfully well constructed Czech lager where the lush malt and zesty, citrus hop get it on in fruity fashion. The flagship beer from a shrewd, highly rated brewery.

Ostravar

Ostrava, Moravian Silesia
www.ostravar.cz

 **Kelt** *Stout* 4.8%

Fitting for a city built on coal, Ostravar is one of the few Czech breweries to shine its headlights on dry Irish-style stout. Light espresso flavors, with a bitterness not just from the roasted malt, but from the hop, too.

Premium *Lager* 5.1%

Ostrava, the Czech Republic's third-largest city, doesn't share the pomp of Prague, but its beers are big, bustling, and brawny. Strapping lager with a biting hop bitterness draped over a tight malt trellis of rich malt.

Pivovar Pernštejn

Pardubice, Pardubice
www.pernstejn.cz

 Pardubický porter 8%

There was a time when Baltic porters blessed many Czech breweries, but then golden lagers came along and the dark beers got lost in their shadow. This peppery, suede-colored and espresso-accented porter made its name during the 19th century and hasn't lost any of its allure.

Pernštejn světlý ležák 5.2%

Of the half-dozen bottom-fermented beers that Pernštejn produces, this golden gulp, signed off with subtle sweetness, is the best showcase for the rich malt taken from the brewery's very own maltings.

Pilsner Urquell/Gambrinus

See Brewery Profile pages 136–137
Pilsen
www.pilsnerurquell.com

 Kvasnicový Pilsner Urquell
Unfiltered Pilsner 4.4%

A hazy, hallowed unpasteurized and unfiltered version of the original pilsner spruced up with a dose of young beer. Available only at the brewery (and in a select few bars) drawn from the barrel straight into the glasses of excited, privileged Pilsner drinkers.

 **Pilsner Urquell** *Pilsner 4.4%*

Before this beer was brewed in 1842, there was nothing but darkness. Saaz hops, succulent Moravian malt, triple decoction, and long lagering times combine to produce the gentle, golden, and velvet-smooth giant on whose shoulders all other lagers and Pilsners stand.

Pivovarský Dům

Prague
www.gastroinfo.cz/pivodum

Pšeničné pivo *Wheat Beer 4%*

Bohemia tends not to take on Bavaria and Belgium in the wheat beer arena, but this fruity and clove-wielding contender could hold its own.

Světlý ležák *Yeast Lager 4%*

As you'd expect from a brewpub situated below the Czech Research Institute of Malt and Brewing, Pivovarský Dům is keen on experimentation, dabbling with innovative ingredients in its seasonal beers. While these funky forays are fun, it's the traditional Czech beers, such as this grassy, grainy golden lager, that pull in the Prague punters.

Platan

Protivin, South Bohemia
www.pivo-platan.cz

Pracheňská Perla *Lager 6%*

Picturesque South Bohemian *pivovar* is surrounded by platan trees, from which the brewery gets its name. Since 2000, its eclectic beers have been in private hands, yet retained their brewing roots, which date back to 1598. With a massive mousse-like head and a honey aroma, this gloopy, golden lager is a decadent drop.

 **Platan Premium** *Lager 5%*

Pilsner-style light lager with a pristine minerally mouthfeel, clipped hop character, and very slight and sweet moreish malt. Perfect as an accompaniment to a light salad, fish, or as a crisp quencher.

Poutník

Pelhřimov, Vysočina
www.pivovarpoutnik.cz

 **Poutník Special** 5.8%

State-owned until 2001, the "Pilgrim" brewery has a turbulent history dating from the 16th century. Since 2003, new owners have secured a return to traditional Czech brewing practices with their unpasteurized beer. An amber-colored, sweet, softly sparkled special lager accented with almonds, biscuit, and traces of candy floss.

Primátor Náchod

Náchod, Hradec Králové
www.primator.cz

 **English Pale Ale** 5%

Located in the charming northeastern town of Náchod, Primator is one for the purists and the past. It's one of the few breweries in the Czech Republic still under the stewardship of the State, and hasn't strayed from traditional techniques. Bizarre as it is for a Czech brewery to brave a British beer style, this bottled pale ale succeeds with an Orval-like fruity sourness, heavy hops on the nose, and tightly packed toasty malt.

Primátor Premium 5%

Brewed by open fermentation, hops from Žatec and Moravian malt come together in an immaculately balanced crisp, herbal lager.

Rebel

Havlíčkův Brod, Vysočina
www.hbrebel.cz

 **Černý Rebel** *Dark Lager 4.7%*

Since the ancestors of the founding family took over the brewery in 1995 and administered some technical tender loving care, Rebel's beers have conformed in terms of consistency. Matured for 50 days, it's a dark brown moreish drop with strongly stewed coffee and scorched caramel on the palate.

 Rebel Tradiční *Light Lager 3.9%*

War, communism, fire, economic turmoil, a monkey with a knife—all of these, apart from the last one, have attempted to bring the brewery to its knees since it was founded in 1834. Like the Czech nationalist and rebel after whom the town is named, this light lager is a dissident, challenging the notion that beers below 4% lack finesse and flavor.

PILSNER URQUELL
SAB MILLER

U Prazdroje 7, 304 97 Pilsen, Bohemia

www.pilsnerurquell.com

"To guarantee that the beer drunk today remains true to the original Pilsner Urquell, we continuously brew a sample batch of beer that's been crafted in the traditional way using the original equipment."

VÁCLAV BERKA
BREWMASTER

If you like lager, raise your glass to Josef Groll: an inspirational rebel—he who taught the world to rise up, stare the forces of bad-tasting, badly brewed beer in the eye, and exclaim: "Enough!" Josef Groll is the man who changed the way the world sees beer. In 1842 he placed a grenade down the pants of traditional European brewing by creating the first ever golden lager in the town of Pilsen in Bohemia. Prior to this, all beer was dark, cloudy and, more often than not, a little lousy.

So lousy in fact that, three years previously, the upstanding pillars of Pilsen society had angrily emptied 36 barrels of rancid beer onto the street in front of the town hall. So disillusioned were they with the quality of the local beer, they decided to build their own brewery capable of producing bottom-fermented beer that would last longer, taste better, and blow the socks off the beer world.

While work began on the Bürgerliches Brauhaus (citizens' brewery), delegates from Pilsen were sent to England to study new malting techniques that were then being honed by English brewers, while Groll was headhunted from Bavaria, and brought to the place we now call the Czech Republic.

A more curmudgeonly and cantankerous chap you'll struggle to meet, but even Groll must have cracked a wry grin on realizing the natural tools he had before him: local Pilsen water softer than a baby's proverbial and ideal for brewing pale bottom-fermented beer; sweet Moravian barley malt; and the deliciously delicate spicy Saaz hop from the nearby Žatec region. He was also gifted a five-and-a-half-mile-long (9 kilometer) labyrinth of chilled tunnels, cut into sandy rock beneath the brewery, that were lined with oak barrels in which the lager languidly matured.

When Groll united these elements, an extraordinary alcoholic alchemy occurred. The transmutation was coppery gold, clear, sparkling, and extremely alluring. Decanted into glass vessels, a novelty at the time, its flame-like luster and indulgent fluffy white head was like nothing seen or drunk before. At a time

when all beer was darker than a coal miner's worst nightmare and drunk from pewter mugs, the prospect of a light beer was a genuinely exciting one. OK, so they may not have had BlackBerries or overhead projectors in the 19th century, but the fundamental principles of marketing still rang true, and before long everyone was reaching for the Pils.

Only 3,600 barrels were brewed in the first year, but word of Pilsner soon spread to Prague and, by the 1870s, it was audaciously rubbing shoulders with Bavarian beers in Munich and earning elbow-bending plaudits in Berlin, Paris, and London. In 1873 it became the first truly international beer when it was exported across the ocean to the United States.

In an unfortunate oversight that would have made Groll's naturally grumpy demeanor all the more unforgiving, the brewery neglected to patent the Pilsner style; so when other brewers from other countries began labeling their light-golden bottom-fermented beers as Pilsners, the original Pilsen was helpless to stop them. They were forced to add "Urquell", meaning "original source", to the name and, more than 160 years later, there are thousands of golden-hued lagers, brewed all over the world, that borrow the pilsner moniker. Today, light-colored lagers make up 80 percent of the world's beers, but the vast majority are pale imitations of the original.

Pilsner Urquell is now drunk in more than 58 countries and continues to be sourced from the brewery in Pilsen. To ensure global consistency, modern brewing techniques and technology have been embraced, but thankfully, painstaking

fidelity to the original beer remains. Brewmaster Václav Berka, a man whose only shortcut is the one he takes from the brewery to the brewery tap every evening, oversees a parallel brewing process that ensures faithfulness to the original beer is rigorously preserved.

"To guarantee that the beer drunk today remains true to the original Pilsner Urquell, we continuously brew a sample batch of beer that's been crafted in the traditional way using the original equipment," says Vaclav. "We make sure that the flavors, aromas, and mouthfeel of both beers are identical and if they are not, we do not let people drink it. No other brewer in the world does this."

What further distinguishes Pilsner Urquell from its imitators is the uncommon brewing process. Its direct-flame heating of the mash tun is used by only one other brewer in the world, and gives the beer its toasted grain bouquet, while its unwavering insistence on triple-mash decoction is both essential and rare.

The technique involves the beer being switched from mash tun to brew kettle three times at gradually rising temperatures, over the course of more than four hours. This lends the beer a fullness of body on the palate and an esoteric aftertaste.

For true lager loyalists, try to get hold of Kvasnicový Pilsner Urquell, the unpasteurized, unfiltered version of its flagship beer. Available only within a modest radius of the brewery and a few select Czech bars, Kvasnicový is a hazy, hallowed drop, best drawn straight from the barrels in the cold, dark, and damp brewery cellars whence golden beer drinking sprung.

Key Beer

Pilsner Urquell 4.4%

Regent

Třeboň, South Bohemia
www.pivovar-regent.cz

Bohemia Regent Dark Lager 4.4%

Founded in 1379, the Regent brewery is one of the oldest in the world and is named after a chap called Jakub Krčín who began life as a Rosenberg accountant and then rose to become not just regent of the large dominion of Vilem, but also the uncrowned king of the entire Bohemian Kingdom. Almost as impressive is this delicious garnet-colored, spicy hop, creamy lager that has a delightfully tasty licorice and almond finish.

Bohemia Regent Jedenáctka *Pilsner* 4.6%

When the Velvet curtain was raised in 1989, Regent was one of the first beers to shine on the international stage and, despite murmurs among purists regarding the sacrifice of traditional techniques, Regent's beers are still regarded as some of the best in South Bohemia. With grassy notes and a grainy base, this barely carbonated beer is a more worthy effort than the brewery's flagship Bohemia lager.

Bohemia Regent Prezident *Premium Lager* 6%

A pale hue of amber and unashamedly hoppy special lager brewed at a high balling rate and aimed squarely at the aficionado.

Richter Brewery

Prague
www.pivovarubulovky.cz

Richter Helles 5.1%

A new wave Prague brewpub which opened in 2004 to huge acclaim. In a marked departure from his Czech counterparts, highly skilled head brewer František Richter embraces a dazzling array of European influences, including stouts, porters, bocks, and Alts. This Helles is deep golden and lightly cloudy, treacle and spice on the nose, honey, estery fruit, and a crisp, lip-smacking finish. Delicious.

Richter Ležák *Lager* 5%

Championing the Czech tradition is this delicious deep copper-colored lager full of floral fragrance and a superb malty body.

Staropramen (Anheuser-Busch/InBev)

Prague
www.staropramen.com

Staropramen *Lager* 5%

Staropramen is the *pivo* most readily associated with Prague. It is now owned by Anheuser-Busch InBev. Brewed with Bohemian malt and Saaz hops, it resembles a Pilsner, but Prague people would never describe it as such. Rich with a buttery nose and a fine, sparky hop finish.

Svatováclavský pivovar

Olomouc, Olomouc
No web address

Weisbier/Pšeničné 5.9%

Since 2006, the Svatovaclavský brewpub has been brewing some new wave Czech beers with a difference in the Moravian student town of Olomouc and in the shadow of the famous Holy Trinity Column. Brandishing Bavarian-style bananas and bubblegum aromas, it's solid and spicy, with a wonderfully wispy white head.

Pivovar Svijany

Svijany, Liberec
www.pivovarsvijany.cz

Svijany Kníže 5.6%

Dating from 1564, the Svijany brewery has changed hands more often than a "jazz cigarette" at a Grateful Dead concert. Following nationalization, it settled down under private ownership in 1998 and has excelled with unpasteurized beers brewed by traditional means. All the beers are worth investigating, but if you like your lagers heady of hop and moreish of malt, then this is the one for you.

Pivovar U Fleků

Prague
www.ufleku.cz

Flekovský tmavý ležák *Dark Lager* 4.6%

No right-thinking beer drinker worth his malt should visit Prague without taking in the Gothic grandeur of the legendary U Fleků pub, the world's oldest brewpub dating back to 1499. It's a stylish stained-glass shrine to one of the world's finest dark beers. Behind the ink-black sheen and beneath the wonderful frothy head lies licorice, creamy mocha coffee, dark bitter chocolate, and the peppery, piquant presence of hops. So sublime, you won't notice the tourists or the oompah band.

U Medvídků
Prague
www.umedvidku.cz

 **X-beer**
Wood-aged Beer 12.8%

From this gigantic Gothic and grandiose brewpub, dating back to 1466, comes this superb, sensuous shape-shifter of a beer. Following a languid lagering period in traditional oak barrels for around seven months, it flirts with a feast of different flavors. On a vinous background lurking beneath the tightly packed head, there are vanilla, tobacco, treacle, woody resins, and a lingering finish. Sensible sipping required.

Velké Popovice
Velké Popovice, Central Bohemia
www.kozel.cz

 **Kozel Premium** 5%

Kozel means "goat" in Czech, and a comical image of one clutching a frothing tankard, designed by a French artist, adorns the brewery logo. Historically, the goat symbolizes strength and power, and is traditionally associated in Germany and Bavaria with bocks, but this fantastically floral Bohemian lager is well worth locking horns with. A very popular brew that is now owned by SAB Miller.

Pivovar Vyškov
Vyškov, South Moravia
www.pivovyskov.cz

 Jubiler 7.5%

Traditional brewery dating back to 1680 and based in the pretty South Moravian town of Vyškov. When it's not being burned down by frequent fires, Vyškov brews some terrific stuff, including this strapping strong lager, brewed at a malt sugar scale of 16:80 in commemoration of the brewery's birth. Imagine a sweet malty Oktoberfest Bavarian beer, but from Moravia.

Žatec
Žatec, Ustí Nad Labem
www.zateckypivovar.cz

 **Lučan Premium tmavé**
Dark Lager 4.3%

Chewy and creamy dark lager which churns a flurry of fruitcake, aniseed, licorice, and black currant flavors.

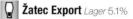 **Žatec Export** *Lager* 5.1%

Sweeter and more subtle in hops, but with a pepper-prickle on the palate sprung from a biscuit base. Now how could the town's residents export it?

 Žatec Premium *Lager* 4.9%

There can be few finer vehicles for the sensual spicy, citrusy Saaz hops than this stunning golden lager firmed up with a fantastically firm malt spine.

Zlatá Labut'
Zvíkovské Podhradí, South Bohemia
www.pivovar-zvikov.cz

 **Zlatá labut' kvasnicové pivo** 4.7%

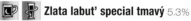

Zlatá, a bucolic brewpub located at the confluence of the Vlatva and Oltava rivers in South Bohemia, hails the ale (mostly ginger-infused), as well as some lovely, lovely lagers. Small and skilled in the science of brewing, it replicates the beers made by a brewery that was once housed in the nearby Zvikov castle, using hops from its own hop field. Aromatic and hazy yeast beer with a touch of banana to balance out the pronounced crisp bitterness.

 **Zlata labut' special tmavý** 5.3%

A brilliant blacker-than-black bottom-fermented beer with a rich presence of dry roasted coffee offset by sweet caramel and a medicinal, elixir-like finish akin to Jägermeister.

Zlatopramen
Ústí Nad Labem, Ústí Nad Labem
www.zlatopramen.cz

Zlatopramen 11 4.9%

Along with Krušovice and Satrobrno, Zlatopramen is owned by Heineken, but don't let big brewery business take away from the balance of a beer that levels the seesaw of hoppy bitterness and juicy, moreish malt. Hugely popular and, for once, understandably so.

Italy

Asking whether Italy is home to an exciting beer scene is like asking whether the Pope is a little bit partial to amusing millinery. Of all the up-and-coming brewing nations in the world, Italy is the one to watch. In fact, it's already arrived.

Having lived for so long in the brewing shadow of its more northerly neighbors, Italy now finds itself at the diamond-cutting edge of new wave brewing. It may have arrived late to the craft beer party, but it's arrived fashionably late, bikini-clad babe on each arm, before coolly tossing a set of Ferrari keys into the party bowl.

Until the appreciation of all things epicurean got the better of it, Italy had remained relatively immune to the microbrewing bug, but a craft-brewing craze that started in the early 1990s, with a few homebrewers opening brewpubs, has now mushroomed into a pioneering movement that's young, energetic, and aiming squarely at the top end of the market—well away from the Euro-fizz peddled by Italy's big brewers.

Working in close association with Italy's Slow Food movement, Italy's craft brewers often work in collaboration with local boutique artisan producers and tend to source as many indigenous—and eclectic—ingredients as possible.

The movement, which consists of more than 150 microbreweries and brewpubs, was strengthened in 1998 with the creation of Unionbirrai, a craft-brewing union designed to raise awareness of the fact that Italy is now home to some insanely inventive unpasteurized ales.

In the past ten years, the likes of Teo Musso at Birrificio Baladin and Agostino Arioli at Birrificio Italiano have taken the common perception of Italian beer, as merely an accompaniment to pizza, and sliced it into pieces. Other pioneers include Lambrate, Panil, and Birra del Borgo, although the list could go on and on and on.

● MILAN

PIEDMONT

1

● GENOA

FLORENCE ●

FEATURED BREWERY

1 Baladin
Piozzo *pages 148–149*

Right: *At Grado Plato in Chieri, Sergio Ormea, who founded the brewery in 2003, personally attends to the brewing process, making sure the copper vessels contain the right mix of ingredients.*

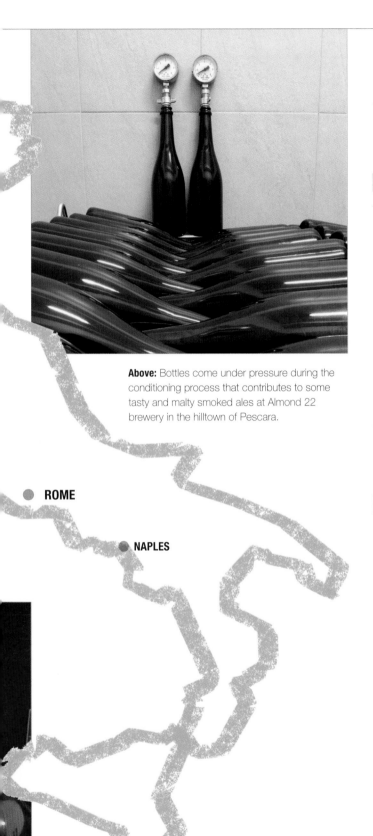

Above: Bottles come under pressure during the conditioning process that contributes to some tasty and malty smoked ales at Almond 22 brewery in the hilltown of Pescara.

ROME

NAPLES

32 Via dei Birrai
Onigo di Pederrobba, Veneto
www.32viadeibirrai.com

 **Audace** *Golden Ale* 8.4%

Award-winning Tripel-style golden ale fuming with herbal aromas, peppery pickle on the palate, and a smooth, sweet malt base. One of several terrific tipples—mostly Belgian in style—turned out by Fabiano Toffoli at his modestly-sized microbrewery that sources fresh spring water.

Almond 22
Pescara, Abruzzi
www.birraalmond.com

 **Torbata** *Smoked Ale* 6.9%

Chestnut honey, orange peel, and cane sugar joining peated smoked malt to brew a superb bottle-conditioned smoked ale from a small microbrewery in the green hills of Pescara in Abruzzi. The brewery's name refers to the year, 1922, when a legion of elderly women worked in the same building as the brewery peeling almonds to produce the world famous *confetti* of Sulmona.

Babb
Manerbio, Lombardia
www.babb.it

Omnia *Pilsner* 5.5%

Funky, forward-thinking microbrewery and brewpub-cum-restaurant near Brescia that warms up its sparse and stark interior with minimalist art, a gleaming brewery that looks as if it's been built in 2099, and a range of unusual yet first-rate beers boasting both style and substance. A Bohemia-leaning Pilsner, Babb leads with brown bready notes and a spiky, sharp hop finish.

Birrificio Baladin

See Brewery Profile pages 148–149
Piozzo, Piedmont
www.birreria.com

 **Elixir 10%**
Strong Belgian Ale 10%

This incredible Belgian ale encapsulates the cutting-edge style for which brewer Teo Musso has become renowned. Scotch whisky yeasts from Islay in Scotland are called upon in the primary fermentation, affording the beer a rampant effervescence and a fruity, flint-like dryness. Drink extremely chilled.

 Super Baladin *Strong Belgian Ale* 8%

Super indeed. Widely regarded as the jewel in Le Baladin's heavily multifestooned crown. Based on a 9th century Belgian monastic recipe and akin to a Tripel, it veers off-piste with the inclusion of English yeast and is fermented a second time in the bottle. Richly perfumed with touches of tropical fruit esters, the palate is dry and long, and warmed up with a rumlike alcohol.

 **Xyauyù** *Barley Wine* 13.5%

An "oxidized" ale, this almost defies definition as it flitters between barley wine and a dry, sherry-like Lambic. Over a period of two and a half years, Teo deliberately allows oxygen into the aging process—a technique more readily associated with sherry and port. A dry, rose-like perfume is accompanied by a touch of sourness. A truly exceptional ale.

Beba

Villar Perosa, Piedmont
www.birrabeba.it

 **Motor Oil** *Dark Beer* 8%

A blacker-than-black, coffee-colored gulp; so gorgeously gloopy, it'll leave your palate feeling like an oil-slicked seabird—but in a good way. Molasses, treacle, and a touch of vanilla. One of several outstanding beers from a Northern Italian brewery that was set up in the mid 1990s by two brothers—Sandro and Enrico Borio.

Bi-Du

Rodero, Lombardy
www.bi-du.it

 **Confine** *Porter* 6%

The Bi-Du brewpub is the brainchild of Beppe Vento. Here, close to the Italian-Swiss border and far from Shoreditch, London, Beppe has replicated a London-style porter extremely well.

 **Rodersch** *Kölsch* 5.1%

As a godfather of the Italian craft-brewing scene, Beppe has been inspired by an array of different brewing traditions and his beers have won many awards. This cool, crisp, and bitter Kölsch has a creamy biscuit palate with pear on the nose. Unfiltered.

Birra del Borgo

Borgorose, Lazio
www.birradelborgo.it

 **Ke To Re Porter** *Porter* 5.5%

In May of 2005, former college brewer and biochemist Leonardo di Vincenzo set up del Borgo in Lazio to the northwest of Rome. His brewing approach is shaped primarily by the brewing traditions of England and Belgium, and he places unusual ingredients and food compatibility at the forefront of much of what he does. This remarkable elixir is a smoky porter that's been infused with tobacco.

Il Bovaro

Florence, Tuscany
www.ilbovaro.it

Titan *Märzen* 6.3%

After a hard day drinking in Florence's rich culture, there's no better way to relax than with a beer from the city's sole microbrewery. Daniele Venturi's ales are extremely aromatic, and the citrus signature of the Amarillo hop shines through even this malty märzen mouthful.

Cittavecchia

Sgonico, Trieste, Friuli-Venezia Giulia
www.cittavecchia.com

 San Nicolò *Amber Ale* 6%

Cittavecchia was first written about by Pliny the Younger in 107 AD when he also wrote about the hop. There's nothing ancient about ex-homebrewing fanatic Michele Barro's beers, however. Since 1999, he's carved a flavorsome local niche with interesting ales packaged in the kind of stylish bottles you'd expect from a former designer. Deliciously dry, copper-colored ale spiced with cardamom.

Il Birrificio di Como

Como, Lombardy
www.ilbirrificio.it

 **Baluba** *Dark Lager* 6.9%

Hugely impressive brewpub located near Lake Como in Lombardy producing some equally impressive beers that merge tradition, off-centered ingredients, and scientific precision. A dark red lager with aromas of nougat, rose, and hazelnut, together with a rounded, spicy full-bodied palate and a long malty, earthy finish. Dried apricot, pineapple, and ginger are added during primary fermentation.

 **Birolla** *Chestnut Ale* 6.5%

Roasted chestnuts and honey harvested from local chestnut and thorn trees give this dark beer its depth of nutty character. The roasted chestnuts are added to the wort, and the thorn tree honey and chestnut tree honey are added to the maturation tank. Honey is also used to spark secondary fermentation.

Grado Plato

Chieri, Piedmont
www.gradoplato.it

 Chocarrubica
Oatmeal Stout
7%

This is a voluptuous, big-boned black beer filled out with an enormous amount of oats in the grist. The addition of Venezuelan cocoa beans sourced from Sicily give the beer its silky, chocolatey, and roast character.

 **Strada san Felice**
Amber Ale 8%

A tiny brewpub that's been brewing beautiful big and balanced beers since 2003 when it was founded by Sergio Ormea. A dry and nutty light orange bottom-fermented beer brewed with chestnuts sourced locally from the Piedmont region and dried over an open fire.

Birrificio Italiano

Lurago Marinone, Lombardy
www.birrificio.it

 **Fleurette**
Spiced Beer 3.7%

Agostino Arioli set up his brewpub in Northern Italy in 1994. This soft, subtle splash brims over with immense aromatics and deep flavor courtesy of citrus bee honey, elderberry, black pepper, whole roses, and violets laid over a grain blanket of rye, barley, and wheat.

Scires *Kriek* 7%

Disillusioned with the humdrum domestic brewing scene, passionate gastronome Agostino Arioli has been inspired by what he has seen across the Atlantic and instructed by a stint working in a brewery in Germany, founded his own venture with his brother Stefano and a few pals. The brewpub is renowned for incredible food and a range of remarkable beers that run a gamut of Italian styles and native ingredients. This sensational, sour dark ale whose cherry and almond flavor is intensified and mellowed with the addition of wood chips, wild yeast, and—at the end of primary fermentation—a dose of fresh wort and ale yeast that sparks a four-month refermentation in the bottle. The resulting brew is one well worth waiting for.

Tipopils *Pilsner* 5.2%

If you like your Pilsners with a hardened hop character, then you'll lap up this wonderfully bitter and dry bottom-fermented beauty. An exquisitely constructed interpretation of Pilsner, this rekindles one's faith in a much-mistreated and maligned beer style.

"Let us drink for the replenishment of our strength, not for our sorrow."

CICERO
PHILOSOPHER & ORATOR 106–43 BC

BIRRIFICIO BALADIN

Piazza 5 Luglio, 15, 12060 Piozzo, Piedmont

www.birreria.com

Jesus may have turned water into wine, but Teo Musso at Le Baladin has gone one step further—by changing beer into wine, according to Ted Thomas.

At his bar in Piozzo, a small village high up in the Piemontese hills above Barolo wine country, he proffers a glass of Xyauyù, a dark, almost black powerfully alcoholic ale that has spent 18 months sitting outside in a container in the courtyard at the brewery. Exposure to air has led to the beer going through a period of oxidization, which in most cases is sudden death to beer, but here the process has alchemically altered the beer in the most sensational way—it has gone through the valley of shadow and death, and come out totally transformed.

Viscous and limpid in the glass, it is warming and sherry-like on the palate, complex, and blessed with a restrained but comfortable sweetness: an elegant and esoteric beer that has taken on the character of wine. It is strong, 13.5% ABV in strength, and the drink-by date on the bottle says, to be consumed by the end of the world. Clearly, Musso is a man with his eyes firmly fixed on beery nirvana.

Even though wine is king in the country of Italy, craft beer is taking pot shots at the throne, especially in the style bars and brewpubs springing up in the north. Even though many will reach for their Peroni or Moretti bottles whenever the subject of Italian beer crops up, this growing band of breweries and brewpubs is challenging the old hegemony.

Baladin, which has been going since 1996, is often seen as the star of the show, with Musso as its leading light. He certainly has the aura of a man who believes his own publicity ("he is the Jim Morrison of beer," says Italian beer writer Maurizio Maestrelli). He is tall and rangy, draped in a long scarf, leather-jacketed, stick thin, heavily stubbled, and blessed with the sort of distressed, windswept hair that must take forever to do in the morning. Even though he's in his early forties, there's

a boyishness about him, an enthusiasm, a sense of adventure or exploration, plus an easy charisma—he greets people in his bar with the sureness of one of those infuriating people who seem to have limitless self-confidence.

The home of Baladin's beery nirvana is the eponymous bar where the brewery first began. Up until 2008 the beer was created in a stand-alone site across the village square and down a side street. Now this is solely for experimental beers, with the regulars being created elsewhere in the village.

Eighty-five percent of Baladin's beers are bottled because Musso believes that this is the best way to present his beer, especially when it appears on the beer list of smart restaurants. Many hail him as a genius, though others of a more conventional stripe might think some of his ideas thoroughly crazy. For a start, most of the fermenting vessels have headphones attached to them. This is due to Musso's belief that, as yeast is alive, it can respond to music, in the way newborn babies like a spot of Mozart. There is even a tango guitarist who has composed movements for the different phases of fermentation.

Along with the regulation barley and hops, various spices, chocolate, coffee beans, and even myrrh go into the brewing pot, while top-fermenting yeasts are joined by strains that usually work with whiskey or wine. Then there is Musso's latest creation, the Casa Baladin, which is a beer restaurant and hotel across the square from the bar, a unique stronghold of beer cuisine and seven luxuriant rooms all individually decorated to a theme. "I want to transmit experiences to people," he says.

In the cellar at the Casa Baladin is beery heaven. This is the sort of room that would be an ideal winter's night experience

Key Beers

Brune *Stout* 4.7%
Nöel *Old Ale* 9%
Super Baladin *Strong Belgian Ale* 8%
Elixir *Strong Belgian Ale* 10%
Xyauyù *Barley Wine* 13.5%

with a glass of the brewery's chestnut-colored Nöel Baladin to hand, sumptuous seasonal Christmas ale that has become so popular it is now brewed all year. In keeping with Musso's brewing contrariness, however, the recipe is changed annually. The 2007 vintage that I tried had coffee beans in the mix, while 2006 had chocolate added. He never knows what the following year will see in his beer.

Challenging perceptions of what beer is and can be is what Musso is about. His Belgian-style witbier Isaac has a tart, sourish edge to the palate; Elixir is an abbey-style ale that is fermented with Scottish distillers' yeast, while Nora contains gingerroot and myrrh, and is hopped as lightly as Italian brewing laws will allow—it's weird, but absolutely delicious. The Italian spirit of adventure and inspiration that drove the likes of Marco Polo and da Vinci are very much alive in Teo Musso. "Every week I think in my head of a new beer and every two months I try and brew one" he says. "A new taste is like a new way of communicating with people. My beers try to communicate new flavors and aromas to people. I never get bored with brewing. I am like a volcano spewing out new ideas. I could never be a wine producer because there I could only expect to be creative once a year, while in beer you can be creative all the time."

Opposite right: Teo Musso is a leading light of the Italian craft-beer movement.
Above left: Musso creates his new brews in Piozzo, high up in the Piedmont hills.
Above right: Sampling one of Baladin's fine brews is one of life's great beery pleasures.
Right: Xyauyù and Super Baladin are among the brewery's highly regarded ales.

Birrificio Lambrate

Milan, Lombardy
www.birrificiolambrate.com

 **Ghisa** *Smoked Stout* 5%

Milan's most eminent brewpub was founded in 1996, in a railway station, and is home to eight excellent ales, of which this jet-black beer, dry like an Irish stout with the smokiness of a gentle German Rauchbier, is the most intriguing. Fabulous with smoked cheese and fish—not at the same time, though.

 Montestella *Kölsch* 4.9%

Cleverly straddling Kölsch and Pilsner styles, it's crisp and floral, with a delicate depth of flavor and a glorious winking white head. Its noticeable bitterness makes it excellent with food.

Birreria Menabrea

Biella, Piedmont
www.birramenabrea.com

Menabrea 1846 *Lager* 4.8%

Old-school Italian brewer based in Biella, a small town with a history of wool trading at the base of the Italian Alps. Founded by brothers Antonio and Gian Battista Caraccio in 1846, it was sold to Giuseppe Menabrea in 1864 and, after passing from father to son for generations, still remains in the hands of the Menabrea family. This extremely clean-tasting lager has a decisive, business-like bitterness. Slightly floral notes on the nose and sweet on the finish, with a high-quality thirst-quenching capability.

Menabrea Christmas Ale 5.2%

An accomplished Christmas ale, full of fruitcake and fig flavors, that gets its depth of Christmas character from maturation beneath the brewery in Slovenian oak barrels.

Menabrea Strong Ale 7.5%

For the first hundred years or so of its existence, this double-malt Munich lager was the beer on which Menabrea's success was built, and it certainly has the skills to pay the bills: dark bronze with a poised balance of caramel malt and restrained hop bitterness. Well rounded.

Maltovivo

Capriglia, Irpina
www.maltovivo.it

 **Noscia** *India Pale Ale* 6%

As well as citrusy Cascade hops and earthy bitter Golding hops, this well-appointed IPA from the Amalfi coast is enhanced with the addition of smoked malt to the mix. Sweet honey, tobacco, and a touch of dried apricot are all present in the brew.

Birrificio Montegioco

Montegioco, Piedmont
www.birrificiomontegioco.com

 **Dolii Raptor**
Strong Barrel-aged Beer 8.5%

Riccardo Franzosi, the star of Italy's exciting craft-brewing scene, set up this brewery in 2006. This dark ale is aged in Barbera wine barrels for more than half a year and given added gusto with the addition of wine yeast. Dark amber in color, its nose gives off prunes, apricot, and sweet hazelnut.

Montegioco Draco *Barley Wine* 11.5%

The sensational malt-accented beers brewed by Franzosi are all packaged attractively in tissue paper à la Liefmans in Belgium. Draco is the brewery's particularly potent barley wine brewed with fresh blueberries, a variety of barley and wheat malt, and fermented not once, not twice, but thrice. Aromas of honey, toffee and fall fruit, with a peppery hop bitter finish all contribute to this stunning brew. The blueberry influence is restrained.

Birra Moretti

Udine, Friuli-Venezia Giulia
www.birramoretti.it

La Rossa *Doppelbock* 7.2%

Founded in Udine in 1859 by Luigi Moretti, this large regional brewer is now a major Italian player on both the national and international markets, principally on the back of its accessible and accomplished Pilsner. It's the richer, darker, and roastier stablemate, however, that's all the more appealing. The chap on the label, a chubby Vincent Van Gogh lookalike, was photographed in 1942, but his identity is still unknown.

Birrificio Panil
Torrechiara-Parma, Emilia-Romagna
www.panilbeer.com

 **Barriqueè**
Sour Red Ale 8%

A marvellous microbrewery in Provincia di Parma—"the larder of Italy" and home to some of the finest food and drink in the world. Son of a winemaker and biology boffin, Renzo Lossi began brewing at his father's winery in 2000 and much of what he does with beer is garnered from grape-based techniques such as wood barrel–aging and the use of sparkling wine yeast. Barriqueè is a moreish sherry-like, sour brew deliberately infected with lactobacillus bacteria and aged in oak for a period of more than 16 weeks.

Panil Enhanced
Strong Belgian Ale 9%

A lovely light blond liquid with an enlivening effervescence and dry fruity esters courtesy of the "spumante" wine yeast. Smoke on the nose, burnt marshmallow malty in the mouth, and earthy, grassy bitterness brought to the finish by English whole hop flowers.

Peroni
Rome
www.peroni.it

Peroni Gran Reserva *Bock* 6.6%

If you're wondering where Nastro Azzurro is, then I'm afraid we ran out of room. Instead, we've opted for this superior malty bock-like lager, created to celebrate Peroni's 150th anniversary. Malty yet with a crisp hop bitterness, it's ideal for washing down a big plate of spaghetti and meatballs.

Piccolo Birrificio
Apricale, Liguria
www.piccolobirrificio.com

 **Chiostro** *Belgian-style Abbey Ale* 5%

A small micro located in the idyllic town of Apricale in Northern Italy. Having come on line in 2005, owners and brewers Lorenzo Bottoni and Roberto Iacono have sourced the local region for interesting ingredients and are renowned for thinking outside the brewing box. Wormwood, the wayward and mayhem-inducing ingredient in absinthe, is used as a spice in this Belgian-style abbey ale, to fine, citrusy effect.

White Dog Brewery
Rocanetta di Giuglia, Modena
www.whitedogbeer.com

White Dog IPA 5.4%

The White Dog Brewery, run by ex-pat Brits Steve and Kelly Dawson, is situated in a 17th-century stone building in the Apennines, between Bologna and Modena. It specializes in hoppy bottle-conditioned and cask-conditioned English ales. This, the hoppiest, is a golden, citrusy, and slightly sweet, splashed with gentle carbonation.

"Sometimes when I reflect back on all the beer I drink I feel ashamed—then I look into the glass and think about the workers in the brewery and all of their hopes and dreams. If I didn't drink this beer, they might be out of work and their dreams would be shattered. Then I say to myself, 'It is better that I drink this beer and let their dreams come true than be selfish and worry about my liver."

JACK HANDEY
AMERICAN COMEDIAN, 1949-

Denmark

Amager Bryghus

Kastrup, Sjœlland
www.amagerbryghus.dk

The Amager Bryghus has been instrumental in transforming Denmark's brewing landscape. Having caught the brewing bug in the early 1990s as part of a college project, the Amager team vowed to create their own brewery. Life, however, got in the way, and it wasn't until 2002 that the dream was rudimentarily realized in the shape of a homemade hand brewing plant in a cellar. Unfettered experimentation followed and, in 2005, Amager found itself on the podium at the Danish Homebrewing Championships and, inspired by drinkers' delight, a foray into full-time was made. Inspired by the US brewing scene, Amager is now a byword for big, bombastic yet balanced beers that take no prisoners.

Dragør Tripel 9%

Yeast is allowed to run riot on the light malt background of this gloopy, golden gulp. Fabulous exotic fruit—mango, passionfruit, and jackfruit —and a smattering of strawberries.

Hr. Frederiksen *Imperial Stout* 10.5%

Goodness, they've gone crazy with the malts in this beer. Eight different varieties were used, and it is the dark and heavily roasted ones that give the beer its blacker-than-black color and its enormously chewy, voluptuous mouthfeel. At 81 IBU, it's remarkably bitter, like an espresso on steroids.

Imperial Stout 10.1%

Warning. This is not a drill. Repeat. Unless you are a seasoned extreme beer enthusiast with an unhealthy infatuation for IBUs and blisteringly radioactive roasted bitterness, then put this beer down and step away.

Rated XX *Imperial India Pale Ale* 9%

Hailed by Amager as something "SERIOUSLY not suited for kids," this hop monster contains, wait for it: Zeus, Mittelfruh, Brewers Gold, Crystal, Simcoe, Perle, Mount Hood, Hersbrucker, Challenger, Fuggles, Liberty, Styrian Goldings, Columbus, Chinook, Amarillo, Bramling Cross, East Kent Goldings, Willamette, Palisade, and Saaz hops (and breathe out). That's 20 hops. An immense, mouth-scrunching IPA, this tastes like liquid potpourri. It is a staggering feat of brewing.

Bøgedal Bryghus

Vejle, Syddanmark
www.boegedal.com

 **Bøgedal Nr** Various %

Brewer Casper Vorting, who makes some of the most expensive beers in Denmark, oversees Scandinavia's sole all-gravity brewhouse and is renowned for championing "Goodbeer", Denmark's rather aptly named traditional beer style. All Casper's beers are brewed to the same formula, but the vagaries of the process mean that no two beers are the same and are distinguished using a numbering system that renders tasting notes obsolete. If you see it, drink it.

Brøckhouse

Hillerød, Hovedstaden
www.broeckhouse.dk

Brøckhouse Epic Stout 10%

An old-style microbrewery near Hillerød to the north of the Danish capital, overseen by Allan Puisen, who in 1996 began brewing beer on a homemade 10.5 gallon (40-liter) copper set in his basement. This stout has an intense aroma of wine-like fruitiness, bitter chocolate, and dark caramel, a pitch-black color and beige bouffant foam head.

Brøckhouse Esrum Kloster
Herb and Spice Beer/Abbey Beer 7.5%

Developed in conjunction with the Esrum cloister, this is a faithful replica of monastery beer from the Middle Ages. It is brewed with a base of wheat, barley, and rye, and Allan adds hops, cane sugar, herbs, lemon balm, meadowsweet, lavender, rosemary, juniper, and anise—all growing in Esrum's herb garden. Aromatic to say the least.

Brøckhouse IPA 6%

Allan Puisen's handcrafted approach to brewing using esoteric ingredients has remained steadfast despite the expansion of his brewery since the early days. This is a very strong hoppy brew that makes full use of Pilsner, caramel, and Munich malt; a residual sweetness softens the prickly, piney presence of three different types of hop.

Carlsberg

Copenhagen, Hovedstaden
www.carlsberg.com/www.carlsberg.dk

 Semper Ardens Abbey Ale *Dubbel* 7.3%

It's sad that this once-pioneering brewery is now associated with mainstream lagers. However, innovation lives on in the shape of the "Semper Ardens" (Always Burning) initiative, with collaborations between Carlsberg's brewmasters and leading Danish gastronomes. This dark, aromatic ale brewed with Müncher malt, caramel malts, and roasted chocolate malt gives way to black currant, apricot, chocolate, anise, and orange.

Bryggeriet Djævlebryg

Copenhagen, Hovedstaden
www.djaevlebryg.dk

 **Son of Nekron** *Porter* 6.5 %

The "Devil's Brewery" began in 2002 as a hobby but after gaining plaudits among the discerning Danish homebrew crowd, the Devil went to work professionally in 2006. Anything but sweetness and light, Djævlebryg's drops are lords of darkness, bitterness, and smoke. Peaty porter brewed with peat smoked malt, roasted malts, and Muscovado sugar, and swathed in chocolate, coffee, and smoky chipotle sauce.

Eastcoast Brewing

Tureby, Sjælland
www.eastcoast.dk

Eastcoast Brewing Imperial Stout 9%

Formerly known as Ellebryg, Eastcoast Brewing is an up-and-coming Danish brewery best filed under "ones to watch". This, its biggest beer, is a seriously toasty fellow with licorice, chocolate, and chipotle.

Eastcoast Sommer Blond 8.9%

Brewed using a Belgian house yeast, it is fabulously fruity with melon, pear, peach, and lychee. Sweet yet strong, like King Kong in a tutu.

Fuglebjerggaard Gardbryggeri

Helsinge, Hovedstaden
www.fuglebjerggaard.dk

 **Kølster Bryg No. 65 Hojsommer** *Saison* 5%

A fabulously resourceful farmhouse brewery, whose brewer vows not to veer far in its search for brewing materials. With its own malting and organic grain, and a commitment to Danish hops, it's a real "think local, drink local" operation. So this traditional beer is brewed using Danish hops, organic spelt, wheat, and barley malt all sourced from the farm.

Halsnæs Bryghus

Hundested, Sjælland
www.halsnaesbryghus.dk

Halsnæs Rode Ran 6%

At the time of writing, brewer Peter Sonne was in the process of setting up his own brewery on the harbor in Hundested, having brewed his beer at the Herslev brewery. Here's hoping that his beers will be as good as this red ale brewed using cara red malt. Sweet but not sickly, and very fruity—raspberry, cherry, and plum.

Hancock Bryggerierne

Skive, Midtjylland
www.hancock.dk

 Old Gambrinus Dark *Doppelbock* 9.5%

A small, independent microbrewery which is enamored of Bohemia's bottom-fermented beers and specializes in lovely lagers. Hancock's beers are brewed at low gravity with long lagering times (between seven weeks and a year) at extremely low temperatures, and showcase the Saaz hop in style. A rich, dark, and plumlike Doppelbock brewed with lager malt.

Herslev Bryghus

Herslev, Sjælland
www.herslevbryghus.dk

Herslev Four Grain Stout 7%

Family-owned farmhouse brewery situated in the small village of Herslev near Roskilde and founded in 2004. The brewery has been growing steadily on the back of its unfiltered, unpasteurized, and naturally effervescent ales, renowned for being brewed with an assortment of different grain types. Barley, rye, wheat, and oats combine in this dark, creamy churn of chocolate and coffee. There is a big bitterness, too.

Herslev Hvede *Hefeweizen* 5.8%

Traditional south German Weizen brewed using a mixture of wheat, malt, and barley sourced from Bamberg, Bavaria. Subdued bitterness allows the full fruity flavors and aromas to frolic and funnel their way to your nose.

Herslev Pale Ale 5.9%

Big mouthfeel and wonderful softness from the use of oats, while Amarillo delivers a highly aromatic, bitter finish. Ideal for spicy food.

Herslev Pilsner 5.5%

Malt and hops from Bavaria give a distinctively Germanic flavor to this crisp, bitter Pilsner. All the full malt and bitter hops you'd hope for.

Hornbeer

Hyllinge
www.hornbeer.dk

 **Caribbean Rumstout**
11%

This seriously strong stout is aged in oak after it's brewed using toasted malt, smoked malt, coffee, and a dash of rum.

 Hornbeer Røgøl *Rauchbier/Smoked Beer* 5.7%

An acquired taste that you may, or may not, feel like acquiring. An intensely smoky sip brewed using six barley malt, wheat malt, and Saaz hops. A loving companion to smoked ham and cheese.

Hornbeer Russian Imperial Stout 8.1%

It's difficult to decide what is more impressive: Jorgen Fogh Rasmussen's huge range of incredibly innovative ales or the wonderful labels, designed by his artist wife, which adorn them. Either way, having burst onto the burgeoning Danish brewing scene in 2008, Hornbeer is well worth checking out. Seriously smooth-operating stout brewed using peat smoked malt and Colombian coffee.

Bryghus Horsens

Horsens, Midtjylland
www.bryghushorsens.dk

Horsens Imperial Oaked Stout 8.2%

A bucolic brewpub and café situated beneath the timbers of a listed 18th-century house. Created in 2006, it's earned a reputation for beers that are traditional with a twist. Horsens' black-as-coal stout has an IBU of more than 80 and a touch of vanilla and cream on the palate. Coffee, chocolate, and dark toasty malt flavors.

Horsens Julebryg *Strong Ale/Barley Wine* 7.5%

A Christmas beer enriched with extra malt and a flurry of festive goodies including orange, cinnamon, and raisins.

Indslev Bryggeri

Nørre Åby, Syddanmark
www.indslevbryggeri.dk

Indslev Sort Hvede *Hefeweizen* 6.5%

The Indslev brewery officially dates back to 1897, but in the 1970s it stopped brewing and began making soft drinks, before losing its fizz and closing in 1990. Anders Busse Rasmussen, a descendant of the original brewer, jump-started the brewery and now specializes solely in wheat beers brewed in a 2,000-liter brewhouse by Bavarian brewmaster Stefan Stadler. A full-bodied, toffee-ish beer with a banana aroma.

Jensens Bryghus

Juelsminde, Midtjylland
www.jensensbryghus.dk

Jensens Brown Ale 5%

Growing rustic farmhouse brewery in Jutland founded by Frede Jensen in 2006. Mahogany-colored, light toasted malt, and sweet caramel. Ballerina-like balance.

Jensens Strong Lager 6%

The beer that Carlsberg Special Brew likes to think it is. Caramel, butterscotch, subdued alcohol on the nose, and enough hop bitterness to break up the syrupy body.

Bryghuset Kragelund

Silkeborg, Midtjylland
www.bryghusetkragelund.dk

Kragelund American Pale Ale 5.5%

A small-batch brewer that is owned by 150 local Silkeborg shareholders and specializes in American-influenced cutting-edge craft beer styles. Piney pale ale crammed with Cascade. Sprinkled malt sweetness on the grapefruit flavor.

Kragelund Natmand Havre Stout 6.8%

A black, flint-dry all-grain stout that is unashamed in its deep, dark malt signature. Mouth-filling oats and chocolate malt make for a "thinking man's" milkshake.

Mikkeller

See Brewery Profile pages 156–157
www.mikkeller.dk

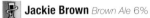 **Beer Geek Breakfast** *Espresso Stout* 7.5%

The beer that put Mikkeller on the world brewing map. A full-bodied, well-hopped oatmeal stout brewed with gourmet coffee.

Beer Geek Breakfast "Weasel" *Espresso Stout* 7%

See above. Just add coffee brewed with weasel droppings. No. Really.

Big Worse *Barley Wine* 12%

A no-nonsense, aggressively astringent American barley wine that eyeballs you up close with heaps of seriously citrusy American hops.

Jackie Brown *Brown Ale* 6%

A lot of brown ales can be a little one-dimensional, but this is not one of them. There are different shades of brown in here, and the use of fresh hops late in the boil gives it an added complexity. A fine all-rounder ale.

Monk Elixir *Quadrupel Belgian Ale* 10%

A sensational, seriously strong celestial liquor inspired by the Belgian Trappist habit of brewing big beers that showcase fruity yeast flavors, grainy malt, and medicinal herbal hop character. Ideal for laying down.

Nørrebro Bryghus

Copenhagen, Hovedstaden
www.nørrebrobryghus.dk

 Ceske Bomber *Pilsner* 5%

A beautifully balanced beer, created in the Bohemian mold, from a brilliant Copenhagen brewpub founded in 2003. Brewer Anders Kissmeyer is widely recognized for the quality and quirkiness of his beer.

North Bridge Extreme *Imperial India Pale Ale* 9.5%

Hugely hoppy American-style IPA with a nose-bleeding IBU count. Best drunk after you've tried everything else since it'll knock out your tastebuds, so they won't be getting up anytime soon.

Old Odense Ale *Sour Ale* 7.5%

Brewed in conjunction with Sam Caglione of the Dogfish Head Brewery in Delaware, USA. Seasoned with milfoil, star anise, short lip, and woodruff, it has a tartness that will tilt your head sideways.

Pacific Summer Ale

Pacific Summer Ale 5.6%

Brewed in association with Brooklyn Brewery's Garrett Oliver, this pale ale showcases aromatic North American hops in style. Crisp, spicy, and fairly bitter with a long-lasting finish of pine needles.

Skärgaards Porter 6%

A proper porter brewed in association with Nynäshamms. Smooth and elegant, with a palate of chocolate and creamy coffee.

Odder Bryghus

Odder, Midtjylland
www.odderbryghus.dk

Esthers Hvede *Weissbier* 5.6%

After years of homebrewing, Frank Lund turned pastime into profession in 2008 and, in a new 400-liter English brewhouse, crafts impressive beers that are unpasteurized, unfiltered, and refermented in the bottle. Fruity Germany yeast esters occupy the front seat of this hazy Bavarian-style weizen, one of his key beers.

Raasted Bryghus

Råsted, Midtjylland
www.raastedbryghus.dk

Raasted Brown Ale 5.5%

English-style brown ale brewed with Fuggles and East Kent Goldings. Earthy hop character gives the malt room to maneuver in the mouth.

Raasted Imperial Stout 10%

When Martin Jensen launched Raasted in 2005, he wasn't just the new kid on Denmark's brewing block, he was, at the tender age of 24, the youngest. There's nothing naïve about his beers, however, brewed on a brewhouse he built himself in a former dairy. Deep black beer with brusque, verging on brutal, bitterness courtesy of four American hops— Chinook, Centennial, Amarillo, and Cascade—the last being used in a late hopping part of the brewing process.

Raasted India Pale Ale Cascade 5.5%

American-style IPA whose body is swelled with some residual malt sweetness and estery fruit flavors. Present are spicy citrus tones with a hint of elderflower, courtesy of Centennial and Cascade.

Raasted Tripel 8.5%

Golden abbey ale brewed with light cane sugar, coriander, orange peel, and the wonderfully fruity Westmalle yeast.

Randers Bryghus

Randers, Midtjylland
www.randersbryghus.dk

Pale Ale 5.5%

Hops, spices, specialty malts, and traditional brewing methods are at the forefront of this 1,000-liter brewery run by brothers Stefan and Kristian Kappel. An Anglo-American-European ale that uses aroma hops from the United States, English yeast, and malt from Continental Europe. Honey, lemon, and lychee all make an appearance.

MIKKELLER

Slien 2, 2. t.v., DK-1766,
Copenhagen V, Hovenstaden

www.mikkeller.dk

**So. Here's the thing. In Indonesia there's
a weasel called a luwak and that means it
may not be a good idea to "wake up and
smell the coffee."**

Otherwise known as a civet or a musang, the luwak is a small
wild, nocturnal mammal much like a mongoose. Thanks to
a noxious odor excreted from its scent glands, situated near
its anus and bearing an uncanny resemblance to testes,
many people associate it closely with the skunk species on
stinkiness alone.

Expert climbers who spend
their lives in trees, these animals

eat small vertebrates, insects, ripe fruits, seeds, and palm sap,
but it's a fondness for coffee berries that is responsible for
luwaks making a rare cameo appearance in a book on beer.

You see, while the outer fruit of the berries is digested, the
coffee beans are passed through the luwak's digestive tract
untouched and excreted as part of
the animal's droppings. The caffeine-
carrying excrement is then collected by

farmers before the resulting cleaned green beans are roasted, sold for as much as $600 per lb, and—this is the crucial bit—used to brew one of the world's strangest yet most sought-after beers.

Danish brewer Mikkel Borg Bjergsø, the man behind the marvelously maverick Mikkeller beers, uses 15½ pounds of Kopi Luwak coffee beans in every 1,057 gallons of an awe-inspiring imperial oatmeal stout called Beer Geek Breakfast (Weasel).

"We brew the coffee in pots and pour it into the beer the day before we bottle it," says Mikkel who, in his thirties and with chiseled Scandinavian features, certainly doesn't look like a brewer. "It costs a lot and makes the beers hugely expensive, but it's worth it."

Even in these days of epicurean adventuring, with brewers unafraid to experiment with unusual ingredients such as gooseberries, Merlot grapes, hemp, poppies, and nettles, it's an outrageous, out-there ale.

Mikkel doesn't even have his own brewery. To avoid being shackled by overheads, Mikkel chooses to trot the globe like a hedonistic hobo, collaborating with the cream of craft brewing and borrowing their brains and equipment to create his unique beers.

"What I find is that I can make a range of different styles by going to the breweries that have a strength in that style," he says. "I rent the equipment and have a good relationship with the whole of the brewing community. I don't have to brew beer that sells well. I just brew beer that I like, as there's very little financial risk. I can think

of flavor rather than customers. It's a huge freedom."

Standing out from the crowd is an oft-repeated mantra among new wave brewers, and it's one that Mikkel, standing knee-deep in Indonesian weasel doo-doo without a home to go to, or many bills to pay, certainly embodies.

"I started homebrewing five years ago," he says. "Throughout the 1990s I had been drinking awful fizzy beer and not thinking about it, but I was really fed up with what was going on in Denmark and was disillusioned with the lack of choice."

Mikkeller's small-batch output is prolific. In 2008 it launched 25 new beers in conjunction with some of the world's most exciting craft brewers, including Cantillon in Belgium, Nøgne Ø in Norway, Brewdog in Scotland, Stone and AleSmith in San Diego, and Jennings in the United Kingdom.

Having begun brewing only in 2003 and still earning a living as a part-time chemistry teacher, he currently enjoys hallowed status among the hardcore beer drinking community for his unfettered experimentation and audacious approach.

Inspired by the eclectic approach of American breweries, Mikkeller runs a huge gamut of styles, including Californian-style Belgian Tripels, chili-infused imperial stouts, Lambics, beers aged in Calvados barrels, smoked ales and single-hop IPAs made with Simcoe and Black which, at 17.5%, is the strongest beer ever brewed in Denmark. His beers are now sent to the USA, Japan, Belgium, and England and he is rated the sixth best brewer in the world.

Opposite above: Mikkel tastes one of his brews at the Nørrebro brewhouse in Copenhagen, where some of his beers are prepared.
Left: Mikkeller's beers are audacious, award-winning adventures in brewing.
Right: Beer Geek Breakfast comes with or without Indonesian luwak droppings.

Key Beers

Beer Geek Breakfast *Espresso Stout* 7.5%
Stateside IPA 7%
Jackie Brown *Brown Ale* 6%
Monk's Elixir *Quadrupel Belgian Ale* 10%
Big Worse *Barley Wine* 12%

Skagen Bryghus

Skagen, Nordjylland
www.skagenbryghus.dk

 Skagen Skawskum *Dunkel* 5%

A micro established in 2005 in an old power station located in Skagen city center. Draws on a wide range of European and American influences and ingredients. Dark Germanic lager whose Munich malt sweetness is clipped off by a finish of brisk German hops.

Bryggeriet Skands

Brøndby, Hovedstaden
www.bryggeriet-skands.dk

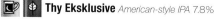 **Bla Chimpanse** *Belgian Ale* 6.5%

A boutique brewery from Brøndby that has kept things small-scale and manageable. This Belgian-style beer has a marked malt sweetness and a funky, fruity aroma, with a low hop bitterness that allows the vinous sweetness and dried fruit to come through.

Elmegade IPA 6.4%

This beer is testament to the success of Skands Brewery's decision to limit growth so as not to compromise its commitment to ingredients, time, and brewing integrity. Elmegade is a softly spoken and subtle American-style IPA brewed using Maris Otter malt and hopped with Northern Brewer and Cascade. Unfiltered and unpasteurized.

Bryggeri Skovlyst

Værløse, Hovestaden
www.bryggeriskovlyst.dk

Skovlyst Skovm Aerkebryg *Spice Ale* 5%

Set in the heart of the woodlands of Hareskoven, what distinguishes this bucolic brewery from others is the way it sources much of its ingredients from the neighboring forest—be it herbs, spices, or plants. Only lightly filtered, this delicate, spicy ale features forest honey and the Hareskoven's handpicked woodruff flowers.

 **Havre Stout** 7%

A sturdy, solid stout made with added roast malt, oats, barley, and rye. Notable licorice character spiced up with the addition of stinging nettles to the boil. Akin to a chocolate after-dinner mint.

Stevns Bryghus

Haarlev, Sjælland
www.stevnsbryghus.dk

Klintekongens Stout 7.5%

A full-bodied, very fruity, and smoky stout from a prolific micro that's on a mission to return craft beer to the head of the Danish dining table. Hopped with Northern Brewer and Centennial, and plumped up on the palate with roasted barley and oats.

Stevns Vaarbrud *Spiced Ale* 6%

If you can taste a hint of French lavender in this spiced ale, then that's probably due to the addition of French lavender. The generous help of the snappy, spicy Saaz hop makes it anything but a soporific sip.

Thisted Bryghus

Thisted, Nordjylland
www.thisted-bryghus.dk

Limfjords Porter *Porter* 7.5%

Thisted has brewed beer in the eponymous town since 1902, but it's only since it started making organic beers in 1995 that those beyond a regional radius of the brewery have been able to access its excellent ales. Baltic porter, known locally as the "gentleman of beers", was introduced in 1989 after seven years of experimentation. Smoked malt and licorice make an upstanding pillar of a porter.

Thy Eksklusive *American-style IPA* 7.8%

Rich on hops and sweet malt that comes from the use of hot lava stones. The inspiring beer label is designed by Danish artist Bjørn Nørgaard.

WinterCoat Brewery

Sabro, Midtjylland
www.wintercoat.dk

Vildmoseøl *Smoked Ale* 5.8%

Wintercoat beer is brewed on a second-hand 800-liter English brewhouse that was first fired up in a barn back in 2003. Brewmaster Niels Jørn Thomsen makes a mockery of his rudimentary equipment with some seriously celestial ales, of which this sensational smoked ale is one. Subtle smoky notes of peat-fumed malt, fresh spicy tones from bog myrtle, and bittersweet fruit flavors of rowan berries.

Finland

Downtown Brewery
Helsinki, Southern Finland
www.stadinpanimo.fi

 **Original Porter** 4.1%

The lone Helsinki craft brewery set up by two serious homebrewing heavyweights back in 2000. Ari Järmälä and Kari Likovuori draw on a huge gamut of international influences and even brew cask-conditioned ales for some of Helsinki's more switched-on beer pubs. Their porter, a terrific toasty beer with a hint of roasted chestnut, is merely one of several first-class Finnish beers.

Finlandia Sahti
Matku, Southern Finland
www.finlandiasahti.fi

Finlandia Sahti 8%

Beer doesn't come much more traditional than Sahti. Brewed using a variety of grain, mostly rye and oats, it's flavored, filtered, and often heated using juniper branches and berries. Once the exclusive domain of quirky home brewers, Sahti is now being produced by a couple of Finnish brewers, as well as some off-centered American boutique beer-making outfits. Fans of Hefeweizen will appreciate its hazy amber misty hue and fruity banana-like yeast esters. Refreshing and strong.

Finlandia Sahti Strong Sahti 10%

This traditional sahti is medicinal and fruity, with a syrupy body and a juniper nose akin to Jenever gin. A terrific digestif.

Lammin Sahti Oy
Lammi
www.sahti.fi

Kataja Sahti 8%

While most Sahti is brewed using baking yeast, which is what gives the beer its Weizen-like charms, Kataja calls on yeast more commonly associated with the brewing of ales at higher temperatures. It's also boiled for an hour. A departure from tradition, but a welcome one, that produces a blood-orange color, with peach, pear, and citrus on the palate and some marzipan on the finish.

Lammin Sahti 7.7%

This was the Sahti that started the revival. It's still brewed in open wooden mash tuns and troughlike sieves known as *kuurnas*, where the juniper acts as the main preservative. Present in the palate are banana, clove, spearmint, and caramel, with notes of aniseed on the nose and notes of juniper in the finish.

Sinebrychoff Brewery
Kerava, Southern Finland
www.sinebrychoff.fi

Karhupanimo Jouluolut Strong Ale 6.5%

Shrewd Finnish beer drinkers know Sinebrychoff for its Karhupanimo microbrewery-cum-brewpub set up in an old electric power station in Pori as part of a joint venture with a major Finnish restaurateur. Its small-batch boutique beers are available only in the cozy venue, but this full-bodied, warming Christmas beer is well worth the visit. Dark red with the softly roasted aroma of chocolate malt and the bitterness of Slovakian hops.

Sinebrychoff Porter 7.2%

Now internationally owned, Sinebrychoff was founded to the north of Helsinki by a Russian called Nikolai Sinebrychoff on October 13th, 1819 and, apart from a brief period when it wasn't allowed, it's been brewing a toasty porter ever since. Slides down on a soothing cushion of chocolate, coffee, and graham cracker.

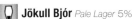

Iceland

Mjöður ehf Brugghús
Stykkishólmur, West Iceland
www.mjodurehf.is

Jökull Bjór Pale Lager 5%

Brewing was legalized in Iceland only in 1989 and Mjöður (an old Icelandic word for beer), located in West Iceland, came on line only in 2008. Crafted by two brewers from Germany and Italy, Jökull is a clean, crisp bottom-fermented "glacial" lager, softer than a pillow full of marshmallows, with a clinical, clean bite.

Norway

Aass Bryggeri
Drammen, Buskerud
www.aass.no

 **Aass Bock** 6.5%

Aass (pronounced "orse") is the oldest brewery in Norway and still brews using traditional methods. This dark, sweet floral beefy bock benefits from double decoction, an extended boil, and months of maturation.

Haand Bbryggeriet
Drammen, Oslo
www.haandbryggeriet.net

Norwegian Wood *Smoked/Spiced* Ale 6.5%

Innovation knows no bounds at this eccentric, forward-thinking operation run by four dedicated amateur brewers who dabble in wild yeast, barrel aging, high IBUs, and unusual indigenous ingredients.

Macks Ølbryggeri
Tromsø, Troms
www.mack.no

Arctic Lager *Light Lager* 4.5%

A very popular Norwegian lager from what claims to be the world's northernmost brewery in Tromsø. Highly refreshing, but tastes pretty much of nothing—the liquid equivalent of licking an iceberg.

Nøgne Ø
Grimstad, Aust-Agder
www.nogne-o.com

Dark Horizon Second Edition Stout 17.5%

Pronounced *"non-yay"* and meaning "barren ale", Nøgne Ø is two former home-brewers who have sown the seeds of creative brewing on a Norwegian landscape otherwise bereft. They brew more than 20 "uncompromising" ales, heavily influenced by American hops beginning with C: Chinook, Centennial, Cascade, and Columbus. This brutally bitter, robust Russian stout is an incredibly impressive beer that should be filed alongside ports and single-malt whiskies under Special Occasions.

IPA 7.5%

Nearly three-quarters of the brewery's production is exported and is held in high esteem among fanatic craft beer followers. This rich, malty, and very bitter ale has a long fruity, spicy finish thanks to much Cascade.

Ut Pa Tur *Sahti* 7.5%

Traditional Norwegian farmhouse ale spruced up with juniper berries and twigs. Limited availability.

Sweden

Carlsberg
Stockholm, Stockholm
www.carlsberg.se

Carnegie Stark Porter 5.5%

First brewed in a Gothenburg back in 1836 and named after the Scottish settler that founded the brewery. Less potent than most Baltic porters, it's a roast coffee-soaked seductive top-fermented mix of chocolate, vanilla, and aniseed. Now owned by Danish brewing giantCarlsberg, but it tastes just as good as ever.

Jämtlands Bryggeri
Pilgrimstad, Jämtland
www.jamtlandsbryggeri.se

Hell *Helles* 5.1%

The mantelpiece of this small yet celebrated Swedish craft brewer sags under the weight of brewing medals. Established in 1996 in the heart of Sweden, it crafts small-batch beers that run a gamut of English and Franco-German beer styles, brewed by an ex-pat Brit. A handsome Helles that's dry, hoppy, and crisp, with a sturdy malt body.

Heaven *Schwarzbier* 5.0%

A deep ebony lager, with an aroma of bitter chocolate and treacle-y malt, slightly oaky yet light palate, with some vanilla-laced coffee tones. Very refreshing.

Pilgrim *Pale Ale* 4.5%

English pale ale with an American accent in which tangy, resiny hops outwit the caramel biscuit base. Lychees and lime on the nose that mellow on the palate.

Närke Kulturbryggeri
Örebro, Närke
www.kulturbryggeri.se

Närke Kaggen Stormakts porter *Various* (circa 9%)

Närke is the rising bubble in Sweden's effervescent craft-brewing scene. Founded in 2003, it has pricked up the ears of the extreme beer lovers with some seriously adventurous ales and is talked about in the same breath as Nøgne Ø of Norway and Denmark's Mikkeller. The jewel in its crown is undoubtedly its vintage Baltic porter, an incredibly deep and complex cacophony of coffee, truffles, chocolate cake, and woody vanilla that pours like viscous motor oil. A must-have.

Nils Oscar

Nyköping, Södermanland
www.nilsoscar.se

American IPA 5.3%

The Nils Oscar microbrewery/distillery was
established in 1996, founded by Swedish
entrepreneur Karl-David Sundberg. He named the
business after his grandfather, Nils Oscar, who
farmed in the same rolling farmland less than an
hour's drive from Stockholm. With its own maltings
and barley fields, it brews a range of ten beers,
many of them award-winning, and distills both
aquavit and vodka. As Nils Oscar is too far north
to grow hops, it calls in heaps of Amarillo to give
this enormously aromatic West Coast IPA its citrusy,
vibrant sensuality.

God Lager 5.3%

A muscular, dry Vienna-style drop with juicy, sweet
malt overlaid with a brisk hop bitterness. Nils Oscar's
bestselling beer—the name isn't blasphemous, it means "good" in
Swedish. Rarely has a beer been more aptly titled.

Barley Wine 9.5%

A big, balanced beer that's full in body and intense in hop aroma, with
a warming, malt body. Balanced toffee sweetness, smoldering hay,
and stewed tea bitterness are all wrapped up in a soothing brandy-like
character. A gold medal winner at the 2000 World Beer Cup, this is a
great beer with cheese.

Nynäshamns Ångbryggeri

Nynäshamns, Södermanland
www.nyab.se

Landsort Lager 5.6%

This small "steam brewery" has been brewing in
the small coastal town of Nynäshamns in southeast
Sweden for more than a decade, in which time its
consistent quality beers, named after geographical
places on the nearby archipelago, have gained a
loyal following and are even exported to the United
Kingdom. A pale-straw well-constructed lager
spruced up with grassy hops. Light, soft, and clean.

Oppigårds

Hedemora, Darlana
www.oppigards.com

Golden Ale 5.2%

Old meets new at Björn Falkenström's farmhouse
brewery where, on a modern brewkit, life is being
breathed back into beer styles once brewed by
the 19th-century Swedish farmsteads. Sweet and
slightly spicy golden ale with citrus bitterness.

Oppigårds Stark Porter 5.9%

Nearer British than Baltic in style, this decadent yet
poised Scandinavian sip delivers chocolate raisins,
scorched caramel and a smidgen of black cherry.

Slottskällans Bryggeri

Uppsala, Uppsala
www.slottskallans-bryggeri.se

Slottskällans Imperial Stout 9%

In 1997 former duty-free salesman Hans Finell
opened Slottskällans after an enlightening beer-
drinking trip to the West Coast of America at the
height of the microbrewing boom. Based in the
university town of Uppsala, 50 miles north of
Stockholm, Slottskällans crafts unpasteurized
classic beer styles with a twist. If you're looking for
rich roasted coffee notes, chicory, molasses, and
port, then you can't go wrong here.

Slottskällans Pale Ale 5%

Certified organic, this citrusy Scandinavian take
on an English pale ale is brewed with Golding,
Fuggles, and Challenger, and slakes a thirst with
rapier-like refreshment. Nutty malty backdrop.

France

Brasserie d'Annoeullin

Annoeullin
No web address

L'Angelus *Wheat Beer* 7%

Located between Lille and Lens in a village of the same name, the rustic and rather rudimentary Annoeullin brewery has been in the hands of the Lepers family since the 1880s. As well as a gently hopped Bière-de-Garde, Annoeullin is well known for waking up the French wheat beer tradition in the late 1980s. L'Angelus is strong and spicy, and gets its syrupy substance from the use of 30 percent unmalted wheat.

Brasserie Castelain

Bénifontaine, Nord-Pas-de-Calais
www.chti.com

Ch'ti Blonde 6.4%

Much like its English equivalent, northern French brewing history is heavily entwined with the region's rich industrial heritage. While the coal mining has waned, the brewing goes on, and Castelain, brewing in Bénifontaine since 1926, is a big brewer of Bière-de-Garde. The biggest seller is this sweet, slightly bitter, and herbal blonde made with four types of hop.

Ch'ti Brune *Brown Ale* 6.4%

Ch'ti is the slightly unflattering nickname given to northerners in France—unfairly stereotyped as alcoholic, depressive, inbred, and unemployed, with an indecipherable local dialect. Despite the name, Ch'ti's beers are anything but backward as this vinous, brunette Bière de Garde can testify. Sloe berry, plums, and sweet caramel malt are all mixed in with the mouthful.

Ch'ti Triple 7.5%

Launched in 1997, this is Castelain's strongest calling card. A feverishly fruity and forceful abbey-style beer, it borrows some of the medicinal, Chartreuse-style notes from its Bière-de-Garde brethren. Packaged in a rather smart corked-and-caged champagne bottle.

Brasserie La Choulette

Hordain, Nord-Pas-de-Calais
www.lachoulette.com

Bière des Sans Culottes
Bière de Garde 7%

Founded in 1885, La Choulette is regarded as the most impressive brewery in France—its feet set firmly in traditional brewing methods but its head very much looking forward. Choulette has championed the Bière-de-Garde style more and better than most, and this authentic brew is simply fantastic—spritzy, spicy with licorice, fennel, and a touch of star anise.

La Choulette Ambrée *Tripel* 8%

Biscuit-base, mousse-like white head, and shimmering gold in color. Toffee, prunes, and a deep, lingering warm alcohol finish.

Coreff

Carhaix, Brittany
www.coreff.com

Coreff Ambrée *Brown Ale* 5%

Not content with berets, lovely cider, and clichéd stripy jumpers, Brittany is also home to one of France's finest microbreweries. It was founded in 1985, when it was the first new artisanal brewhouse in France for 30 years and the first Breton brewery for more than fifty. Spicy and warm, with a dry, lingering malty brown sugar finish.

Brasserie Duyck

Jenlain, Nord-Pas-de-Calais
www.duyck.com

Jenlain Ambrée *Bière de Garde* 6.5%

Duyck is the second largest independent brewer in France and almost single-handedly revived the Bière-de-Garde style. Imperiously packaged in Champagne bottles, Jenlain is one of France's most recognizable and revered beers, and is still in the hands of the Duyck family, who hail originally from the Belgian side of Flanders. A distinguished, dark amber dinner companion.

Jenlain Blonde 6%

Faced with a notoriously fickle French beer-drinking consumer, Duyck threw its beret into the blonde beer ring back in 2005 in an attempt to lure in lager-suppers. Golden, medium-bodied, and slightly syrupy with plenty of fruit and floral hop.

Fischer
Schiltigheim, Alsace
www.heineken-entreprise.fr

Fischer Tradition *Lager* 6%

Enormous Alsatian brewery owned by Heineken and guilty of giving birth to Desperados, a beer made with tequila flavoring. One doubts whether Jean Fischer, who created the brewery back in 1824, would approve. He'd probably prefer Fischer's prestige lager—nicely balanced with delicate caramel and a refreshing citrus kick.

Gayant
Douai, Nord-Pas-de-Calais
www.brasseurs-gayant.com

La Bière du Demon *Strong Ale* 12%

Devilish beer brewed by medium-sized commercially minded microbrewery in French Flanders. It is fermented for two weeks, lagered for a month, and best drunk when you have absolutely nothing planned for the next day. A dense yet drinkable golden beer.

Brasserie Grain d'Orge
Hombourg, Alsace
www.grain-dorge.com

Belzebuth *Strong Ale* 13%

The strongest beer in France, brewed by a small artisanal, family-owned brewery established in the town of Ronchin in 1898. Formerly known as Brasserie Jeanne d'Arc, it has made its name with this potent beer of maple syrup, cotton candy, and a long, sweet finish.

Grain d'Orge Cuvée *Strong Wheat Beer* 8.5%

A fruity, hazy resuscitation of a recently discovered recipe dating back to the date of the brewery's foundation in 1898. Bruised bananas, melon, and cloves. Ideal with dessert or as a digestif.

Karlsbrau
Saverne, Alsace
www.kasteelcru.com

Kasteel Cru *Champagne Beer* 5.2%

There's not much romance to this incredibly efficient Alsatian brewer, but it's easy to fall for its sprightly, spritzy champagne beer. Incredibly clean and crisp, with a slightly acidic flourish on the palate. With no strong malty or hoppy influences, a massive 95 percent of the flavor, not to mention the gorgeous mousse-like head, is attributable to the unique yeast, according to the brewer. Best served in a Champagne flute and accompanied by cheese straws and other smart canapés.

Pelforth Brewery
Lille, Nord-Pas-de-Calais
www.pelforth.fr

Pelforth Brune *Brown Ale* 6.5%

In the past decade or so, the northern town of Lille has undergone a massive and welcome transformation, thanks in no small measure to the Eurostar terminal. It often surprises beer lovers on their way to Brussels from London that it's a rather decent beer town, too. One of its finest local beers is Pelforth Brune, a deep russet-colored ale full of figs, prunes, and warming alcohol, with a portlike finish.

Pelforth George Killian's *Red Beer* 6.5%

The French have a bit of a thing for Irish red beers, and there's a touch of Irish whiskey to this amber-colored ale first brewed in County Wexford as far back as the 15th century. The bowl-beaked pelican on the label refers to the former name of the brewery, which was founded in 1914.

"You foam within our glasses, you lusty golden brew, whoever imbibes takes fire from you. The young and the old sing your praises; here's to beer, here's to cheer, here's to beer."

BEDŘICH SEMETANA
A TOAST FROM 'THE BARTERED BRIDE' OPERA 1866

Pietra Brewery

Furiani, Corsica
www.brasseriepietra.com

 Colomba *Wheat Beer* 5%

This wonderfully refreshing unfiltered, bottom-fermented wheat beer is perfect for when the sun puts his hat on and comes out to play—something that happens quite a lot in Corsica. It gets its immense aromas from the Corsican maquis—a spicy herbal blend of tree strawberry, myrtle, and juniper that's sunk into the worth like a big teabag.

Pietra *Amber Lager* 6%

When husband-and-wife team Dominique and Armelle Sialelli opened the Pietra microbrewery in 1996, it was the first commercial brewery to set foot on the gorgeous Mediterranean island of Corsica. Indigenous chestnuts are used in the brewing of Pietra's eponymous flagship beer. Crushed into flour and added to the grist, they afford the amber-colored lager a dry and voluptuous mouthfeel and a certain amount of spice on the finish. Nutty malt sweetness deftly drawn to be just the right amount of hop bitterness.

Brasserie St. Sylvestre

St. Sylvestre, Nord-Pas-de-Calais
www.brasserie-st-sylvestre.com

3 Monts *Bière de Garde* 8.5%

The "three mountains" name is a bit of an in-joke in this hop-growing part of northern France. The landscape is flatter than a super skinny stingray and the hills are more mound than mountain. Corked like a bottle of wine, it's fairly vinous, too, with undulating flavors of dry apricot, grapefruit, toffee, and sherry. Not surprising given its location. It's highly hoppy, too.

Gavroche *Strong Amber Ale* 8.5%

A sweet generously hopped copper-colored and bottle-conditioned ale brewed with a variety of malt and a showboating yeast given free, fruity reign. Named after the rebellious Parisian urchin character in the Victor Hugo novel Les Misérables.

Brasserie Theillier

Bavay, Nord-Pas-de-Calais
No web address

 **La Bavaisienne** *Bière de Garde* 7%

Only a few miles from the border with Belgium, in the little town of Bavay, the Theillier family has been making some rather beautiful Bière de Garde for generations. The charming brewery is part of the Theillier's 17th-century family home. Dark amber with a dense head, this beer is hearty, malty, and spicy, with a minty fresh finish.

La Bavaisienne *Blonde Ale* 7%

This lesser known sister of La Bavaisienne is just as enchanting. A softer palate of malt and spice allows the yeast to clamber into the front seat and takes your taste buds for a spin through cloves, pear, and sweetened grapefruit. Both beers are exported to the United States.

Brasserie de Thiriez

Esquelbecq,
Nord-Pas-de-Calais
www.brasseriethiriez.com

L'Ambrée d'Esquelbecq
Farmhouse Ale 5.8%

Uninspired by a career in the "human resources profession", Daniel Thiriez gave up his job in 1996 and decided to turn his passion for Belgian beer styles and hobby homebrewing into a business. Since then he hasn't looked back. The Ambrée has been brewed since 1997 and majors in roasty malts accented with a hint of spice. A lively mouthfeel completes the drinking experience.

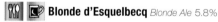 **Blonde d'Esquelbecq** *Blonde Ale* 5.8%

This was the first beer Daniel Thiriez produced when he set up his brewery in an old farm building in the small town of Esquelbecq near Dunkirk. It is the brew that was responsible for establishing his reputation as a brewer of note and this zesty blonde has not lost its lively orange-peel appeal. The Belgian influence is clearly discernible.

 **La Maline** *Abbey Ale* 5.8%

Almost as dark, seductive, and tasty as the rather sexy brunette with smoldering eyes that adorns the label, this Belgian dark ale cradles sweet chocolate, some cherry sourness, and coffee.

Austria

Schloss Eggenberg

Eggenburg, Niederösterreich
www.schloss-eggenberg.at

 Hopfen König Pils 5.1%

Locals love this light straw-colored, grassy pils that proves Eggenberg can do delicate drops as well as bombastic bocks.

Mac Queen's Nessie
Bock/Rauchbier 7.3%

One of the more unusual beers brewed by this family-owned bock specialist. A smoky kilt-wearing bock brewed using peaty Highland Scotch malt and lagered for two months.

Samichlaus Bier *Doppelbock* 14%

One of the strongest beers in the world, this Christmas beer was originally made in Switzerland at the Hurlimann brewing company, until it was closed in 1997. Three years later, it was taken across the border and revived, only brewed on December 6th, matured for a year, then released in time for festive frivolity. Rather aptly, flavors include Christmas cake and figgy pudding drenched in alcohol.

Urbock 23 *Doppelbock* 9.6%

Mention Austrian beer to any beer lover worth their malt, and it won't be long before there's talk of this delicious doppelbock. The "23" refers to the Plato degrees, but everything gets mellowed during a nine-month maturation period. A seriously strong beer disguised under a cloak of candy floss, pear, cloves, mixed spice, orange, grapefruit, and melon. An ideal digestif.

Forstner

Kalsdorf bei Graz, Steiermark
www.forstner-biere.at

 **Styrian Ale** *Premium Bitter* 5.6%

A modern-thinking brewpub which takes a different tack from the older, more traditional breweries in Austria. Gerhard Forstner draws inspiration from off-centered American ales and Belgian beers for his hard-to-pigeonhole liquids, such as this russet-brown drop that skips between a hoppy Californian pale ale and a Belgian Dubbel.

Gösser Brauerei

Leoben, Steiermark
www.goesser.at

 **Gösser Märzen** 5.2%

Gösser is part of the vast Heineken group and boasts an enormous following among Austrian beer lovers, especially for its malty, mellow Märzen—the most popular beer style in Austria, where it is typically lower in alcohol than its German namesake.

Hirt Brauerei

Micheldorf, Kärnten
www.hirterbier.at

 **Privat Pils**
Pilsner 5%

An excellent unpasteurized straw-colored Bohemian-style pilsner from Austria's oldest brewer, whose origins date from as far back as 1270. A grassy hop aroma with a long, soft butter and caramel velvety body, followed by a delicate and gentle short, dry bitter finish courtesy of Saaz and Hallertau hops.

Hofbräu Kaltenhausen

Kaltenhausen, Salzburg
www.edelweissbier.at

Gamsbock *Weissbier* 7.1%

Nestled in the bosom of the Austrian Alps, Edelweiss first began brewing in 1475, but began brewing weissbier only in the 1980s. It still cold-conditions and ferments its ales naturally in mountain-embedded caves. In this Gamsbock there is lots of boozy brawn and brisk bitterness, plus some sweet banana-caramel pie flavors and a deceptively dry finish.

Schremser Brewery

Schrems, Niederösterreich

www.schremser.at

 Roggen *Rye Beer* 5.2%

Small independent brewery created in 1410 in one of the most bucolic regions of Austria. The modern set up, in Trojan family hands since 1838, has revived the long-forgotten and once-forbidden brewing of rye beer. Light brown, fruity, pithy, and dry.

Siebensternbräu

Wien, Vienna

www.7stern.at

Rauchbock
Lager 7.9%

A sensational, sweet, strong, and smoky lager from a long-running Viennese brewpub that attaches electrodes to the nether-regions of long-neglected beer styles and gives them an almighty jolt. Also produces a chili beer and a hemp ale if you're feeling adventurous.

Stiegl Brewery

Salzburg

www.stiegl.at

Stiegl Goldbrau *Premium Lager* 4.9%

This is Austria's biggest private brewery, based in Salzburg, and once a favorite of the composer Wolfang Amadeus Mozart. When in Austria, you can't miss the red-and-white Stiegl (Steps) logo, although the beer's ubiquity is by no means a byword for bland. Crisp, clean, and with a clipped bitterness.

Stiegl Spezial *Pale Lager* 5.5%

This is the favorite beer of Heinrich Kiener, who saved the Stiegl brewery from closure in the 19th century. Stiegl Spezial is a full-bodied well-balanced beer specialty brewed to the original recipe from yesteryear. Dark golden in color, this beer has a rich almond aroma, with a sweet honey malt and biscuit taste. The smooth, full mouthfeel is followed by a light bitter farewell.

Trumer Brewing

Salzburg, Salzburg

www.trumer.at

 Trumer Pils 5.5%

When the Pilsner bandwagon first began rolling in the mid-19th century, Trumer was quick to clamber aboard and shift the focus toward the new golden beer and away from the traditional Bavarian bottom-fermented beers it had been brewing since 1601. Steadfast adherence to open-fermenting and lagering times is still maintained, and the brewery dabbles in seasonals and the occasional wheat beer. A good clean Pilsner.

Zipfer Brauerei

Zipf, Oberösterreich

www.zipfer.at

 Sparkling *Champagne Beer* 5%

Located in a rather idyllic area of Upper Austria, Zipfer was first founded in 1858 by a banker called Franz Schaup. Now owned by Heineken, the latest in a long list of proprietors, it's nationally renowned for whole-hop brewing of lighter lagers and the occasional seasonal ale. While Zipfer Urtyp is its strongest straw-colored seller, Sparkling is much loved for its flint-dry finish, quenching capabilities, and copious carbonation.

"From man's sweat and God's love, beer came into the world."

SAINT ARNOLD OF METZ
AUSTRIAN BISHOP AND PATRON SAINT OF BREWERS, 580–640

Switzerland

Brasserie des Franches-Montagnes

Saignelégier, Jura
www.brasseriebfm.ch

 Abbaye de Saint Bon Chien
Wood-aged Beer circa 11%

Based in the Jura mountains, BFM is the microbrewery that kick-started the microbrewing revolution in Switzerland and, in turn, it's this beer that put Switzerland back on the world beer map. World-class stuff, showing skills at wood aging way above the average level shown by brewers dabbling in barrels. Not just surfing on a trend, this one skillfully treads the line between port, wine, and beer. Sublime.

 Cuvée Alex le Rouge 10.27%

A "Jurassian imperial stout" with Lapsang souchong tea, Sarawak pepper, and other idiosyncrasies. A contemplative, meditative, and incredibly complex, slightly smoky dark beer, but not too massive in the mouth. It enjoys good sales in the United States.

La Meule *Blonde Beer* 6%

Dry, hoppy blonde beer with an almost gingery edge from the addition of sage leaves. A quirky and original quencher that's rich yet with an easy-drinking quality and a floral, honeyed finish.

Brauerei Locher

See Brewery Profile pages 168–169
Appenzell, Appenzell Innerrhoden
www. appenzellerbier.ch

 Holzfass Bier *Oak-aged Amber Lager* 5.5%

An oak-aged amber lager; butterscotch, vanilla, chewy toffee, and some green apple hop notes.

Schwarzer Kristall *Black Lager* 6.3%

A lovely yet rather unorthodox schwarzbier; black, malty, rather mouthfilling, with a solid chocolatey roast malt backbone, almost saline notes, decent hopping, and a nice dash of smoked malt in it. Very pleasant, rich yet not too heavy, and a bold move for a Swiss-German brewery. Great with sushi.

 Vollmond Bier *Lager* 5.2%

Organic Swiss lager brewed only when there is a full moon. Grainy yet clean, with caramel and lemony hop character.

Trois Dames

Sainte-Croix, Vaud
www.brasserietroisdames.ch

 **La Fraîcheur** *Wheat Beer* 4.6%

In 2004, "Three Ladies" was created in the mountains north of Lausanne, a thousand meters above sea level, by former skate- and snowboard shop owner Raphael Mettler who, prior to a trip to the US, had no interest in beer. Having initially brewed British and German beers, he is now renowned for his Anglo-American creations. This is a Belgian wit-style beer that's not bubble-gummy, watery, and sweetish but crisp, dry, with a clear-cut citrusy, hoppy edge, and ends up somewhere between a typical Belgian Blanche and a British wheat ale.

 IPA 6.5%

This Californian IPA brewed using Centennial, Simcoe, and Cascade hops is a floral, aromatic, and beautifully bitter example of Mettler's successful Anglo-American brews.

La Semeuse Espresso Stout
7.5%

A solid chocolatey imperial stout with a wonderful wakey-wakey espresso coffee edge courtesy of coffee beans from Vietnam, Ethiopia, and Brazil. Like all Trois Dames' beers, it comes packaged in a terrific-looking bottle.

BRAUEREI LOCHER AG

CH-9050 Appenzell, Appenzell Innerrhoden, Switzerland

www.appenzellerbier.ch

If Switzerland was a cuckoo clock or a rather expensive watch face, then Appenzell could be found at about half past one. Appenzell is about as Swiss as you can get: surrounded by *Sound of Music* hills and chocolate-box pretty houses, with heart-shaped shutters.

Appenzell is also the butt of Swiss urbanite jokes because as it is situated in the least populated region of Switzerland, where cows outnumber people (15,000 to 1) and where women were given the regional vote only in 1991.

The local brewer is unashamed in proudly circumventing convention. The Locher family has been brewing at its eponymous brewery since 1886, but Karl, the fifth generation of the family to run it, wears the weight of history lightly by doing some fairly extraordinary things with his beer.

Locher's flagship beer, Vollmond, meaning "Full Moon", is a quirky case in point. Borrowing biodynamic techniques more readily associated with wine making, Karl brews the clean and crisp Pilsner only when the moon is at its most rotund. "People in this region believe the moon has supernatural powers and that it determines much more than you think. Many only cut their hair on a full moon," says Karl with the wide-eyed, infectious zeal of a mad professor. "If winemakers can use biodynamics, why can't we do something similar with beer? Some people say it is mumbo-jumbo, but all I know is that when this beer is brewed at full moon it simply tastes better."

Vollmond is by no means Locher's only left-field liquid. There's Hanfblüte, brewed using hemp flowers and leaves, and a fragrant reminder of cannabis's close kinship with the hop; a mellow chestnut beer called Castégna and an unorthodox black lager called Schwarzer Kristall. And then there's Holzfass-bier, an oak-aged amber lager that delicately doffs a cap to Locher's Germanic roots.

But it's not just in the brewhouse where Locher does things differently. A few years ago, Karl teamed up with Appenzell's rather fancy Hotel Hof Weissbad spa resort to extoll beer's many health-giving talents.

There are beer Jacuzzis where yeast and wheat germ oil swirl around you on powerful liquid jets; there's an all-over body cleansing using malt mash and beer residue that leaves your backside baby-smooth; there's a hop massage that soothes the mind, body, and soul with soporific powers; and you can even get a hair care treatment and scalp massage using Ninkasi Beer, a low-alcohol lager that tastes better than anti-dandruff lotions.

"Beer has ingredients that are great for your body," says Karl. "The various types of vitamin B found in beer have a favorable effect on the skin, as well as hair and nails. Hop baths are a great relaxant, too."

Above right: Sharp, refreshing, and in a glass of its own, Holzsfass amber ale lager is one of Locher's key brews.
Opposite bottom left: Taking a sample of the beer to check that everything is as it should be.
Opposite bottom right: Volmond is brewed only when there is a full moon, as locals believe that it has supernatural powers.

Left: Appenzell is not averse to a spot of advertising. This beer transporter comes complete with a scenic Swiss mural and, of course, some of Locher's brews.

"It's not a new thing," he adds. "Egyptian women used beer foam to improve the freshness of their complexion. All we've done is take the nutritional benefits of beer and combined them with the latest research in health science. It may sound bizarre, but it works."

If it's good enough for humans, then it's good enough for cows, too. Local farmer Sepp Dahler, Locher's grain supplier, is given the brewery's by-products (grains, first runnings, and yeast) to produce beer-fed beef, a delicious fall-off-your-fork delicacy that's served at the beer spa.

Twice a day, Sepp and his wife Magdalena treat their happy herd to a sensual massage. "The beer itself doesn't come through in the taste but it makes the cows really relaxed and raises the quality of the meat," says Sepp, lovingly scrubbing the yellow goo under the neck of an increasingly content calf. "It makes it tender, richer, and a little spicier."

Not only is the flavor enhanced by the myriad of nutrients present in the beery sludge, but by slapping it onto cows with a clothes brush it makes the herd more relaxed and content.

The method to his moo-like madness is rooted in Japan, where farmers marinade and massage their cows in sake to produce the revered kobe beef, considered the most exclusive beef in the world and renowned for its flavor, tenderness, and fatty well-marbled texture.

"The Japanese feed their cattle with sake and beer products, but they do lots of other things that aren't very nice. We don't do that."

Even their inevitable slaughter is carried out as humanely as possible, with Sepp walking his cows the ten miles to the abattoir rather than shoehorning them into a bloodcurdling cattle truck. "It's so they don't get stressed out or panicked," he says. "It's nicer for them, and the meat also tastes better."

Key Beers

Castégna *Chestnut Beer* 5%

Hanfblüte *Hemp Beer* 5.2%

Holzfass-Bier *Oak-aged Amber Ale* 5.5%

Schwarzer Kristall *Black Lager* 6.3%

Vollmond Bier *Organic Ale* 5.2%

The Netherlands

Brouwerij De 3 Horne
Kaatsheuvel, North Brabant
www.de3horne.nl

 Meibock 7%

Well-balanced seasonal spring sip seasoned with Tettnang and Northern Brewer from one of Netherland's most technically sound new wave micros—founded in 1990 and expanded a few years later. From a small efficient brewery-cum-bar, brewer Sjef Groothuis flies the flag for fruity Belgium-leaning bottle-conditioned beers.

Budelse Brouwerij
Budel, North Brabant
www.budels.nl

Bock 6.5%

One of the larger Dutch microbreweries that, having been created in 1870, has a longer history than most. Dynamic but not outrageously so, Budelse's signature style is influenced by Germany and predominantly bottle-fermented. A sweet-tongued malty, dark maroon beer with upbeat tones of toffee and molasses. Best drunk from a brandy balloon, slowly.

Grolsch
Enschede, Overijssel
www.grolsch.com

 Grolsch *Pilsner* (bottled) 5%

Grolsch is the Netherland's second biggest brewer after Heineken, with a history that dates back to the 17th century and now based in a state-of-the-art brewery in Enschede. Recognized the world over for its iconic swing-top bottle, it has much more charisma than most mainstream Pilsners—especially from the bottle rather than on draft. Light Hallertau hop aroma with apple and banana notes.

Grolsch Weizen 5.3%

Tucked away in a corner of the vast, newish brewery in Enschede, you'll find the brewery team eagerly experimenting on a smaller (yet still state-of-the-art) pilot brewery that most microbrewers would give their left arm for. It was here that this wonderfully zesty Weizen was born in 2005 as a limited-edition beer. Fuller-bodied than Belgian witbiers but with more spice than Bavarian Weizen, it is now available all year round and abroad.

Gulpener Bier Brouwerij
Gulpen, Limburg
www.gulpener.nl

 Korenwolf *Wheat Beer* 5%

A multigrain, moreish, and unpasteurized Dutch witbier. It was first brewed to raise aid for a dwindling local population of korenwolf (field hamsters) until it was discovered that, rather than dwindling, they had merely moved across the border.

Heineken (Amstel)
Zoeterwoude, South Holland
www.amstel.nl

Amstel Bock 7%

Breweries don't come much bigger than Heineken. Its eponymous lager is recognized all over the world and so too is Amstel, its more session-friendly stablemate. It's under the Amstel umbrella that a range of discerning drops is released with this nutty, black cherry-tinged Bock being the most intriguing.

De Hemel
Nijmegen, Gelderland
www.brouwerijdehemel.nl

 **Nieuw Ligt Grand Cru** *Barley Wine* 10%

The delightfully named Herm Hegger is a veteran of the Dutch brewing scene, having set up the Raaf microbrewery in 1983, where he introduced the first Dutch wheat beer. Having sold it to Oranjeboom brewery, he started De Hemel (Heaven) in a splendid 12th-century cloister in the town of Nijmegen where, as well as mighty fine ales, vinegar, mustard, gin, and brandy are made from the beer. Matured for more than a year in cellars, it's a firm-bodied, vinous barley wine with stewed hop resin aroma, a mellow touch of malt vinegar and an everlasting arid endgame.

Hertog Jan
Arcen, Limburg
www.hertogjan.nl

 **Grand Prestige** *Barley Wine* 10%

A strong, vinous Dutch barley wine is one of a number of intriguing ales from an old Arcen-based brewery that's had more comebacks than a boomerang. Expect a vinous fusion of pears, plums, dried apricot, and warm alcoholic tones of spiced dark rum.

Jopen
Haarlem, North Holland
www.jopen.nl

Bokbier 6.5%

Jopen, located in the lovely town of Haarlem just a half-hour outside Amsterdam, revels in re-creating the Dutch beer styles of yesteryear and has received critical acclaim for doing so. An authentic interpretation of an indigenous, once-ubiquitous Dutch brown beer: smoky, spicy with a sharp tongue of licorice.

Hoppenbier *Pale Ale* 6.8%

Brewed to an early 16th-century recipe of barley malt, oats, and wheat. Sweet, spicy, and—thanks to the addition of oats—superbly smooth, there's grapefruit, orange peel, coriander, and spruce.

Klein Duimpje
Hillegom, South Holland
www.kleinduimpje.nl

Blue Tram *Tripel* 7.5%

Klein Duimpje, which translates as Tom Thumb in Dutch, is a small yet incredibly prolific brewery. Drawing inspiration from all over the world, former hedonistic home brewer Erik Bouman doesn't let diversity dilute the character of his small-batch beers. A jauntily angled Tripel which flashes elements of pear, clove, tropical fruit, and shortbread.

Maasland Brouwerij
Oss, North Brabant
www.maaslandbrouwerij.nl

D'n Schele Os (Dizzy Cow) *Tripel* 7.5%

An udderly tremendous sour and estery orange-colored Tripel from a small barnyard brewery-cum-brewing school located in the west of the Netherlands.

Brouwerij De Molen
Bodegraven, South Holland
www.brouwerijdemolen.nl

Amerikaans *Bitter* 4.5%

A delicate drop among De Molen's roster of full-bodied palate-punchers. American hops add a citrus, grassy character to an English-style bitter for the best of both the Old and the New World. A sensational session beer of a sensible strength.

Rasputin *Imperial Stout* 10.7%

Established in 2004, "The Mill Brewery" is a dynamic Dutch micro based in a 300-year-old windmill in the town of Bodegraven, about 20 miles north of Rotterdam. Brewing small-batch beers in a modestly-sized brewhouse that uses former dairy equipment, brewmaster Menno Olivier is a proponent of big interpretations of traditional global beer styles. Rasputin is a limited-edition imperial stout loaded with warming molasses, rich roasted coffee notes, and a touch of vanilla and spice. This beer is brewed only once or twice a year, so grab it if you see it.

Pauw Bier
Ommen, Overijssel
www.pauwbier.nl

 **Bokbier** 6.5%

The De Pauw brewery was founded by Johan Drenth and Henk Smit in the middle of the Netherlands' no-mans land, 140 years after the last brewery in the small town of Ommen closed. Keep your eye out for the brewery's peacock logo because, while harder to find than most, its beers are really rather good—especially this cloudy copper-colored Dutch bokbier; herbal, spicy, and a dash of brown sugar.

De Pelgrim
Rotterdam, South Holland
www.pelgrimbier.nl

Mayflower Tripel 7.8%

A terrific brewpub and restaurant located on the historic Delfshaven harbor, just a few doors down from the church where the Pilgrims last said prayers before setting sail for America in 1620. Opened in 1996, De Pelgrim brews beers inspired by Belgium and also uses the beer in the recipes for its in-house produce such as cheese, butter chocolates, and mustard. Mayflower Tripel, named after the ship sailed by the pilgrims, bobs up and down on an aromatic golden sea of flavor derived from orange zest, coriander, and herbal hop.

Brouwerij De Prael
Amsterdam, North Holland
www.deprael.nl

Willy *Dark Dubbel* 9%

Co-founder Arno Kooij set up this small, ramshackle brewery in Amsterdam after working in a rehabilitation center helping recovering psychiatric patients to look for work. With suitable work opportunities scarce, he created De Prael and, using government funding, employed his former clients. Brewed with English yeast and esoteric ingredients, all the beers are named after Dutch singers. Willy, a dark Dubbel, is a blend of dark malt and peppery hop.

Brouwerij De Schans
Uithoorn, North Holland
www.schansbier.nl

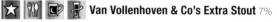 **Van Vollenhoven & Co's Extra Stout** 7%

A fancy-footed romp through roasted coffee, soft-toned blackberries, and scorched caramel, courtesy of a boundary-bending brewery set up in 1998 and run by former engineer Guus Rooijen.

Schelde Brouwerij
Gravenpolder, Zeeland
www.scheldebrouwerij.nl

 **Strandgaper** *Amber Ale* 6.2%

"Beach-yawner" is the best-recognized beer brewed by this traditional brewery located in the southwest coastal town of Gravenpolder in Zeeland. The use of the clean, spicy Saaz and Hallertau hops shakes up the mellow malt. Such a beer is designed to match perfectly with mussels.

Sint Christoffel B.V
Roermond
www.christoffelbier.nl

 **Christoffel Blond**
Pilsner 6%

Dutch diktat has it that if you want to drink delightful lagers, then you should choose Christoffel. Set up in 1986 in the former coal mining town of Roermond, Christoffel brews according to the Reinheitsgebot purity laws and uses fresh hop flowers in the boil and for dry-hopping. No denying the hop character here—peppery tones of marmalade, fennel, and cut grass, all in unfiltered form.

 **Christoffel Robertus**
Munich Lager 6%

A Munich-inspired meze of rich caramel, chocolate, and cookies on the palate. Bitter snap and bite at the back end. A terrific ruby-red beer.

Stichting Noordhollandse Alternatieve Bierbrouwers (SNAB)
www.snab.nl

 **Snab Pale Ale** 6.3%

SNAB doesn't have its own brewery, relying instead on other carefully chosen outfits to turn its eclectic brewing recipes into reality. It's an unusual approach, but one that seems to work, as SNAB's beers are serial international award-winners. A case in point is this truly superb American-style Pacific Northwest pale ale which is brewed with American Cascade hops and yeast from Oregon.

Texelse Bierbrouwerij
Oudeschild, Texel, North Holland
www.speciaalbier.com

 **Wit** *Wheat Beer* 5%

Recognized by its Lighthouse logo, Texelse has endured a rocky time since it was formed in 1994, but now, under secure ownership, is conjuring up some quality craft ales on the Friesian island of Texel. A tasty wit that ticks all the right boxes of spice and fruit, resulting in a parch-reducing drinkability.

Brouwerij 'tIJ
Amsterdam
www.brouwerijhetij.nl

 **Columbus** *IPA/Barley Wine* 9%

The "ostrich and egg" emblem on the bottles is a play on the fact that "ij" sounds like the Dutch word for "egg". In Dutch "to find the egg of Columbus" means "I've done something rather clever" and 'tIJ has certainly done that: Copper-toned ale imbued with heaps of hops and a bright, zesty bitterness. A heavyweight IPA that caresses rather than clobbers.

 **Natte** *Dubbel* 6.5%

There can be no microbrewery more quirky or quintessentially Dutch than the extraordinary 'tIJ in Amsterdam. Located in a converted bathhouse, loomed over by a windmill, the brewery is named after a squat where the owner first brewed his beers. Unlike other Dutch micros, which often take their cues from Belgium, the 'tIJ beers are distinctly Dutch in their character. This Dubbel is a deliciously delicate, dry drop.

Zatte *Dubbel* 8%

Delicious Dubbel sprawling with sweet toasted aromas and ripe summer fruit. Gentle spiciness in the finish.

La Trappe (De Koningshoeven)
Berkel-Enschot, North Brabant
www.latrappe.nl

La Trappe Tripel 8%

The only Trappist brewer outside of Belgium. In 1999, it was stripped of its Trappist status after the monks relinquished their brewing responsibilities but, after an almighty fuss with its Belgian Trappist brethren, it was allowed back in under the condition that the monastery got back into the habit of at least overseeing the brewing. Subsequently, the beers have improved immensely, with the Tripel being especially celestial stuff.

"God has a brown voice as soft and full as beer."
ANNE SEXTON
AMERICAN WRITER 1928-1974

Luxembourg

Bofferding
Bascharage
www.bofferding.lu

Bofferding Christmas Béier 5.5%

Bofferding, the brewery with the largest share of the Luxembourg beer market, was formed in 1975 by the merger of Bofferding and the Brasserie Funck-Bricher of Luxembourg City, in the southwest of Luxembourg. As well as a neat and tidy Pilsner, it has branched out with this festive brunette lager that's bread, nutty, and a little earthy.

Simon
Wiltz
www.brasseriesimon.lu

Simon Prestige
Champagne-style Beer 5%

Traditional methods, dating back to 1824, are still strictly adhered to at this medium-sized micro nestled in the woody hills of the Ardennes. If a solid but unspectacular lager is the brewery's bread and butter, Prestige is the smart silverware brought out only on special occasions. Champagne-style beer brewed using spelt, open fermentation, and Crémant de Luxembourg sparkling wine.

Portugal

Sociedad Central de Cervejas
Vialonga, Lisbon
www.centralcervejas.pt

Sagres Dark *Munich Lager 4.3%*

While rival Super Bock pours supreme in northern Portugal, Sagres lager is the beer of the south and very much seen as the liquid of Lisbon. The pale lager may refresh, but this malty Munich version, introduced in 1940, is the finer example of Sagres' German influence.

Spain

Cerveza Artesenal de Tarragona
Tarragona, Catalonia
No web address

Rosita *Pale Ale 5.5%*

From a small micro in the Mediterranean coastal town of Tarragona in southern Catalonia comes this top-fermented bottle-conditioned hazy pale ale with a superb soft sparkle and citrus hop bitterness. It also has a pretty lady on the bottle, which is always nice from a marketing perspective.

Cervezas Alhambra
Granada, Andalusia
www.cervezasalhambra.com

 Alhambra Negra *Black Lager 5.4%*

Negra pours dark reddish black with a modest off-white head. Sweet biscuit nose with a little licorice note and a fresh, accessible aroma. Provides a medium-bodied palate with blackberry flavors and a touch of background toasty malt.

Alhambra Premium 4.6%

A top-selling sunshine-sipper with a buttery nose and fresh and fruity palate, with a little honeyed malt. In the mouth it is full and richly textured.

Alhambra Reserva 1925 6.4%

Two brewers, Carlos Bouvard and Antonio Knorr, founded the brewery in Granada in 1925 and named it after the city's impressive Alhambra Palace. It's situated on the outskirts of Granada at the base of the snow-capped Sierra Nevada from which it sources its water. Presented in a terrific old-style green bottle, 1925 is Alhambra's showpiece sip and pours dark amber color with a thick, fluffy head. Powerful dark caramel-like malt aromas and full-textured body, with a tight, terse hop bite. A rounded grassy finish.

La Cervesera Artesana
Barcelona, Catalonia
www.lacervesera.net

 Iberian Stout 5%

A Barcelona brewpub brewing "beer fit for the gods" since the early 1990s. Given Spain's embryonic beer scene, Artesana's ales are impressively ambitious and include a honey beer and a fruity number brewed with tangerine. The best, however, is the Iberian Stout. Bellowing roasted barley and coffee are cut with crisp citrus flavors, courtesy of Cascade, Galena, and Northern Brewer.

Cruzcampo

Seville, Andalusia
www.cruzcampo.es

 Cruzcampo 5.0%

Meaning "Cross of the Field" Cruzcampo has been charming the throats of Spain since 1904 when it was founded in Seville by brothers Roberto and Agustin Osbourne. Golden and light with a touch of honey on the nose, it's now owned by Heineken and is one of Spain's best-selling beers—especially in the Andalusian region.

Damm

Barcelona, Catalonia
www.damm.es

Bock Damm *Dunkel* 5.4%

Not only is it's Dunkel packaged in a groovy gothic bottle with a grand-looking goat on the label, but it also has some of the smoothest coffee and dry chocolate tones in all of Spain.

Estrella Damm *Pilsner* 5.4%

To say that Damm is drunk a lot in Barcelona is to say that the sun's a wee bit bright. Founded in 1876 by an Alsatian brewer called Auguste Kuentzmann Damm, Damm's range of beers is predominantly German-influenced and, now owned by Anheuser-Busch InBev, widely available all over Europe. A darn drinkable dry Pilsner that swigs easier than its strength suggests.

Inedit Damm *Witbier/Pilsner* 4.8%

In 2008, Damm joined forces with El Bulli restaurant (see page 264) to design a food-friendly beer. A pioneering blended beer that's a marriage of a Pilsner and a wheat beer plus orange peel, coriander, and licorice. The two are married together at the end of the brewing process, then packaged in a slick-looking 25 oz (75cl) bottle in which it undergoes secondary fermentation. An aroma of bitter orange, gently perfumed with aniseed and mellow estery fruit is present, together with a honey smooth palate, a touch of banana, and a satin-smooth malt base. This is a versatile companion to a wide range of food dishes.

Voll Damm *Märzen/Oktoberfest* 7.2%

An impressive Iberian Oktoberfest beer that has a far fuller body than its flagship stablemate. It has a grassy bitterness, aniseed, caramel, and a frisson of ripe fruit on the finish.

Keks

Girona, Catalonia
www.keks.cat

 **Keks** 5.0%

A quasi-wheat beer brewed using special fajol wheat, a grain that grows exclusively in the Catalonian rural region of Garrotxa. Massive mousse-like head and amber-hued haze, with a bitter lemon nose and a pitter-patter of pear-drop candy on the palate.

Mahou Brewery

Madrid
www.mahou-sanmiguel.com

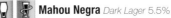 **Mahou Negra** *Dark Lager* 5.5%

A malty Munich-style dark lager first launched in 1908 from a Madrid-based brewery founded in 1890 and now owned by the same people who make the ubiquitous summer sip that is San Miguel. There is bitter chocolate and treacle on the nose, with a hoppy tang and a dry coffee finish.

Mahou Selecta XV *Strong Lager* 6.5%

Positioned as the most discerning lager in San Miguel's locker, Selecta is aged and cold-conditioned for a lot longer. A full-bodied, chunky, and muscular lager with a moreish malt on the palate.

Montseny

Saint Niquel de Balenya
www.ccm.cat.

 **Blat** *Weissbier* 3.5%

Unfiltered and unpasteurized refreshing wheat beer with low alcohol. As much in common with the Low Countries as the big banana Weizen beers of Bavaria and one of four bottled beers brewed by a little-known micro founded within the El Montseny national park in 2007.

Poland

AMBER – ŻYWIEC

Browar Amber

Kolbudy

www.browar-amber.pl

KOŹLAK

 Amber Koźlak *Dunkel Bock* 6.5%

A demonic-looking ram on the label and an intense toffee-nose with sweet tones of licorice and plums and dates on the palate. Port-colored beer brewed by a well-established medium-sized brewery near Gdansk that prides itself on using local ingredients.

Browar Staropolski

Zduńska Wola, Łodzkie

www.browarstaropolski.pl

Mocne Ciemne *Strong Beer* 8.5%

Staropolski was established in 1892 by Zenon Anstadt, a member of a well-known family of entrepreneurs and brewers. Its biggest beer by far is this Baltic black-red beauty full of vinous fruit, espresso and vanilla.

Carlsberg Polska

Galicia

www.okocim.com.pl

Okocim Mocne *Lager* 7%

Formed in 1845 by Viennese Jan Gotz, the Okocim Brewery is one of the most grandiose in Europe and its beers reach beyond Poland thanks to Carlsberg's distribution. A sweet, strong lager with a spicy finish.

Okocim Premium Pils *Pilsner* 5.6%

A quaffable Czech-style lager that is amber in color, with a clean, crisp flavor. It leads with soft, sweet apple and pear notes and is medium-bodied with a long, dessicated finish. Extensively available throughout Europe, Okocim's beers have a good following.

Witnica

Witnica

www.browar-witnica.pl

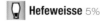

Black Boss Porter 9.4%

An archetypal Polish Baltic porter from a brewery that was founded in 1848 and was state-owned from the end of World War Two until 1992. Pours dark brown to shiny jet black with a sweet licorice aroma—scorched coffee beans and oily dark rum.

Żywiec

Żywiec, Bielsko-Biala

www.zywiec.com.pl

Hevelius Kaper *Strong Lager* 8.7%

A deceptively potent and creamy pilsner first brewed in Gdansk in 1690, named after the region's most famous brewer Johannes Hevelius and, legend has it, drunk often by King John Sobieski III. Now part of the Żywiec family.

Żywiec Porter *Baltic Porter* 9.5%

A meze of dark malts make up the sweet, buttery backbone of this black peppery Baltic Porter first brewed in 1881, 29 years after the Żywiec brewery was founded by the Hapsburg family.

Hungary

Dreher Brewery

Budapest

www.dreher.hu

Dreher Bak *Dark Bock* 7.3%

A sizable Budapest brewery that was once the workplace of Anton Dreher, who was the pioneer of low-temperature bottom-fermentation. Today, under the auspices of SAB Miller, Dreher belies both its size and the commercial concerns that come with it by making some rather respectable bottom-fermenting beers such as this malty, sweet dark bock.

Ilzer

Monor, Pest

www.ilzer.hu

Hefeweisse 5%

Ilzer began life as a distillery before branching out into brewing in the mid 1990s. Brewed to the German Reinheitsgebot purity laws, the range of beers includes a kosher beer called Shalom, a rye beer and numerous pilsners and wheat beers of which this lively, cloudy refresher is the most well known.

176 A WORLD OF BEER

Estonia

A Le Coq
Tallin, Harju
www.alecoq.ee

Estonian Porter 7%

In the 19th century, Belgian Albert Le Coq carved a rather profitable commercial niche by exporting strong porter from Britain to the Baltic. Then, in 1913, he moved production closer and bought a brewery in Estonia where he began brewing Porter. But, by the 1970s, demand for the style had waned and production ceased. About ten years ago, however, new owners of the Saku brewery breathed life back into the toffee-tinged, spicy dark lager and, in doing so, they've done Albert proud.

Double Bock 8%

Pay heed to the dangerous-looking goat on the label because this is a deceptively strong beer. Paler than most bocks, but full in body with a sweet, mellow finish.

Le Coq Joulu Porter 7.5%

A Christmas porter that is full of festive, spicy fruitcake aromas and with a rich, velvety texture. Pours black as a winter's night with a fluffy snow white head. It comes with a set of Christmas poems on the label that, if read out, will ensure you get all the presents you wish for.

Turkey

Efes
Istanbul
www.efesbev.com

Efes Dark Lager 6.5%

Top Turkish tipples are a little tricky to find but this dark, nutty Munich-style lager from the Efes Beverage Group, founded in 1969 and with an 80 percent share of the domestic beer market, is the best of the bunch.

Malta

Simonds Farsons Cisk
Mriehel
www.farsons.com

Lacto Milk Stout 3.8%

Well-worn trade routes between the UK and Malta meant the locals had a taste for milk stout well before it was first brewed on this Mediterranean Island by Simonds Farsons Cisk after World War Two. A marvelous milky mouthfeel, enlivened with a dose of lactose in the bottle, with dark fruity, chocolate charms.

Hop Leaf Pale Ale 3.8%

Quality, quintessential summer quencher brewed using English hops and malt. A liquid equivalent of a handkerchief on the head for cooling.

Russia

Baltic Beverages
St. Petersburg, Northwestern Federal District
www.eng.baltika.ru

Baltika Porter 8%

It's taken just 30 years for Baltika to gain a Vulcan-like grip on the Russian beer market. Originally based in St. Petersburg, Baltika is now brewed all over the country and makes a number of mainstream international beers under license. The core Baltika range is numbered from one to nine and ranges from non-alcoholic to this black-crimson chocolatey porter.

Baltika #8 Wheat 5%

Unfiltered yet pasteurized, this cloudy yellow wheat comes in a fine-looking bottle and delivers dry, bready notes with plenty of bubble gum, banana and clove.

A WORLD OF BEER
THE AMERICAS

USA Western States

The West Coast is the birthplace of American craft beer. California, Oregon, and Washington are where American beer sowed its seeds of recovery in the 1970s and these states remain lush and fertile beer drinking territory.

The Pacific Northwest is especially bountiful, rightly regarded by many as America's most diverse and devout beer-drinking region. Within the borders of Oregon, or "Beervana" as it is often known, there are more than 80 breweries including several of the nation's top 50 craft outfits (Deschutes, Full Sail, Bridgeport, Widmer, and Rogue to name but a few).

Left-leaning Portland, the jewel in Oregon's beer crown, is arguably America's greatest beer city. Dubbed by the late, great beer writer Michael Jackson as "Munich on the Willamette", it is home to more than 30 breweries and brewpubs and craft beer has a 45 percent share of the Portland beer market—compared with the nationwide figure of just 4 percent.

Given the natural resources bestowed upon Washington, it is little surprise that it's blessed with such a rich craft-brewing scene. Washington is America's heartland of hops, growing 75% of the entire nation's yield and ranked fourth among the nation's top barley-growing states. Brewers can also call upon some terrific natural water, courtesy of its mountain ranges.

Seattle is a brilliant beer town, home to the likes of Elysian, Pike Brewing, and Hale's Ales, but many of Washington's 82 breweries are scattered across the state, with the vast majority being small craft enterprises or brewpubs.

California, in particular the northern part, is the spiritual home of American craft beer. When New Albion opened in the Northern Californian town of Ukiah in 1976, it was the first American microbrewery to do so since Prohibition. Even though it was unable to survive by itself, it still enjoys hallowed "martyr" status among the craft beer community, and New Albion's original sign hangs in pride of place at the nearby Russian River brewpub—one of several widely admired North Californian micros.

Much, too, is owed to Fritz Maytag, who, by preserving San Francisco's Anchor Brewery in the late 1960s, kept craft beer's wavering plate spinning. The city's cool Californian climate and liberal attitude has been harnessed by the Bay Area's thriving

beer culture. As befits the epicenter of today's larger artisan food and drink movement, San Francisco is home to some brilliant brewpubs, beer bars, and envelope-pushing breweries.

The Pacific Coast Highway is inundated with innovative breweries, and there are some hidden gems amid the gridlock of Los Angeles. San Diego, meanwhile, may have arrived late to the scene, but no other city hails the hop in such a high-octane fashion. No other city cranks up the IBU knob with quite the same wide-eyed passion and the city's brewers—AleSmith, Stone, and Green Flash—are being rightly wreathed in awards.

Above: The Deschutes Brewery in Bend, Oregon is the sixth largest craft brewery in the US and its most celebrated beer, a dark one.

Left: In Olympia, Washington, Fish Brewing Company produces beers based on British Bitters and German- style lagers.

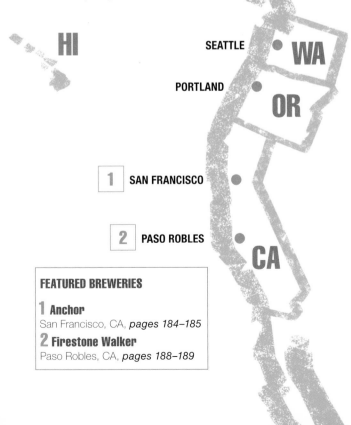

AK

● ANCHORAGE

CANADA

HI

SEATTLE ● WA

PORTLAND ●

OR

1 SAN FRANCISCO ●

2 PASO ROBLES ●

CA

FEATURED BREWERIES

1 Anchor
San Francisco, CA, *pages 184–185*

2 Firestone Walker
Paso Robles, CA, *pages 188–189*

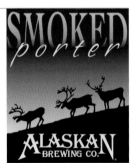

21st Amendment Brewery
San Francisco, California
www.21st-amendment.com

Watermelon Wheat *Wheat Beer 5.5%*

A curve-ball beer produced by a terrific Bay Area brewery, which is located just minutes away from the San Francisco Giants baseball stadium. Wonderfully refreshing wheat beer brewed using 200 lbs of fresh watermelon and available in cans.

Alameda Brew House
Portland, Oregon
www.alamedabrewhouse.com

Irvington Juniper Porter 5.1%

From the achingly trendy part of Portland known as Beaumont-Wilshire comes this smooth, full-bodied porter finished with a flurry of juniper spice. Imagine a thinking drinker's gin-inspired "depth charge".

Alaska Brewing Company
Anchorage, Alaska
www.alaskanbeer.com

Alaskan Smoked Porter 6.5%

An enchanting Alaskan interpretation of German Rauchbiers and a classic vintage ale that improves with age. Brewed with malt that has been languidly smoked over indigenous alder wood for three days, it conjures up caramel, prunes, and port flavors, yet thankfully sidesteps the stifling smokiness of its German counterpart. Incredible.

Alaskan Amber 5%

An early amber-hued pioneer of American craft beer which has been in the grizzly grip of locals since the 1980s. An accessible Alt bier alternative, with an easy-drinking allure.

AleSmith Brewing Company

San Diego, California
www.alesmith.com

 **AleSmith Wee Heavy** 9.5%

Brewer Peter Zein specializes in hoppy, West Coast warps of Belgian and British ales. Anything but wee, this big, brawny, and beautifully balanced Scotch ale will put some bellow in your bagpipes.

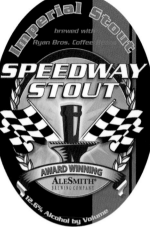

Speedway Stout (Barrel-aged) 12%

Nothing gets a Californian beer boffin more animated than this divine dark and velvet-textured imperial stout. After it's brewed in small batches using copious quantities of coffee beans, it is matured in bourbon barrels. Espresso astringency softened by vanilla notes, a touch of wood, and a smug mellow alcohol glow. A signature classic from an excellent artisan aficionado of ale.

Alpine Beer Company

Alpine, California
www.alpinebeerco.com

Chez Monieux *Fruit Beer* 5.8%

A cracking kriek beer chock-a-block with Michigan cherries and decanted into oak barrels that had previously housed red wine. Fifteen months of maturation tames the face-twisting tartness. Sweet, sour, and seriously fruity.

Exponential Hoppiness 10.5%

Situated in a quirky cabin in the woods outside San Diego, Alpine is not big, but it's very clever. An ever-doubling dose of American hops infuses this IPA with a herbal high, mellowed by the late addition of oak chips and measured maturation. Devilishly drinkable.

> "I am a firm believer in the people. If given the truth, they can be depended upon to meet any national crisis. The great point is to bring them the real facts, and beer."
>
> ABRAHAM LINCOLN
> AMERICAN PRESIDENT 1809–1865

Anchor Brewing Company

See Brewery Profile pages 184–185
San Francisco, California
www.anchorbrewing.com

A San Francisco specialty, steam beer dates from the 1890s California Gold Rush, but was close to extinction in the 1960s when global beer hero Fritz Maytag revived the failing Anchor Steam Brewery. It now produces one of the world's best beers, made from Northern Brewer hops to produce a complex, thirst-quenching brew.

Liberty Ale *IPA* 6%

Here come the hops. Anchor's nod to IPA is a measured, marked departure from the loony lupulin efforts of its West Coast neighbors. Brown sugar-dusted grapefruit flavors sprung from a biscuit base.

Anchor Small 3.3%

A rare thing indeed is a Californian session beer. Small in strength but not in flavor, this classic brewmaster's beer is cut from the mash of Anchor's Old Foghorn Barley Wine.

Anchor Steam *Steam Beer* 4.9%

First brewed in 1896, Anchor Steam hasn't always been this good. In fact, until Fritz Maytag knocked it into shape in 1971, it was pretty lousy. Not any more. A San Franciscan classic brewed using fresh citrusy North American hops and conditioned like an ale, but just at a slightly lower temperature.

Anderson Valley Brewing Company

Boonville, California
www.avbc.com

Anderson Valley Hop Ottin' *IPA* 7%

Anderson Valley is a bucolic solar-powered brewery in beautiful Boonville, where locals speak their own dialect. A classic Californian IPA, but unlike many it holds back on the hops, is blessed with balance, and makes for "Bahl Hornin' " (good drinking). For more hornin' action, check out the Boonville Beer Festival every spring.

Ballast Point Brewing

San Diego, California
www.ballastpoint.com

 Calico Amber Ale 5%

Malt-accented copper-colored British bitter with an American Northwest hop twang. Mellow mouthfeel with a backbone of rich toffee spruced up by citrus and pine.

 **Yellow Tail Pale Ale** 4.6%

This is the brewery that Jack White built, and its soaring success owes much to this West Coast take on a German Kölsch. Citrus-sweetness on the nose and slightly tangy, it's adorned with five percent wheat, Tettnang and Liberty hops, and yeast collected in Cologne, Germany. All in all this pale specimen is a real catch.

Bear Republic Brewing Company

Healdsburg, California
www.bearrepublic.com

Racer 5 IPA 7%

The joy of Racer 5 is in its immaculately hoarse hoppiness, mineral mouthfeel, rasping middle, and a comforting warm finish. An idolized, intelligent IPA from a brilliant brewpub, whose brewer Richard Norgrove also races stock cars.

BridgePort Brewing

Portland, Oregon
www.bridgeportbrew.com

Black Strap Stout 6%

Smoother than a cashmere codpiece, Black Strap Stout brims with rich, dark molasses, cocoa, and an acerbic Northwest hop finish. Capped off with a thick, mustache-bothering creamy white head.

Bridgeport IPA 5.5%

Set up by the winemaking Ponzi family and head brewer Karl Ockert, Bridgeport was a pioneer of Portland's utopian beer scene. Its IPA, first brewed in 1996 and considered by many to be the northwest's finest, accounts for three-quarters of the brewery's production. Double-fermented and brewed using a quintet of hops, it offers glorious balance when compared with other west coast efforts . Simple, elegant, and damn drinkable.

Craftsman Brewing Company

Pasadena, California
www.craftsmanbrewing.com

 **Triple White Sage** 9%

Never mind the Botox, Los Angelinos should be stuffing their faces with the creative quaff of Craftsman Brewing. Brewer Mark Jilg has been casting pearls before swine for more than a decade, braving the grim, glitzy gridlock in a 1940s Studebaker delivery truck and brewing some awesome idiosyncratic ales. Set alongside a pale ale brewed with poppy seeds, Cabernale brewed with grapes, a pre-Prohibition lager, and a smoked dark lager, Triple White Sage is a bombastic Belgian ale that brings honey, coriander, sage, grassy hops, and a touch of mint to the party. Fantastic.

Deschutes Brewery

Bend, Oregon
www.deschutesbrewery.com

 **Black Butte Porter** 5.5%

Deschutes is the sixth-biggest craft brewery in the United States but the only one whose success has been founded on a dark beer. Beautifully balanced bitterness; chocolate-tinged sweetness. A slightly smoky finish like coffee brewed on a bonfire.

Mirror Pond Pale Ale 5.5%

Deschutes champions the use of whole, fresh hops (as opposed to vacuum-packed pellets) and sprinkles locally grown Cascade into this archetypal American twist on a British pale ale. Strong and hoppy, but nowhere near as aggressive as other Northwestern neighbors. Drenched in beer festival gongs, it was also named one of the United States' top ten beers by none other than *Playboy* magazine.

Drake's Brewing Company

San Francisco, California
www.drinkdrakes.com

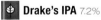 **Drake's IPA** 7.2%

The nautically themed Drake's brews some big, buccaneering beers, many of them barrel-aged, yet lupulin-loving landlubbers will walk the plank for this hearty, heavily hopped swashbuckling sip. Aye!

ANCHOR STEAM BREWING CO.

1705 Mariposa Street, San Francisco, CA 94107

www.anchorbrewing.com

Fritz Maytag is talking about the weather. It's the kind of chit-chat you'd expect from someone you've just met, but Fritz, an austere yet extremely engaging chap, is not one for small talk. On a dog-eared piece of paper, he's frantically drawing the Californian coastline. There are arrows here, isobars there, and, it seems, areas of high pressure everywhere.

Over the course of our meeting, he sketches pot stills and brewing kettles, dusts down antique tomes by Louis Pasteur, and exudes all the infectious enthusiasm of a schoolboy showing you his toy soldiers.

But first up was the weather. Sitting in his brewery office, neither pen nor notebook is out before the climactic questions are raining down like heavy hailstones. Do I know what the average temperature is in San Francisco? Can I tell him the knot speed of the local on-shore wind? How does the deep ocean off Monterey affect the Californian climate? I erect my umbrella of ignorance, but Fritz is far too busy eagerly making a point to require my meager meteorological input.

"The reason Anchor Beer survived so long has an awful lot to do with the climate," he says in conclusion. "It helped prolong the shelf-life of the beer. The low here is 55° or 56° Fahrenheit all year round, and it's a lot cooler than the rest of California. San Francisco weather saved Anchor beer."

A blushing Mother Nature aside, it was Fritz that really saved the Anchor Brewery. In 1965, on a complete whim, he bought a majority stake in the Steam Brewery. It was, if truth be told, a ludicrous idea. For a start, Fritz had no prior knowledge or experience in brewing of beer, nor even a particular interest in the stuff. "I was never into beer really. I drank light US beers such as Lucky Lager, Olympia, and Dos Equis and didn't think much about what I was drinking."

What's more, his new brewery was a shambles, selling just 100 kegs a year. "It was the last medieval brewery in the world," chuckled Fritz. "There was no refrigeration at all; everything was pumped and gravity-pulled. It was dusty, rundown,

ramshackle, very primitive, and the beer tasted pretty bad. I first set eyes on it on a Wednesday and had bought it by the end of the week. "

To buy any small brewery, let alone a tumbledown one, producing an odd long-forgotten "Steam" beer style, was pure folly. During the 1950s, a wave of consolidation had swept through the American beer scene and culled the number of breweries from 407 in 1950 to just 280 in 1961, with only half of those independently run. The likes of Pabst, Schlitz, and Miller were gobbling up market share like hungry Pac-Men and, quite frankly, it was no time to be a minnow, in the 1960s.

But Fritz, heir to the famous Maytag washing-machine empire, had some money in the family coffers and an appetite for a challenge. But the beer's historical lousy reputation initially hamstrung sales, while some restaurant and bar owners even went so far as to inform Fritz that the Anchor Brewery had in fact closed some years before.

"People enthused about Anchor, but that had more to do with the history than the beer," he recalls. "We were a tiny little brewer making quite a traditional beer, but standards had slipped and it wasn't as traditional as I thought it should be. It was sour, and I wasn't happy with it."

By 1968, Fritz had acquired sole ownership of Anchor and set about restoring some pride in the beer. He sought advice from other brewers—both big and small, and attended brewing conferences where he listened and learned while, back at the brewery, he buried his head in brewing tomes and transformed it from a "medieval" operation into one of the most modern brew houses in the world.

Key Beers

Anchor Steam 4.9%
Liberty Ale 6%
Anchor Porter 5.6%
Old Foghorn 8%
Summer Beer 4.6%
Anchor Bock 5.5%
Christmas Ale Varies

"We were very proud of how we modernized things," he says. "Modern technology is a wonderful thing when used right. We centrifuged. We flash pasteurized—it heated the beer, sending it from ice cold to 160°F and back again without harming the beer at all. Beer can become like stale bread. If you don't keep it fresh, then it's no good".

Fritz went back to traditional basics. Sugar was taken out of the brew kettle, whole hops—and lots of them—were introduced alongside two-row imported barley, while additives and adjuncts were unceremoniously shown the door. The new beer made its bottled debut in 1971 and, consistency being the key, sales shifted ever upward. Fritz's vision dovetailed neatly with California's counterculture.

Disenchantment with corporate food and drink was growing, the Vietnam War had undermined trust in the Establishment and people—especially on the West Coast—were rejecting the large, corporate, and impersonal philosophy in favor of the small, local, and authentic.

Fritz began making other beers. A porter was unleashed in 1972, Liberty Ale followed in 1975, alongside an Old Foghorn barley wine and a Christmas Ale. In the same year, Anchor began turning a profit, but demand was beginning to outstrip what the original brewery could supply. Determined to maintain local links, Fritz chose a site in San Francisco—a former coffee roastery in the Potrero Hill district—and built a brand-new brewery in 1979.

Anchor and Maytag's tale has become folklore among North America's craft beer movement, and quite right, too. By proving that the small guy can thrive in the shadow of big business,

Anchor's success laid the foundations on which a thriving craft brewing movement has been built. Having cut a lonely swathe for so long, it was with open arms that Fritz welcomed the craft-brewing cavalry in the eighties. "We've been doing it for years, and we were saved by the competition," admits Fritz. "Between us all, we've met the tremendous demand for small craft beer. This is a great time for beer drinkers. There's integrity, passion, and variety. All in all, it's a wonderful time."

"But it's very hard to do anything in the brewing world that's earth-shaking today," he adds. "We were humble, but we were wild back then and, when we did porter and barley wine, there was nothing like it in the world. But, today, if you make a chocolate huckleberry stout people will just say 'oh yeah, there's another one.'"

Once the pacemaker, Anchor has now been overtaken by the likes of Sierra Nevada and Firestone Walker in terms of size, sales, and brewing capacity. Fritz, though, isn't worried one bit. "I like small things, and I don't want to lose control or sell out," admits Fritz. "I know what it feels like to risk a lot of money. I would rather be small and comfortable, keep our growth modest and keep doing what we're doing. I just have a wild enthusiasm for making stuff."

Opposite: Fritz Maytag revived the Anchor Brewery in San Francisco in 1965, and it has been going strong ever since.

Opposite above right and above: Steam Beer and Liberty Ale are some of Anchor's bestselling brews.

Above right: Gleaming copper vessels house hops and wort that are added at regular intervals to the vessel through a hatch in the top.

Elysian Brewing Company

Seattle, Washington

www.elysianbrewing.com

 🍺 **Dragonstooth Stout**

Seattle may be famed for its coffee, but it's this multi-award-winning rich, smooth mocha-accented stout is the dark brew to seek out. The 20-barrel Elysian Brewing brewpub, perched at the top of Seattle's trendy Capitol Hill neighborhood, makes for essential ale-drinking attention.

Firestone Walker Brewing Company

See Brewery Profile, pages 188–189
Paso Robles, California

wwwfirestonewalker.com

⭐ 🍺 **Firestone Walker Pale Ale 31** 4.6%

Plowing a lonesome yet seriously lovely furrow amid the vineyards of Californian wine country, Firestone Walker pays tribute to British beer styles. It has pioneered a barrel brewing system similar to the Burton Union which, during primary fermentation, amplifies the hop character and softens the malt with vanilla and wood notes taken from the oak. All the best bits of British and American brewing can be found in this phenomenal pale ale.

Fish Brewing Company

Olympia, Washington

www.fishbrewing.com

🍺 **Organic Wild Salmon Pale Ale** 5.5%

Petite but prolific producer of powerful beers, Fish's organic ales take their cue from British brewing while their lagers are lederhosen-slapping fellows. A particularly pleasant pale ale in which

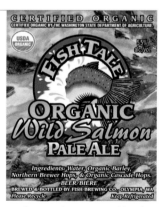

Cascade hops leap high amid a stream of caramel sweetness. It's crisp, it's refreshing, and it raises money to protect our aquatic brethren.

Full Sail Brewing Company

Hood River, Oregon

www.fullsailbrewing.com

🍴 **Full Sail Amber Ale** 5.5%

Full Sail converted a brewery from a former fruit cannery on the banks of the windsurfing wonderland that is Hood River in 1987 and is now the tenth-biggest craft brewer in the States. It is owned by a 47-strong employee cooperative, and the wind in Full Sail's sails has been this excellent amber ale, an eight time-gold medal winner at the World Beer Cup. Robust yet refreshing.

 🍺 **Session Premium Lager** 5.1%

In the heartland of heavy-hopped ales, this retro Pre-Prohibition lager does what it says on the label. Ideal for sipping on the brewpub's spectacular sundeck after a long day pretending that you can windsurf.

Hair of the Dog

Portland, Oregon

www.hairofthedog.com

⭐ 🍺 🍺 **Hair of the Dog Adam** 10%

Only the brave or bonkers would hazard Hair of the Dog's behemoth, boutique bottle-conditioned beauties at breakfast. Drooled over by discerning drinkers, Adam is a complex interpretation of Adambier, an elusive German beer style. A warm, smoky, fruity, constantly evolving ale that flirts with barley wines and harvest ales.

⭐ 🍺 🍺 🍺 **Hair of the Dog Fred** 10%

A golden-hued malt-driven tribute to renowned beer writer Fred Eckhart that betters in the bottle. Brewed with rye grain, ten hop varieties and, when it comes to maturation, scant regard for Father Time.

⭐ 🍺 **Hair of the Dog Rose** *Tripel* 8%

Honey-cloaked take on a Belgian Tripel with a hoodwinking drinkability. Like all Hair of the Dog's beers, Rose gets better if left alone for a while, then smugly consumed in celebration of one's restraint.

Hale's Ales
Seattle, Washington
www.halesales.com

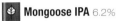 **Mongoose IPA** 6.2%

Having first poked his mash-fork about at the now-defunct Gale's Brewery in Hampshire, England, Mike Hale brews upstanding English ales of impeccable character of which the rounded, malty Mongoose IPA is one. Visit the brewery and you can drink it in a genuine double-decker London bus. But, remember, don't drink and drive. In fact, don't even putt.

Kona Brewing Company
Honolulu, Hawaii
www.konabrewingco.com

 **Pipeline Porter** 5.2%

Rich, roasty, and, when chilled, refreshing in the heat of Honolulu. Brewed using Kona coffee beans. Thinking drinker's energy booster after a hard day catching tubes and partaking in other gnarly nonsense.

Lagunitas Brewing Company
Petaluma, California
www.lagunitas.com

 Lagunitas Czech Pils 5.3%

A robust Pilsner from Lagunitas (pronounced "lah-goo-knee-tuss"). Founder Tony Magee describes it thus: "While an ale might steal your car or try to date your daughter and keep her out all night for who-knows-what purpose, this well-bred Pilsner would offer to clean your house while you're on vacation and leave fresh biscuits and coffee for you when you return."

Lagunitas IPA 5.7%

Renowned as much for his extremely amusing tasting notes as his collection of gorgeous giggle juice, Lagunitas' creator Tony Magee has built his esoteric ale empire on this excellent IPA. Pine needles, eucalyptus, and marmalade, with maple sweetness.

Lagunitas Maximus IPA 7.5%

Imperial IPAs don't come much more imperial than this. It will water your eyes, terrorize your taste buds, and put hairs on your body where there shouldn't really be any.

Lost Abbey Brewing
San Diego, California
www.lostabbey.com

 **Cuvée de Tomme** 11%

In search of enlightening Belgian-style elixirs, Lost Abbey's brewmaster Tomme Arthur pushes more envelopes than a postman on crack. One of several sought-after seasonal releases, Cuvée is the bourbon-barrel-aged baby of bonkers Brettanomyces yeast and sugars sought from sour cherries, barley, raisins, and candy sugar.

Lost & Found Abbey Ale 8%

A deep amber abbey-style beer brewed from a blend of six malts, sugar, and a special raisin purée. Discover its many flavors, including bananas, spice and a bon-bon backbone.

Magnolia Pub & Brewery
San Francisco, California
www.magnoliapub.com

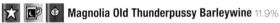 **Magnolia Old Thunderpussy Barleywine** 11.9%

Dave McLean, one of San Francisco's main microbrewing missionaries, crafts Californian-accented British beer styles on legendary Haight. It's a terrific brewpub, and this rich and fruity extreme IPA is a terrific tawny-tinted beer. Seek it out if you can.

Midnight Sun Brewery
Anchorage, Alaska
www.midnightsunbrewing.com

 **Panty Peeler**
Tripel 9%

Alaskan brewer with attitude, artistic labels, and a bevy of seasonal Belgian beers and casks. With a French name of Epluche-Culotte, meaning panty peeler, this knee-knocking tripel brings dry, fruity, spicy, and earthy notes to the beer-tasting table.

FIRESTONE WALKER BREWING COMPANY

1400 Ramada Drive, Paso Robles, California CA 93446

www.firestonewalker.com

Anyone who has driven through California will know that it is daunting drinking territory for anyone more used to drinks and flavors that emanate from a smaller, perhaps subtler, European sensibility.

The state's beers, like its burgers, cars and scenery, are a lot bigger than they are on the other side of the Atlantic. A lot bigger.

For a more timid palate, the West Coast infatuation with intense IPAs is particularly intimidating. Bombastically bitter, aggressively astringent, and heavily hopped and hostile, Californian IPAs will knock your bowler hat off with Oliver Hardy-esque disdain and give your senses the kind of warm Californian welcome last witnessed when Reginald Denny drove into town.

They will have your nostrils whimpering in the corner, shivering and shell-shocked; reduce your tastebuds to flinching, cowering fools begging for forgiveness; and leave your livers in the fetal position, rocking back and forth, bubbles protruding from their nostrils and with their underpants on their head. It is pretty heady stuff.

But fear not, for respite and refuge from these beefy beers can be found at an Anglophile ale-making enclave, deep in Californian wine country, between Los Angeles and San Francisco.

Surrounded by vineyards, the Firestone Walker brewery goes against the grain—and the grape—by brewing beautiful, balanced beers laced with clichéd British restraint. "We really focus on drinkability and balance and that can be a little pedestrian for the beer geeks, but we're a traditional regional brewer," says Matt Bryndilson, Firestone Walker's head brewer. "We tend to stick with cleaner hop flavors and not the earthy, grassy and vegetal aromas that you can find in other Californian beers."

Adam Firestone, the grandson of the

Key Beers

Firestone Walker DBA *Pale Ale* 5%
Firestone Walker Pale Ale 31 4.6%

Right: Head brewer Matt Bryndilson is proud of Firestone's traditional regional brews such as DBA and Walker Pale Ale 31 (opposite).

eponymous tire-making titan, and his English brother-in-law David Walker set up Firestone Walker in 1996. They had witnessed the Californian wine boom of the 1980s, in particular the harmonious marriage of Old Word winemaking traditions and New World techniques, and thought that what worked for a tulip glass would work for a tankard, too.

Sadly, Adam and David's first attempt at brewing was far too ambitious. "They wanted to do oak-fermented ales. So the original concept was to take Chardonnay barrels and use beer in them," recalls Matt. "But the beer oxidized and it was basically all malt vinegar."

The wayward wine barrels were subsequently dispatched from the brewery in favor of a unique adaptation of the iconic 19th-century Burton Union system, which was favored by 19th century British Burton-on-Trent-based brewers.

The system, which separates beer from surplus yeast using a row of linked oak casks and troughs, was tweaked by Firestone Walker and christened (rather aptly) the "Firestone Union". Using forty 60-gallon, medium-toast American oak barrels, the system amplifies the hop character and the oak imparts delicate notes of vanilla, chocolate, and wood.

"There are a lot of brewers who are working with wood but we're different because we use oak for the primary fermentation," says Matt. "We're closer to Burton than California and we're the only brewery in America to use the Union system. The biggest difference between Firestone and Burton is that we use new oak and different types of barrels."

Batches of oak-fermented beer are blended into all Firestone's beers. The Double Barrel Ale, or DBA, is the system's signature beer and Firestone Walker's most successful. Rich, fragrant, bracing, and brisk, it's classic English-style pale ale piqued with hop spice and underscored with soft, warm malt flavors. "Double Barrel Ale represents 50

percent of our production," adds Matt. "It's a very English beer in its origins—in fact, it's as English as American beer gets."

As well as Double Barrel, Adam and David have rolled out the bright-eyed, bushy-tailed Firestone Pale Ale, Firestone Lager, the opaque Walker's Reserve overloaded with espresso and chocolate aromas, and—to placate the hop-hungry masses—Union Jack, an intense, dry-hopped yet drinkable IPA that shakes you by the hand, not the neck.

Yet it is Firestone's vintage ales and bespoke barrel-aged beers that have pricked up the ears of craft ale connoisseurs. In 2006, to commemorate a decade of brewing, a limited-edition Strong Ale was released called "Ten"; a glorious gathering of high-gravity beers aged in different barrel formats and blended using the expertise of local winemakers. Part barley wine, part port, it is highly complex, rich, and teeming with tannin, molasses, roasted chestnuts, fall fruit, and a dry, roasty bitter finish.

Matt, who was honored in 2007 by the Brewers Association for his innovative barrel-ageing techniques, released further vintages in 2007 and 2008 to huge, "we're not worthy" acclaim.

"We've learned a lot from winemakers about toast levels, oak and we're moving beer in and out of barrels," says Matt. "We're not trying to make Belgian beers with fruit or bugs, but I'm interested to see what oak ageing does to the beers. So we're taking very clean beer and ageing them in all kinds of whiskey and wine barrels, blending them like wine and experimenting with racking and different toast intensity. The consumer is pushing breweries to go outside of the lines," he adds. "But we don't intend to lose sight of drinkability."

If you swing by the brewery or the nearby taproom in Buellton, there's bound to be limited-edition barrel-aged brews on tap, as well as a 100 percent wood-fermented version of the Double Barrel Ale. Enjoy.

Moonlight Brewing Company

Santa Rosa, California
www.moonlightbrewing.com

 Death & Taxes 5%

Breweries don't come much more bucolic than this. Set in a wonderfully rustic corner of the Sonoma Valley, Brian Hunt's one-man operation brews top-class beers, of which this bracing black lager, adorned with mild molasses and a nutty finish, is very much one.

Ninkasi Brewing Company

Eugene, Oregon
www.ninkasibrewing.com

 **Total Domination IPA** 6.9%

Named after the ancient Sumerian goddess of fermentation, Ninkasi Brewing was set up by former president of the Oregon Brewers Guild Jamie Floyd. He does a great line in hip hop beers of which Total Domination, endowed with pine citrus and grapefruit, is my favorite. Hedonistic hop heads, meanwhile, hark after the demon Tricerahops Double IPA. Seriously out there.

North Coast Brewing

Fort Bragg, California
www.northcoastbrewing.com

Brother Thelonious 9%

North Coast's brawny beers may share their coastal home with a former US military fort dating from the Civil War, but they're lovers not fighters. This robust and dark homage to jazz legend Thelonious Monk is as smooth as his musical vibes and spirals up on notes of mole-like spicy chocolate, figs, and fall fruit.

Red Seal Ale 5.5%

Clap your hands and bark in appreciation of this excellent copper-colored amber ale that batts its eyelids in the direction of American pale ales. A nutty nose, moreish mouthfeel, and lingering lupulin length at the end.

Rogue Ales

Newport, Oregon
www.rogue.com

Old Crustacean Barleywine 11.4%

Long in the tooth, Rogue specializes in unpasteurized, small-batch heavily hopped and highly irreverent ales packaged in tall screen-printed

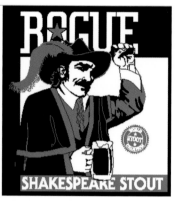

650 ml bottles and marketed across the United States and beyond with a mischievous glint in their eye. The strongest is a beast of a barley wine. Unfiltered and unfined, it's intense, immense, malty, and dark.

Shakespeare Stout 6%

Ebony liquid with a towering ivory head lacing long into the glass. Dark chocolate bitterness, mellow mocha, and a delicate roasted malt accent. Such stouts as dreams are made of. Have too many, though, and you may be "bard".

Smoke Ale *Rauchbier* 7%

Inspired by the fall of the Berlin Wall, brewmaster John Meier has built a German Rauchbier using delicate smoke aromas, an orange-amber hue, peaty malts, and a spicy hop finish.

Russian River

Santa Rosa, California
www.russianriverbrewing.com

Blind Pig IPA 6%

Bringing orange, peaches, grapefruit flavors, and a bag full of balanced bitterness to the party, Blind Pig is believed to be the original Double IPA. If you're a hardened hophead, you'll be like a pig in the proverbial sense.

Pliny the Elder *India Pale Ale* 8%

This is the beer all Double IPAs want to be when they grow up. Intoxicating hop oils on the nose, a cacophony of citrus fruit on the palate and a peppery, tang finish that stays longer than the mother-in-law. A lupulin-lover's wet dream.

Supplication *Brown Ale* 7%

Blissful bottle-conditioned Belgian brown ale. Aged with sour cherries and wild and crazy yeast in French oak Pinot Noir barrels for a year. Tart, oaky, and complex.

Sierra Nevada Brewing
Chico, California
www.sierranevada.com

 **Sierra Nevada Celebration Ale**
6.8%

Cockle-warming winter ale with one foot in the IPA family. Comforting, hoppy, and earthy chocolate notes mingle with lots of lemon and lychee hop flavors. Best drunk in the glow of a roaring fire or surrounded by other warming festive clichés.

 **Sierra Nevada Pale Ale** 5.6%

Having sown the seeds of the now-blossoming West Coast beer scene, this quintessential American pale ale enjoys, and deserves, legendary status among the craft-brewing community. A superb showcase for the spicy, fruity Cascade hop. A classic. Don't miss it.

Sierra Nevada Porter 5.6%

It may be a "plain" porter but it's anything but plain. Lovely smooth mouthfeel laden with caramel, coffee, and chocolate. Dark fruit finish courtesy of Golding and Willamette hops. Brilliant.

Stone Brewing Company
Escondido, California
www.stonebrew.com

 **Arrogant Bastard Ale**
7.2%

This unapologetically hedonistic, herbaceous ale oozes resin aromas and oils. Enormously astringent, it's an in-your-face IPA that dares you to drink it. Yes, you.

 **Stone Pale Ale** 5.4%

The beer on which the Stone empire has been built. Full-bodied, muscular, and copper-colored with an IBU of 41. At Stone, that's a laid-back lupulin liquid.

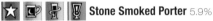 **Stone Smoked Porter** 5.9%

Colossal in character and big in both attitude and flavor, Stone's unashamedly aggressive beers blew the doors off a subdued San Diego beer scene in 1996. Malts smoked over peat shape this shimmering ebony-hued twist on German rauchbier. A thinking drinker's Islay Scotch depth charge.

Terminal Gravity Brewing
Enterprise, Oregon
www.terminalgravitybrewing.com

Terminal Gravity IPA 6.7%

Amid the uplifting oblivion of Eastern Oregon, Terminal Gravity conjures up some seriously superb beers from a modest brewhouse shoehorned into a garage. The brewpub serves an awesome abbey ale, a big, ballsy barley wine and this flagship brew; a brawny bottle-conditioned beer with a weighty texture, notes of citrus, ginger, and rosemary, and a finish so beautifully bitter it'll tilt your head sideways.

"Not all chemicals are bad. Without chemicals such as hydrogen and oxygen, for example, there would be no way to make water, a vital ingredient in beer."

DAVE BARRY
AMERICAN HUMORIST AND COLUMNIST 1947–

USA Central States

The central United States is derisively called "flyover country" by some, and those who aren't familiar with the region still consider it a beer desert. That is certainly not the case, according to **Maryanne Nasiatka** and **Paul Ruschmann**.

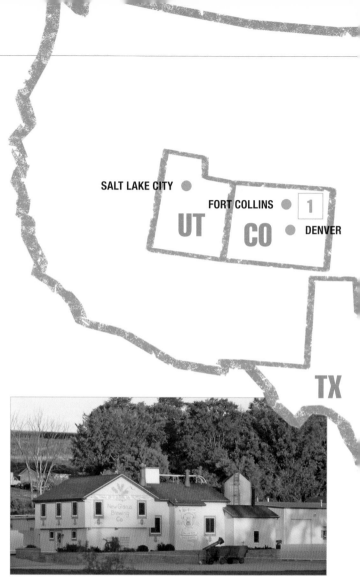

SALT LAKE CITY

FORT COLLINS

1

UT   CO   DENVER

TX

Admittedly, the central states came late to the craft-brewing party—for one thing, the liquor laws were slow to change—but they've been busy making up for lost time. In much of the region, the craft brewing movement was really a rediscovery of pre-Prohibition beer culture.

In the 19th century, an area roughly bounded by Cincinnati, St. Louis, and Milwaukee took in millions of Germans, and a culture that celebrated beer. A brewery, preferably with a beer garden, was as essential to a Midwestern town as a church, a schoolhouse, and a grain elevator. The local tavern remains a central feature of community life, both in farming towns on the prairie and in the ethnic neighborhoods of Chicago. Wisconsin, which boasts a heavy and lingering German influence, ranks fifth in the nation for its number of breweries. Milwaukee's mega breweries—Blatz, Pabst and Schlitz—have closed their doors, but Miller soldiers on; elsewhere in the state you'll find everything from regional survivor Leinenkugel to adventurous micros such as Capitol and New Glarus. Michigan ranks right behind Wisconsin in brewery population. The state that once

put "muscle cars" on the road is now gaining a reputation for potent, characterful "big beers". Some of the biggest beers come from Dragonmead, Founders, and New Holland (see Eastern States, pages 202 and 204).

The other Great Lakes states are dotted with breweries new and old: Minnesota's August Schell is a generations-old operation that found a second life as a regional craft brewery; Three Floyds, in Indiana's industrial northwest (see Eastern States, page 203), attracts a cult following to its Dark Lord Russian Imperial Stout release party; and Ohio is the home of quirky brewpubs that allow customers to come in and brew their own beer. Missouri earns a place on the brewing map, thanks to St. Louis-based headquarters of global giant Anheuser-Busch InBev, America's largest brewery; and the Show-Me State is bookended by St. Louis's Schlafly Bottleworks and Kansas City-based Boulevard Brewing.

Kansas endured bouts of prohibition even before the "Great Experiment" went national, but Lawrence's Free State Brewing has revived the state's brewing tradition—with liberal amounts

MN

WI

ST PAUL

MILWAUKEE

CHICAGO

IL

DALLAS

August Schell Brewing Company

New Ulm, Minnesota
www.schellsbrewery.com

 **Caramel Bock** 5.8%

A toffee-tinged, copper-colored, sweet-tempered tipple from the United States' second-oldest brewery, dating back to 1860. Easy to drink and ideal for Bock-drinking neophytes and mainstream lager swiggers looking to take a leap.

Avery Brewing Company

Boulder, Colorado
www.averybrewing.com

 **Avery IPA** 6.3%

Amid the laid-back, tofu-munching locals of bohemian Boulder, family-owned Avery crafts some terrific, bombastic beers—especially the high-octane Belgian ales. The IPA is richly resinous, and copious Columbus, Simcoe, Cascade, and Centennial hops deliver a pine-powered punch. A holy mother-pucker.

FEATURED BREWERY

1 New Belgium
Fort Collins, CO, *pages 196–197*

of indigenous wheat. Farther south, a lingering "Bible Belt" influence and the locals' preference for national-brand beer have posed a double-barreled challenge for craft brewers, but good beer has made its way there as well. Louisiana's Abita is known nationwide, thanks in part to its association with Chef Emeril Legasse. In Texas, Spoetzl Brewery's Shiner Bock can be found far beyond its tiny hometown.

Wherever you go in the nation's midsection, you aren't far from a brewpub. And if you do a bit of looking, you'll find a store stocked with good locally brewed ales and lagers.

Flossmoor Station Restaurant & Brewery

Flossmoor, Illinois
www.flossmoorstation.com

Pullman Brown Ale 6%

Multi-award-winning brown ale from a multi-award-winning small brewpub. Molasses, three different hops, and myriad malts make up this deep mahogany downy English-style ale that is richly delicious.

Above left: Hefty mash tuns are well used at the New Glarus Brewing Company in Wisconsin.

Above right: The brewhouse at New Glarus is indeed a micro, set among the undulating hills of Wisconsin in an area akin to a Little Switzerland, even down to its German-style beers.

Goose Island Beer Company
Chicago, Illinois
www.gooseisland.com

★ ⊕ **Goose Island IPA** 5.9%

An intelligent, accessible copper-hued IPA. Sidesteps saccharine malt sweetness in favor of a deliciously dry biscuit base, upon which a rich, succulent, herbal hop character is laid.

★ ⊕ **Honker's Ale** Bitter 4.3%

In 1988, when few other Midwestern micros were flying the flag for flavor, Goose Island provided a breath of fresh air for the windy city's beer drinkers. Its array of European-style ales pour from white-necked tap handles all over Chicago and beyond. Honker's, a brusque British bitter, is sweet, spicy, and superb as a session beer.

Great Divide Brewing Company
Denver, Colorado
www.greatdivide.com

★ ⊡ ⊠ **Oak Aged Yeti Imperial Stout** 9.5%

An enormous yeti walks into the Great Divide brewery tap, an old dairy in north Denver, pads up to the bar, and says: "Can I get some nachos, a glass of milk, some beef jerky, two pale ales, and .... er .... erm .... a bottle of your opaque, opulent, and robust Russian imperial stout, the one that's had its intense coffee and chocolate character mellowed by French oak ageing?" "Sure thing," replies the barman, "but why the big paws?"

⊕ **Titan Indian Pale Ale** 6.8%

Deep golden heavyweight hop hitter that'll throw your taste buds on the ropes with jabs of grapefruit, freshly cut grass, and fruity esters thrown from a sweet, shortbread canvas.

Left Hand Brewing
Longmont, Colorado
www.lefthandbrewing.com

⎍ ⊠ **Juju Ginger** 4.2%

Ginger gently bops you on the nose, tickles the tongue and burns up the bitterness born out of Cascade, Golding, and Saaz hops. A soothing thirst-quencher and a model midrange microbrew.

Minneapolis Town Hall
Minneapolis, Minnesota
www.townhallbrewery.com

⊕ **Masala Mama India Pale Ale** 5.9%

Piney, resinous, and piquant proof that the West Coast doesn't have the monopoly on perfectly poised IPAs. Brewed with a trio of American hops, several caramel malts, and mash-fork magic.

New Belgium Brewing Company
See Brewery Profile, pages 196–197
Fort Collins, Colorado
www.newbelgium.com

⊡ **Abbey** Dubbel 7%

When it's not hanging about on podiums at major beer competitions, this delightful Dubbel keeps itself busy being auburn-hued and smooth. Conjures up banana cream pie flavors and some herbal notes.

★ ⊡ ⊠ **La Folie** Sour Red Ale 6%

Wood-aged red sour Flanders ale that dawdles about in French oak for up to three years. Brewed in homage to New Belgium's "Follow your folly"; it's dry, tremendously tart, and an ideal apéritif.

New Glarus Brewing Co.
New Glarus, Wisconsin
www.newglarusbrewing.com

⎍ ⏍ **Dancing Man Wheat** 7.2%

Quaint and quirky amid the undulating hills of Wisconsin, New Glarus is the United States' Little Switzerland, complete with chocolate, fondue, chalets, useful pen knives, cuckoo clocks, and other lazy national stereotypes. And this German Hefeweizen, big on bubblegum, banana, and nuts on the finish, is representative of its premier brews.

★ ⏍ ⊠ **Wisconsin Cherry Beer** 5%

More than a pound of Montmorency cherries make it into each 750ml bottle. Arguably the United States' finest fruit beer also hosts Wisconsin-farmed wheat, Belgian-roasted barley, unruly Belgian yeasts, and year-long aged Hallertau hops that have mellowed and mingled in oak. A textured tart, sparkling, almond-tinged cherry explosion best sipped slightly chilled from a Champagne flute.

Odell Brewing Company
Fort Collins, Colorado
www.odellbrewing.com

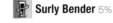 **5 Barrel Pale Ale** 5.2%

A strapping 36 IBU aromatic pale ale filtered through a bed of whole flower hops before being inundated with even more of the little green blighters. Lovely.

Cutthroat Porter 4.5%

Odell, situated an hour's drive outside Denver, has been crafting cracking quaff for 20 years now and exports to half a dozen states. Smoother than a velvet tuxedo on a sledge, this dark plum-colored porter combines coffee, chocolate, and a frisky hop finish. Try some when you can.

Saint Arnold Brewing Company
Houston, Texas
www.saintarnold.com

Saint Arnold Divine Reserve
Weizenbock 8.4%

One can't imagine a problem that Houston has not solved, or at least eased, by the Divine Reserve series of beers. Saint Arnold, founded in 1994 and Texas' oldest brewery, releases a Divine Reserve every year to huge acclaim. Following in the footsteps of a first-class barley wine and impressive IPA comes this Weizenbock, well endowed with flavours of bananas, chocolate, and spice.

Sprecher Brewing
Glendale, Wisconsin
www.sprecherbrewery.com

Black Bavarian
Schwarzbier 5.86%

A jewel of a German-leaning brewery founded in 1985 by Randy Sprecher and making some of the best microbrews in Milwaukee. A creamy cultured and midnight-black mash-up of coffee, caramel, molasses, and chocolate.

Surly Brewing Company
Brooklyn Center, Minnesota
www.surlybrewing.com

Surly Bender 5%

Deftly bridges the gap between a brown ale and a porter. Aromatic American hops conspire with some Belgian malt and, to give it added texture, oatmeal to produce a very drinkable dark beer.

Tommyknocker Brewery
Idaho Springs, Colorado
www.tommyknocker.com

Tommyknocker ButtHead Doppelbock 8.2%

Do not be hoodwinked by the chirpy goat-riding, slightly camp guys on the label because this big, bucking bock is a German giant of a beer. Auburn-colored and medium-bodied, with nutty chocolate and a sweet malt finish. It rocks.

Tyranena Brewing Company
Lake Mills, Wisconsin
www.tyranena.com

Devil Over a Barrel Bourbon Imperial Oatmeal Coffee
Oatmeal Porter 8%

In addition to some top-class core and seasonal beers, this whimsical Wisconsin brewery has earned acclaim for its limited-edition "Brewers Gone Wild" collection—a series of "big, bold, and ballsy beers." While this cracking coffee stout, infused with vanilla and peppery spice, is hard to get hold of, the BGW beers are well worth hunting down.

Wasatch Brew Pub and Brewery
Park City, Utah
www.wasatchbeers.com

Polygamy Porter 4%

If you are going to survive as a brewery in a state where 70 percent of the population does not drink, then the beer has to be mighty fine. Which this Mormon-mocking mellow mocha-flavored porter, complete with "Why just have one?" tagline, certainly is.

NEW BELGIUM BREWING

500 Linden, Fort Collins, Colorado, CO 80524

www.newbelgium.com

Do you detest your job? Spend your "working" day staring into the distance half-heartedly shifting desktop icons from one corner of the computer screen to the other? Wish you could do something, absolutely anything, else? Well, may I suggest you go to work at New Belgium?

Located in the lovely, laid-back town of Fort Collins, voted *Money* magazine's Best Place to Live 2006, New Belgium is a utopian, environmentally friendly beervana where everything and everyone appears to have been smeared in a high-definition cinematic "happy" visual sheen.

The sun shines; the flowers bloom; the trees blossom; there are young, smiley pretty things and cool dudes; there is laughter and high-spirited hubbub; and there is even a Director of Fun, a man whose task it is to ensure that employees enjoy enough tomfoolery in their lives.

Every Thursday, tools are downed, and everyone heads off for volleyball night on the floodlit court behind the brewery. The staff owns a third of the company, there's a climbing wall installed in the brewhouse, and, if you work there for 12 months, you receive a New Belgium cruiser bike to pedal cheerily to your day's "work".

As many as a third of the company's employees own them but the bikes symbolize more than merely a merry mode of transport. For it was while on a cycling trip through Belgium, back in 1985, when founder Jeff Lebesch first became enchanted by the country's eclectic beer.

Enlightened, inspired, and armed with a souvenir strain of brewer's yeast, Jeff returned to Colorado and began homebrewing some Belgium beers of his own. Six years later, he and his wife Kym Jordan turned pastime into profession and began brewing commercially from their basement and kitchen.

Abbey, a Belgian ale, was the first beer to be brewed and bottled, followed by Fat Tire, an amber ale inspired by the Belgian beer Palm. Such was Fat Tire's initial success, driven

by word-of-mouth and funky labels, that it was soon being peddled faster than it was being brewed and, before long, the newfangled New Belgium had outgrown its basement and moved into a local rail depot, where it stayed for two years.

But sales kept going upward and onward. In 1995, Jeff, Kym, and a handful of eager employees moved into the current home—a state-of-the-art brewery that employs traditional brewing principles. In less than 20 years, New Belgium has metamorphosized from a basement producing a humble, eight and a half barrels-a-week into the third-largest craft brewer in America with an enviable reputation for its eco credentials.

Not content with being the first brewery in the United States to be entirely reliant on wind power (using wind turbines in Wyoming) and one of the largest single users of wind power in North America, it also collects methane from the brewing wastewater and converts it into electricity; recyclable bins are littered throughout the brewery; light tubes channel natural light into the warehouse; refrigeration is driven by ammonia; everything is insulated; solar power is rife; and there are bikes.

But what of the beers? Well, first and foremost, there's Fat Tire. The sweet-sided malty, mainstream amber ale has an enormous following across more than 16 states. It's responsible for two-thirds of New Belgium's sales and while some connoisseurs regard its reputation as somewhat inflated, its phenomenal popularity has afforded head brewer Peter Bouckaert the freedom to experiment elsewhere.

Peter has hailed himself the "Jackson Pollock of brewing."

"I take my can of paint and drip it all over the canvas," he says. "We do everything different here. There's no rule book

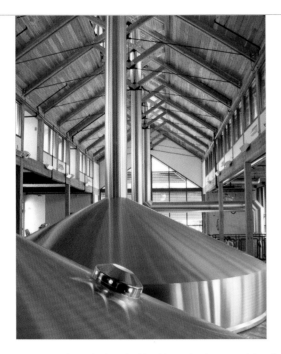

Key Beers

1554 *Brussels-style Black Ale* 5.5%

Abbey *Belgian Dubbel* 7%

Blue Paddle *Pilsner* 4.8%

Fat Tire *Amber Ale* 5.3%

La Folie *Belgian Brown Sour Ale* 7%

Mothership Wit *Organic Wheat Beer* 4.8%

Sunshine Wheat *Wheat Beer* 4.8%

or parameters. Instead of looking at a beer as lots of separate influences, our beers are greater than the sum of their parts. We use a lot of different yeasts and spices."

Bouckaert, a Belgian-born brewer formerly of Alkan-Maes and Rodenbach breweries, brews more than a dozen beers, mostly with a distinct Belgian accent. "The brewing process can be a little one-dimensional. You need to think about it from a different angle", adds Peter. "Just putting more hops in doesn't make a more interesting beer—it's more involved. You can tweak any one thing in the brewing process—people ignore the mash process but that's absolutely key."

Unbeknown to the vast majority of Fat Tire followers, Peter brews a brace of refreshing wheat beers (Sunshine Wheat and Mothership Wit), an excellent ester-emboldened abbey ale, a Flemish ale named 1554, a top-class Tripel, an American pale ale, as well as an authentic Czech Pilsner called Blue Paddle.

But it's the liquid embodiment of New Belgium's "Follow Your Folly" mantra that excites the beer buffs the most. A wood-aged Flemish sour ale, La Folie is a spontaneous fermenting ale, very much in the Rodenbach mold, aged in French oak for up to three years with the help of wild yeast strains. Blended and released as a limited-edition vintage every year, La Folie is a forceful yet delicately tart frisson of fruit flavors. "Some of the older Belgians think I'm a traitor, selling their secrets and stealing their share of the export market. But we are interpretations. We're new Belgium and, if anything, we're rolling out the red carpet for Belgium beers by introducing people to new flavors and tastes. It raises awareness, I'm helping the Belgians come in."

Opposite top: New Belgium employees are entitled to a company bicycle after 12 months' service.

Top left: Even the brewhouse is constructed from eco-friendly materials, with solar and wind power providing energy.

Above: Fat Tire and La Folie are two of the Belgian-inspired brews developed by founder Jeffe Lebesch and head brewer Peter Bouckaert.

USA Eastern & Midwestern States

American East–West rivalry is not just about colleges and rap music. Craft brewers are at it, too, claims **Lew Bryson**. But the contest's usually framed to favor the West: Who makes the hoppiest beers?

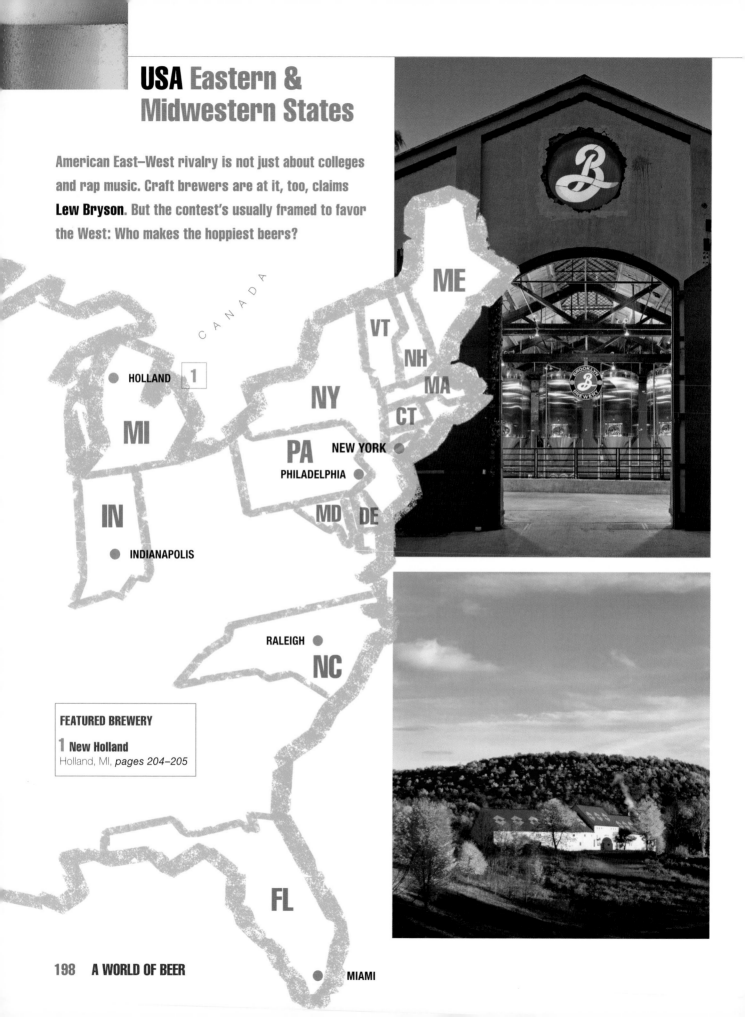

CANADA

HOLLAND 1

MI

IN

INDIANAPOLIS

ME

VT

NH

NY

MA

CT

PA

NEW YORK

PHILADELPHIA

MD DE

RALEIGH

NC

FL

MIAMI

FEATURED BREWERY

1 New Holland
Holland, MI, *pages 204–205*

The East has been working at a disadvantage in that arena because that is the West's identity: take a beer and hop it to the hilt. The East has a different, more complex identity, and it should arrange to fight on its own turf more often.

The East's strengths are tradition and variety. Eastern brewers generally tend toward brewing established European types of beer: Pilsner, pale ale, and Tripel. Maybe it's because of the people that settled here maybe it's because of Europe's relative proximity. And maybe it's due to the old pre-Prohibition breweries in the East: the United States' oldest, Yuengling, is in Pennsylvania, and Matt's in Utica, New York state, is successfully making the move to craft beers with its Saranac line. Whatever the reason, the East represents variety created by more than 1,000 years of European brewing experimentation.

Except, that is, when they tweak it. Eastern brewers do make absolutely traditional beers—fine examples such as Allagash White that can stand up to the originals. Then they'll get a wild hair up their butt, and decide to put German hops in their pale ale, IPA-level hopping in their weissbier, or throw an English ale yeast in to their Belgian Tripel recipe. They experiment with all the elements of beer, not just hopping rates.

That may sound like no big deal compared to wildly ridiculous, insane amounts of hops, but it's a breadth of experimentation that finds its zenith at Dogfish Head, where the brewers take the East Coast mix of tradition and variety farther than anyone. They sometimes make beers based on beer pot residue found in 5,000-year-old tombs.

Who else is here? The country's biggest craft brewer, Boston Beer Company, makes Samuel Adams, from Sam Adams Light to the whopping 26% ABV Utopias. There are brewpubs from the early years of craft brewing: Gritty McDuff's, Northampton, MA, and Portsmouth, NC, have been open for 20 years or more. You'll find more lagers here—mostly in the New York–Baltimore–Pittsburgh triangle—and the ubiquitous Ringwood yeast, a classic love-it-or-hate-it experience. There are also plenty of Belgian-type specialists, such as Allagash and Brewer's Art, plus Wolaver's, an organic brewer.

Variety in the East, it's not just the spice of beer life. It is life.

Opposite top: The Brooklyn Brewing Company in New York is at the forefront of adventurous, small-scale brewing.

Opposite below: In upstate New York, Brewery Ommegang is built on a former hop farm and brews five Belgian-inspired flagship beers.

Allagash Brewing
Portland, Maine
www.allagash.com

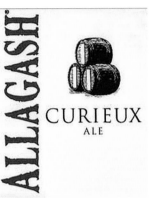

 **Allagash Curieux**
Bottled Tripel 9.5%

Synonymous with beautiful boutique Belgian-style beers, the East Coast–based Allagash made its name on the back of a wonderful wheat beer. But it's this bourbon barrel-aged Tripel, in its swanky corked bottle, and touched with vanilla and a smidgen of smoke, that charms the discerning connoisseur.

Bar Harbor
Bar Harbor, Maine
www.barharborbrewing.com

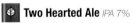 **Cadillac Mountain Stout** 6.7%

Dark, dry stout from a marvellous Maine-based micro. As if it's been brewed to the soothing, soulful sounds of Barry White. Smooth, slightly smoky, and satin-black like the Walrus of Love's smoldering bed sheets.

Bell's Brewery
Kalamazoo, Michigan
www.bellsbeer.com

Bell's Kalamazoo Stout 6%

Bell's, in existence since 1985, is one of the United States' longest running breweries and previously brewed under the name Kalamazoo. This eponymous stout is darker than a miner's nightmare, with espresso roast flavors, mocha, and a viscous, velvety texture.

Two Hearted Ale *IPA 7%*

This hoppy and impressive IPA opens with orange, gives it a bit of grapefruit, then finishes off with a fine floral flourish. Hearty indeed and very tasty.

Boston Beer Company
Boston, Massachusetts
www.samueladams.com

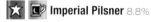 **Imperial Pilsner** 8.8%

Like a Pilsner, just bigger. And badder (in the Michael Jackson sense of the word). A lager with legs, it hails the Hallertau hop and, with a rich mouthfeel and plenty of warm alcohol, treads on the toes of a Tripel-style Belgian ale.

Samuel Adams Boston Lager 4.8%

When craft brewers stormed the gates of big, bland beer in the mid-1980s, the Boston Beer Company's Jim Koch was in the front chariot, holding the reins in one hand and this Vienna-style lager in the other. Accessible yet authentic, with a sweet mellow middle, herbal aroma, and beautifully tight finish.

Utopias 25%

It's a beer, Jim, but not as we know it. It's the strongest beer ever brewed, possibly the most unusual, and perhaps the most expensive. Utopias' peers are not pilsners, bocks, or weiss biers but ports, brandies, and whiskies. Utopias doesn't look like a beer, it doesn't smell like a beer, and it certainly doesn't taste like a beer, but … beer it is. Crimson in color, with the texture and taste of a fine brandy, Utopias is brewed with a trio of noble hops, three varieties of malt, several different types of yeast, and a splash of maple syrup before being aged and matured in whisky, cognac, or port barrels for up to ten months. After-dinner snifter territory, where pint glasses fear to tread.

Brewery Ommegang
Cooperstown, New York
www.ommegang.com

 **Ommegang Three Philosophers** 9.8%

A Belgian-style farmhouse built on a former hop farm in upstate New York, Ommegang bangs the Belgian-style ale drum with zeal and gusto. Of the five flagship beers, Three Philosophers is the funkiest and fruitiest. A luscious, languidly matured love child of Lindemans cherry Lambic and a dark ale, it's all chocolate, dark fruit, and toasted malts matured and delivered in a beautiful bottle. Check it out with cheese or a cigar. Or even both.

Brooklyn Brewery
New York, New York
www.brooklynbrewery.com

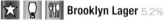 **Brooklyn Black Chocolate Stout** 10.1%

Some of the flavors in this velvet-smooth imperial stout: chocolate, port, prunes, a bit more chocolate, coffee, chocolate again, figs, chocolate, mocha, chocolate, hints of toast, and, last but not least, more chocolate. Did I mention the chocolate?

 **Brooklyn Lager** 5.2%

In 1996, when the brewery breathed life back into Brooklyn beer, it led with this assertive amber-gold Viennese-style lager. Wonderful floral, sturdy bitterness, a kiss of caramel, and a long, smooth finish.

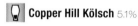 **Brooklyn Local** 9%

German hops, sugar from Mauritius, Belgian yeast, and some Big Apple attitude. They're all in this lovely 100 percent bottle-fermented Lowlander-style liquid—coriander, spice, pear-drop candy and cloves shaking their booty.

Cambridge House Brewery
Granby and Torrington, Connecticut
www.cbhbrew.com

 **Copper Hill Kölsch** 5.1%

Killer Kölsch from Connecticut that cranks up the IBU a little. Restrained hops, citrus sweetness, easy-drinking, esters, and a butterscotch back end.

Dogfish Head Craft Brewery
Milton, Delaware
www.dogfish.com

 **90 Minute IPA** 9%

In the late 1990s, while other brewers were adding hops once, twice or thrice during the brewing process, Sam Caglione experimented with continual hopping. A continual stream of hops was added using a converted American football tabletop game that languidly shook the little green blighters into the boil over the course of 90 minutes. The result? An IPA that's absurdly hoppy without being overly bitter. If you think this is big, there's a 120 minute IPA at 21%. Golly gosh.

 **Chateau Jiahu** 9%

Properly mental and a little oriental, this barley wine is a living liquid legacy of 12th-century China taking the sugars from rice, honey, muscat grapes, hawthorn fruit, and chrysanthemum flowers and feeding them to sake yeast during a month-long fermentation.

Raison d'être *Strong Belgian Ale* 8%

Dark, ruby-red Belgian ale fermented with Belgian yeast, Belgian beet sugar, and raisins. Smoke and no small amount of poke, funky and phenolic, vinous and voluptuous. Lovely.

Duck-Rabbit Craft Brewery
Farmville, North Carolina
www.duckrabbitbrewery.com

 Duck-Rabbit Milk Stout 5.7%

Duck-Rabbit prides itself as a prized peddler of cracking (or should that be quacking?) ales from the dark side, such as this opaque, silky stout.

 **Duck-Rabbit Porter** 5.7%

Another shadowy sip from North Carolina's dark beer brewers. Creamy mouthfeel courtesy of the oatmeal addition to the grist, licorice notes, chocolate, and an astringent coffee finish.

Flying Dog Brewery
Frederick, Maryland
www.flyingdogales.com

 **Doggie Style Pale Ale** 5.5%

Loved by the late "gonzo" journalist Hunter S. Thompson and labeled by his artist Ralph Steadman, Flying Dog's brilliant beers cock a leg on the fire hydrant of conformity. In 2008, the brewery left Denver, Colorado for Maryland but, as this dry-hopped hooch proves, the move from the mountains hasn't tamed the beers' tenacity. Crisp and full-bodied, brewed with copious amounts of Cascade, and brought back to heel using crystal malt.

Old Scratch Amber Ale *Lager* 5.5%

An ace multi-award-winning amber ale whose subdued toffee-apple sweetness makes it superb in the summer.

Founders Brewing
Grand Rapids, Michigan
www.foundersbrewing.com

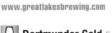 **Dirty Bastard** *Scotch Ale* 8.3%

A chewy sasquatch-sized Scotch ale that'll lift your kilt, toss your caber, and perform other innuendo-laden Scottish clichés, thanks to the use of ten different malts and no small amount of spicy hops. A peaty, potent pal.

Great Lakes Brewing
Cleveland, Ohio
www.greatlakesbrewing.com

 **Dortmunder Gold** 5.8%

Greener than a queasy Kermit, Great Lakes' unrivaled environmental awareness has not been at the expense of brewing excellence. As proved by this distinctively dry Dortmund-style lager, bronze in color, laced and lathered in head with a minerally middle and a robust, crisp flourish.

Harpoon Brewery
Boston, Massachusetts
www.harpoonbrewing.com

 **Harpoon Ale** 5%

Harpoon was one of the leading chariots fighting for choice in the early 1990s having been inspired by the ales of Europe. This archetypal, balanced American pale ale was the first in the family and the prototype for the countless pales that have followed.

Magic Hat Brewing Company
South Burlington, Vermont
www.magichat.com

 **Magic Hat #9** *Pale Ale* 4.6%

Liquids as laid-back and left wing as the liberal-leaning town in which they brew, Magic Hat does deft drinks running a gamut of styles including raspberry-infused stouts and big Belgians. This pale ale contains a "secret ingredient" that we reckon is apricot. How do we know? It tastes of apricot.

Jolly Pumpkin's Artisan Ales
Dexter, Michigan
www.jollypumpkin.com

 La Roja *Flanders Red* 7.2%

Ales aged for anything between eight weeks and ten months come together for jolly japes in an amber-colored tart toffee-tainted peppery embrace. Jolly reviving.

Oro de Calabaza *Belgian Ale* 8%

Barrel-ageing, open fermentation, and bottle conditioning are what carves a smile on the face of Jolly Pumpkin, with this Franco-Belgian fusion of esters, bananas, spice, and citrus zest being a prime—and potent—example.

Matt Brewing Company
Utica, New York
www.saranac.com

Saranac Adirondack Lager
Amber Lager 5.5%

Founded in 1888 in Utica, NY, at the foothills of the Adirondack Mountains, Matt Brewing launched this reasonably hoppy amber ale in its centennial year. Back then, it was a bold move, but the brewery believed in the beer, and it's worked out amazingly well for it. Today, it makes some pretty aggressive beers, but the Adirondack is still good, and makes just as remarkable a statement.

New Holland Brewing
See Brewery Profile, pages 204–205
Holland, Michigan
www.newhollandbrew.com

Dragon's Milk 9%

Worshippers of barrel-aged beers flock to Holland, a town with more than 150 churches, to kneel at the altar of this creative craft brewer. Dragon's Milk plucks up some Dutch courage with tannins and toffee, raisins, vanilla, and a complex finish.

Pilgrim's Dole *Weizen/Barley Wine* 10%

Wonderful "wheat wine" brewed with a 50/50 blend of wheat and barley malt. This rich and fascinating brew includes citrus and caramel flavors akin to a fruity crème brûlée.

Kuhnhenn Brewing
Warren, Michigan
www.kbrewery.com

Raspberry Eisbock 10.8%

Serve in a Champagne flute. An exceptional viscous elixir resplendent in more than just a feast of fruit. Hazelnut, chocolate, and almonds vie for attention alongside licorice, pepper on the nose, and a decadent disappearance of warm alcohol at the end. Outstanding, unique, and ever-so elusive.

Smuttynose/Portsmouth Brewery
Portsmouth, New Hampshire
www.smuttynose.com and www.portsmouthbrewery.com

 Bottle Rocket IPA 6.5%

Extremely well-constructed IPA that pours at the Portsmouth Brewpub, the sister company of Smuttynose. Light mahogany in color, with a tan head that laces all lovely, it springs grassy herbal aromas, orange jelly, and spice from a base of rich malt.

Shoals Pale Ale 5%

Named after a rocky archipelago and brewed in New Hampshire since 1994, Smuttynose beers are not to be sniffed at. Stick your hooter in this, though, and you'll be sure to get plenty of floral American hop oils wafting in. Milder than most pale ales, but no less complex.

Schmaltz Brewing Company
Brooklyn, New York
www.schmaltz.com

 **He'Brew Genesis Ale** *IPA* 5.2%

Oy vey, oy vey. One for the chosen ones, this "interdemoninational" IPA stuffs five American hop varieties under its skull cap alongside some mellow malt sweetness. Great with a salty beef bagel. Proper Kosher.

St. Somewhere Brewing Company
Tarpon Springs, Florida
www.brewery.com

Saison Athene *Saison* 7.5%

One of very few brewers flying the flag in Florida, St. Somewhere brings boutique Belgian-style ales to the sun-kissed hordes. This Saison, brewed using chamomile, rosemary, and black pepper, pours a sunny gold and exudes herbs, spice, and all things nice.

Stoudts Brewing Co.
Adamstown, Pennsylvania
www.stoudtsbeer.com

Gold *Munich Style Helles* 4.7%

A fiercely traditional brewer created more than 20 years ago by Carol and Ed Stoudt and specializing in Germanic and, later, Belgian beers. When it comes to brewing, Carol's the one who wears the lederhosen, and this five-times' winner at the Great American Beer Festival is a hell of a Helles. It showcases the perle, Hallertau, and Saaz hops with spice up front followed by a brusque, bitter conclusion.

Three Floyds Brewing Company
Munster, Indiana
www.threefloyds.com

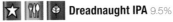 **Dreadnaught IPA** 9.5%

Mention Three Floyds to well-informed beer boffins, and they will start drooling and pinging eyeballs from their faces. Probably. Since beginning life in an Indiana warehouse back in 1996, where the beers were fermented in open vessels shaped like Samuel Smith's famous Yorkshire Squares, Three Floyds has embraced innovation, none more so than in this massive, muscular mouthful that stuns the senses with cluster bombs of citrus, grapefruit, and freshly cut grass. A cult classic.

Gumballhead 4.8%

Capable of slaking a thirst from a hundred yards, Gumball bounces about the tongue leaving a trail of coriander, lemon, lime, and dry-hopped bitterness in its wake. Drink it when the sun comes out to play.

Troegs Brewing Co.
Harrisburg, Pennsylvania
www.troegs.com

 **Nugget Nectar** 7.5%

Long-running Pennsylvanian purveyor of enigmatic artisan ales with a loyal following both locally and in the ethereal land of beer bloggers.

Victory Brewing
Downingtown, Pennsylvania
www.victorybeer.com

 HopDevil Ale *IPA* 6.5%

Begun by two childhood friends, Bill Covaleski and Ron Barchett, Victory now enlightens educated elbow-benders in two dozen states and beyond with a hugely diverse range of excellent ales. While famed for its first-rate pilsners, it is this voraciously hopped IPA that many marvel at. Wonderfully nuanced toasted maltiness, floral hop aroma, and a clipped, bitter finish.

 **Golden Monkey** 9.5%

This peppery, warming, and herbal take on a Belgian Tripel does nothing to dispel the notion that there are very few scenarios in life that are not improved by the presence of a monkey. Especially a golden one.

NEW HOLLAND BREWING CO.

66 E. 8th Street, Holland, Michigan 49423

www.newhollandbrew.com

The folks at New Holland Brewing believe that craft brewing is an artistic pursuit. Their logo, "Art in Fermented Form", speaks volumes. They're genuine, and they're on a steady course, making good, reliable, balanced beer.

New Holland is a story of two childhood friends, Brett VanderKamp and Jason Spaulding, who roomed together at Hope College, a small liberal arts school in the west Michigan town of Holland. Jason studied physical therapy, and Brett studied geology. After graduation, Brett headed to Colorado, where he realized the potential of craft beer and decided to introduce it to his home state.

So, in 1996, Brett came back to Michigan and teamed up with Jason again. The two pursued their dream of brewing beer in the unlikeliest of places. Holland is a staunch conservative Dutch Reform community. It's located in Ottawa County, which until recently even banned the sale of beer and wine on Sunday. Most people contemplating a brewery would stop right there and look someplace else.

But young people have the gifts of optimism and determination, not to mention a different perspective. They reasoned that the area was starving for new business; besides, a new bar hadn't opened in Holland for years. Yes, money was an obstacle, but Brett and Jason said to themselves, "This is America. Let's do it."

Lo and behold, they did. It turned out that as strait-laced as Holland was, starting up a brewery there was very easy. By June 1997 they were open for business, brewing beer in an old factory they'd converted to a brewhouse. They opened a small taproom and, before long, word spread about New Holland Brewing Company's liquid gold. It gained a following, not just in the Holland area but also across the state.

In September 2002 John Haggerty came on board as head brewer. John, who's originally from Indiana, attended brewing school in Berlin and had brewed in various parts of the country. Having been part of large-scale brewing, John wanted to work

at a smaller operation where he could have an influence over what was brewed. He and New Holland are a perfect match.

The slow, steady growth that New Holland had enjoyed so far was about to explode. In December 2002 they opened a second facility in downtown Holland with a small brewery for making experimental batches, 20 taps to serve their fresh beer, and a restaurant. By 2006 they outgrew their original production facility and opened another across town.

Meanwhile, John Haggerty has been busy expanding New Holland's offerings. The brewery now turns out four year-round beers, four seasonals, and a rotating series of six high-gravity beers. But the brewing fun really begins with the ten to twelve experimental beers it produces, plus the ones that it brews for special occasions only, such as Holland's annual Tulip Festival and Fall Festival.

New Holland was one of Michigan's first breweries to join both the barrel-ageing and high-gravity brewing trends. Sitting in storage are more than 220 bourbon barrels filled with beer in various stages of fermentation. The plan is to develop a library of beers that customers can someday enjoy while comparing the same label across multiple vintages.

Several years ago, New Holland also added a two-barrel distillery to its operation. In addition to a line of artisanal spirits, it is applying a brewer's unique perspective to distilling. Imagine the possibilities—and the fun—of tasting a style of beer, then tasting that same beer distilled as a spirit.

In 2008, Brett and other local business owners started a grassroots effort to overturn local restrictions banning the sale of beer on Sundays. The "Say Yes to Sunday" campaigners had to negotiate a convoluted procedure that required them to win two separate elections: the first to put the question of

BARLEYWINE STYLE ALE MADE WITH WHEAT
Brewed and bottled by
New Holland Brewing Company, LLC
Holland, Michigan

Key Beer

Dragon's Milk *Wood-aged beer* 9%

Sunday sales on the ballot; the second to actually lift the ban. In the end, voters sided with Brett and his friends, and another silly beer law has disappeared from the books.

Early 2009 brought yet another change. Matt Millar, a well-known and highly respected local chef, joined the New Holland team. His mission: take an artistic approach in the kitchen using local foods. It's casual dining with a very creative flair. The continual stream of thirsty, hungry customers speaks volumes about what these artisans have accomplished.

Now that it's firmly established—they shipped over 9,500 barrels, a very respectable amount for a Midwest brewery, to 12 different states in 2008—expect even more interesting things to come out of New Holland. Stay tuned for more art in fermented form.

Above left: New Holland opened a small tap room in 1997 next to the brewery, as word of its classy brews spread.
Above and right: Simple but effective posters for New Holland beers advertise their wheat and wood-aged brews.
Right above: Dragon's Milk is the signature brew.

Brewed and bottled by
New Holland Brewing Company, LLC
Holland, Michigan

Canada

Much as the nation itself has been likened to a cultural mosaic, the Canadian brewing industry is a rich tapestry of influences, trends, and innovations, encompassing as many as two hundred or more breweries and certainly well over a thousand individual brands. Viewed in very general terms, however, there are some definite regional tendencies, maintains Stephen Beaumont.

The area comprised of Nova Scotia, New Brunswick, Prince Edward Island, and Newfoundland, known as the Atlantic Provinces, was slow to come to craft brewing and still today trails all other regions—save, arguably, the Prairies—in both number of breweries and the degree of their influence on the overall beer market. British beer styles dominate, with best bitters, pale ale, and porters prominent, and Halifax remains the region's brewing epicenter.

In Québec, the home of avant-garde brewing in Canada, you'll find cutting-edge beers such as ales flavored with vanilla beans and cocoa and wheat beers fermented with fresh citrus fruit, together with the strongest Belgian influence. While this iconoclastic approach to the brew kettle does at times yield beers of questionable worth—ersatz "Gueuze" and mint-flavored beer spring to mind—it has also blessed the province with some truly great breweries.

Notorious for their conservatism, the brewers of

<table>
<tr><td>FEATURED BREWERY</td></tr>
<tr><td>1 Unibroue
Chambly, Québec, pages 212–213</td></tr>
</table>

HUDSON BAY

CHURCHILL

EDMONTON

VANCOUVER

1 MONTREAL

USA

TORONTO

Canada's most populous province, Ontario, have long directed their efforts toward interpretations of such traditional German, Czech, and British styles as blonde lager (Helles), wheat beer, Pilsner, and pale ale, largely with success. Where experimentation has been allowed to flourish of late, however, the results have been, to put it kindly, mixed.

The Prairies, although generally well populated with brewpubs, is where most of the small-scale brewing operations in Alberta, Manitoba, and especially Saskatchewan exist to take advantage of the off-sales license that accompanies the brewpub permit in at least two of the provinces. As such, the market for craft-brewed beer remains decidedly immature, despite the efforts of a handful of truly inspired breweries and a lone, long-established regional craft brewer.

A long time in coming, the influence of the vibrant brewing scene of the American Pacific Northwest is finally being felt in British Columbia, with a resulting surge in the brewing of hoppy, characterful pale ales, IPAs, and so-called "double" IPAs. This recent swing aside, the more general trend in B.C. brewing is toward British beer styles.

Above top: The Big Rock Brewery in Calgary is one of the longest established craft breweries in Canada.

Above: In its Montreal brewpub, Dieu du Ciel! serves its own award-winning microbrews to a highly appreciative clientele.

Alley Kat Brewing Co.
Edmonton, Alberta
www.alleykatbeer.com

 **Fireside Mild** 3.5%

Who says winter seasonals need all be big beers? This annual offering has an appealingly sweet, malty nose that carries a hint of chicory coffee, plus a balanced and malty body that's neither too sweet nor disappointingly thin, with notes of molasses, carob, and weak coffee.

 **Full Moon Pale Ale** 5%

Perhaps it's the power of suggestion—the brewery also makes an apricot beer—but there's a distinct note of apricot to this fragrant, fruity, and pleasingly bitter pale ale. From the soft start to its dry and bitter finish, this is a wonderfully crafted session pale ale.

Olde Deuteronomy Barley Wine 10%

Given the paucity of barley wines in Canada, it's inexplicable that this splendid example is only sporadically brewed. Toffee-ish malt blends with spicy hop in the foreground, while sweet and complex fruitiness in the body segues to moderate bitterness and a lengthy, warming finish. Ideal for cold northern Alberta winters.

Big Rock Brewery
Calgary, Alberta
www.bigrockbeer.com

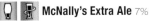 **McNally's Extra Ale** 7%

One of Canada's first classic craft-brewed beers, from one of the nation's original microbreweries, this Irish-inspired brew has a caramel apple nose and malty, plummy notes throughout the body. A quaffable strong ale.

Black Oak Brewing Company
Toronto, Ontario
www.blackoakbeer.com

Black Oak Nut Brown Ale 5%

Although it lacks the wininess or appealing minerality of some British brown ales, this Toronto creation is considered a local jewel, with a distinct nuttiness, sweetish, and food-friendly maltiness, and sessionably dry finish. Very appealing.

Bushwakker Brewpub

Regina, Saskatchewan
www.bushwakker.com

 **Bushwakker Palliser Porter** 5.8%

Regina's pride and joy offers one of the nation's best porters in this, a wonderfully balanced blend of roasted malt and coffee notes, drying hop, and flavors of both dark and lighter chocolate. A versatile food beer.

Microbrasserie Charlevoix

Baie St. Paul, Québec
www.microbrasserie.com

 Dominus Vobiscum Triple 9%

The name of this fine tripel translates from Latin to "The Lord be with you" and after a couple of half-liter bottles, perhaps He or She will be! A spicy-fruity aroma foretells of the tropical fruitness and peppery spice flavors to come, all of which wrap up in a drying, warming finish.

Cheval Blanc

Montréal, Québec
www.lechevalblanc.ca

 Bock 6.8%

Not to be confused with the Brasseurs RJ brands of the same name, this Ontario Street brewpub is Montréal's original, and still among its best, as evidenced by this complex toffee-ish bock with a light spiciness and notes of apple and brandy on the finish.

County Durham Brewing Co.

Pickering, Ontario
www.ontariocraftbrewers.com
/brewery.php?brewery=durham

Patrick's Oyster Stout 4.8%

You can drink it only at one place, Starfish Oyster Bed and Grill in Toronto, but it's worth the trip. Starfish proprietor Patrick McMurray provides pasteurized oyster liquor that is added to Durham's Black Katt Stout, thus creating a rich and silky, faintly briny, roasty delight.

Crannóg Ales

Sorrento, British Columbia
www.crannogales.com

 **Back Hand of God Stout** 5.2%

Easily one of the best beer names in Canada, there's much more to this organic Irish-style dry stout than novelty, with a note or three of pipe tobacco in the nose and a mild, enticing, and thoroughly appetizing roastiness in the body.

Denison's Brewing Co.

Toronto, Ontario
www.denisons.ca

Denison's Weissbier 5.4%

A draft-only offering available primarily at better Toronto beer palaces, this excellent Bavarian-style wheat draws from the pedigree of the late and lamented brewpub of the same name. Classic spice and banana in the nose, with a mild clove accent on a softly sweet and fruity body.

Dieu du Ciel!

Montréal and St. Jérôme, Québec
www.dieuduciel.com

⭐ **Péché Mortel** 9.5%

This "mortal sin" is an intense experience, with real coffee providing the espresso accents to a full, rich, and formidable imperial stout already rife with notes of chocolate, roasted malt, and dark fruits such as prune and fig.

Rosée d'Hibiscus Wheat Beer 5%

As the name might indicate, hibiscus flowers provide the flavoring for this rose-colored wheat beer, imbuing it with a suitable floral character and light notes of citrus and gooseberries leading to a dry, appetizing finish.

Route des Épices Spiced Ale 5%

While the start is reminiscent of the spicy flavors of Mayan cocoa, by the time it reaches the back of your throat, there's no doubting the black pepperiness of this beautifully balanced ale. Spiced to be intriguing and enjoyable, never overwhelming.

Garrison Brewing Co.
Halifax, Nova Scotia
www.garrisonbrewing.com

Grand Baltic Porter 9%

Deep regal purple in color, this big beer has a nose that speaks to the molasses added to the boil, plus sweet black coffee, dark chocolate, and a whiff of burnt toast. In the body, it's rich and coffee-ish, with notes of blackstrap molasses, burnt toffee, and black licorice.

Imperial Pale Ale 6.9%

Odd, perhaps, for an "Imperial" IPA to be defined by its biscuity malt rather than its hops, but so it is with this ale. Piney, spicy, and citrusy hoppiness is definitely present, and perhaps a bit unbalanced, in fact, but it's the malt front and the almost chewy finish that will keep you coming back for one more.

Granite Brewery
Toronto, Ontario
www.granitebrewery.ca

Best Bitter Special 4.5%

As fine a cask-conditioned bitter as you'll find in North America, this is a gem of a beer available only at the midtown Toronto brewery pub or in takeaway growlers. Beautifully balanced, it hits the palate with a suggestion of fruity malt, before segueing into a drier, leafy quaffer. As refreshing as a walk in the woods in fall.

Half Pints Brewing Co.
Winnipeg, Manitoba
www.halfpintsbrewing.com

Burley Wine 10.5%

Like many of Half Pints' beers, this has a duality to it, with a more malty, British style front and a singularly American, peppery, citrusy middle. A formidably warming and bitter finish leaves the distinct impression of a bracing Barley Wine, regardless of inspiration.

Humulus Ludicrous Double IPA 8%

This big beer announces itself with a full and perfumey nose carrying notes of burnt orange peel and a malty, caramely front. Hops arrive in force soon thereafter, but always in balance and never quite dominating, all the way to a gently bitter, slightly toffee-ish finish. Such subtlety in a so-called "double" IPA is rare indeed.

Hopfenstark
L'Assomption, Québec
www.hopfenstark.com

Post-Colonial IPA 6.5%

Amber-colored American-style IPA with complex perfumey aroma, pungent flowery citrus notes preceded by caramel-y malt held in check by fresh lemon and grapefruit notes. Fruity, brisk, and fantastically funky.

Saison Station 55 5%

Who would think to combine aspects of a Belgian-style Saison and American-style IPA? Fred Cormier of Hopfenstark, that's who. Hazy gold with a nose that almost redefines "hoppy spice," this starts with spicy citrus notes, turns faintly sweet in the middle, and ends with a bitter, slightly funky flourish.

King Brewery
Nobleton, Ontario
www.kingbrewery.ca

King Pilsner 4.8%

King by name and king by nature, this Bohemian-style Pilsner is unquestionably the finest pale lager Ontario has to offer, with a fresh and floral aroma, a stylistically sound hint of buttery malt in the body, and a crisp, dry finish.

McAuslan Brewing Co.
Montréal, Québec
www.mcauslan.com

St-Ambroise Oatmeal Stout 5%

Pretty much as good as oatmeal stout gets, this ebony offering has a rich aroma of coffee, raisin, and plum, followed by a silken, mocha-ish body, with plenty of gentle roast and a hint of smoke. Simply an outstanding pint of black.

St-Ambroise Vintage Ale 9.2%

First brewed to mark the new millennium, and still ageing well, this annual-edition ale is full of fruit and malty sugars in its youth, but matures to a complexity of tanned leather, toasted spice, prune, high-cocoa-content chocolate, and burnt orange. Definitely worth waiting for.

Mill Street Brewery
Toronto, Ontario
www.millstreetbrewery.com

 Tankhouse Ale 5.2%

Although identified as neither bitter nor pale ale, this is certainly more the former, with a lightly roasty, faintly cocoa-ish nose and fruity (raisins, red apple), earthy, hoppy body that ends with a satisfying bitterness.

Les Brasseurs du Nord
Blainville, Québec
www.boreale.com

Boréale Blanche *Wheat Beer* 4.2%

The brewery is coy about the extra spice they add to this Belgian-style wheat beer, but one sip is enough to let you know it's ginger, and a fairly generous portion at that. Mixed with the orange peel and coriander, it makes for a truly thirst-quenching summer tipple.

Phillips Brewing Co.
Victoria, British Columbia
www.phillipsbeer.com

 **Amnesiac Double IPA** 8.5%

This dangerously quaffable "imperial" pale ale doesn't taste anything near its strength, with a soft and faintly chocolate-y start and full, malty body of more chocolate, cinnamon, walnut, lime zest, and rising bitterness. All in all, a fine if oddly restrained interpretation of the style.

Propeller Brewing Co.
Halifax, Nova Scotia
www.drinkpropeller.ca

 **Propeller IPA** 6.5%

This highly sessionable IPA strikes a fine median between the hop-out assault of some American IPAs and the more reserved maltiness of some Brits. Citrusy and spicy American hops certainly assert themselves here, but never to the detriment of the dryly fruity malt.

Pump House Brewery
Moncton, New Brunswick
www.pumphousebrewery.ca

 **Pumphouse S.O.B.** 5%

"Special Old Bitter" is what the irreverent name stands for, although CAMRA purists might disagree. The start is very British with a leafy hop aroma and dry maltiness, but it's not long before citrusy American hop notes take hold and dominate, leading this quencher to a fine bone-dry finish.

Brasseurs RJ
Montréal, Québec
www.brasseursrj.com

 Snoreau *Winter Ale* 7%

This spicy winter ale draws its tart, quenching character from the addition of cranberries, which produces a beer equal parts fruity, spicy, and warming. A fascinating take on a winter warmer that not surprisingly pairs well with roasted poultry.

Spinnakers Gastro Brewpub & Guest Houses
Victoria, British Columbia
www.spinnakers.com

 **Mitchell's Extra Special Bitter** 5.2%

From a pioneering brewpub still going strong with restaurant, off-premises sales, and even lodging comes this full-bodied floral-fruity ESB with a faint smokiness in its dry finish.

Storm Brewing Co.
Vancouver, British Columbia
www.stormbrewing.org

 Hurricane IPA 7.5%

Sitting on the precipice between pleasing complexity and a riot of out-of-control flavors, this hazy and happening IPA melds citrus fruit notes with a softer fruitiness (peach, apricot) and an aggressive spicy hop character. Available only on tap.

Unibroue

See Brewery Profile,
pages 12–213
Chambly, Québec
www.unibroue.com

⭐ ☕ **Fin du Monde** *Tripel* 9%

Filled with fruitiness, bracingly
strong, and afforded great depth by
a solid spiciness and drying rather
than bittering hop, this is less a Belgian-style Tripel than it is a Belgian-
inspired very Québécois interpretation. Uniquely delicious.

⭐ ☕ ✕ **Maudite** *Amber Ale* 8%

Generously spiced with coriander
and possibly something else
unidentifiable, this strong Belgian-
inspired ale possesses sufficient
fruity malt to qualify as a great dinner
accompaniment, yet enough spicy,
warming strength to work also as a
fitting nightcap.

⭐ ☕ **Terrible** *Spiced Ale* 10%

Ignore the Québécois tongue-in-cheek, this
wonderfully potent ale is anything but terrible.
Expect notes of black licorice, Asian spice, molasses, and alcohol
in the aroma and a complex body offering spice, dark chocolate,
espresso beans, and blackstrap molasses.

Vancouver Island Brewery

Victoria, British Columbia
www.vanislandbrewery.com

⭐ 🍷 🍺 **Hermann's Dark Lager**
5%

An early, enduring Canadian classic,
this crisp, lightly earthy, and mocha-ish
beer may have actually grown in body
in recent years, although it remains only faintly sweet and never cloying.
Recommended for those who remain inexplicably wary of dark lagers.

Wellington Brewery

Guelph, Ontario
www.wellingtonbrewery.ca

 **Arkell Best Bitter** 4%

A long-established star on the British-influenced
side of Canada's craft beer renaissance, Arkell is a
floral and nutty bitter best enjoyed on cask in one
of several southern Ontario pubs. A dry and mildly
bitter finish completes this session ale.

🍷 🍺 **Iron Duke Strong Ale** 6.5%

The yin to Arkell's yang, or vice versa, is this malty
delight of an ale, with an almost syrupy toffee nose
and a winey body that offers stewed fruit, hints of
cocoa, and just a touch of coffee on the warming,
satisfying finish.

Wild Rose Brewery

Calgary, Alberta
www.wildrosebrewery.com

 Cherry Porter 6.5%

With a dark chocolate-y nose imbued with black cherry
notes, this ale hints of what might be—and actually
is—an impressive mix of cherry fruit, mocha, sweet
spice, toasted malt, and concentrated plum. Pour it
beside a slice of chocolate cake or over some vanilla
ice cream and enjoy the sensation.

Yukon Brewing Company

Whitehorse, Yukon
www.yukonbeer.com

 **Lead Dog Ale** *Winter Ale* 7%

You'd have to expect that a brewery based deep
in the Canadian north would know a thing or two
about crafting a winter ale, and you'd be right. The
aroma is rich raisin and plum, while the body adds
some spice and bittering hop to the mix. Altogether
a satisfying winter warmer.

UNIBROUE

Chambly, Québec

www.unibroue.com

Without question the most widely recognized Canadian craft brewer in the world today is Unibroue. Born in the suburbs of Montréal, the Québec brewer of beers with such irreverent and, to some, impenetrable names as Maudite ("Damned"), Eau Bénite ("Holy Water"), and Fin du Monde ("End of the World") is sold far and wide, from Los Angeles to Paris, says Stephen Beaumont.

Although today known for brewing strong Belgian-inspired ales, Unibroue has origins going back to one of Québec's earliest craft breweries, the Massawippi Brewing Company of the Montréal area Anglo enclave of Lennoxville. Known for a pale ale of dubious reliability, Massawippi was on the precipice of failure in 1991, when it was rescued from near bankruptcy by a retired Francophone hardware magnate named André Dion.

Once an owner of the Rona chain of hardware stores, Dion was looking forward to at least semi-retirement when he sold off his holdings in 1990. Restlessness took its toll, however, and he was soon listening to offers from other businesses, including a coalition of Québec microbrewers with an interest in organizing a distribution network for their brands. Would Dion, they inquired, consider getting behind the idea? He would, he did, and Unibroue was born.

Although the distribution idea ultimately went nowhere, the brewing bug had bit Dion, and it was not long before he found himself traveling Belgium in search of beers he could import to Québec. It was during one of these trips that he discovered the Riva Brewery in West Flanders.

Recognizing the potential in Riva's wheat beer, Dion decided that his interests would be better served by buying the recipe for the beer and brewing it on the other side of the Atlantic, rather than merely acting as importer. When he returned home recipe in hand, however, he found that the provincial government had placed a moratorium on the issuing of new brewery licenses. Luckily, Massawippi was ripe for picking.

Not long after, Massawippi Pale Ale fell by the wayside in favor of brands such as Blanche de Chambly—the wheat beer modeled after Riva's original—Maudite and Fin du Monde, and the brewery itself was relocated to the Montréal South Shore community of Chambly. Dion's apparent strategy was simple: Hire young people with no brewing industry experience —"So they have no bad habits," he once said—brew beers of unusual character, and market them heavily using beautiful imagery, Québécois symbolism, and, after a short time, the star power of famed French singer Robert Charlebois, who became a minority partner in the business.

It didn't take long for Dion's new brewery to make its presence felt internationally, selling in the United States, France

Key Beers

Chambly Noire Dark Ale 6.2%

Don de Dieu Triple Wheat Ale 9%

La Fin du Monde Tripel 9%

Maudite Amber-Red Ale 8%

Seigneuriale Amber Ale 7.5%

Terrible Spiced Ale 10%

Trois Pistoles Dark Ale 9%

Left: Unibroue's beers have been inspired by Riva in Belgium, yet are produced in the suburbs of Montreal.

and, audaciously, Belgium, as well as in other European nations. But it was in the rough-and-tumble world of Québec beer sales that Unibroue made the most noise, going toe to toe with the country's third-largest brewing company, the Ontario-based Sleeman Breweries.

Best known for a golden Cream Ale packaged in a clear glass bottle, Sleeman was desperate to make a name for itself in the Québécois market, and Dion appeared equally determined to stop them, launching a competing and rather out-of-character golden lager, called simply U, and bottling it in clear glass. Animosity between the two companies was at one time so great that office walls at Unibroue were decorated with humorously defaced Sleeman posters.

Ultimately, John Sleeman, founder and CEO of Sleeman Breweries, made Dion an offer he couldn't refuse, and Unibroue joined the Ontario company's stable of regional cross-Canada breweries in 2004. Two years later, the hunter became the hunted, and Sleeman, along with its Unibroue subsidiary, fell to the control of Japan's Sapporo Breweries.

Most Unibroue aficionados will assert that little has happened to change the character of the brewery's beers since the Sapporo purchase, although there has been some shake-up in the structure of the company, most specifically with the departure of one-time Chimay brewer Paul Arnott. Replacement Jerry Vietz put any concerns about continued quality largely to rest, however, when Unibroue released its first post-Arnott ale in the form of Quatre-centième, an impressive strong ale brewed in 2008 to commemorate the 400th anniversary of the provincial capital, Québec City.

And so, with U still selling in Québec, although no longer in clear glass, and a sizable stable of well-known and appreciated brands sold around the globe, the future for Unibroue appears as bright as ever.

Above: La Fin du Monde is Unibroue's fine Tripel, full of Belgian-style spice and hops.

Below: Painterly labels and witty beer names are all part of the Unibroue story.

Cervecería Mexicana

Tecate
www.molsoncoors.com

 **Potro** *Porter* 4.7%

Stouts tend to wilt in the sun, so this Mexican interpretation is more like a porter or a dark lager. Very drinkable with chocolate, spice, and a touch of chipotle—one can imagine it finds favor with spicy Mexican food as a molé substitute. Special mention must be made of the eye-catching azure-colored blue bottle.

Cervecería Moctezuma

Monterrey, Nuevo León
www.ccm.mx

Bohemia *Pilsner* 4.8%

While many associate the big Moctezuma brewery with the global phenomenon that is Sol and, to a lesser extent, Dos Equis, it's the Czech-style Bohemia that has been garnished with the most gongs. Using Saaz hops sourced from the Czech Republic, it's a rich Pilsner with a kiss of cocoa on the palate and a sweet, silky swallow.

Casta *Dark Ale* 4.8%

Tawny-brown testament to the fact that it's not all parch-thrashing Pilsners in Mexico, Casta is a dark ale with one foot in Scotch ale and the other in the malty beers of Belgium. There are plums and toffee on the palate, with an acidic citrus finish.

Noche Buena *Strong Ale* 6%

Full-bodied and full of warm alcoholic festive fireside cheer, Noche Buena translates as "Good Night" and is a soft and gentle dried fruit-filled Christmas lager released every year in time for yuletide fun.

Grupo Modelo

Mexico City
www.gmodelo.com

Negro Modelo *Pilsner* 5.3%

While Corona Extra is clearly the priority for the gargantuan Mexican brewer Grupo Modelo, it is certainly not the only string to its bow. Of the other beers in its cupboard, Modelo Especial is a stronger, fuller-bodied pilsner that packs more punch than Corona while the supremely satiating Pacifico Clara has traditionally been a favorite among Mexican fishermen. Negro Modelo, however, is the most impressive; a dark Munich-style lager with hints of bitter chocolate.

Carib Brewery TRINIDAD & TOBAGO

Champs Fleurs, Trinidad
www.caribbeer.com

 Royal Extra Stout 6.5%

Sweet stouts don't come much more "TNT" (dynamite-like) than this full-bodied thick, creamy black brewed to a recipe inherited from the Walters' Brewery, Port of Spain, in 1952. This couldn't be more different from the light Carib lager.

Desnoes & Geddes JAMAICA

Kingston, Jamaica
www.jamaicadrinks.com

 **Dragon Stout** *Foreign Stout* 7.5%

A rambunctious sweet and syrupy stout with a color akin to navy rum. Mostly drunk chilled in Jamaica, it gains complexity when taken slightly warmer. Toast and roasted malt, chocolate, and a dry bitter finish.

 **Guinness Foreign Extra Stout** 6.5%

Never mind all that twee fiddle-fiddling Oirish, "do-you-know-the-way-to-Tipperary" nitro-keg nonsense, if drinkers want a proper Guinness then this black cherry-flavored, jet-black sweet, and slightly sour stout is genuine, uncut liquid craic.

Red Stripe *Lager* 4.7%

Here's a joke for you: "My wife went to the West Indies to drink a crisp, clean lager first brewed in 1927 and named after the Red Stripe that runs down the uniform trousers of the police force." "Jamaica?" "No, she went of her own accord". She likes slightly malty lagers, especially when it's hot.

St. John's Brewers VIRGIN ISLANDS

St. John, Virgin Islands
www.stjohnbrewers.com

Tropical Mango Pale Ale 4.5%

When college buddies Chirag Vyas and Kevin Chapman moved to the Virgin Islands, they realized that there wasn't enough good beer to soak up the sunsets, so they founded the brewery in 2001. Mango is not the only fruit in this aromatic, slightly sweet pale ale. There are pear, lychee, and a touch of pineapple too. Now available on the US mainland.

Argentina

Antares Brewing
La Plata, Buenos Aires
www.cervezaantares.com.ar

 **Imperial Stout** 8.5%

US and English-influenced chain of brewpubs
producing this immense full-bodied, sweet, spicy stout brewed with
Pilsner, chocolate, and caramel malts, and Cascade and Fuggles hops.

Barba Roja
Buenos Aires
www.cerveceriabarbaroja.com.ar

Negra *Dark Lager* 4.5%

Bavarian-style bottom-fermented black beer from a Buenos Aires
brewpub with a swashbuckling pirate theme. This smooth, silky Munich
lager is all malt and sweetness.

Buller Brewing Company
Buenos Aires
www.bullerpub.com

Oktoberfest 5.5%

September and October may be spring in Argentina, but this malty
Munich mouthfiller tastes just as fine, especially when sipped in Buller's
sun-bathed beer garden in the center of Buenos Aires.

Cervecería Fueguina
Ushuaia, Tierra del Fuego
No web address

 Beadle Negra *Stout* 7.8%

The southern-most brewery in the world produces excellent bottle-
conditioned Beagle ales, named after Darwin's ship of the 1830s.
These include a bitter/pale ale, IPA, and this tawny-colored fruity stout.

Cervecería Jerome
Mendoza, Mendoza
No web address

Cerveza Diablo *Belgian Dubbel* 7.5%

A small five-barrel craft brewer situated in the wine-growing region
of Mendoza run by Eduardo Maccari. But it's a micro with macro
ambitions and exports its ales, brewed with Patagonian Cascade hops,
to both the US and the UK. As well as a superb stout and a red and a
blonde ale, it brews Diablo, a Belgian Dubbel with a tangy sweetness.

Brazil & Peru

Cervejaria Eisenbahn BRAZIL
Blumenau, Santa Catarina
www.eisenbahn.com.br

 Eisenbahn Lust *Champagne Beer* 5%

The nearest you'll get to Brazilian bubbly, Eisenbahn
Lust is the first beer in Brazil to be produced using the
méthode champenoise. After the first fermentation at the
brewery the beer is sent to a winery, where it stays for
three months and undergoes a secondary fermentation in
the bottle. Slightly acidic, crisp, and citrusy.

 Eisenbahn Rauchbier 6.3%

Part German/part Brazilian, Blumenau is an affluent town. Founded in
1850 by German settlers, it is Brazil's biggest brewing town and even
hosts an Oktoberfest each year. It may seem incongruous, but when
you drink this sweet, malty smoked lager with traditional churrasco
grilled meat, it all makes complete, delicious sense. This beer is known
as "Defumada" in the United States.

 Eisenbahn Weizenbock *Doppelbock* 8%

Named after a Blumenau brewery that opened and closed in the early
1900s, Eisenbahn has become the largest craft brewery in Brazil. It was
built in 2002 by Juliano Mendes, a disillusioned beer drinker with a love
for ambitious European beers such as this effervescent unfiltered wheat
double bock with toasted wholegrain bread, bananas, and chocolate.

Cervejaria Sul Brasileira BRAZIL
Santa Maria, RIo Grande do Sul
www.amazonbeer.com

Xingu *Dark Lager* 4.7%

An opaque black silky lager laced with sweet treacle on the palate,
a tight tan-head and licorice aromas. Pronounced "Shin-goo", it is
apparently inspired by ancient Amazonian tribes who brewed black beer
as far back as 1557.

Cervesur PERU
Lima, Lima
www.cusquena.com.pe

Cusqueña *Malt Lager* 5%

"The brew from Peru" draws on mountain water from the
Andes and a German ancestry dating back to 1898. Now
owned by SAB Miller and enjoyed in Europe and the US.

Cusqueña Malta *Dark Lager* 5%

Cusqueña Malta is darker and slightly sweeter but just
as refreshing. It has a chocolate-y, scorched sugar cane
character, a rich mouthfeel, and a dry coffee finish.

A WORLD OF BEER
AUSTRALASIA

Australasia

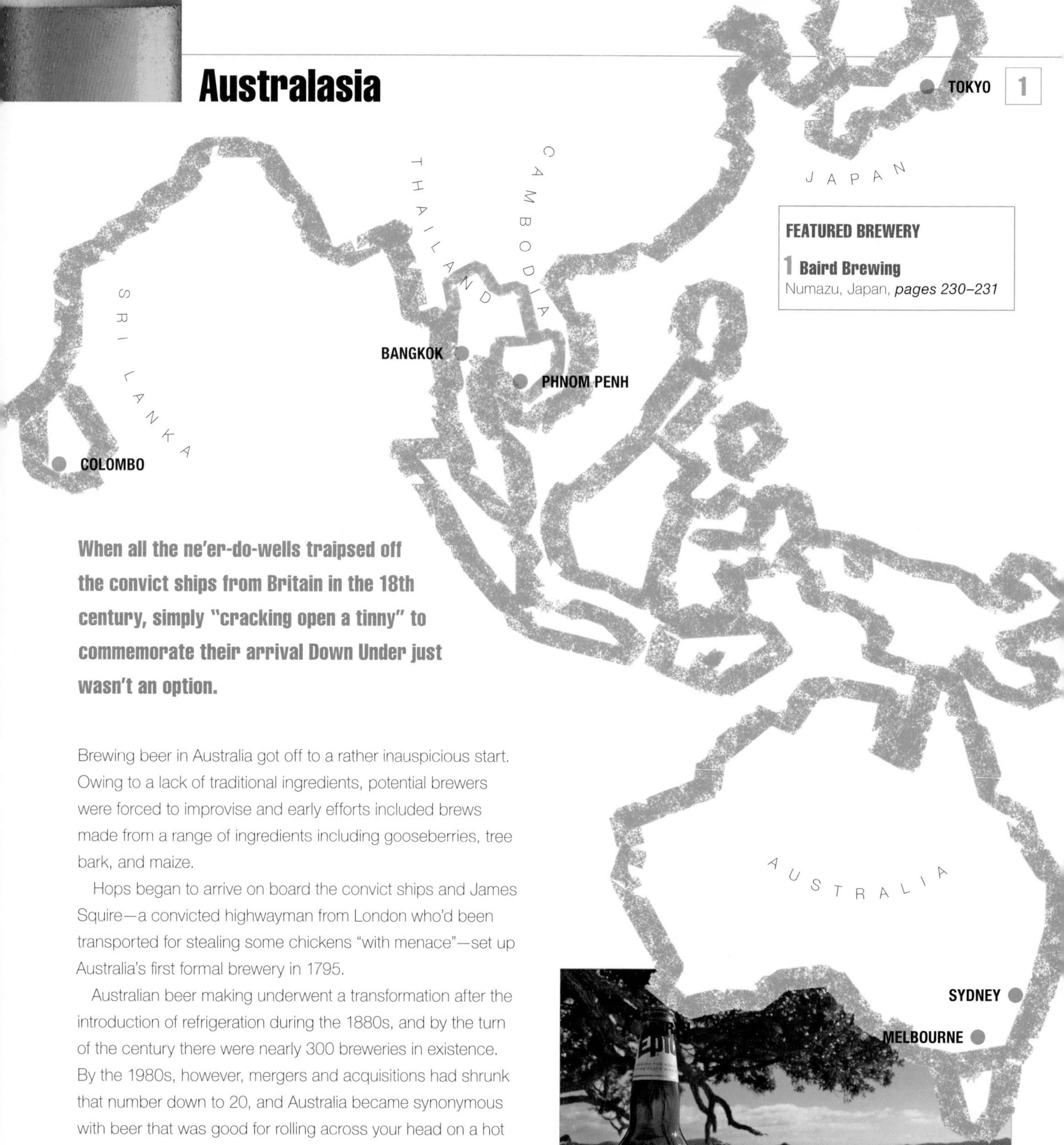

FEATURED BREWERY

1 Baird Brewing
Numazu, Japan, *pages 230–231*

TOKYO 1

JAPAN

THAILAND

CAMBODIA

SRI LANKA

BANGKOK

PHNOM PENH

COLOMBO

AUSTRALIA

SYDNEY

MELBOURNE

When all the ne'er-do-wells traipsed off the convict ships from Britain in the 18th century, simply "cracking open a tinny" to commemorate their arrival Down Under just wasn't an option.

Brewing beer in Australia got off to a rather inauspicious start. Owing to a lack of traditional ingredients, potential brewers were forced to improvise and early efforts included brews made from a range of ingredients including gooseberries, tree bark, and maize.

Hops began to arrive on board the convict ships and James Squire—a convicted highwayman from London who'd been transported for stealing some chickens "with menace"—set up Australia's first formal brewery in 1795.

Australian beer making underwent a transformation after the introduction of refrigeration during the 1880s, and by the turn of the century there were nearly 300 breweries in existence. By the 1980s, however, mergers and acquisitions had shrunk that number down to 20, and Australia became synonymous with beer that was good for rolling across your head on a hot summer's day but little else.

Today, the domestic Australian beer market is almost entirely controlled by Foster's and its "Kiwi" rival Lion Nathan, but the number of craft breweries and brewpubs has reached triple figures and the likes of Coopers, Little Creatures, Barons, and Redoak are doing much to challenge the unfair associations with Australian beer.

A burgeoning microbrewing scene in New Zealand means that there are nearly as many beers as there are sheep, but not quite. Pioneered by Robert Emerson, the variety of Kiwi quaff has exploded in the past decade or so, and a number of New Zealand winemakers are applying their New World daringdo to beer brewing.

Of all the Asiatic nations, Japan is the most exciting when it comes to beer. The beer scene is polarized between the big players, Asahi, Kirin, and Sapporo, and an embryonic yet incredibly innovative Japanese craft-brewing movement that, in 2009, celebrated its 15th anniversary, so it's still in its infancy.

In 1994, regulations on the issuance of brewery licenses were eased, and small regional breweries began to open in Japan, albeit at a slow pace. By the turn of the century, more than 300 had been opened, many of them by sake brewers, and Japan is now fusing American and European influences with indigenous ingredients to impressive effect.

● WELLINGTON

NEW ZEALAND

Above: The Japanese bottling line of Asahi is suitably high-tech.

Opposite Right: Epic Pale Ale is the flagship beer of this New Zealand brewer, based in the suburb of Otahuhu, Auckland.

Australia

Barons Brewery Co
Sydney, New South Wales
www.baronsbrewing.com

Barons Black Wattle Original Ale *Amber Ale* 5.8%

Wattle is a spiky shrub native to the Australian bush. Barons prides itself on making beer that is the most "Australian" in the wo rld and often usurps hops with different native herbs and spices. Thankfully, it's not done in a deliberately wacky way; they have to work in the beer. This light ebony-colored toffee-sweet beer is easier to drink than it is to say, especially after a few. A brilliant beer for barbecued meat.

Billabong Brewery
Perth, Western Australia
www.billabongbrewing.com.au

4 Hop Ale *Best Bitter* 3.8%

This is a misleading name because the beer actually contains eight different hops, but this tasty best bitter is hopped at four different stages of the boil. Remarkably balanced.

Billabong Pale Ale 5.5%

Born out of a brew-your-own bar begun in 1993, Billabong has been winning awards and weaning Western Australians off bland bubbly booze for a few years now. As well as brewing some gorgeous craft beers such as this zesty, citrusy American-style pale ale, Billabong has gone against the grain, quite literally, with some award-winning gluten-free beers that you don't have to suffer wheat allergies to enjoy.

J. Boag & Son
Launceston, Tasmania
www.boags.com.au

James Boag Premium Lager 5%

Now part of Lion Nathan, Boag livened up its lager line a few years ago with some delectable Tasmanian beers. This devilish beauty is fermented at a lower temperature, lagered longer, and has a big dose of late hopping.

Bootleg Brewery
Margaret River, Western Australia
www.bootlegbrewery.com.au

Raging Bull *Strong Ale* 7.1%

Surrounded by vineyards in the staunch wine region of Margaret River, Bootleg has been converting cork-sniffing, plonk-spitting tourists since 1994. This dark brunette ale will prick up the ears of Malbec and Musar drinkers, with notes of sweet caramel, coffee, chocolate, and prunes.

Bridge Road Brewers

Beechworth, Victoria

www.bridgeroadbrewers.com.au

 ### Beechworth Bling IPA 4.8%

Bridge Road is an innovative small-batch brewery in the "historic" town of Beechworth, founded by former winemaker Ben Kraus after an inspirational beer-drinking sojourn in Europe. However, he can do American-style IPAs, too, as this rasping, herbal hop refresher proves.

 ### Chevalier Bière de Garde 7.5%

This Australian interpretation of a French farmhouse beer is a rare yet rather wonderful thing, layered in spice, herbs, and plenty of quenching power. Ben's homage to this lesser known European style includes packaging the Chevalier range in smart Champagne bottles.

Carlton & United Breweries

Melbourne, Victoria

www.fosters.com.au

Sheaf Stout 5.7%

From the very same people who "brew" Foster's and Victoria Bitter (commonly known as VB) comes this rough and ready stout. It's the black sheep of the Foster's family that flexes it malt muscle. Sweet and strong, Sheaf Stout is sadly even harder to find than a needle in the remote Outback.

Cascade Brewery

Hobart, Tasmania

www.cascadebrewery.com.au

Cascade Pale Ale 5%

Now also part of the Foster's family, Cascade's history dates back further than any other working brewery in not just Tasmania, but all of Australia. Brewing since 1832, its creation was devised by Peter Deagraves while doing time in a Hobart jail. Cascade is renowned for its better-than-most lager, but it's the trio of specialty beers that get the beer buffs excited—especially, this fruity, aromatic pale ale.

Colonial Brewing Company

Margaret River, Western Australia

www.colonialbrewingco.com.au

 ### Colonial IPA 6.6%

Another small-batch brewing infiltrator working its magic in wine country, Colonial began beer-making in 2004 and excels in the crafting of artisan ales. This is an awesome piney, grassy American-style IPA steeped in a cacophony of citrusy hops.

Colonial Kölsch Ale 4.5%

Crisp, clean, and creamy, this cracking Kölsch is remarkably refreshing.

Coopers Brewery

Adelaide, South Australia

www.coopersbrewery.com.au

Coopers Best Extra Stout 6.3%

Roasty and grainy with a creamy chocolate-coffee nose and a flourish of vanilla on the palate, with a finish drier than the Ashes.

Coopers Original Pale Ale 4.5%

Fruity, robust, and brewed in the "Burton-on-Trent" style, its mineral mouthfeel has lively carbonation and gentle, grassy hop notes and a yeasty sign-off. The cloudy residue can be dissipated by rolling the bottle on the table.

 ### Coopers Sparkling Ale 5.8%

While other big Australian breweries have jumped on the bland bottom-fermenting bandwagon, Coopers of Adelaide has steadfastly kept hailing the bottle-conditioned ale in style and, in doing so, provided inspiration for the legion of new wave breweries in Australia. This is the beer that Coopers is built on. A deep auburn-colored cloudy beer with lots of sediment, it is brewed using a top fermentation that Thomas Cooper implemented in 1862. A "honeyed" hop aroma followed by a full-bodied fruity, raspberry-ish note, with a mild hop bite.

Coopers Vintage Ale 7.5%

Christmas pudding, port, and dark toffee are just some of the tasting notes adorned to vintage batches of what is arguably Australia's finest beer. Packed with cooked plum and toffee-like flavors, and balanced by hints of sour cherry and chicory, and it is reckoned by Cooper's that two years of rest will bring out the best in it.

Enterprise Brewing

Clare Valley, South Australia
www.lion-nathan.com.au

Knappstein Reserve Lager 5.6%

When the Knappstein winery moved into the former home of Enterprise Brewery in 1970, it was surely only a matter of time before the winemakers succumbed to curious temptation and breathed life back into the building's brewing past. In 2006, nearly a hundred years after the brewery first fired up its kettles, this luscious grapefruit-tinged lager with notes of lychee and pear was unleashed in a fantastic-looking bottle with a sharply designed label. Maybe those pesky winemakers aren't so bad after all.

Feral Brewing Company

Swan Valley, Western Australia
www.feralbrewing.com.au

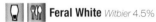

Feral White *Witbier* 4.5%

Don't be put off by the wild hog on the label, as the beers from this western Australian micro are anything but …ahem…boorish. Hazy, lightly hopped and spicy Belgian wit.

Feral Hophog *American-style IPA* 5.8%

True to the brewery's "undomesticated yet sophisticated" slogan, this American-style IPA will drive hopheads wild with its spike of pine needle, searing citrus aroma and bready malt background.

Fish Rock Brewery

Bowral, New South Wales
www.fishrockbrewery.com.au

Fish Rock Red Emperor Ale

Amber Ale 4.5%

Yet more booze-making gurus who've swapped the grape for the grain, Fish Rock is the brewing arm of Artemis wines and excels in crafting beers under the Reinheitsgebot purity law. Cascade and Amarillo hops laid over a sweet, toffee-base. Apple pie anyone?

Leather Jacket Lager *Pilsner* 4.5%

A sensational Saaz hop showcase brewed using a decoction mash. Little surprise that it was named Australia's best lager in 2006 at the Australia Beer Awards.

Gage Roads Brewery

Fremantle, Western Australia
www.gageroads.com.au

Gage Roads IPA 5.1%

Go-getting micro with beers "brewed by fussy bastards" that first caught the brewing bug working in a brewpub. They set up their own brewery after becoming frustrated by the fact that the number of people who could experience their esoteric ales was severely limited. This dry-hopped IPA firmed up with five Australian malts, is just one of its fine brews.

Hahn

Sydney, New South Wales
www.lionnathan.com.au

Hahn Premium *Lager* 5%

A nice, easy-drinking beer made with Munich hops from a brewery that can boast Germanic roots. Purists may scoff at this beer, but when things are hotter than a flaming cockatoo, its crisp, back-of-the-throat bitter bite is a simply superb thirst quencher.

Hargreaves Hill

Steels Creek, Victoria
www.hargreaveshill.com.au

Pale Ale 4.9%

Tiny brewery run by a former pianist and his opera-singing wife who have swapped warbling and ivory-tinkling for making melodious malty lagers and ales in the Yarra Valley. Hits top grapefruit and citrus notes with a biscuit-backing vocal.

Jamieson Brewery

Jamieson, Victoria
www.jamiesonbrewery.com.au

Beast IPA 7%

It's only little, but the Jamieson family-run hotel brewery has made a big impression in Melbourne and beyond with a range of impressive, adventurous bottled ales. The biggest and most boisterous is this IPA, inspired by the ales of the Pacific Northwest and heaving with five hop varieties. Bitter yet balanced.

Lion Nathan Brewing

Sydney, New South Wales
www.lion-nathan.com.au

 **Southwark Old Stout** 7.4%

An ink-blank imperial stout inherited by Lion Nathan as part of its buy-out of South Australia Brewing. Coffee with a dash of navy rum on the nose, full-bodied toast and toffee on the palate, and a portlike vinous mocha-flavored, billowing mouthfeel.

Little Creatures

Freemantle, Western Australia
www.liitlecreatures.com.au

 **Little Creatures Pale Ale** 5.2%

Inspired by the American craft-brewing revolution, especially the Sierra Nevada business model, Little Creatures began fashioning an array of intriguing ales on the shore in Fremantle back in 2000. This, the biggest Little Creature, has made its way to the United States and Europe on the back of a hazy hue, succulent malt, and lychee citrus-flavored finish.

Little Creatures Rogers' 3.8%

A low-gravity, easy-sipping celebration of sweet malt, a dash of pepper, and a tingle of hop bitterness. A wonderfully well-constructed amber that competes well above its weight in terms of depth of flavor.

Lord Nelson Brewery Hotel

Sydney, New South Wales
www.lordnelson.com.au

Nelson's Blood Porter 5%

Pours black with a portlike red shimmer; rolling roasty mouthfeel and a rich espresso finish.

Old Admiral Strong Ale 6.7%

A barnacle-blistering big beer that's fruity, juicy-malted and comforting. Full of plum, fig, and a touch of almond with the strength to sweep your sea-legs from under you.

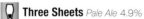 **Three Sheets** Pale Ale 4.9%

This big, grandiose brewpub is somewhat of a Sydney beer-drinking institution, having been around since the 1980s, longer than any other on-premise institution. In a building that dates back to the 1830s, it brews half-a-dozen year-round ales. Three Sheets, a golden aromatic pale ale, is the most popular of the Lord Nelson offerings.

Malt Shovel Brewery

Sydney, New South Wales
www.maltshovel.com.au

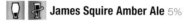 **James Squire Amber Ale** 5%

When the Malt Shovel name was revived in the late 1990s, this was the ale that announced its arrival. A creamy caramel-tinged copper-tinted ale with nutmeg, spicy notes, and a fruity hop finish.

 **James Squire Porter** 5%

Malt Shovel's beers are named after James Squire, a convict, a nefarious highwayman and, allegedly, Australia's first brewer who—in the 1780s—had a pub called the Malt Shovel. With a mouthfeel swelled by the use of roasted barley and wheat, this chocolate-y porter undergoes a long maturation, during which it picks up some prune and figlike flavors. Criminally tasty.

 Malt Shovel IPA 5.6%

Having helped "develop" Coors Light while brewing in his native United States, brewmaster Chuck Hahn arrived at Malt Shovel in 1998, and he's been digging himself out of a hole with some excellent craft ales ever since. An intense yet not overly outrageous IPA, earthy, dry-hopped with English Fuggles and robust malt, and a floral finish.

Matilda Bay Brewing Company

Fremantle, Western Australia
www.matildabay.com.au

 Dogbolter Dark Lager 5.2%

A sweet, malty mongrel that snaps at the heels of bock beers. Beneath the off-white tan lurks roasted coffee, mocha, chipotle and a touch of dry bittersweet chocolate.

 **Redback** Hefeweizen 4.7%

When this Fremantle trailblazer first stuck its head above the parapet in the dark beer-drinking days of the 1980s, it caused a stir with this hazy Hefe full of yeasty fruit and spice. Even though it's now owned by Foster's, its penchant for pioneering hasn't waned, so keep an eye out for Matilda's more maverick efforts.

McLaren Vale Brewing Company

McLaren Vale, South Australia
www.valeale.com

 Vale Ale *Pale Ale* 4.5%

A gorgeous pale ale from the McLaren Vale grape country, packaged in a seriously stylish and well designed vessel that deserves an admiring glance before being broached with the bottle-opener. Drinking in its contents is an even more pleasurableexperience: citrus aromas provided by Saaz and Cascade, light estery fruit, and a dry, delicate finish brought through by Brewer's Gold.

Mildura Theatre Brewery

Mildura, Victoria
www.mildurabrewery.com.au

Desert Premium *Pilsner* 4.5%

A brewpub based in an impressive 1930s theater whose beers tread the boards of taste with confidence. Given the region's meager rainfall and warm, temperate climate, it's little surprise that locals love this aromatic lager brewed with an array of Australian malts and a duo of delicate Kiwi hops. Quite delicious.

Storm Cloudy Ale *American-style Pale Ale* 4.5%

US-influenced blood-orange pale ale that is heavily flavored with Amarillo and Cascade hops. It is assertive and a little astringent, but with enough malt to balance it out.

Mountain Goat Brewery

Melbourne, Victoria
www.goatbeer.com.au

Pale Ale 4.5%

Cam Hines and Dave Boningham began this Melbourne micro in the late 1990s after originally brewing in Dave's backyard. It accrued its moniker because it's "a big, hairy animal that's never going to fall over" and it's forever on the front hoof in terms of marketing and flavorsome brewing, A golden straw-colored gulp full of sweet floral aromas, lemon marmalade notes, and a dry fruity finish.

Surefoot Stout 5%

Evenly balanced dark brown beer with a beige head. Full-roast flavors include charcoal, fruitcake, and a late lashing of licorice.

Murray's Craft Brewing Company

Taylors Arm, New South Wales
www.murraysbrewingco.com.au

Murray's Best Extra Porter 8%

Since founding the brewery in 2006, craft beer enthusiast and owner Murray Howe has not been scared to drag Australian drinkers out of their schooner-swilling comfort zone, and this polar-opposite imperial porter does just that with its creamy combination of rich bittersweet chocolate, roast, and warming alcohol.

Murray's Grand Cru *Tripel* 8.8%

Murray brought in the Belgian yeast especially for this titanic Tripel. Pours like golden treacle with a feathery cockatoo-white head, intense fruity esters, and Hallertau-hopped dry bitterness sprung from a juicy sweet malt base. Terrific.

Murray's Nirvana Pale Ale 4.5%

One of the most adventurous, envelope-pushing craft breweries in the country located, rather incongruously, in a pub called: "The Pub with No Beer" . This, the flagship ale, packs in the piney hops and herbaceous resins. Plenty of lupulin for such a low-alcohol pale ale.

Paddy's Brewery

Sydney, New South Wales
www.paddysbrewery.com.au

Chocolate Porter 5%

Located in a bustling mainstream pub next to the Olympic site in Sydney's Homebush Bay, Paddy's installed a brewery in 2001, and within three years it was named Champion Small Brewery of the Year. More recently, it has got its hands on a gong at the prestigious World Beer Cup. This beautifully rich porter with a palate of bitter chocolate, toffee, caramel, and mocha coffee aroma is the connoisseur calling card.

Paddy's Original Pilsner 5%

Spicy, floral pale-straw-colored Czech Pilsner swathed in distinctive spicy Saaz hop and reputedly using a yeast from a brewery in Pilsen. A cultured, educated alternative to VB and Foster's.

Pale Ale 5%

A homage to English pale ale interpreted with an American twist. The floral grapefruit signature of the Cascade hop springs from a grainy, biscuit base. A long, dry resinous finish.

Redoak Boutique Brewery
Sydney, New South Wales
www.redoak.com.au

Belgian Chocolate Stout 5.1%

Brewer David Hollyoak founded Redoak in 2004 and is the king prawn on Australia's boutique beer "barbie". This oatmeal stout, with coffee, chocolate, and spice notes pairs with crème brûlée.

Blackberry Hefeweizen 5.2%

David is a passionate proponent of beer and food matching, and pairs all of his beers with suitable dishes at the Redoak Boutique Beer Café in Sydney. Dessert beers don't come much better than this tart, fruity, and toffee-nosed Hefe.

Framboise Froment 5.2%

Redoak has for more than five years continued to stoke the coals of craft ale convention by bravely brewing a hugely ambitious and award-winning range of unusual beer styles. This 2008 World Beer Cup winner is Redoak's flagship beer, brewed with handpicked raspberries from Victoria's Yarra Valley. Tart, sweet, and sour with a flint-dry fruit finish, it is definitely one you must try.

Redoak Special Reserve 12%

From a range of limited-edition small-batch Redoak specialty beers comes this seasonal barley wine. A Celestial liquor that undergoes triple fermentation and matures in a variety of oak barrels for more than two years, and brings oak aromas, vanilla, prunes, figs, and leathery spice.

Scharer's
Picton, New South Wales
www.scharers.com.au

Burragong Bock 6.4%

Inspired by the German brewing tradition, Geoff Scharer was one of a handful of trailblazing Australian brewers during the 1980s and broke new ground when he set up an on-premise brewery on the rural outskirts of Sydney. This big, ballsy bock blew the doors off the Australian ale scene in 1987, and its malty muscle, pungent hop, and sticky toffee pudding character has certainly not dated.

Scharer's Lager 5%

Geoff handed over the reins to the younger duo of David Wright and Luke Davies in 2006, but the new owners have not let the flagship lager lose any of its legendary luster. It is Bavarian in character, with herb-like hop and yeast aromas, a peppery bitterness, and a piney finish.

Snowy Mountains Brewery
Jindabyne, New South Wales
www.snowymountainsbrewery.com

Charlotte's Hefeweizen 4.7%

Inspired by his native US and a passion for skiing, Kevin O'Neil opened Snowy Mountain so that skiers could sip superior suds after a day on the slopes. A full-bodied, fruity Hefe brewed with four malts (wheat, pale, Munich, and caramel) and a mix of Willamette and Cascade hops.

Crackenback Pale Ale 4.9%

It may sound like a tear-inducing treatment at a male waxing parlor but worry not. It's a perky, pine-needle pale ale with measured malt and a touch of orange blossom, late-hopped with three different hops.

Southern Bay Brewing Company
Moolapi, Victoria
www.southernbay.com.au/

Bearings Ale Bitter 4.5%

A well-rounded aromatic bitter from a mid-sized micro that was formerly known as the Geelong brewery and dates back to 1987.

Steel River Brewery
Newcastle, New South Wales
www.steelriverbrewery.com

Platts Old Folly World Lager 4.7%

Young yet ambitious craft brewery making malt beer in accordance with the German purity laws. Inspired by the pre-Prohibition lagers of 19th-century North America, it's triple-hopped, fermented at warmer temperatures than the flagship Steel River lager, and available in bottles.

Wig & Pen Brewing
Canberra, Australian Capital Territory
www.wigandpen.com.au

Brewers IPA 6%

In the relatively terse timeline of Australian craft brewing, Wig and Pen head brewer Richard Watkins is a veritable veteran, having manned the handpumps in this bustling brewpub since 1993. Ten different beers are brewed on-premise, many of them cask-conditioned, including this superb, seasonal IPA. Earthy rich malt offset by a piney, resinous hop.

Kamberra Kölsch 4.8%

An ever-so-easy-to-imbibe golden ale with a creamy mouthfeel, a hint of graininess, and fruity aroma. Available all year-round in one of Australia's best beer pubs.

New Zealand

Emerson's Brewing Company
Dunedin, Otago
www.Emersons.co.nz

 **Emerson Pilsner** 5%

Energized by what he drank as an 18-year-old on a jaunt to Europe with his father, founder and brewer Richard Emerson has been at the forefront of New Zealand craft brewing since 1993, and his beers are permanently on the podium at national and international brewing competitions. A crisp and citrusy "Kiwi classic" using Saaz hops that are grown in New Zealand.

London Porter 5%

A voluminous velvet mouth-filler that's a lot chunkier and richer in character than the ABV would suggest. Brewed using malt plumped with sweetness, rather than parched, it makes for a delightful milk chocolate-laden dessert beer.

Epic Brewing Company
Otahuhu, Auckland
www.epicbeer.com

Epic Pale Ale 5.4%

Brewing beers that are "bigger, badder and better", Epic is a brash Auckland brewer that's clearly inspired by the high-octane United States craft-brewing community. The claim to fame of its flagship pale ale is that each bottle is imbued with the equivalent of 15 hop flowers and, judging by the explosion of grapefruit on both the nose and palate, it may well be true.

Invercargill Brewery
Invercargill, Southland
www.invercargillbrewery.co.nz

 **Biman** Pilsner 5.2%

New Zealand's southernmost brewery was created by father-and-son team Gerry and Steve McNally back in 1999. Initially installed in a cowshed, the brewery outgrew its original home and moved into bigger premises in Invercargill. The four core beers, supplemented by a flurry of seasonal ones, include a pale ale, a superb stout, a honey Pilsner, and this sprightly hopped floral Pilsner that impresses with fruity traces of lychees, melon, and lime.

Mac's Brewery (McCashin's)
Nelson, Nelson
www.bonz.co.nz

Macs Hop Rocker Pilsner 5%

Mac's beer has been around since the early 1980s, when former rugby AllBlack and agriculturalist Terry "McCashin" set up a brewery of the same name in Nelson. In 2000, the ex-egg chaser decided to "cash in" by selling the brand to Lion Nathan and leasing the brewery. A number of different, and often innovative, ales are now being brewed under the Mac's banner, including this perky Pilsner with New Zealand-grown, Cascade and Sauvin hops.

Monteith's
Greymouth, West Coast
www.monteiths.com

Black Lager 5.2%

Monteith's brewery in Greymouth, on New Zealand's west coast, dates back almost 150 years. In 2001, it was closed by new corporate owners but, following public outcry, reopened four days later. The brewery still uses boilers fueled by coal and open fermentation, and the beers remain unpasteurized. Light-bodied lager, soft and mellow with malty licorice, biscuit, and a nutty finish.

Renaissance Brewing
Blenheim, Marlborough
www.renaissancebrewing.co.nz

Elemental Porter 6%

Prize-winning porter, with chocolate and cappuccino notes, courtesy of a small micro based in Marlborough. Set up in 2005 by Brian Thiel and Andy Deuchars, brothers-in-law from San Diego, Renaissance brews four quality craft ales and distributes them locally to Christchurch and Wellington.

Three Boys Brewery
Christchurch, Canterbury
www.threeboysbrewery.co.nz

 **Three Boys Wheat** 5%

Another micro, this time headed up by former scientist Dr. Ralph Bungard, who caught the brewing bug after a holiday romance with Yorkshire real ales. Packaged in seriously dapper bottles, Three Boys taste as good as they look, especially this hazy straw-colored slightly sour wit brewed with coriander and citrus zest.

Tuatara Brewing
Waikanae, Wellington
No web address

 **Ardennes** *Belgian Ale* 6.5%

Situated 40 miles north of Wellington on the Kapiti Coast, Tuatara was set up in 2002 by Carl Vista, whose disillusionment with New Zealand's myopic attitude to beer was hardened on a trip to England. Tutara was named New Zealand's best brewery at the 2008 BrewNZ Awards thanks to this tangy, spicy Belgian ale inspired by Westmalle.

Twisted Hop Brewery
Christchurch, Canterbury
www.thetwistedhop.co.nz

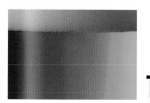 **Twisted Ankle** *Dark Ale* 5.9%

A boutique brewery and bar in central Christchurch run by a pair of young ex-pat English mash-fork-waving beer missionaries. Martin Bennett and Stephen Hardman, who source ingredients from New Zealand and England, champion other Kiwi craft brewers in their bar. Ankle is the strongest, a savory carbonated plum-colored brew.

Wanaka Beerworks
Wanaka, Otago
www.wanakabeerworks.co.nz

Brewski *Pilsner* 4.8%

A small but well-established microbrewery located near the South Island mountain resort of Wanaka. The Bohemian-style brewski shows the Saaz hop off in style. Zesty citrus nose and refreshing dry finish.

Cambodia

Cambrew Brewery
Sihannoukville
No web address

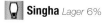 **Black Panther Stout** 8%

First commissioned by the Cambodian Government in the 1960s about 170 miles (273 kilometres) west of Phnom Penh, the Angkor Brewery was knocked off its stride in the 1970s and bought by Carlsberg in 1991. Surrounded by bland lager beers, this punchy, rich toffee-tainted stout is one of Southeast Asia's more complex contributions to world beer.

Sri Lanka

Lion Brewery
Biyagama
www.lionbeer.com

Lion Stout 8.2%

In a country where humidity and heat are high, it's a wonder why Sri Lankans love their stouts so much, but they do—a lot. Perhaps it's because this is one of the world's most impressive stouts, brewed high up in the mountainous tea-plantation region. Rich and chocolatey, with licorice, spice, prunes, and cappuccino.

Thailand

Boon Rawd
Bangkok
www.boonrawd.co.th

Singha *Lager* 6%

Thailand's first-ever lager was the brainchild of Thai nobleman Pyrya Bhirom Bhakdi and his son Prachuap—the first Thai to gain a brewmaster diploma from Munich's Doemens Institute. The brewery was built in 1934 as a way of heading off foreign imports, and the beer, still owned by third, and fourth, generation members of the Bhakdi family, is brewed using Saaz hops, German yeast, and a mixture of European and Thai malt. Sturdy sweetness and herbaceous hop on the nose, it's well positioned to pair with the spice, heat and texture of Thai cuisine.

Thaibev
Bangkok
www.changbeer.com

Chang *Lager* 5%

Chang is Thailand's bestselling domestic beer. Sweeter than the bone-dry, clipped character of most Asian beers and lighter than Singha, it's the ideal refresher after a hard day dodging ping-pong balls.

Japan

Asahi

Osaka, Osaka
www.asahibeer.com

Asahi Black *Dark Lager* 5.0%

Now the biggest brewer in Japan, Asahi dates back to 1889, when it was known as the Osaka Beer Brewing Company. Originally launched in 1995 in Japan as "Kuronama", Asahi Black is brewed in Osaka, lagered for a month, and brewed using three different dark malts, as well as hops, rice, and maize. Nutty, sweet, and creamy with a distinct espresso flavor and slight carbonation, it has been used in the UK as an ingredient in some left-field cocktails that mix Asahi Black with Asahi Super dry; a thinking man's "Black Velvet" with Champagne.

Asahi Stout 8%

Perhaps the bestselling Asahi beer is Asahi Super Dry which has taken the Japanese mainstream market by storm, but this one, Asahi Stout, is the brewery's really super beer, one to delight the discerning beer drinker. Pitched with both *brettanomyces* and top-fermenting yeast, it's fiercely fruity in flavor with hints of dark prunes, figs, and a melted marshmallow mouthfeel.

Baird Brewing Company

See Brewery Profile, pages 230–231
Numazu, Skizuoka
www.bairdbeer.com

Baird Kurofune Porter 5.5%

Robust yet refined smooth porter decked in dry chocolate and spicy bitter coffee.

Baird Rising Sun *Pale Ale* 5.1%

West Coast American pale ale with all the heavily sugared grapefruit character one would expect. Tastes just as good on the other side of the Pacific Ocean.

Echigo Beer Brew Pub

Niigata, Niigata
www.echigo-beer.jp

Echigo Stout 7%

When Japanese brewing laws were relaxed in 1994, an established sake brewer was one of the first to take advantage. Within a year, Echigo became Japan's inaugural brewpub, and four years later, brewing began on a bigger scale at a larger brewery site. The brewpub is a little out of the way, but Echigo's beers are widely available in cans and the sleek stout, all muscular malt and creamy coffee notes, is the pick of a pretty good bunch.

Fujikankokaihatsu Co/Sylvans Restaurant

Kawaguchiko
No web address

Fujizakura Koougen *Hefeweizen* 5.5%

Set in the shadow of Mount Fuji, the Sylvans Restaurant is a massive brewpub, restaurant, and gardened complex inspired by German brewing traditions. Its excellent beers can be found in Tokyo, so if you see this hazy Hefe, with its big banana-y esters and fruit finish, try one.

Hakusekikan Beer/Stone Iwamoto Co.

Ena-Gun, Gifu
www.hakusekikan-beer.jp

Fujizakura Rauchbock *Smoked Beer* 5.5%

A medium-bodied beer with a full waft of beech wood smoke plus earthy malt and peppery hops.

Crystal Ale *Golden Ale* 12%

Fermented with French wine yeast, this gargantuan golden ale packs a big fruit punch, with pear, peach, melon, pineapple, and lychee dampened with Fuggles and uplifting effervescence. A sublime sour brew.

Hakusekikan Hurricane *Mead* 14%

Remember mead? Course you don't, as Soshi is one of very few brewers who makes the medieval honey-based elixir anymore. Using wild yeast taken from Kyushu honey, Hurricane is a storm of warming alcohol, sweet fruit flavors, and a sweet Demerara sugar base.

Super Vintage Ale *Barley Wine* 14.3%

This boundary-breaking brewery is one that beer boffins salivate most over. Brewmaster Satoshi Niwa brews Japan's version of Belgian Lambic by harnessing wild yeast exclusive to the rural prefecture of Gifu to wonderful effect. Brewed with red wine yeast, this tart barley wine is fruity, portlike, and intoxicating.

Hida Takayama Brewing Agricultural Company

Takayama-Shi, Gifu
www.hidatakayama.co.jp

Hida Takayama Karumina *Brown Ale* 10%

Brilliant brewery in the little town of Takayama, perched high up in the idyllic mountains of the Gifu prefecture, which makes beers with attitude at altitude. This dark Belgian ale won silver at the World Beer Cup in 2002 for its deep flavors of rum-soaked, figgy pudding.

Hida Takayama Weizen 5%

Soft, spritzy Bavarian-style banana-laden beer. Like all its beers, it is delivered in a stubby Red Stripe-style bottle with a scarf-like neck label.

Hitochino Nest

Naka City, Ibariki
www.kodawari.cc

Hitochino Espresso Stout 7.5%

An unbelievably moreish and mellow coffee stout brewed with caramel, roasted, black, and chocolate malt. Deep dark fruit flavors on the finish. Superb.

Hitochino Japanese Classic Ale IPA 7%

A Japanese IPA made with an Anglo-American hop combination of Kent Golding, Challenger, and Chinook, then mellowed in cedar casks. A woody, spicy sensation anchored with just the right amount of biscuity malt.

Hitochino Nest White Ale Saison 5%

The Kiuchi Shuzou company was established in 1823 in the tiny hamlet of Kounosu (Nest) as a producer of Japanese Sake. But in 1996, the company branched out into brewing beer. Having won numerous international awards, its range of bottle-fermented beers and bottles adorned with a funky looking owl, have developed a strong following in the United States. Winner of the Gold Medal in the Herb & Spiced Beer Category at the 2000 World Beer Cup, Hitochino Nest White Ale is a refreshing mildly hopped Belgian-style Saison brewed using coriander, orange peel, and nutmeg.

Hitochino Red Rice Ale Spice Beer 7%

The skills of a sake producer are called upon to brew this delicious hazy dark pink beer. Rice grains used for sake are blended with Pilsner malt, Hallertau hops are added, then two strains of yeast—one used for sake and the other for beer—are let loose on the wort. Filtered but unpasteurized, the result is a spritzy and refreshing sip that blows raspberries, cherries, and almond on the palate and the nose.

Hyouko Yashiki No Mori Brewery (Swan Lake)

Agano-Shi, Niigata-Ken
www.swanlake.co.jp

Swan Lake Amber Ale 5%

Located in the Niigita-Ken prefecture of Japan, Swan Lake's stock is continually on the rise, having scooped several medals at the prestigious World Beer Cup. Misty reddish copper, tight off-white head, and gentle aroma of biscuity malt, fresh peach, and prunes. Perfumed hop bitterness and caramel tang.

Isekadoya Brewery

Ise, Mie
www.biyagura.jp

Imperial Smoked Porter 8%

Making all manner of stuff ranging from food to miso and wine, Isekadoya is a jack of all trades and, having tasted its lovely beers, a master of at least one. Ink black, vinous, and velvet smooth. Toasted, charred malt flavors with cherry tartness and an espresso bitterness.

Peach Lambic 5.5%

While Isekadoya made its latest brewing bow in 1997, it claims that its beer-making heritage dates back to the late 19th century. One wonders what they would have made of this tart, funky white peach sour beer, but we certainly like it, especially as a light apéritif.

Iwatekura

Ichinoseki, Iwate
www.sekinoichi.co.jp

Iwate Kura Oyster Stout 7%

The Iwate prefecture, situated at the northern tip of Japan, is renowned for its oysters, and the brewery is said to cast the local mollusks into the brewing of its smooth, satin stout. The oysters help to clarify the beer and add to the slightly salty, metallic mouthfeel.

Landbeer/Kinshachi

Nagoya City, Aichi
www.landbeer.jp

Kinshachi Red Miso Lager 6%

In 1996, Kinshachi was installed in a disused factory in the suburbs of Nagoya city, from where it excels at brewing rather unusual yet strangely arresting beers. Red miso paste, made from fermented soy bean, is what gives this maroon lager its chewy toffee flavor. Ideal with dishes flavored with sweet soy such as miso kushikatsu.

Moku Moku

Nishlyubune, Iga-Shi
www.moku-moku.com

Smoked Ale 5%

Owned by a farm cooperative and located to the east of Osaka, Moku Moku is well known for making beers with a smoky signature, hence the brewery name: a reference to the smoke screen used by Ninja warriors. This awesome ale is the smokiest of them all, but not outrageously so. Smooth, a little syrupy, and brewed with Scottish peated malt.

Nasu Kogen Beer Company
Nasu-Gun, Tochigi Ken
www.nasukohgenbeer.co.jp

 **Ninetailed Fox Barley Wine** 11%

Rarer than rocking horse doo-doo and as hard to get hold of as a seal smeared in grease, it's a cunning British Barley Wine, brewed just once a year at Japan's most English brewery, with a rich, honey-like palate and sherry aroma that intensifies when left to mature in its eyecatching ceramic bottle.

Otaru Beer
Otaru, Hokkaido
www.otarubeer.com

Otaru Dunkel 5.2%

Look closely under Otaru's kimono and you'll find a pair of German lederhosen. Founded in 1995 by Akio Shoji, Otaru headhunted German brewmaster Johannes Braun, who brews according to the Reinheitsgebot laws using Otaru's extremely soft, Pilsen-esque water. Slow decoction brewing gives this dark brown Dunkel caramel and toffee apple tones.

Otaru Weiss *Wheat Beer* 5.4%

Brewed using more than 50 percent wheat in the grain mix, the yeast has plenty to get its teeth into and its appreciation is expressed in huge banana aroma that wriggles its way through the mountainous white head, then reappears on the palate. A touch of toffee, too.

Otaru Pils *Pilsner* 4.9%

Otaru's biggest-selling beer. Robust, clean, and crisp with grainy malt and grassy hop bitterness.

Sapporo
Sapporo, Hokkaido
www.sapporobeer.jp

Sapporo Yebisu Black 4.3%

Sapporo was founded in the northern city of the same name back in 1876 and claims to be Japan's oldest brewery. Its flagship lager, often drunk from a funky-looking can, wrestles with Asahi and Kirin in terms of sales, but thinking drinkers prefer this Germanic Dunkel with drawn- out toffee and prune flavors, a touch of aniseed, and molasses.

Sapporo Yebisu *Lager* 5%

Now brewed in Tokyo, Yebisu is positioned as a cut above other mainstream lagers and rightly so. It declines the use of rice in favor of an all-malt recipe and has the solid sweet malt profile and a zesty hop profile akin to a Dortmunder.

Shiga Kogen Brewery
Nagano, Nagano
www.tamamura-honten.co.jp

Kogen House IPA 8.2%

Shiga Kogen is new on the Japanese brewing scene, only branching out from sake production in 2004. Named after Japan's largest ski resort, it's not afraid to experiment, and its ales are the subject of increasing admiration among enlightened enthusiasts. This enormous tikka-tinged American-style ale has huge eucalyptus and mint aromas, with earthy undertones.

Miyama Blonde *Saison* 6.7%

Piquant, fruity proof that rice in beer isn't always a bad thing. Rice used in the production of sake is thrown into the boil alongside specialty malt and spruced up with a healthy dose of hops.

Yo-Ho Brewing Company
Karuizawa, Nagano
www.yohobrewing.com

Yo-Ho Brewing Company is one of the best-known craft breweries among mainstream beer drinkers and synonymous with head brewer Toshi Ishii—a leading figure in Japanese craft brewing. With a surname that means "stone", it was destiny that Toshi should spend nearly four years brewing at the Californian brewer of the same name. Inspired by the big beers of West Coast America, Toshi has been instrumental in changing perceptions back in his homeland.

 Yo-Ho Yona-Yona Barley Wine 8%

Brewed in one-off single batches since 2001, the year Toshi joined Yo-Ho Brewing, the hop formula for this blissful Barley Wine is tweaked every year, but the dedication to strength, smoothness, balance, and eye-popping IBUs runs constant.

Yo-Ho Yona-Yona Real Ale *Pale Ale* 5.5%

Cascade and Perle-infused American-style pale ale whose name, "every night", points toward its immense drinkability. The floral character of the cascade hops dances on the subtle malt base. Japan's answer to Sierra Nevada Pale Ale.

Yo-Ho Yona-Yona Tokyo Black Porter 5.0%

Very dark brown, almost black porter-style beer. It has a lightly tanned, long-lasting head. The aroma is a pleasant mix of chocolate, espresso coffee, and roasted malt, with a hint of woodiness, giving a slightly oaky smell and a slightly sweet floral element from the hops. Texture is smooth, medium-to-full bodied, and crisp, with a dry feeling on the palate. Carbonation is medium, giving a slight bubbly sensation on the tongue.

BAIRD BREWING COMPANY

The Fishmarket Taproom,19-4 Senbonminato-cho,
Numazu, Shizuoka 410-0845, Japan

www.bairdbrewing.com

The Japanese craft-brewing industry is only around 15 years old and Baird Brewing, established in 2000, is a relative newcomer to this young, thriving beer scene. Bryan Harrell tells us more.

In 1994, regulations on the issue of brewery licences were eased from a required two million liters, around 530,000 gallons of annual production to just 15,850 gallons (60,000 liters) making it possible for small breweries to start up. While 60,000 liters yearly is a bit much for a brewpub, small regional breweries began to open in Japan, albeit at a slow pace. By the turn of the century, more than 300 had opened, most being operated by joint ventures between local governments and private interests, or additional new businesses that had been set up by sake brewers.

The intent of the Japanese Government was that small breweries would revitalize local economies, although many were unaware that fine-quality brewing ingredients, small-scale brewing equipment, and even brewmasters themselves had to be imported, as the illegality of homebrewing in Japan left the country without a solid base of experienced home brewers ready to "go pro" when the opportunity arose.

As a result, craft beer in Japan was unnecessarily expensive (owing to the 222 yen/liter tax on all beer sold), while inexperienced management was ill equipped to deal with basic sanitation issues. Despite most breweries having access to trained European or American brewers, regular employees could not maintain the methods necessary to make beer of a quality similar to that of mass-produced products from the four big brewers: Asahi, Kirin, Sapporo, and Suntory.

While the public was interested in trying the new "local" beers, most fell short and, by the end of the decade, the stage was set for a talented American brewer to steal the show.

Getting a Start

Bryan Baird, a native of Ohio, opened Baird Brewing in 2001 together with his business partner (and wife) Sayuri Baird, a native of Southern Japan. They chose the town of Numazu in Shizuoka Prefecture, on the Pacific Coast two hours south of Tokyo, where the pace of life is slow and the winters are warm and clear. They found a small storefront just opposite the town's thriving fish market, building a brewpub on the second floor with a small brewery in the back.

Baird initially brewed on a tiny setup, in 8-gallon (30-liter) batches. A visit to the Baird "Fishmarket Taproom" was akin to going over to the house of a great homebrewer whose wife happened to be a great cook. Sayuri ran the kitchen, turning out interesting dishes that combined the best parts of Japanese and American home cooking, reaching a high level of culinary synergy wherein the total eating experience exceeded the sum of the two parts. Fresh local fish and vegetables combined with American-style seasonings and cooking techniques to make perfect matches with Bryan's well-balanced ales of distinctive character.

Baird still insists on using top-quality floor-malted Maris Otter malts and whole flower hops, along with a variety of brewing techniques inspired by the US homebrewing revolution of the 1970s. He had apprenticed at Redhook, near Seattle, and brought with him to Japan a high level of passion to brew the best beer possible. Baird Brewing is known in Japan as the best of the best, with outstanding quality by international standards, and is recognized by Japanese craft beer enthusiasts as one of the country's best producers.

Primary Motivations

"I never thought of launching this craft-brewing business in the USA. I've been a long-time student of Japan, and have lived here a while. My primary motivation, before beer even, was to create a business endeavor in Japan," explains Baird. "So, pursuing craft brewing in Japan is how I can marry two of my great life passions—characterful beer and Japanese culture."

Baird notes that Japan is a well-educated and affluent society with a huge population in a small area. The social environment is also favorable because there is a great reverence for craftsmanship, and no pseudo-moral demonization of alcohol in Japanese society. As such, Japan has a fairly relaxed and uncomplicated legal structure regarding alcoholic beverage production. Specifically, there are no restrictions on shipping, distribution, and sales between prefectures, and no limitations on the ability to both manufacture and retail beer or on internet sales of beer.

Country Discomforts

"Numazu, as a regional city, poses great sales challenges for us," Bryan relates. The people of Shizuoka prefecture tend to be quite middle-of-the-road, and the area is known as a test market for the products of industrial manufacturers. "Our beer is extremely flavorful and distinct, and anything but middle-of-the-road. So far, we haven't exactly set the Numazu market on fire," he adds.

On the other hand, Numazu is not far from Tokyo, which makes it easy for the large numbers of beer enthusiasts in a metropolitan area approaching 30 million people to visit Baird at weekends. The response has been so great that Baird opened a taproom in central Tokyo in the spring of 2008, with all beer being supplied from the Numazu brewery, which itself had undergone two significant expansions within five years.

As a brewery location, Numazu is outstanding because of its low costs compared to Tokyo and because of its position at the foothills of Mount Fuji, ensuring superb water as an ingredient for the beer.

Balance + Complexity = Character

When asked what approach Baird Brewing has taken to achieve its remarkable success, Bryan explains it in very simple terms. "Craft beer, to me, means beer of character. My own equation for this when I create a new beer is that character is the sum of balance and complexity. This is a simple equation but, as with most simple things, it is easier to said than done."

But there must be secrets? Techniques? Obsessions? "I

work towards this goal by solid commitment to three things: the best ingredients, natural carbonation, and appropriate temperature. I use ingredients that are as flavorful and unprocessed as possible. This means exclusively whole flower hops and only floor-malted barley as a base malt. All of my beer is unfiltered, and naturally carbonated through conditioning in the keg or bottle. Finally, I store and serve the beer at the appropriate temperature. At our own taproom, we are fanatical about refrigerating kegs and dispensing only at cool, not cold, temperatures. To us, this means 46.4–53.6°F (8°–12°C). We will not sell Baird Beer in kegs to bars that do not agree to refrigerate the product. In Japan, most bars cannot do this because of limited refrigeration capability."

What's Next

Baird has had a number of brewery workers over the years, most notably Molly Browning, who now brews at Jolly Pumpkin in rural Michigan. He has recently hired a remarkably talented home brewer, Chris Poel, who gladly left his university teaching position for the romance and challenges of brewing. Poel is more edgy as a brewer than the comparatively conservative Baird, so I expect new Baird offerings to reflect the trend toward high-gravity "extreme beers", all the rage in the US. "As for the business," Bryan explains, "we plan to expand our beer production in tandem with opening more company-operated taprooms in Japan, aping our Nakameguro Taproom in Tokyo."

Opposite Top: Bryan Baird and his Japanese wife, Sayuri, started Baird Brewing in 2001.
Above: Baird Brewing's Rising Sun Pale Ale is a US-inspired brew.

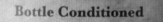

Bottle Conditioned

EAST COAST
⇒ ALE ⇐

Refreshing South African
Golden Ale

ROBSON'S

A WORLD OF BEER
MIDDLE EAST
& AFRICA

The Middle East

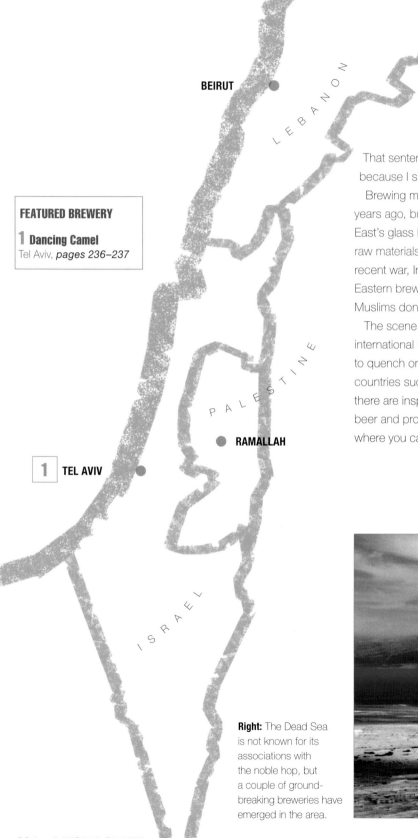

The Middle East is home to one of the most exciting beer cultures in the world, with hundreds of craft breweries and marvelous micros making magical beer.

BEIRUT

LEBANON

PALESTINE

● RAMALLAH

ISRAEL

FEATURED BREWERY

1 Dancing Camel
Tel Aviv, *pages 236–237*

1 **TEL AVIV**

That sentence is, of course, a complete lie, but bear with me because I shall explain.

Brewing may have been born in the region more than 8,000 years ago, but the froth has been blown from the Middle East's glass by a number of factors, including a dearth of local raw materials, a hot anti-brewing climate, conflict (up until the recent war, Iraq had been one of the last bastions of Middle Eastern brewing), and, last but by no means least, the fact that Muslims don't drink very much, if at all.

The scene is dominated by big, often state-owned or international breweries making lager-style beers that tend to quench one's thirst rather than seduce one's throat. In countries such as Israel, Palestine, and Lebanon, however, there are inspirational craft breweries flying the flag for good beer and proving that there are very few places on the planet where you can't get your hands on some kind of quality brew.

Right: The Dead Sea is not known for its associations with the noble hop, but a couple of groundbreaking breweries have emerged in the area.

Israel, Lebanon, & Palestine

Dancing Camel ISRAEL
*See Brewery Profile
pages 236–237*
Tel Aviv
www.dancingcamel.com

 **American Pale Ale** 5.4%

Brewer David Cohen has
purposely reined in the bitterness
of this kosher Californian-
style pale, but the grassy hop
character is there, at the finish.
Very drinkable.

IPA 7.5%

Tempered for the Tel Aviv tongue
with the addition of sweet date
honey, this IPA has a slight nose of aniseed and a firm malt backbone.

961 Beer LEBANON
Beirut
www.961beer.com

 **961 Traditional Lager** 5.2%

With Lebanon embroiled in the Hezbollah war with Israel, 2006 was not
the ideal time to start a business, but that didn't stop four entrepreneurs
from creating a Beirut boutique brewery. Named after Lebanon's
international dialing code, 961 brews six organic beers, with this, a
spick-and-span lager, the bestseller.

Taybeh Brewing Company PALESTINE
Ramallah
www.taybehbeer.com

Taybeh Golden Beer *Pilsner* 5%

Undaunted by the unlikely business model of
selling alcohol in a Muslim community,
Nadim Khoury has been brewing German-
style beers amid political and commercial
conflict since 1993. The brewery, 20 miles
or so outside Jerusalem in the village of
Taybeh (which means "delicious" in Arabic),
makes a trio of beers that sell in parts of the
West Bank, Israel, the United Kingdom and
Germany. This crisp golden pilsner with a
distinct sweet malt character leans toward a
Dunkel in style.

> "Beer is living proof that God loves us
> and wants us to be happy."
>
> BENJAMIN FRANKLIN
> AMERICAN SCIENTIST & POLITICIAN 1706–1790

DANCING CAMEL BREWERY

Hataasiya 12, Tel Aviv, Israel
www.dancingcamel.com

It may boast Belfast's defiant edge, the solar-powered spirit of Rio de Janeiro, an insomniac party attitude akin to New York City, and Cairo's clement climate but, for those seeking fine beer, Tel Aviv is hardly the "Promised Land" for serious beer lovers.

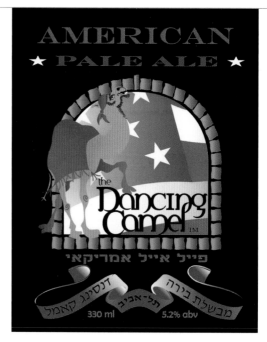

The city is a magnificent metropolis, but it's certainly not "Beer Town." The legacy left by the German immigrants who arrived in the 1930s is some stunning Bauhaus architecture that, incongruous against the ancient edifices of neighboring Jaffa, gleams bright in the Middle Eastern sun. History, however, intervened before the Germans could begin to impart their passion for brewing beer.

It's little surprise that, given Tel Aviv's balmy climate, beer variety rarely strays beyond a lager duopoly—Goldstar and Maccabee. As a rule, beer cultures tend to wilt rather than prosper in places where the mercury rides high, but it's not just the weather that's to blame for the barren beer scene. Tel Aviv simply doesn't have a brewing history to speak of. In fact it hardly has a history at all—having celebrated its centenary year only in 2009.

Discounting Islamic countries, Israelis drink less beer than any other nation in the world, and in Tel Aviv the local imbibing inclination leans heavily toward coffee. Intelligently brewed beer imports are thin on the ground, the tax on beer is prohibitively high for budding brewers and, lest we forget, the opportunity for exporting to neighboring countries is, at best, a scant possibility.

It was in 2006 that Dancing Camel strode bravely into this arid beer-drinking desert in the form of David Cohen, an chartered accountant from New York. From a funky warehouse in the southern, insalubrious, and industrial quarter of Tel Aviv, David plows a valiant and solitary furrow, hailing esoteric ales in a city where the idea of flavorsome beer has hitherto gone down like a pork chop at a Bar Mitzvah.

"You have to develop a very thick skin to sell this kind of beer in Tel Aviv," admits David. "I've got used to people doing that contorted face when they first drink it," he adds, screwing up his features as if he's just licked a battery.

In a land of light lackluster lager, Dancing Camel boogies to a different beat: ambitious, audacious ales brewed using English and American hops, grain from Germany and Belgium, French yeast, and the local hard Tel Aviv water, which furnishes the beer with a fuller body.

The beers are unashamedly modeled on those of the US craft-beer scene. Inspired by both the wave of West Coast craft brews wandering east and the burgeoning local brews in New York during the 1980s, the former accountant first began brewing at his Brooklyn home. "After years of putting up with lousy stuff, I realized what beer should taste like. I fell in love with Samuel Smith and began replicating Tadcaster Porter."

David's part-time pursuit turned into a potential profession when he joined Heavyweight Brewing Company in New Jersey. "It was a great brewery, and we brewed a cask-conditioned Baltic porter that won a medal at the Great British Beer Festival," he says. "My time there was really instrumental, a turning point, as it's a massive jump from homebrewing to running your own brewery."

Yet David's ultimate plan was to fuse his passion for brewing with a lifelong ambition "to make Aliyah" (translates as "going up" to Israel). So, in July 2003 he left for Israel, scoured the country for a suitable brewing site, and, having found one in Tel Aviv's blue-collar quarter, bought a ten-barrel brewery, formerly owned by the Flying Pig Brewery in Washington State.

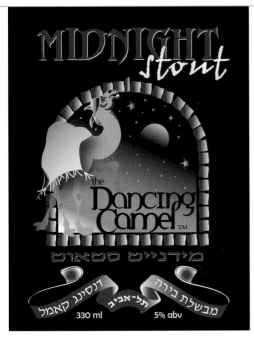

In the summer of 2006, he began brewing and now produces around a thousand barrels a year. His beers, all of them completely kosher, are often influenced by ingredients indigenous to Israel. "Part of our mission is to introduce the concept of a local brewery that uses local produce, as long as it works well, that you wouldn't expect to find in beer," he adds, citing his Dancing Camel IPA as a quirky case in point. An esoteric US-Israeli amalgamation, it's brewed using classic American Cascade hops and native date honey. "Israelis don't have a palate for bitter flavors," says David. "When we brewed the IPA at a high IBU, it didn't go down as well as it would in America. So we added silan, a date honey that mellows out the hop influence. We changed the hopping regiment and toned the bitterness down. It's still high in hops but outside Israel we don't call it an IPA."

The IPA is Dancing Camel's second biggest-selling beer behind the lightly hopped Pale Ale, which accounts for 40 percent of its sales. A smooth-sipping, nutty Midnight Stout and a fruity hefe-wit, which bestrides the Bavarian and Belgian styles, complete the quartet of all-year round ales.

But it's with a series of seasonal beers that Dancing Camel showboats. "We brew around a dozen limited-edition beers every year and play around with different ingredients. "These include a "Caribbean" stout laced with Carib beans, a spicy summer sip made using real chili peppers, and Golem, an intoxicating elixir brewed like an Eisbock to 15%, then diluted down to 10.5%.

To celebrate Rosh Hashanah, the Jewish New Year, David produces a pomegranate beer called 613—"there are 613

Jewish laws and 613 seeds in a pomegranate," while Sukkot, a Jewish festival that takes place in the fall, is observed with "Trog Wit", an American-style Belgian wheat beer starring the Etrog lemon in a fragrant and fruity cameo role. "Etrog is an archetypal Israeli fruit," explains David. "It's bigger than a lemon, much more flavorsome, oily, and incredibly aromatic, and works wonderfully well with wheat beer."

In 2007, Dancing Camel began bottling its beers, no bad thing in a nation where 75 percent of beer sales take place in supermarkets and liquor stores, and, slowly but surely, its ales are wheedling their way into all the right bars and boutique supermarkets. "We're getting there. It's hard, but the American ex-pat audience helps and so, too, does the increase in Belgian and British imports,"says David. "There's also an embryonic homebrewing culture, which is always a good sign."

Key Beers

Dancing Camel IPA *India Pale Ale* 7.5%

Dancing Camel American Pale Ale 5.4%

Dancing Camel Midnight Stout 5%

Dancing Camel Caribbean Stout *(seasonal)* 7.5%

Dancing Camel Golem 10.5%

Dancing Camel Six Thirteen-5768 Pomegranate Ale 6.1%

613 Pomegranate Beer 5.8%

Dancing Camel Trog Wit *Belgian-style Wheat Beer (seasonal)* 6%

Africa

Even though beer cultures tend traditionally not to thrive in countries with hot climates, Africa is certainly no beer-drinking desert and it boasts a long and rich brewing heritage in several of its larger countries.

Lagers that are light and refreshing, and often brewed with corn or maize, play a leading role in most people's beer-drinking lives on this continent, but you'd be mistaken if you assumed that they drank nothing else. Stouts command a strong following, due in no small measure to Europe's colonial influence, and so does an indigenous drink called sorghum beer.

As much a food as a drink, sorghum has a thicker consistency than conventional beer. It's sweet and cloudy, uses wild yeast for fermentation, and is brewed using millet and sorghum grain because there are few places on the continent where barley and hops can be easily grown.

South Africa is one of the few countries where hops can grow successfully, and it's here, predominantly under the stewardship of behemoth international brewer SAB Miller, where more than half the continent's beer is brewed.

While there is a handful of craft breweries in South Africa, the big global breweries are also dominant in Africa's other major brewing nations such as Namibia, Kenya, and Nigeria.

CASABLANCA

MOROCCO

ETHIOPIA

ADDIS ABABA

NAIROBI

NAMIBIA

KENYA

S. AFRICA

WINDHOEK

1 DURBAN

FEATURED BREWERY

1 Shongweni Brewery
Durban, S. Africa, *pages 240–241*

Above right: South Africa, despite a population of 50 million, can boast only a handful of microbreweries.

African countries

Kombolcha Brewery ETHIOPIA
Addis Ababa
No web address

 Bati Beer *Lager* 4.5%

Ethiopia's oldest brewery was founded in 1922 and is located in central Addis Ababa, where it can get really rather hot and where this pale lager, crisp and refreshing, can come in rather handy.

East African Breweries KENYA
Nairobi
www.eabl.com

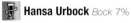 **Tusker Lager** 4.2%

This consistent Kenyan thirst-quencher is the largest beer brand in East Africa. Pale gold and instantly refreshing, with a delicate citrus nose, it's an ideal "sunset" beer and named in memory of the brewery's founder George Hurst, who was killed by a rogue elephant a year after the brewery was founded. Brewed with barley grown in Kenya.

Brasseries du Maroc MOROCCO
Casablanca
www.1stmaroc.com

Casablanca Beer *Lager* 5%

This clean and simple lager is not to be drunk with one's thinking fez on, as it is a simple-thirst quencher, but is none the worse for that.

Namibia Breweries NAMIBIA
Windhoek
www.nambrew.com

Hansa Urbock *Bock* 7%

A robust and earthy bock with a chewy, no-nonsense malt profile. Not what you'd expect from a country where the mercury soars, but the legacy of the two German founders, who started brewing in the 1920s, lives on. Brewed only once a year in May.

South Africa

Castle/SABMiller
Sandtona
www.sabmiller.com

 Castle Milk Stout 6%

Until a merger in 2002 with SAB Miller, this sturdy, sweet stout was part of South African Breweries—set up back in 1895 to satisfy the thirst of the mining community in the Johannesburg region. Despite the decline in mining and a climate that lends itself to light lagers, it remains huge in South Africa and is still a top-five selling beer.

Mitchell's Brewery
Western Cape
www.mitchellsknysnabrewery.com

 **Ninety Shilling** *Scotch Ale* 5%

It's been more than 25 years since Lex Mitchell kick-started Africa's first microbrewery in the Western Cape town of Knysna. This Scotch-finished leathery homage to the Mitchell's family's Perthshire roots is one of several predominantly British-style unpasteurized beers.

Raven Stout 5%

Creamy and soft lactose-imbued ebony ale firmed up with plenty of hops. Other beers are session lagers and ales around the 4% mark.

Shongweni Brewery
Durban *See Brewery Profile, pages 240-241*
ww.shongwenibrewery.com

Durban Pale Ale 5.7%

A dark, fuller-bodied interpretation of an American-style ale brewed with an added measure of crystal malt. Fruity and crisp like a Kölsch.

 East Coast Ale *Golden Ale* 4%

A lovely, light pale ale brewed with Brewer's Gold and Challenger hops, boldly aimed at luring local mainstream lager lovers into a new arena.

 Mango Fruit Beer 4%

Belgian in style, but with the brakes put on for a less cloying consistency to suit the more temperate climate. Brewed using locally sourced mangoes and matured for a hundred days.

Wit *Wheat Beer* 4%

Lemon-influenced Low Countries wheat beer brewed with unmalted grain sourced from the Free State about a hundred miles away. Stuart recommends serving it with a typical Durban dish, the bunny chow, a mutton or beef curry, very spicy and rich, which is served in a hollowed-out loaf of bread with the leftover bread placed on top.

SHONGWENI BREWERY

Shongweni Brewery Estate, B1 Shongweni Valley,
Shongweni, Near Durban, KwaZulu-Natal, South Africa
www.shongwenibrewery.com

South Africa is definitely not a big, bountiful land of beer, at least not in terms of diversity or choice. In a nation of more than 50 million people, just three breweries command a 98 percent share of the entire beer market, and there are only a dozen microbreweries.

Yet, on the outskirts of Durban, Englishman Stuart Robson and his wife, Sherene, are single-handedly dragging South Africa, kicking and screaming, onto the global craft-brewing map from their small Shongweni Brewery set up in 2006.

Shongweni's bottle-conditioned ales and fruit beers are inspired by Europe and the United States using fresh, local ingredients and brewed using infusion mashes and ale yeasts in open fermentation vessels. All the beers are matured in the brewery for one hundred days. Stuart provides this background to his brewing philosophy:

What brought you to South Africa?

Sherene is South African and used to live in Durban when she was younger, and I'm from London. I had previously worked in the environmental sector, and Sherene had worked in the business management function of financial institutes while pursuing her MBA qualification. The main reason for coming to Shongweni was that we wanted a change in lifestyle. We're based in the "Valley of a Thousand Hills" with views across the ocean. Imagine the Lake District or Scottish Lowlands, but in a subtropical setting.

Given that South Africa is bereft of diverse beer, what inspired your decision to open a microbrewery?

Wherever Sherene and I had traveled, we'd try to discover new, local beers and pair them with great food. Unfortunately, when we came to South Africa, the beer choice was limited to variations on a mass-produced lager and the occasional stout.

We realized that the local market was crying out for alternatives and, influenced by the beers we'd experienced on our travels, we knew we could meet that demand.

What brewing experience did you have?

I made my first "beer" from a homebrew kit when I was 16, as a present for my dad's birthday, and just continued the passion through my two degree studies in biology and later, when we had made the decision to set up the brewery, at Brewlab in the United Kingdom. We also spent time with UK microbreweries before coming to South Africa, exchanging ideas.

When was your first beer "moment"?

As a young man I was fortunate that my local pub sold a variety of cask beers. I remember, especially around Christmas, casks standing on the bar counter, but my introduction to a wider world of beer came with a holiday to Europe where I first encountered Belgian abbey beers and French beers such as Jenlain. I haven't looked back since, but just as important was Sherene's discovery that beer was as diverse in flavor as wine and something that can be drunk at dinner and appreciated as a connoisseur drink, to rival fine wine and whiskey.

Have any other breweries been an inspiration?

Adnams Brewery has always been a favorite, and we even got engaged there! But one or two stand out. We can certainly relate to Garrett Oliver's experience of returning from Europe to the United States and being faced with just mass-produced beer. His passion for beer and food also parallels our own. The brewers from the Tunnel Brewery in Northamptonshire also gave us some great ideas and inspiration.

Which countries have shaped your brewing?

The major styles that have influenced us here are British IPA, the wheat beers from Germany and the Low Countries, the "California Common" style, and the golden ales from the United

Far left: Shongweni beers are inspired by European and North American beer styles.
Left: Stuart Robson uses local malt and fruit, together with some imported yeast and hops, as ingredients in his craft beers.
Right: The small brewery is situated on the outskirts of Durban.

Kingdom and Europe. Our fruit beers take inspiration from Belgium, but are brewed with the sub-tropical climate, so tend toward refreshment rather than heavy, jammy palates.

What ingredients do you use?

We use yeast and imported hops from Europe and America, including Challenger, Cascade, Brewer's Gold, First Gold, Saaz, Hallertau, and Northern Brewer. Most of our beers are made with local pale malt, often referred to as "African Gold". Our unmalted wheat is sourced from the Free State, about 120 miles (200 kilometers) away, and we also import selected specialty malts that are not produced locally. All of the fruit that we brew with is from local farmers, within a 45-mile (75-kilometer) radius. We are currently waiting for our first crop of brewery-grown pineapples.

Why bottle-conditioned beers?

They're unique in South Africa, and it gives us control over the quality of the beer. Beer here tends to be keg beer and often suffers at the hands of the bar staff that dispense it.

Are you fighting a lone brewing battle?

There is a vibrant homebrewing scene in RSA, and we hope that the next commercial micros will come from their ranks. SAB Miller have installed a few small (+/- 10 gallons/40 liter) brewplants at some universities to get graduates into brewing.

What does the future hold for you and the beer?

In five years we'd like to be recognized across South Africa as the brewers of the best, most diverse range of beers in the country and to encourage others to brew commercially. We have developed a vintage ale, and are considering a brew utilizing molasses and possibly sorghum.

East Coast Ale

Brewed like a golden ale but served "fruitier" at lager temperature, it is loved by locals for its lager-style appeal and, having tried it and overcome their ale aversion, they're now moving on to try our other beers.
Food match: It was brewed with the most popular South African food in mind, the "Braai" or BBQ. It goes well with any BBQ food especially the traditional "Boerewors" farmers sausage, served with maize pap (a kind of maize "mashed potato") and tomato and onion gravy.

Wheat Beer

Inspired by both Germany and the Low Country classics, it has less clove and more citrus because of the lack of unmalted wheat in South Africa.
Food match: This beer is ideal with a typically Durban dish, the bunny chow. This is usually a mutton or beef curry, very spicy and rich, which is served in a hollowed-out loaf of bread.

Durban Pale Ale

Based on British IPAs which, on their journey from England to India, stopped over in Durban where they were drunk by British garrisons.
Food match: Goes well with a *potjie*. This is a traditional cast-iron cooking pot (think witch's cauldron) that is often used for cooking over smoldering coals. The *potjie* is like a big stew, using meats such as beef, mutton, or game such as springbok or kudu and plenty of local vegetables and also barley. A "potbread" is often cooked on top of the *potjie*, so that the final meal is a hearty stew, topped with fresh bread and accompanied by a Durban Pale Ale.

West Coast Ale

A darker, South African version of Californian Common ales such as Anchor Steam from San Francisco.
Food match: It goes well with spicy East Coast crayfish (lobster), particularly when you use the beer to cook the crayfish in, with added chili and spice.

Mango Fruit Beer

Using local fruits, our fruit beers tend towards lighter interpretations of the Belgian style.
Food match: A rich and syrupy traditional cake known as a "Malva pudding".

BEER & FOOD

History of beer and food

Beer and food matching is all the rage. Breweries have begun hosting beer and food dinners; beer labels are adorned with increasingly elaborate food matching recommendations; ales and lagers are being brewed specifically to accompany food; and many of the world's most remarkable restaurants—from Le Gavroche in London to the magnificent El Bulli in Spain—are turning to beer in their ongoing quest for groundbreaking gastronomic experiences. It's all rather exciting.

But matching beer with food is not a new phenomenon. In fact, it's very old. The two have been close culinary companions since medieval times, when brewhouses and kitchens were one and the same. The beer tankard, not the wine chalice, graced the dining tables of both the affluent and the pauper for centuries. While the multi-layered synergies between beer and food were seldom the talk of the table, it was most definitely the grain and not the grape that sat at its head.

It was the Romans, the original oenophiles, who were first to develop the "wine and dine" myth that has been propagated ever since. While beer was busy fueling industrial revolutions, quenching the thirst of the masses and making sure that the world kept spinning, wine was having dinner.

Stealthily, by degrees, wine has usurped beer as the foodie's favored friend. But don't, whatever you do, be hoodwinked by this Roman ruse. Yes, wine dovetails delightfully with a whole host of dishes and flavors, but certainly not all of them and not always the ones you'd think.

In the ultimate tome on the art of beer and food matching, *The Brewmaster's Table: Discovering the Pleasures of Real Beer with Real Food*, American author and brewer Garrett Oliver writes: "If you love food, but you only know wine, then you're trying to write a symphony using only half the notes and half the orchestra". He's so right. A bon vivant who shuns beer is, strictly, just a vivant—a vivant scoffing at the dinner table of denial.

What beer lacks in tannin and acidity, two of wine's weapons, it makes up for in copious other culinary qualities; it has bitterness, it has sweetness, it has bubbles, it leads with less alcohol, and it has an enormous array of flavors, many of which are absent from wine's wide repertoire. Beer has the caramelized character to find favor and further flavor with charcoal-checkered meat and desserts; where spicy, heat-emitting foods shoot wine down in flames, beers, such as robust India Pale Ales and brusquely bitter Pilsners, have the firefighting bitterness and fat-lifting carbonation to rescue and revive flavors from the overpowering inferno.

Irish stouts and porters envelop the acidity of oysters and seafood in a dark, roasty, and toasty cloak, peaty Rauchbiers smolder with smoked cheese and meats, and wheat beers woo salads and herb-encrusted fish with their spicy citrus charm and tempered tartness.

Herbal, spicy German weissbiers chase succulent roast chicken down with zest and zeal; fruit beers are a fine, faithful friend to chocolate, foie gras, and duck; and British best bitters are, by divine appointment, betrothed to battered fish and chips, succulent pork pies, sausage and mash, and, of course the classic British pub dish, a plowman's lunch.

If you're looking for something to accompany game, then the spicy, herbal French Bière de Garde is a winner; fruit beers go with chocolate desserts; chocolate beer goes with fruity desserts and, of course, beer goes with all pizza. And the same goes for nuts and chips.

These fusions of flavor are just a few examples of beer and food's delightful possibilities. The culinary combinations are endless and, unlike wine, pleasantly affordable. While wines worry wallets, beer's epicurean enlightenment is well within the grasp of everyone's fiscal fingertips. So, open your eyes, awaken your senses, and bask in the brilliance of beer and food.

Concise guide to beer & food matching

Pilsners, Kölsch and Light Lagers

These beers know all about delicate flavors and so won't trample over finely-tuned food flavors. Shellfish; Cajun; mildly spicy Indian; smoked meats or fish; tapas; or spicy Vietnamese or Thai.

Brown Ales

Made for a meat feast, malt-driven brown ales belong with Cajun food, chilli, burgers, steaks, meat casseroles, and barbecue ribs.

Fruit Beers

Great companions to sweet and savory dishes. Chocolate dessert is exquisite with kriek (cherry) beers while frambozen (raspberry) is simply sublime with foie gras. Strangely, these beers don't go well with fruit dishes. It seems that too much fruit can, maybe, be a bad thing.

Pale Ale/Bitters

A loving and devoted partner to pub grub, pale ales will gild bangers and mash, fish and chips, pizza, pies, pasta (not tomato-based sauces), or also a Reuben sandwich with panache.

Trappist/Abbey Ales

Dubbel ales (all caramel, chocolate, dark fruit, and warming spice) lend themselves heartily to dark meat dishes with fruity sauces such as ribs, steaks, game, and strongly smoked fish.

Tripels (floral hops, spicy aromatics, and fruity flavors) have a foodie fetish for herb-crusted dark meats, swanky sausages, and foie gras.

Witbiers & Weissbiers

Wheat beer is food's flexible friend. Light and zesty, witbier complements salads, white meat, and pasta dishes, and links up citrus flavors in salads, light fish courses, or moules marinière. Bavarian weissbier is fantastic with fishcakes and fruity North African dishes.

Indian Pale Ale/Double IPA

Think rich. IPAs have the bitterness to cut through fat like a knife through, er … butter. Roasts—especially beef or pork—are a good starting point; curries also suit (and not just because they're from India); chili con carne; enchiladas; spicy sausages and gourmet hamburgers, too.

Porter/Stout

Stout is a dessert beer: terrific with vanilla ice cream, fruit tarts, chocolate cakes and mousses, pannacotta, cheesecake, and plum pudding. It's also excellent with cheese, especially Stilton.

Porters make ideal BBQ beers, anything caramelized or chargrilled is ideal, but don't forget porter and oysters. Sublime.

Barley Wines & Bocks

Say cheese! Or say rich desserts, indulgent ice creams, or a slice of pecan pie drenched in cream. Please.

Stephen Beaumont: Four ways to pair beer & food

Canadian **Stephen Beaumont** is widely regarded as one of the world's best beer and food writers. These are his four guidelines for pairing beer and food. As with all gastronomic guidelines, there are exceptions, sometimes significant ones, to each of these general rules. In getting started in food and beer pairing, however, they constitute a helpful first step.

1 Think of ale as red wine and lager as white wine

As most people have at least a passing familiarity with how to partner wine and food, this is a useful place to start. When beef, lamb, or any other dish that you would usually pair with red wine is on the menu, select an ale to serve with it, looking for one with characteristics that might parallel those you would desire in a wine for that particular food. Conversely, if the main course is a "white wine food" such as fish or poultry, try a lager.

2 Hoppiness in beer = acidity in wine

Anywhere that you would seek high acidity in a wine—such as with spicy, salty or oily food—you will have best luck choosing a beer with significant hoppiness, such as a German-style Pilsner, pale ale, or IPA. The more intense the spiciness, fattiness, or saltiness of the dish, the hoppier you will want the beer.

3 Complement or contrast

As much as possible, try to match foods to beers with complementary characters, such as a robust stew with a full-bodied ale or the subtle taste of pan-fried whitefish with the relative delicacy of a wheat beer or pale lager. To mix things up, try a directly contrasting flavor, such as a crisp, dry lager with a cream soup or an assertive stout with the briny taste of oysters.

4 Keep the beer sweeter than the dessert

Nothing kills the flavor of a beer like the overpowering sweetness of a dessert, much in the same manner that mint toothpaste will make even the sweetest apple taste sour and off-putting. Keep the sugar contents of both beer and dessert balanced, however, and the pairing will work tremendously.

Beers that work well with food: Seafood

Beer and seafood have been entwined in maritime matrimony ever since humans took to the sea. Seldom would sailors set sail without bunging barrels of beer on the boat first.

Not only did beer provide valuable ballast in the bows, but it was a lot safer to drink than water. Jam-packed with hops to preserve it and brimming with protein, vitamins, and morale-boosting alcohol, beer was less vulnerable to infection and contamination and would be washed down with fresh catches.

Today, gastronomic adventurers are able to cast their net far and wide when looking for suitable beers to accompany the myriad of flavors offered by crustaceans, shellfish, and other fruits of the ocean.

Matching Suggestions

Oysters Dubbel, porter, schwarzbier, altbier, strong brown ale

Mussels Amber lager, Pilsner, American pale ale, Märzen

Shrimp, scallops, crab, and lobster Bock, dry Irish stout, amber lager, Vienna lager, ESB, Altbier

Fish Porter, stout, strong bitter, Dubbel, Dortmunder, dunkel

Sushi Premium English bitter/ESB, Barley Wine, oatmeal stout, Scotch ale, Bière de Garde

Fish pies and fishcakes Abbey beer, Trappist ale, dark lager

Battered fish and chips Maibock, Dunkelweizen, Tripel, blonde ale, Vienna lager, Pilsner (highly hopped)

Gammon/Ham Smoked ale, Gueuze, Oude Bruin, sweet stout, brown ale, Mild

Smoked/pickled fish Premium bitter, American-style IPA, Doppelbock, Dubbel, Trappist ale, Bière de Garde, abbey beer, Schwarzbier

Oriental Roast Sea Bass

Lobster Thermidor

King Shrimp Brochettes

Pressed Sushi

Rick Stein's Beer & Seafood Pairings
for recipes see pages 250–251

Fish & chips with Sharp's Chalky's Bite

This classic British dish calls for a catch-all accompaniment to break through the batter, lighten the texture of both the meaty fish and mouth-filling fries, and, of course, hold the tangy tartar sauce at bay. While many drinkers will reel in traditional British bitters, one beer that fulfills all these flavor hooks is Chalky's Bite, a British take on a French Bière de Garde, brewed on the Cornish coast with citrus hops, and a saison-like finish.

Monkfish Vindaloo with Meantime IPA

It makes sense that a nation's food is betrothed to its drink but that's not why this "Indian" ale is paired with this intensely flavored Indian dish. A genuine, heavily hopped IPA is one of the few beer styles willing to stand up to the heavyweight heat and roaring spice of a vindaloo. But, unlike some American hop monsters, this bottle-conditioned firefighter doesn't overpower the monkfish. It's a bittersweet knockout combination.

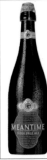

Shangurro Crab with Saison Dupont

OK, so it's not often you see crabs in Belgian farmhouses, but this sublime, slightly sour summer thirst-quencher parries the piquancy of the dish perfectly and cuts a swathe through the texture without leaving a trail of destruction. Wheat beers, usually wonderful with crab dishes, may wilt a little under these circumstances.

Gremolata Shrimp with Duvel

A stunning Belgian golden ale that mirrors the citrus zest, herbal notes and bitterness in the dish, acting in the same way as a crisp white wine would in complementing the subtle and delicate flavors of the seafood.

Moules Marinière with Boon Oude Geuze

Both in the pot and on the palate, nothing flexes the mussel's flavors like an elegant gueuze. The acidity and effervescence temper the seafood's thickset texture and counterbalance its sweetness.

Rick Stein: The marriage of beer & seafood

Rick Stein OBE is one of Britain's most famous celebrity chefs. He has presented numerous popular globetrotting gastronomic series on television and runs a handful of restaurants and pubs, as well as a cooking school, in Cornwall.

"In Britain, we don't champion our beer enough and far too many of us are unaware of the excitement and innovation that's brewing on our doorstep."

Having recently designed his own beer in association with Cornish brewer Sharp's, Rick has become a passionate proponent of matching beers with local produce—especially seafood.

"Beer works brilliantly well with fattier fish dishes and deep fried fish in particular," he says. "Chilli-based dishes are better suited to beer too and anything with vinegar as that will blow wine clear out of the water. A British bitter with fish and chips? There's nothing better."

"In Britain, we don't champion our beer enough and far too many of us are unaware of the excitement and innovation that's brewing on our doorstep. When I talk to British brewers now, it reminds me very much of New World Australian winemakers, who were reinventing wine more than ten years ago."

"Just as people in Britain have woken up to the wealth of local ingredients and producers with regards to food," says Rick, "so, too, are they realising that there's some magnificent beers on their doorstep."

Fish & Chips with tartar sauce

Serves 4

8½ oz. plain flour
3½ teaspoons baking powder
9 fl. oz. ice-cold water
2 lb floury potatoes,
such as Maris Piper
Sunflower oil, for deep-frying
4 x 6 oz. pieces of thick cod fillet,
cut from the head end, not the tail
Salt and freshly ground black pepper

Method

For the batter, mix the flour, 1 teaspoon salt and the baking powder with the water. Keep cold and use within 20 minutes of making.

Preheat oven to 300°F/150°C. Line a baking tray with plenty of kitchen paper and set aside.

Peel the potatoes and cut them lengthways into chips ½ in (1 cm) thick. Pour some sunflower oil into a large deep pan until it is about a third full and heat it to 260°F/130°C. Drop half the chips into a frying basket and cook for about 5 minutes, until tender when pierced but not colored. Lift them out and drain off the excess oil. Repeat for rest of the chips.

Heat the oil to 325°F/160°C. Season the cod fillets with salt and pepper and then dip into the batter. Fry, 2 pieces at a time, for 7–8 minutes, until crisp and golden brown. Lift out and drain on the paper-lined tray.

Raise temperature of the oil to 375°F /190°C and cook the chips in small batches for about 2 minutes, until crisp and golden. Lift out of the pan and shake to remove the excess oil. Sprinkle with salt and serve with the cod.

Left and Above: Sharp's Brewery in Rock, Cornwall has developed a new beer, Chalky's Bite, together with Rick Stein. It will be served at his Padstow restaurant.

Monkfish Vindaloo

Serves 4

3–4 tablespoons groundnut
or sunflower oil
1 onion, chopped
2 tomatoes, roughly chopped
10 fl. oz. water
4 medium-hot green chilies
2 lbs. skinned monkfish tail,
sliced across
1-inch thick steaks
Coconut or white wine vinegar, to taste
Sea salt

For the vindaloo curry paste:
1½ oz. dried Kashmiri chilies
1 small onion, unpeeled
1 teaspoon black peppercorns
1½ teaspoons cloves
3-inch cinnamon stick
1 teaspoon cumin seeds
1-inch piece of fresh ginger
4 tablespoons roughly chopped garlic
A walnut-sized piece of tamarind pulp
1 teaspoon soft brown sugar
2 tablespoons coconut
or white wine vinegar

Method

For the Vindaloo paste, cover the chilies with hot water and leave them to soak overnight.

Preheat oven to 450°F/ 230°C. Place the unpeeled onion on the middle shelf of the oven, and roast for 1 hour until the center is soft and the skin is caramelized.

Remove and leave to cool, then peel off the skin. Drain the chilies, squeeze out the excess water and then roughly chop. Put the peppercorns, cloves, cinnamon and cumin seeds into a mortar or spice grinder and grind to a fine powder. Tip the powder into a mini food processor and add the roasted onion, chilies, ginger, garlic, tamarind pulp, sugar, and vinegar. Blend to a smooth paste.

Heat the oil in a large, deep frying pan. Add the onion and fry until richly browned. Add the

tomatoes and cook to a deep-golden paste. Stir in 4 tablespoons of the paste and fry gently for 5 minutes, stirring, until it has slightly caramelized. Add the water and leave to simmer for 10 minutes, stirring occasionally.

Slit the green chilies open along their length and scrape out the seeds. Add the monkfish steaks and chilies. Simmer for 10 minutes, turning the fish if necessary. Lift out the steaks then boil the sauce rapidly to reduce. Add vinegar and salt to taste, return the steaks to the sauce and reheat. Serve with rice.

Pilau rice

In Goa they sometimes add crisply fried shallots to their basic aromatic spiced rice. It goes particularly well with the Monkfish vindaloo. This recipe gives you the option to do it either way.

serves 4

6 large shallots, thinly sliced (optional)
12 oz. basmati rice
2 tablespoons sunflower oil
3 cloves
3 green cardamom pods,
cracked open
2-inch piece cinnamon stick
1 bay leaf
½ teaspoon salt
1 pint boiling water

Method

If you wish to add some crisply fried shallots to your rice, heat ½ inch (1 cm) sunflower oil in a large frying pan. Add the shallots and fry them, stirring now and then, until they are crisp and golden. Lift out with a slotted spoon on to plenty of kitchen paper and leave to drain and cool.

Shangurro *Basque-style Stuffed Crab*

Serves 4

2 large cooked brown crabs,
or approximately
1 lb. fresh white crab meat and
4 oz. fresh brown crabmeat
3 tablespoons olive oil
2 onions, finely chopped
9 garlic cloves, finely chopped
8oz. plum tomatoes, skinned,
seeded and chopped
2 fl.oz. dry white wine
1 teaspoon caster sugar
¼ teaspoon dried chili flakes
3 tablespoons chopped parsley
2oz. fresh white breadcrumbs
½ oz. butter, melted
Salt and black pepper

Method

Preheat the oven to 400°F/200°C If using cooked crabs, remove the meat from the shell. Wash out the back shells and then break away the edge along the visible natural line to make a flat open shell. Set aside.

Heat the oil in a heavy-based frying pan, then add the onions and all but 1 chopped garlic clove. Fry over a gentle heat for 2 minutes, until softened.

Increase the heat, add the tomatoes, wine, sugar, chili flakes and some salt and pepper and simmer for about 4 minutes, until the mixture has reduced to a thick sauce.

Stir in 2 tablespoons of the parsley and the flaked crab meat and spoon the mixture into the crab shells or individual gratin dishes. If using crab shells, rest them in a shallow ovenproof dish.

Mix the breadcrumbs with the melted butter and the rest of the parsley and garlic, sprinkle this mixture over the crab and bake in the oven for 10 minutes until the topping is crisp and golden.

Gremolata Shrimp

Serves 4

1 large lemon
2 tablespoons olive oil
20 unpeeled large raw shrimp
Cayenne pepper (optional)
3 garlic cloves, finely chopped
4 tablespoons chopped
flat-leaf parsley
Coarse sea salt and
freshly ground black pepper

Method

Peel the zest off the lemon with a potato peeler. Pile the pieces up a few at a time and then cut them across into short thin strips.

Heat the oil in a large frying pan. Add the shrimp and toss them over a high heat for 4–5 minutes, seasoning them with some cayenne pepper or black pepper and sea salt as you do so.

Cut the lemon in half and squeeze the juice from one half over the shrimp. Continue to cook until the juice has almost evaporated — the prawns should be quite dry. Take the pan off the heat and leave for about 1 minute to cool very slightly.

Then sprinkle over the lemon zest, chopped garlic, parsley and ¼ teaspoon of salt and toss together well. Pile the shrimp into a large serving dish and serve with plenty of napkins.

Moules Marinières

Serves 4

3 ½ lb.
or 7 pints mussels
2 oz. unsalted butter
1 medium onion, chopped
2 fl. oz. gueuze
1 tablespoon roughly chopped
fresh parsley
1 quantity Mustard mayonnaise

Method

Wash the mussels in plenty of cold water. Scrape away any barnacles with a short-bladed knife. Pull off all the beards and wash the mussels again. Discard any that are open and do not close when tapped sharply.

Take a large lidded pan that is big enough to hold all the mussels. Add the mussels, butter, onion, beer, and half the parsley and set over a high heat. Turn the mussels over every now and then as they start to open. Keep the lid on the pan in between turning them. When they are all open, remove from the heat and leave for 30 seconds or so to let all the grit settle to the bottom of the pan.

Scoop out the mussels with a big spoon and divide between four large, deep plates. Wide soup plates are ideal but you can use deep bowls as well. Pour all the juices from the pan over the mussels holding back the last tablespoon or so which will be full of grit. Sprinkle the rest of the parsley over the mussels and serve with the mayonnaise and chips.

Right: The watery setting of Padstow is where Rick Stein's restuarant empire first began. He now owns several gastronomic ventures in the town.

Beers that work well with food: Meat

While one's epicurean instinct is to reach for red wine when looking for an alcoholic accompaniment to meat, beer works just as well, if not better.

Beer and meat have a close culinary affinity that stretches well beyond the backyard barbecue. Unlike wine, beer is armed with the fat-lifting carbonation to alleviate mouth-coating fatty textures, the caramelized flavors to dovetail with those found in roasted and grilled dishes and the versatility of style to accommodate a variety of glazes, gravies, and sauces.

In dark meat dishes such as pies, stews, and casseroles, beer—mostly malty dark beers—is used as an essential ingredient and can also step in to play a role in marinades too.

Meat's flavor and texture can fluctuate wildly according to the beast, the cut, and the way it's cooked but, as a rule of thumb, the beers should—once again—match the intensity and strength of the entire dish and all its accompanying ingredients. A beer that suits a hamburger, for example, may not be suitable for New England pot roast.

Matching Suggestions

Steak Dubbel, Porter, Schwarzbier, Altbier, strong brown ale

Burgers Amber lager, Pilsner, American pale ale, Märzen

Kebabs Bock, dry Irish stout, amber lager, Vienna lager, ESB, Altbier

Meat pie Porter, stout, strong bitter, dubbel, Dortmunder, dunkel

Casserole/stew Premium English bitter/ESB, barley wine, oatmeal stout, Scotch ale, Bière de Garde

Calf's liver Abbey beer, Trappist ale, dark lager

Pork chops Maibock, Dunkelweizen, Tripel, blonde ale, Vienna lager, Pilsner (highly hopped)

Gammon/ham Smoked ale, Gueuze, Oude Bruin, sweet stout, brown ale, Mild

Roast lamb Premium bitter, American-style IPA, Doppelbock, Dubbel, Trappist ale, bière de garde, abbey beer, Schwarzbier

Roast beef Scotch ale, amber lager, Saison, Dunkelweizen, bitter, ESB, pale ale

Roast Pork Amber lager, Vienna lager, Oktoberfest/Märzen, Dortmunder, Bière de Garde

Sausages Trappist ale (especially Orval), Oktoberfest/Märzen, bitter, ESB, Pilsner, Vienna lager, Saison, porter, Schwarzbier... the list goes on and on

Wild boar Barley Wine, Double IPA, oak-aged beers, ESB

Venison Brown ale, ESB, Barley Wine (not too hoppy), American IPA, Dubbel, Dunkelweizen, porter

Veal Tripel, premium bitter, imperial pilsner, Bière de Garde/saison, weizenbock, smoked beer, stout

Fritas with Cuban Avocado Salsa

Wood-grilled T-Bone Steak Florentina Style

Prime Roast Rib of Beef with Thyme Yorkshire Pudding

Beer & Meat Pairings

Bacon & cheeseburger with Sierra Nevada Pale Ale

Beer has a lot to get its head around here: The gratifying squelch of succulent beef, the stringy bacon and the soft spongy cheese, the clean crunch of the salad, and the cacophony of flavor from the myriad relishes. It needs something hoppy yet balanced, something refreshing, citrusy and slightly sweet, something that's drinkable yet distinctive. That something is Sierra Nevada Pale Ale.

Pork Belly with Spaten Oktoberfestbier

A lighter meat than most, pork requires a beer that won't overpower the subtlety of flavor. But don't just think about the white meat, as there's lovely, rather indulgent, crackling to consider and the addition of applesauce. Go with, rather than against, the flavors, and choose something sweet and fruity that rises above the slight fattiness, but stays in touch with the nuances.

Lamb Chops with Terminal Gravity IPA

Wine often bleats in complaint when asked to deal with the mouth-coating fattiness of lamb, not to mention the rich gravy and herby, mint sauce that traditionally accompanies roast lamb. American IPAs can be a little too boisterous for the dinner table sometimes, but this excellent ale from eastern Oregon, with perfect herbal hop character, sweet strength, and carbonation, is well worth a gamble.

Gammon with Manns Brown Ale

There's a well-known gammon recipe that involves boiling gammon for a couple of hours in cola. It may sound like culinary blasphemy, but it actually works and is incredibly simple. Gammon shines next to sweetness, and Manns, one of England's most underrated brown ales, is very sweet. It's fruity, malty, and won't overpower the dish with too much alcohol.

Smoked Ribs with Alaskan Smoked Porter

Beer can cope manfully with barbecued food. Especially beer brewed with darker malt, or a malt that's been smoked over oak or beech wood. Rauchbiers from Bamburg would be the obvious choice, but they can be a little heavy-handed and lack the refreshment drivers. This Alaskan smoked porter, however, sends all the right smoke signals.

Beers that work well with food: Chicken & game

Beer has the versatility to capture chicken in all its various guises. Its white meat is a blank canvas on which many flavors, spices, and sauces can be daubed, so the beer-matching possibilities are endless.

Other birds, from goose to pheasant and duck to partridge, work equally well with beer. Darker beers work especially well with darker meats and fleshier birds. When matchmaking chicken it is best, like meat and fish, to stick to the basic premise of pairing taste intensities and to bear in mind the other ingredients in the dish.

Matching Suggestions

Roast chicken American pale ale, Bière de Garde, bitter, Saison, Gueuze, Märzen

Fried chicken Pilsner, Vienna lager, Dortmunder, Kölsch

Chicken pie Golden ale, Helles, Kellerbier, summer ale, bitter, Vienna lager

Roast duck Weizenbock, Doppelbock, Märzen, ESB, Schwarzbier

Aromatic duck American pale ale, Doppelbock, porter, kriek, framboise, Flanders red

Duck confit ESB, porter, Dubbel, Doppelbock, brown ale, Altbier

Foie Gras Framboise, kriek, Scotch ale, sweet stout, Doppelbock, ESB, Gueuze, Lambic, Barley Wine

Goose Strong Belgian ale, abbey/Trappist ale, Weissbock, Bière de Garde, Vienna red

Partridge Saison, abbey ale, Altbier, amber lager

Pheasant Premium bitter, American brown ale, Bière de Garde, dubbel

Quail American pale ale, Bière de Garde, bitter, Tripel

Turkey Dunkel, Dunkelweizen, Vienna lager, framboise, Märzen, best bitter

Caesar Salad

Chermoula Burgers with Minted Harissa Salsa and Preserved Lemon and Artichoke Salad

Roasted Chicken with Olives, Almonds, and Preserved Lemons

Beer & Chicken & Game Pairings

Chicken Caesar Salad
with Hopback Summer Lightning

A citrusy, zesty, and refreshing summer sip that won't trample all over the delicate chicken nor be pushed around by the lemon, anchovies, or Parmesan.

Roast Chicken & all the Trimmings
with Timothy Taylor Landlord

Chicken has soft, delicate flavors and makes a great partner for soft, gentle bitters, but the presence of Brussels sprouts, roast potatoes, and stuffing calls for something a little hoppier. IPA, especially an American, is too much, but a brusque, fruity bitter such as Timothy Taylor Landlord is spot-on.

Foie Gras with Liefmans Kriek

I defy you to unearth a more instantly incredible food and drink pairing than this. Liefmans has the requisite sweetness to match that of the foie gras, yet unlike Sauternes, which is the age-old wine drinker's choice for this dish, it cuts through the fattiness and doesn't complicate things with a coating mouthfeel. The textures are wonderful, too. The rich carbonation contrasts brilliantly with the smooth buttery feel of the foie gras.

Coq-au-Bière with Jenlain Ambree

When they're not munching on cheese and surrendering, the French like nothing more than making this classic chicken casserole. In the south, they opt for red wine in the sauce but in the north, they often use dark beers or farmhouse ales. This bronze bière de garde, full of stewed prune and caramel flavours, is delicious.

Honey-glazed duck with Kwak

You'd be forgiven for thinking this pairing is included solely for the shocking pun. You'd be almost right as there are a lot of Belgian ales that can deal with duck. But Kwak can match the sweetness and has the strength to shake off the greasy textures.

Honey-glazed Roast Barbary Duck

Beers that work well with food: Cheese

Beer pays homage to *fromage* far better than wine. Wine and cheese may be a traditional pairing, but it is nowhere near as happy a marriage as that of beer and cheese, which are perfect partners. Ask any self-respecting sommelier and they'll tell you as much.

Both beer and cheese are traditional farmhouse products with similar agricultural ancestry. Cheese is made from the milk of animals that munch on grass not grapes, while barley, essentially another kind of grass, is what brewers use to make beer. Cheese and beer are both fermented, aged, and shaped by tiny little organisms. Both can be enjoyed at their most youthful—displaying simple, clear flavors—or with some maturity, when a range of complex characters comes to the

fore. Not convinced? Ask a plowman whether he'd like a pint of bitter or a glass of Bordeaux with his lunch, or go to a Trappist monastery, where beer and cheese are always eaten.

Unlike wine, beer has the varying textures and bubbles to lift cheese's rich, indulgent textures off the palate, while cheese, in return, mellows out beer's bitter hoppiness. Citrus and herbal hops, meanwhile, are endowed with the flavors of fruit chutney, quince jelly and raw apple—all common accompaniments to a cheeseboard.

Whether it's butterscotch and biscuits, or wintry spice and dried fruits, the easiest and most successful rule for beer and cheese pairings is to match their intensities of flavor.

Cheese and Beer Pairing Guidelines

Soft-rinded cheese Harvest/summer ale, Helles, Kölsch, Pilsner, tart fruit beer

Mild cheese/goat's cheese Wheat beers, honey beers, amber lagers, champagne beers

Blue cheese Barley Wine, porter, Imperial Pilsners, American IPA

Hard cheese Medium to strong British bitter, Belgian golden ale, American pale ale, Oude Bruin

Sheep's cheese Saison, Bière de Garde, amber lager, Vienna lager, Märzen

Wash-rinded (pongy) cheese Trappist/abbey ale, Doppelbock, Tripel, Gueuze

Mountain cheese Dunkelweizen, fruit Lambic, Doppelbock, Dubbel, sour red ale

Smoked Gouda-style cheese Rauchbier, smoked porter, barrel-aged beer

Keen's Farmhouse Cheddar (UK) with Bath Ales Gem

The delightful West Country bitter has its hoppy edges softened and malty tang enhanced by the firm flavors of the vigorous cheese. In response, the beer brings out the rich, nutty character in the Keen's. A well-established symbiotic relationship in which the total sum is far greater than its considerable parts.

Camembert Fermier (France) with Mort Subite Oude Kriek

Plates fly and doors slam with this powerful pairing. Yet the beer's sour and sharp effervescence counteracts the massive, earthy richness of the cheese and the bubbles peel away the sticky texture of the paste to ensure a clean, complex finish.

Epoisse (France) with Orval

A clash of the classics. A wonderful aromatic, brine-washed cheese with a melting mouthfeel requires a robust, fruity beer that won't freeze in the face of its full-on flavors. The portlike, almond-tinged Trappist ale fits the bill perfectly.

Ossau (southwest France) with Pilsner Urquell

Ossau is a semi-hard cheese with a brine-rubbed crust and a firm yet supple texture that crumbles, and it has a complexity of tastes that tingle on the tongue. Both the beer and cheese are slightly grainy and nutty with a bitter, lingering finish.

Bonde (France) with Saisis Wheat

Smooth, fruity, and delicate goat's cheese with spice and fruity tang seeks lively, like-minded individual for gastronomic good times.

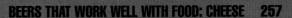

Beers that work well with food: Dessert, fruit, & chocolate

Toward the latter end of the meal, when things get sweet, sticky, and a little self-indulgent, beer starts punching above its weight, with sweetness in one hand and bitterness in the other. Beer has an ambidextrous ability that dessert wine simply doesn't possess.

If you discard the grape connection, fruit has a much tighter relationship with beer than it does wine, and fruits such as cherries, raspberries, apricots, bananas, strawberries, and oranges are often incorporated into the brewing process. Nowadays brewers are even experimenting with mangoes and avocado honey.

But when matching fruit desserts with beer, temper the inclination to pair fruit with fruit, as they tend to cancel each other out. Unless there's a symbiotic sweet versus sour/tart relationship, then things can become far too fruity and sickly. Often the dreamiest date for a fruit dessert such as cheesecake is a dry beer with a chocolate, coffee-ish character such as stout or porter, while sweeter krieks and framboise are excellent partners for chocolate desserts.

The pairing of beer and chocolate, meanwhile, is more than just a mischievous indulgence. There are many wine styles and grape varieties that have a problem when drunk with chocolate, but beer and chocolate make a natural double act with many shared taste nuances.

Chocolate malt and other barley that's been given a slight roasting provide beer with flavors with which wine simply cannot compete. No amount of oak-ageing will give wine the same kind of burnt or roasted character as silky-smooth stouts and velvety porters. Brewed with these roasty-toasty malts from the dark side, stouts and porters taste delicious with chocolate, especially those rich variants made, not primarily from vegetable fat and sugar, but with a real cocoa content.

But it's contrasting, not just corresponding, flavors one should be seeking to unite beer and chocolate. For example, the hop-derived marmalade qualities of India Pale Ales will match any orange-like flavors so often present in after-dinner chocolate, while the IPA trademark bitterness can stand up to chocolate's buttery decadence. The lightly malty and floral aromas of some Pilsners and Märzens work, too.

Strawberry Sandwich Cake

White Chocolate and Mandarin Soup with Spiced Bread

Banana, Dark Chocolate, and Pecan Semi-freddo

Raspberry Sorbet

Matching Suggestions

Apple pie Russian imperial stout, porter, oatmeal stout

Banana cream pie Weissbier, imperial stout, scotch ale, Scotch-barrel-aged beer

Cookies/brownies Brown ale, sweet stout, porter, Doppelbock

Cheesecake Porter, cream stout, Imperial stout, (sweet) fruit beer, Schwarzbier

Chocolate stout (all kinds), strong Baltic porter, fruit beers, champagne beer, tripel, India Pale Ale (with orange chocolate)

Fruitcake Barley Wine, imperial porter, American porter, stout

Crème Brûlée Stout, porter, Scotch barrel-aged beer, sweet fruit beer

Fruit flans/tart Cream ale, porter, stout, espresso stout

Ice cream Fruit Lambic, imperial stout, oatmeal stout, milk stout, fruit beers (both tart and sweet), honey beer

Sticky toffee pudding Baltic porter, imperial stout, strong, dark Trappist ale

Pumpkin pie Strong dark farmhouse ale, stout, porter, cream stout

Tiramisu Tripel, imperial stout, porter, Dubbel, Eisbock, Schwarzbier

Yogurt Sweet fruit beer, spiced ale, honey beer, amber lager, porter, stout

Beer & Dessert, Fruit, & Chocolate Pairings

Crème Brûlée with Harviestoun Ola Dubh 30-year-old

A utopian after-dinner union. Brimming with immensely indulgent chocolate, caramel, orange, and smoke, Ola Dubh seduces the burnt, singed sweetness of the brûlée and complements the creamy texture with its bulbous mouthfeel. An incredible pairing further enhanced by a "chaser" of Highland Park 30-year-old Scotch.

Valrhona Porcelana Chocolate with Schneider Aventinus

A sublime partnership involving one of the most expensive chocolates in the world. You'd expect the dark chocolate to overpower the beer but you'd be mistaken. Coming through instead are banana tones, hints of elderflower, and a powerful desire to keep eating.

Vanilla Ice Cream with Pipeline Porter

Opposites attract here in terms of taste, color, and temperature. The deep black Hawaiian coffee-tinged porter, akin to an espresso, is given the freedom to really shine by the frozen, creamy tabla rasa.

Apple Pie with Titanic Stout

Port-like with chocolate, hazelnut, and a touch of dark cherry, Titanic Stout is a decadent accomplice to apple pie, especially when drunk slightly warm. It softens the sharpness and acidity of the apple, catches on to the caramelized sugar and, if you're feeling adventurous and can overlook the unfortunate pun, can even perform a delicious cameo role in ice cream.

Cherry Tart with Harvey's Imperial Stout

The culinary matrimony of cherry and stout is a reliable, long-lasting one, but for the best pairing, the beer needs to have the strength of body and alcohol to mellow the fruity flavors of the tart.

Beers that work well with food: Spicy food

Beer goes well with spicy food. It is a flameproof friend to curry, chili, and spicy food, whether it hails from the Indian subcontinent, Southeast Asia, Latin America, or the Caribbean.

What unites hot and spicy cuisine is that a few dishes tend to be eaten together, like tapas or meze, and this represents a challenge when looking to find the most suitable beer, you need to find a style that gets on well with a wide range of dishes, each with a distinctive flavor.

The temptation, as witnessed in Mexican restaurants and British curry houses, is to try to extinguish the fire with a beer that's refreshing, but this tends to provoke rather than placate the prickle on the palate.

Besides, dishes deserve better than just being washed down with bland beer and its role should be more than one of a mere firefighter. While wine wilts in the heat of fiery foods and is left panting for breath, beer has the carbonation to scrub the palate clean, a soothing sweetness, a lower level of alcohol that suits quenching, and a calming mouthfeel that turns the heat down.

Hops in beer are a hook that stokes the subtle flavors at the heart of highly spiced food, while in return spice and herbs in piquant dishes spike the citrusy, herbal, grassy notes in the beer. Even with matches that fight fire with fire, the key to harmony in the heat is providing balance. It should be a sizzling embrace, not a sweaty one.

Along with wheat beers, IPAs are probably one of the most perfect beers to lift a wide gamut of foods to the sensational. It's the hops that do it, strutting their stuff like the most catwalk-friendly grape. Lychees, lemon, lime, marmalade, apricot blossom—all are flavors that can be demonstrated by India Pale Ales. On the overriding principle that strong beer flavors need strongly flavored dishes, IPAs and spicy tandoors are perfect bedfellows—the IPA's hops being the perfect foil for the rasping capsaicins in the marsalas and curry and bringing clean citrus fruit flavors, like liquid chutney, to the dish. But beware. Softer flavored South Indian dishes would be ruined by the IPA.

Lamb chops with Spinach and Peppercorn

Aubergine Salad wth Coriander and Yogurt, accompanied by Olives

Potatoes with Cumin

Matching Suggestions

Biriyani Bière de Garde, Maibock, abbey ale, premium bitter

Burritos Brown ale, Schwarzbier, Dunkelweizen, chocolate beer, American pale ale

Cajun food Pilsner, amber lager, brown ale, Kellerbier, French farmhouse ale, whisky barrel-aged beer

Tandoori/dry spiced chicken Pale ale, moderately hopped American IPA, Tripel, Maibock, amber lager, strong bitter

Chilli con carne Smoked ale, Mild, brown ale, Tripel, ESB, Scotch ale, dark abbey ale, porter

Fajitas Saison, Märzen, amber lager, Vienna lager, Munich lager, doppelbock

Mole Chocolate beer, brown ale, stout, porter, espresso stout

Mild Indian curry Best bitter, hoppy pale ale, Pilsner, Helles, Märzen, witbier, weissbier, blonde ale, Saison

Hot Indian curry IPA, American IPA, Barley Wine, Dortmunder, bock

North African dishes Pale ale, American pale ale, Kölsch, Pilsner, Bière de Garde, Dortmunder

Singapore noodles American pale ale, IPA, Tripel, blonde ale, Imperial Pilsner

Thai Curry Witbier, weissbier, Bière de Garde, coconut beer, amber lager

Beer & Spicy Food Pairings

Chicken Fajitas with Bell's Kalamazoo Stout

OK, it may sound unusual, but when it comes to a traditional Mexican dish, a dark smooth stout can perfectly mimic the role of mole, the rich, deep, smoky sauce that has a chocolate and chili hit.

Chicken Bhuna with Worthington White Shield

A bhuna is big on spice and is looking for a liquid lover to act as a chutney substitute. White Shield, with its marmalade notes and soothing citrus notes of lychees, lemon, and lime, is just perfect here. It also has the stamina and hop strength to survive.

Jerk Chicken with Mongozo Coconut Beer

Rubbed with a range of aggressive spices, Jamaican jerk chicken can rub beers up the wrong way, but the dulcet, heat-dampening tones of the coconut, a staple in Caribbean cuisine, mellows out everything marvelously.

Sichuan Twice-cooked Pork with Little Creatures Pale Ale

This delicately balanced Australian craft brew, hoppy and gently effervescent, soothes the sizzle with citrusy sparkle and some much-needed sweetness.

Pad Thai with Adnams Explorer

Brewed with American Chinook and Columbus hops, Explorer aerates the palate with aromatics, bitter hop nuttiness, and a sweetness to match the noodles.

Beers that work well with food: Snacks

All this talk of beer's classy kinship with haute cuisine is all very well, but beer and food are also perfect companions in a more informal environment, where nourishment comes in nibble form.

Beer is essentially a laid-back layman's liquid with the versatility and modest alcohol content to get on with salty snacks and sharing foods, whether it's pork scratchings and peanuts in

Britain, pretzels in Germany, Belgian charcuterie, the pickled sausages of Czech Republic pubs, Italian antipasti and Middle Eastern meze, or dipping chips in salsa in front of the TV.

Matching Suggestions

Nuts Pilsner, light lager, Kölsch,

Cheese straws Best bitter, cold German Pilsner, Kölsch, Helles

Olives Saison, Tripel, Dubbel, Vienna lager

Dim sum Weissbier, witbier, Bière de Garde, Helles

Falafel American pale ale, bock, Märzen, Dortmunder

Guacamole Pale ale (both English and American) , India Pale Ale, premium bitter

Hummus Märzen, Doppelbock, ESB, weissbier, witbier

Chips Pilsner, Helles, Kölsch, best bitter,

Chorizo Pale ale, strong bitter, Bière de Garde, strong Pilsner

Charcuterie Saison, Oktoberfest, amber lager, Schwarzbier, blonde ale, Kölsch

Crudites Weissbier, Pilsner, Saison, Dunkel

Focaccia with Figs and Proscuitto

Falafel

Pizza and Pasta

So, there's good news and there's bad news. The bad news is that, in general, tomato-based pasta dishes are not beer's best buddy. Red wine tends to work better with pasta (although lasagne is rather smashing with a Dunkel or an amber lager), and it seems only fair that we leave the grape-guzzlers with something.

The good news, however, is that beer and pizza were born to be together. It doesn't matter which beer you choose to go with which pizza, as all beer goes with all pizza. That's a fact. Some people may suggest otherwise, but they're wrong.

As American author Dave Barry once famously wrote: "Without question, the greatest invention in the history of mankind is beer. Oh, I grant you that the wheel was also a fine invention, but the wheel does not go nearly as well with pizza."

Bresaola

Small Savory Lebanese Pastries

Beer & Snack Pairings

Charcuterie with Peroni Gran Reserva

While lesser lighter lagers would suffocate in the gristly grip of a cold meat assortment, Peroni's premium dark and refreshing drop has more than enough tangy sweetness and greasy texture-slaying bitterness to accommodate the piquancy and powerful flavors that may come knocking.

Nachos with Bear Republic Racer 5 IPA

Jalapeños. Melted cheese. Salsa. Salty chips. Sour cream. Guacamole. It's a mash-up of flavors, textures, and sensations in the mouth. What is required is something robust and refreshing to knock the taste sensations into shape, but in a way that doesn't leave bruises. Some Californian IPAs are too firm of fist, but Bear Republic's flagship beer is just right.

Cheese Straws with Kasteel Kru

Crumbly cheese straws and a champagne beer make for a perfect pre-dinner pairing because they're both delightfully dry and won't peter out one's palate with too much flavor. The impressive effervescence and slight acidity keep the taste buds on their toes.

Dry roasted peanuts with Žatec Premium

Traditionalists may harrumph at the prospect of pairing such a quintessentially English pub snack with a Bohemian lager but, having experimented at length with various combinations, I can assure you that Žatec is one of very few beers with the bubbles and bitterness to successfully scrub the palate of the piquant, peppery peanuts. Some English bitters and lesser lagers simply don't have the fizz-ique for it.

Pork Scratchings with Brakspear Bitter

Pork scratchings, deep-fried pieces of pig fat with hairs sticking out of them, are arguably Britain's finest culinary contribution to the world and best washed down with a fellow countryman that, rather than interfere with their subtle finesse, keeps the palate poised and ready for another bite. And another…. and so on and so forth.

The science of beer & food matching at El Bulli, Spain

El Bulli in Northern Spain is widely regarded as the greatest restaurant in the world, where chef **Ferran Adrià**, a pioneer at the cutting-edge of avant-garde cooking, was the first to adventure into molecular gastronomy, merging the culinary arts of the kitchen with scientific techniques more readily associated with the laboratory.

El Bulli receives more than two million reservation requests a year, yet only eight thousand souls are fortunate enough to experience its volcanic culinary creativity and an intensely imaginative epicurean approach that's steeped in science, design, history, and art.

Ferran Centelles and **David Seijas**, El Bulli's head sommeliers, offer this approach to beer and food matching.

Couture Beer and Food Matching

"Polyvalence" is the key word that comes to mind when we think of matching food with beer, whose ability to enhance a huge range of culinary preparations is it's most important attribute.

Finding a perfect food match is never an easy task, but beer can embrace many of the most difficult taste elements. Before we start talking about perfumes and flavors of certain types of beers, it is important to consider the kind of matching we would like to do. There is a range of options: we could look for a match where the dish and the beer work together in harmony, through the palate and flavor receptors. Or we can try matching by contrasting completely opposite tastes and flavors, thereby creating something new to savor.

When thinking about a general matching concept, our main aim is to find dynamism and to obtain concord and discord between beer and food in order to balance sensations. We reckon that an acidic beer can complement a soft dish by combining two opposite sensations. But, on the other hand, an astringent beer can do something notoriously difficult: complement bitterness in a dish, as well as heighten the matching by delivering two similar sensations. Dynamism + (concord) and – (discord): this is our main point when looking for a specific match.

Beer can also be present in different ways: in a regional alliance of local beer with local dishes, through a psychological matching, or by using it as an ingredient of the recipe that will result in several interesting combinations.

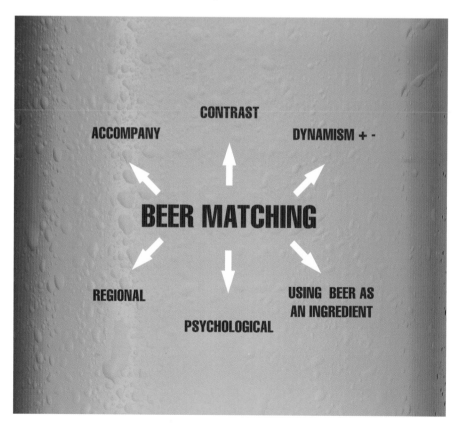

Beer Aromas—Bridge Ingredients

The existence of some bridge ingredients can help in the preparation of recipes in order to get closer to a perfect union. Due to the huge range of beer styles, we have created a list of ingredients that could be used to improve the overall connection.

*

WHEAT BEER

Apple citrus

Elderflower

Flavored butter

*

PALE ALE

Red fruits

Curry

Smoked products

*

STOUT/PORTER

Chocolate

Dried fruits

Toasted bread

*

TRAPPIST

Meat sauce

Caramel

Hazelnuts

*

LAMBIC/GUEUZE

Dried citrus peel

Honey

Mushrooms

*

Main Food Tastes and their Influence on Beer Matching

The main food taste in a dish will often influence our final match decision, as the general tendency of a specific dish will provide the prime parameter for finding the correct beer association.

Food structure and flavor intensity are the first items to be evaluated. In that case, food structure and aromatic intensity have to be equally balanced with beer. Therefore a light dish needs to be tasted with a light beer, and an extremely perfumed dish requests a highly flavored beer.

High salinity food such as cod fish, seafood and processed cold meat will combine perfectly with a refreshing, floral beer like a wheat beer or pale ale.

Bitterness needs to be balanced with the same sensation in beer; food such as asparagus, endives, or strongly grilled meat can find a good combination in highly hopped beers such as some abbey beers, Trappist ales, and traditional Lambic.

Dishes with high acidic overtones such as citrus or vinegar-based preparations work best with an opposite soft taste because acidity is a harsh sensation and requires an oily soft beer with a velvety texture. In the same way, mature heavily malted beers with low carbon dioxide would be ideal partners for punchy dishes because they reduce the feeling of acidity.

Sweet food loves residual sugar and smooth beers. In order to obtain that, it could prove interesting to combine stouts, porters and some silky fruity Lambic beer with various sweet dishes.

The temperature of the dish can be related to beer alcohol strength, taking into account that hot dishes demand drinks with higher alcohol content than cold ones do.

Last but not least, food texture is important, too: rich and oily food demands to be balanced with a full-bodied beer, while succulent meat would be well complemented by a rich, tasty abbey or Lambic beer; additionally, a high degree of effervescence would help to give dynamism.

These are just a few guidelines. However matching is not an exact science and the most important maxim is to follow your own palate.

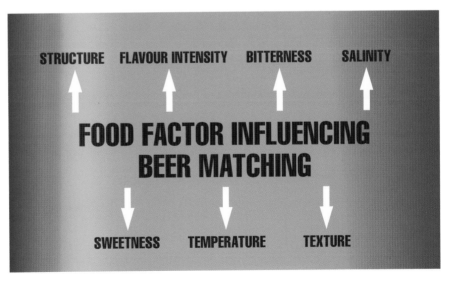

STRUCTURE   FLAVOUR INTENSITY   BITTERNESS   SALINITY

FOOD FACTOR INFLUENCING BEER MATCHING

SWEETNESS   TEMPERATURE   TEXTURE

A beer banquet at El Bulli, Spain

Beer and Food pairings from El Bulli in Northern Spain, created by chef **Ferran Adrià**.

DISH 1177
Turtle dove with tuna medulla, enokis and samphire

BEER: ABBEY/TRAPPIST

Match: This is a powerful match. Here, structure, creaminess and low carbon dioxide joins hunting meat, saltiness, and bitter taste without losing their own personality. Turtle dove's succulence combines perfectly with the full-bodied beer leaving a never-ending flavor.

DISH 1022
Stuffed giant morel and flowering wild garlic

BEER: LAMBIC (not fruity style)

Match: Fresh moist forest and mushrooms aromas come together with the deliciously oxidized aromas of authentic Lambic beer. The earthy texture of the mushrooms enhances the deep flavors of the beer.

DISH 1002
Spherical raviolo of elderflower with muscovado sugar

BEER: WHEAT BEER

Match: This is a clear example of how two products can highlight each other by creating a synergic flavor that enhances the taste. The typical freshness of wheat beer is balanced with the sugary taste of muscovado.

DISH 1154
Tender walnuts, smoked tea, and wasabi

BEER: PALE ALE

Match: This is acomplementary match where the nutty taste of the beer enhances the walnut flavor. Due to the tea astringency the delicate hop flavor is extolled and the beer's delicate texture softens the hot wasabi sensation.

DISH 1198
Frozen chocolate and hazelnut praline crumbs with passionfruit sweet

BEER: STOUT / PORTER

Match: Stouts, having deep flavors and a full-bodied structure, combine perfectly with the bitterness of a black chocolate. Due to the fact that this combination is vigorous, we add passion fruit which revitalizes the overall structure of this dessert.

The perfect marriage of beer and food

Garrett Oliver, brewmaster of Brooklyn Brewery in New York and described as the "Robert Parker" of beer, selects his favorite beer and food matches.

As much as I love wine, it's a simple fact that craft beer has a far wider range of flavor. Beer can taste like almost anything—smoke, oranges, coffee, chocolate, caramel, lemongrass—the variety is endless and so are the pairing possibilities.

Over the past 20 years, I've hosted more than 600 beer dinners and tastings in 10 countries, yet beer still surprises me. Some pairings are obvious, but what sticks in the mind are the pairings you don't see coming—the ones that open a window on the world of flavor.

In Bavaria, the hazy wheat beer known as Hefeweizen, or weissbier, is a morning mainstay. At around 10AM, Munich's cafés fill up with people enjoying their second breakfast, known as "brotzeit." Bavarians pair the beer with a bland veal sausage called weisswurst, but it's actually even better with some classic brunch dishes. Weissbier is light, briskly tangy, slightly sweet and fruity, with flavors of bananas, cloves, and a hint of smoke. At brunch, it's like the ultimate mimosa, making a fine pairing with eggs benedict. It's even better with "oeufs poche royale"—eggs benedict with smoked salmon instead of rashers.

Perhaps the most intimidating audience I've ever had was at the Association of Westchester Country Club Chefs. I had 60 chefs in the room, each with their own ideas about pairings. The second dish of the dinner was a seared diver scallop in brown butter, a classic dish. The temptation is to go for something light and pale, but the flavors of the dish are actually about caramelization—the sear on the scallop, the browning of the butter. So I served a soft, dark British porter, showing caramel

and chocolate flavors wrapped around a slightly buttery core.

In Orlando, Florida, I hosted a beer dinner at a terrific restaurant called The Ravenous Pig. The chef wanted to serve a dish I'd never heard of before—risotto carbonara. I cook linguine carbonara all the time at home, but I'd always paired this Italian dish with red wine. This time I paired it with my own Brooklyn Local 2, a dark, dry, fruity Belgian-style abbey ale with Champagne-like carbonation. As it turned out, the beer was actually much better with the dish than wine is.

Some of the best pairings are inspired by sauces. Duck confit is a mainstay of French cuisine, but it's usually served unadorned. But we all know that duck works well with fruit—think duck á l'orange. The same principle applies to beer pairings—I really enjoy duck confit with Belgian fruit lambics. The sweetest ones are best saved for dessert, but those with good acidity and plenty of fruit—Boon Kriek or Girardin Kriek—work wonders.

Some great pairings, I have to admit, I've stumbled upon by accident, or perhaps even "incident." Several years ago I took part in a series of tastings where chefs and food purveyors showcased some of their favorite pairings. I'd looked at two possibilities. Either I would pair Colston-Basset Stilton with our rich, malty, powerful barley wine, Monster Ale, or I'd pair dark chocolate truffles with our strong, chocolate-y imperial stout, Brooklyn Black Chocolate Stout. As the presenter before me finished up her caviar tasting, I realized I had a problem—they'd sent the Stilton and the Black Chocolate Stout. Wrong pairing. Cheese instead of truffles. I started to panic. I had about three minutes before I had to face the crowd. What would I do? I opened the beer and tasted it with the cheese. It was absolutely perfect. In fact it was better than either of the matches I'd contemplated. I was stunned. And then I went out and presented the pairing. It remains among my favorites and I use it all the time now. Many of my best pairings were not planned—they just happened. Dutch witbier and a grilled salmon and gouda sandwich by an Amsterdam canal; a pint of Adnams Extra with fish & chips at a Suffolk coastal pub. Get the beer right and magic can happen.

Matches Made in Heaven

Eggs Benedict with Schneider Weisse

Weissbier is brilliant with eggs (often said to be the bane of wine), the smoky character is great with bacon and sausages, and the high carbonation really refreshes the palate. Weissbier is perfectly capable of handling the full Sunday cooked breakfast too, and that's a rare talent.

Scallops with Carnegie Stark-Porter

The roasted malts of the porter harmonize nicely with the browned surface of the scallop, while the malt sweetness meets the scallop's own sea-sweetness.

Carbonara with Brooklyn Local 2

Carbonara is based around smoky, bacony guanciale, egg yolks, butter, pungent cheese, and plenty of black pepper. The beer also brings smoke, caramel, and dark fruit, but then lightens the heavy dish with its palate-cleansing carbonation. The harmonies are beautiful.

Duck confit with Girardin Kriek

This is an almost wine-like pairing of strong contrasts, with the beer's acidity and bitterness providing cutting power, while the fruit flavors provide a pleasing and complementary counterpoint to the duck's gamey richness.

Stilton with Brooklyn Black Chocolate Stout

The Stilton reveals a huge and unexpected chocolate-y underpinning, and the beer wraps itself around the cheese in a profound, powerful embrace.

Glossary

Abbey ale
Belgian strong ale brewed by or under license from monasteries, although not all have monastic links.

ABV (alcohol by volume)
A measurement of the alcoholic strength of beer, it is expressed as a percentage, e.g. 5% ABV.

Adjuncts
Any ingredient other than barley, hops, yeast, or water that is added to beer. It usually refers to cereals and sugars that may be introduced for special flavors.

Alpha acid
The naturally occurring acid present in the cone of the hop plant. It gives bitterness to beer during the brewing process.

Alt, Altbier
Old-style beer from the Düsseldorf area of Germany, similar in style to British bitter or pale ale.

Aroma
The "nose" of a beer is that which gives an indication of the malt, hops, and possible fruit content of a beer. Combined with finish and mouthfeel, it is used to assess the taste and flavor of a beer.

Barley
The most commonly used grain for brewing and one of the four main ingredients in beer.

Barley Wine
Extra-strong ale that originated in Britain, but is now produced by brewers worldwide, particularly in Belgium and the United States.

Bière de Garde
French "keeping beer" was a style originally associated with the farmer brewers of French Flanders, who brewed in spring and stored the beer for use during the summer to refresh farm laborers. It is now brewed year-round.

Bitter
British-style beer that is usually well hopped. Best Bitter is a stronger version.

Blonde/Blond Ale
European name for a light-colored golden ale, often French or Belgian in origin.

Bock
German term for a strong beer that was once brewed only seasonally. Stronger versions include Doppelbock and Eisbock.

Bottle conditioning
A process in which beer is bottled with live yeast in order to improve in condition, to mature, and to develop additional strength over time.

Brettanomyces
A semi-wild form of yeast used in the brewing of Belgian Lambic beers and some porters and stouts.

Brew kettle
Vessel used to boil wort with hops during the brewing process.

Brew pub
A pub that brews and sells its own beer on the premises.

Brown ale
A traditional British beer, low in alcohol, which was often mixed with Mild. Newer versions of the style made by US brewers tend to have a higher hop content.

Burtonize/Burtonization
A process of adding salts such as gypsum and magnesium to ape the hard brewing water found in Burton-on-Trent, England.

Carbon dioxide (CO$_2$)
A gas that is naturally produced during fermentation of beers that are conditioned in either the cask or bottle. When beers are filtered in a brewery, carbon dioxide may be added.

Cask ale
Ale that is brought to maturity in the cask, either at a brewery or in a pub cellar. Maturation times can vary from a week to more than a year.

Condition
A beer's condition is denoted by the level of carbon dioxide (CO$_2$) present, which gives the brew its sparkle.

Copper
Vessel used in the brewing process to boil the sugary wort with hops. Traditionally made of copper, it is now often made of stainless steel instead, and is also known as a brew kettle.

Decoction
Part of the brewing process in which some of the wort is removed from the vessel then heated to a higher temperature and returned to the vessel in order to produce more complex flavors by improving enzyme activity and increasing sugar levels.

Doppelbock/Double bock
An extra-strong German-style bock, often of an ABV around 7.5% or more.

Dortmunder
A style of bottom-fermented golden ale originating in Dortmund, Germany.

Draft beer
Beer that is served direct from a cask or bulk container and drawn to the bar. Also known as "draught" in the United Kingdom and elsewhere.

Dry hopping
A process of adding hops to the finished brew to improve the beer's bitterness, aroma, and flavor.

Dubbel/Double
A Belgian-style abbey ale that describes a strong dark ale.

Dunkel
Means "dark" in German and describes dark lagers and dark wheat beers.

Eisbock
The strongest available version of bock.

Enkel
Means "single" in Dutch and describes a beer of modest strength.

Esters
Natural flavoring compounds that impart fruit and spice flavors by turning sugars into alcohol and carbon dioxide (CO_2).

Extra Special Bitter (ESB)
A bigger and bolder version of bitter, often with additional hop character, this beer style is enjoying a renewed popularity in the UK and USA, with new brews appearing quite regularly.

Extreme beers
A phrase originating in the United Kingdom to describe beers that push the limits by means of taste and flavor due to unusual ingredients, wild yeast fermentation, oak-barrel ageing, or a very high hop or alcohol content.

Fermentation
The process that converts malt sugars to alcohol and carbon dioxide by the action of yeast. Ale is made by warm fermentation, lager by cold fermentation, often called top and bottom fermentation, respectively.

Finish
The aftertaste of a beer; the impression that is left at the back of the tongue and the throat.

Foeder
An oak barrel used to mature beer, used in particular by Rodenbach in Belgium.

Golden ales
Pale ales with a moderate hop content, rarely exceeding 5%. These accessible ales straddle the line between lager and bitter, introducing many "novice" beer drinkers to the delight of craft brews. These ales are referred to as blonde ales in the United States.

Grand Cru
A term often used by Belgian brewers to describe their finest brew and one that is typical of their house style.

Grist
The name applied to ground malt (or other grains) and warm water that, when combined, forms the wort used in the brewing process.

Gueuze/Geuze
A type of beer formed by blending young and old Belgian Lambic beers to produce a refreshing beer.

Hefeweizen
Hefe means "yeast" in German, and this is a naturally conditioned German-style wheat beer with yeast sediment.

Helles
A German-style beer, meaning "light", applied to a pale beer, either a lager or a wheat beer.

Hops
A climbing plant with cones containing acids, resins, and tannins that produces aroma and bitterness in beer, to complement the natural sweetness of malt. There are many different varieties, each of them known for their different flavoring properties.

IBU (International Bittering Units)
A scale for measuring the bitterness of beer, which is a complex calculation that is based on the ratio and weight of hops, alpha acids, wort, and alcohol in a brew.

IPA (India Pale Ale)
Short for India Pale Ale, a heavily hopped beer which was first brewed in Burton-on-Trent, England, in the 19th century to survive the long journey to India, bound for soldiers and administrative officials based there. Now produced by several brewing nations, including the heavily hopped versions found in the United States.

Kellerbier
German for "cellar beer", this is a hoppy, lightly carbonated lager, often unfiltered.

Kölsch
A type of top-fermented light golden ale first brewed in and around the city of Cologne in Germany.

Kräusen
The addition of partially fermented wort to beer in the lager cellar, to stimulate a strong secondary fermentation.

Kriek
A Belgian Lambic beer in which cherries are fermented, imparting a tart, fruity flavor.

Lager
A range of beer styles created by bottom-fermenting (or cold-fermenting) in tanks where the temperature is just above freezing. As yeast settles at the bottom of the tank, a slow secondary fermentation occurs, carbonation increases, and a thirst-quenching beer emerges. Lager means "to store" in German.

Lambic
A style of Belgian beer originating from tiny, rural breweries in the Payottenland region. It is fermented using airborne wild yeasts that cause spontaneous fermentation. When cherries or raspberries are added, the beers are known as kriek and framboise, or frambozen.

Lauter

A vessel used to run off and filter the wort from the grain once the mashing has taken place.

Liquor

The term used by brewers for the water that is used during the mashing and boiling process.

Maibock

A German beer style usually denoting a strong, often pale, lager that is brewed to mark the beginning of spring.

Malt

Grains, usually barley, that have undergone partial germination, and are then dried and cured, or toasted in a kiln, when the seed contains high levels of starches. It is the starches that are converted into fermentable sugars during the brewing process.

Märzen

Traditional Bavarian seasonal larger brewed in March and stored until fall when it is drunk at the Munich Oktoberfest. These days it is also brewed year-round.

Mash

The mixture created when the grist is steeped in hot water during the beer brewing process.

Mash tun

Vessel in which malted grain is mixed with "liquor" to start the brewing process.

Méthode champenoise

A form of bottle conditioning that follows the method for making Champagne by going through a secondary fermentation using added yeast and fermentable sugars. Beers made in this way are usually produced in champagne-style bottles and can mature for several years.

Microbrewery

A small brewery brewing small batches of beer for local distribution and consumption. The craft beer revival in the United Kingdom and the United States began in such breweries 20-30 years ago.

Mild

A British beer style, low in alcohol, developed to quench the thirst of farmer types. Since the 1960s it has become less available in British pubs, although CAMRA (Campaign for Real Ale) has been instrumental in ensuring its survival as a beer style.

Mouthfeel

The taste sensation on the tongue that can detect sweetness, sourness, saltiness and bitterness as the beer flows over it.

Noble hops

Name given to a group of German and Czech hops hailed for their aroma rather than bitterness: Hallertau, Zatec (Saaz), Spalt, and Tettnang.

Nonic glass

A smooth-sided beer glass in both half pint and pint sizes. It has a characteristic bulge two-thirds of the way up to aid grip.

Oktoberfest

An enormous annual two-week beer festival held in the Bavarian city of Munich, with some beers even brewed specially for the occasion.

Oud bruin

A Belgian beer style from Flanders meaning "old brown." These beers have an ageing period of up to one year.

Pasteurization

A heat treatment process that kills bacteria and stabilizes beer. It can sometimes dull the final flavor.

Pilsner/Pils

A golden, hop-filled lager first brewed in the Bohemian city of Pilsen, now part of the Czech Republic.

Porter

A dark beer that is characterized by dark chocolate malty flavors and a rich, strong hop flavoring.

Rauchbier

German-style lager originating from the Franconia area, made from malt and smoked over beech wood fires.

Reinheitsgebot

The German beer purity law of 1516 stated that beer must not contain anything other than water, yeast, malt, and hops. It is still adhered to by many German beer makers today.

Sahti

One of the world's oldest beer styles, developed in Finland using juniper twigs and berries in the brewing process. Extreme brewers are rediscovering this style in an attempt to explore and preserve semi-extinct beer styles.

Saison

A Belgian-style beer that was traditionally brewed in winter for drinking in the summer months. Nowadays it is often produced all year round.

Schwarzbier

Meaning "black beer" in German, this is a dark, opaque style of lager.

Scotch ale

Strong, malty beer style that originated in Scotland as a "pint of heavy," but is now more likely to be brewed in France, the United States and Belgium, where some of the strongest versions are produced.

Seasonal beers

Beers brewed for a limited period each year, traditionally produced to suit climatic seasons, examples include German Märzens and French Saisons, or to celebrate a holiday (Christmas seasonals), or an event, such as Oktoberfest.

Sour ales

Beers from Flanders that undergo an ageing process of between 18 months and 2 years in oak tuns, resulting in a sharp, acetic flavour.

Sparge

"Esperger" in French means to "sprinkle". This is a process by which the grain is rinsed after mashing, to flush out any remaining malt sugars.

Steam beer

Amber-colored, all-malt beer known as Californian Common and introduced to the US West Coast in the latter part of the 19th century. Synonymous with San Francisco, where Fritz Maytag revived the style at his Anchor Brewery.

Stein

A traditional glass or ceramic German drinking tankard seen in bierkellers all over the country. "Stein" means stone.

Stout

A strong dark beer style, usually top-fermented, that is made using highly roasted grain.

Trappist beers

Beers made in seven breweries controlled by Trappist monks in Belgium (Achel, Chimay, Orval, Rochefort, Westmalle, Westvleteren) and one, La Trappe (Koningshoeven), in the Netherlands.

Tripel

The strongest beer of the Belgian abbey ale style, although a few quadrupels have been developed in the United States, especially to fit the extreme beer mold. Generally used as a description for a very strong ale.

Tun

A vessel in which the mash is steeped (mixed with "liquor") during the brewing process.

Urbock

The strongest of bock beers and among the strongest beer in the world.

Urtype

Meaning "original type" in German, this is a term used for a beer that is an authentic interpretation of an established style.

Vienna red/lager

Reddish lager with sweet, malty aroma was the first lager beer brewed in Austria during the 19th century.

Vintage ales

Connoisseur beers that benefit from being cellared, laid down, and left to improve over time, becoming more complex in flavor over the years. The fine port and cognacs of the beer world.

Weiss, weisse

"White" in German, meaning a wheat beer.

Wit, witbier

"White beer" meaning wheat beer, used to describe some Belgian and Dutch beers.

Wheat beer

Beer made from a blend of wheat and barley malt. Also known as "Weizen" (wheat) or "Weiss" (white) in German, "blanche" in French, or "wit" in Dutch and Flemish. Often pale and cloudy in appearance, creamy in texture and sweet on the finish.

Wood-aged beers

Beers stored and aged in wooden rather than metal kegs to add flavor. Scotch whisky, sherry, port, and bourbon barrels have all been used to create beers that are enjoying increased popularity, particularly in the United States, United Kingdom, and Belgium.

Wort

An extract created by the mashing process in brewing, and containing fermentable sugars. It is boiled with hops, then cooled prior to fermentation.

Yeast

A natural fungus that is an active agent in the brewing process, attacking sweet liquids such as wort 'Pac Man'–style, to convert malt sugars into alcohol and carbon dioxide (CO_2).

Yorkshire squares

Square fermenting vessels associated with traditional brewing in Yorkshire, England. Still used at Samuel Smith's brewery and at Black Sheep in Masham, Yorkshire. They are said to produce fine well-balanced beer.

Zoigl beer

An old-fashioned farmhouse lager beer style brewed only by communal breweries in five towns in the Oberpfälz wald region of Germany, close to the Czech Republic border. The towns are: Eslarn, Falkenberg, Mitterteich, Neuhaus, and Windischeschenbach.

Beer directory

BEER BLOGS

The Beernut Blogspot
www.thebeernut.blogspot.com
Dublin-based blog whose tagline is "Made fresh from only four natural ingredients: beer, opinion, travel and unspeakable pubs. Please enjoy responsibly. "

Boak and Bailey's Beer Blog
www.boakandbailey.com
London-based pair who blog about craft beer and food from all over the world, as well as London pubs.

Pete Brown's Blog
www.petebrown.blogspot.com
Beer writer and author of several books about beer, including *Man Walks into a Pub*, *Three Sheets to the Wind* and *Hops and Glory*.

Called to the Bar
www.maltworms.blogspot.com
Adrian Tierney-Jones writes about beer and the countryside.

A Good Beer Blog
www.goodbeerblog
Canadian Alan McLeod's entertaining and informative blog about international beers.

Stonch's Beer Blog
www.stonch.blogspot.com
"Stonch" runs a pub in London's Clerkenwell and blogs daily about beer and running a pub.

Zythophile
zythophile.wordpress.com
Beer historian Martyn Cornell's is the author of *Beer: The Story of a Pint*. His e-book *Amber Gold and Black* is available from this site in electronic format only.

BEER WEBSITES

BELGIUM
Belgian Beer and Travel
www.belgianbeerspecialist.blogs
Belgian Beer Board
www.belgianbeerboard.com
**The Burgundian Babble Belt—
All about Belgian Beer**
www.babblebelt.com
**Podge on Beer:
Podge's Belgian Beer Tours**
www.podgebeer.co.uk

CANADA
www.worldofbeer.com
Canadian Stephen Beaumont is frequently cited as one of the world's leading writers on beer. Author of *The Great Canadian Beer Guide*.

CZECH REPUBLIC
Beer Culture
www.praguemonitor.com/beer
Evan Rail, journalist and beer expert, writes regularly for the *Prague Monitor* on the subject of Czech beer and brewing.

GERMANY
www.europeanbeerguide.net
and
www.germanbeerguide.co.uk
Ron Pattinson is a Netherlands-based expert on German beer and brewing history.

ITALY
www.microbirrifici.org
Online resource of Italian microbreweries.

NORWAY
Knutalbert.wordpress.com
Norwegian blog about brews, pubs, and travel.

JAPAN
www.jibeer.com
Japan-based American duo offering advice about where to find Japanese craft beer.

USA
appellationbeer.com /www.lewbryson.com
Lew Bryson is an East Coast—based beer writer.

Beeradvocate
www.beeradvocate.com
Website devoted to craft beer.

Beer 4 Chicks
www.christinaperozzi.com

Beer Haiku Daily
www.beerhaikudaily.com

Ratebeer
www.ratebeer.com
The best beers in the world by country.

BEER MAGAZINES

Ale Street News
www.alestreetnews.com
Beer newspaper founded in 1992. Also online.

All About Beer
www.allaboutbeer.com

Beer
Quarterly magazine of CAMRA (Campaign for Real Ale), also available online to CAMRA members.

Beer Advocate
www.beeradvocate.com
US-based monthly beer magazine.

Beers of the World Magazine
www.beers-of-the-world.com

Celebrator
www.celebrator.com
Bi-monthly beer magazine with an online presence.

WORLD BEER ORGANIZATIONS

USA
Brewers Association
736 Pearl Street
Boulder
Colorado 80302
USA
Tel + 1 (303) 447 0816
www.beertown.org
Organizers of the annual Great American Beer Festival, held each September in Denver, Colorado.

EUROPEAN BEER CONSUMER'S UNION (EBCU)
European association that promotes craft and quality beer. Its aims are to preserve the European beer culture, promote craft beer, support traditional producers, and represent beer consumers. Members are as follows:

AUSTRIA
BiergIG: Iteressen-Gemeinschaft de Bier-Konsumenten
www.bierig.org

BELGIUM
Zythos VZW
Hoevestraat 30, 3850 Nieuwerkerken
www.zythos.be

CZECH REPUBLIC
Přátel Piva
www.pratelepiva.cz

DENMARK
Danimarca
Danske Ølentusiaster
www.ale.dk

FINLAND
Olutiito
www.olut.org

FRANCE
ATPUP: Association pour L'Union des Biérophiles
Association Atpub
14 rue de Bergues
59000 Lille, France
www.atpub.org

UNITED KINGDOM
Campaign for Real Ale (CAMRA)
230 Hatfield Road
St. Albans
Herts AL1 4LW
Tel: + 44 1727 7998454
www.camra.org.uk
A volunteer-led consumer group which campaigns for the preservation of cask ale and pub-goers' rights. Organizes the annual Great British Beer Festival each August at Earls Court, London.

ITALY
Union Birrai
Via Celoria 2
20133 Milano
Italy
Tel: +39 02 87394893
www.unionbirrai.com
Italian beer consumer's organisation

www.microbirrifici.org
Online resource of Italian microbreweries.

NETHERLANDS
Paesi Bassi
Vereniging Promotie Informatie Traditioneel Bier (PINT)
Postbus 3757
1001 AN Amsterdam
Netherlands
www.pint.nl

NORWAY
Norske Ølvenners Landsforbund (NORØL)
Federation of Norwegian Beer Consumers
Postboks 6567 Etterstad
N-0607 Oslo
Norway
www.nor-ale.org

POLAND
Bractwo Piwne
www.bractwopiwne.pl

SWEDEN
Svezia
Svenska Ölfrämjandet (SÖ)
Stockholm
www.svenskaolframjandet.se

Brewery index

277

"The church is near but the road is icy, the bar is far away but I will walk carefully."

RUSSIAN PROVERB

Beers index

Index

"A fine beer
may be judged
with only one sip,
but it's better to be
thoroughly sure."

CZECH PROVERB

Publisher's acknowledgments

Picture credits

The publisher wishes to thank the many breweries from around the world that kindly provided the images of their beers, beer labels and brewery facilities reproduced here.

Special photography
by Simon Murrell:

Cover image; pages 1-9, 20-29, 50-55, 62-63, 94-95, 177-178, 216-217, 232-233, 242-243, 256-257.

The publisher would also like to thank the following people who helped in the production of this book:
Beers of Europe;
Fuller's Brewery for the loan of beer and glasses for photography;
Rupert Ponsonby of R & R Network;
Riedel and Dartington Glass for the loan of glasses for photography;
Catherine Ball, Bryan Harrell, Mona Mahmoud, Evan Rail and Melissa Smith for picture research.
Siobhan O'Connor for proofreading.

Rick Stein's recipes are reproduced on pages 250-251 with kind permission of BBC Books from the following titles:

Fish and Chips, Gremolata Prawns, Moules Marinière, Shangurro Crab:
Rick Stein's Seafood
published by BBC Books,
hardback £25.00 paperback £15.00;
Monkfish Vindaloo:
Rick Stein's Coast to Coast
published by BBC Books, £20.

Images on pages 250-251 appear courtesy of **RickStein.com**, Padstow, Cornwall.

Images on pages 266-267 appear courtesy of **El Bulli Restaurant**, Spain. The image on page 268 appears courtesy of **Brookyln Brewery**, New York.

The photographs listed below are reproduced from the following titles published by Jacqui Small LLP:

Page 245: Hot Beef Satay with Herbs and Skewered Potatoes from Barbecues by Clare Ferguson, photography by Jeremy Hopley & Martin Brigdale. Page 247: *Top to bottom* Beef Wellington from Steak by Paul Gayler, photography by Peter Cassidy; Oysters on Ice from Fish Cook by Aldo Zilli, photography by David Munns; Mango and Tomato Chutney from Curry by Roopa Gulati, photography by Richard Jung; Red Mullet with Bay Leaves from Fish Cook by Aldo Zilli, photography by David Munns; Strawberry Semi-freddo from Ice Cream by The Tanner Brothers, photography by Peter Cassidy. Page 248: From Fish Cook by Aldo Zilli, photography by David Munns, *Above* Oriental Roast Seabass *Below* Lobster Thermidor. Page 249: *Above* King Prawn Brochettes from Barbecues and Picnics by Clare Ferguson, photography by Peter Cassidy; *Below* Pressed Sushi from Sushi by Emi Kazuko, photography by Gus Filgate. Page 250: Photography from Rick Stein, Cornwall and Sharp's Brewery. Page 252: *Above* Fritas with Cuban Avocado Salsa from Burgers by Paul Gayler, photography by Gus Filgate. *Below* Prime Roast Rib of Beef with Thyme Yorkshire Pudding from Steak by Paul Gayler, photography by Peter Cassidy. Page 253: Wood-grilled T-bone Steak Florentina Style from Steak by Paul Gayler, photography by Peter Cassidy. Page 254: *Above* Caesar Salad from Burgers by Paul Gayler, Photography by Gus Filgate; *Below* Chermoula Burgers with Minted Harissa Salsa and Preserved Lemon and Artichoke Salad from Burgers by Paul Gayler, photography by Gus Filgate. Page 255: *Above* Honey-glazed Roast Barbary Duck from Tools for Cooks by Christine McFadden, photography by David Munns; *Below* Roasted Chicken with Olives, Almonds and Preserved Lemons from Barbecues by Clare Ferguson, photography by Peter Cassidy. Page 258: *Top* Strawberry Sandwich Cake from Small Cakes by Roger Pizey, photography by Sian Irvine; Centre White Chocolate and Mandarin Soup with Spiced Bread from Chocolate by The Tanner brothers, photography by Peter Cassidy; *Bottom* Banana, Dark Chocolate and Pecan Semi-freddo from Ice Cream by The Tanner Brothers, photography by Peter Cassidy. Page 259: Raspberry Sorbet from Ice Cream by The Tanner Brothers, photography by Peter Cassidy. Page 260: *Left* Aubergine Salad with Coriander and Yoghurt from Barbecues by Clare Ferguson, photography by Peter Cassidy; *Right* Lamb Chops with Spinach and Peppercorn from Curry by Roopa Gulati, photography by Richard Jung. Page 261: Potatoes with Cumin from Curry by Roopa Gulati, photography by Richard Jung. Page 262: *Left* Falafel by Sam Clarke from Tools for Cooks by Christine McFadden, photography by David Munns; *Right* Focaccia with Figs and Prosciutto from Steak by Paul Gayler, photography by David Munns. Page 263: *Above* Bresaola from Steak by Paul Gayler, photography by Peter Cassidy; *Below* Small Savoury Lebanese Pastries from Steak by Paul Gayler, photography by David Munns. Page 269: *Top to bottom* Breakfast Steak Hash with Fried Eggs and Black Bean Salsa from Steak by Paul Gayler, photography by Peter Cassidy; Pan-fried Scallops from Fish Cook by Aldo Zilli, photography by David Munns; Carbonara from Cheese by Patricia Michelson, photography by Lisa Linder; Duck Confit with Cannellini Beans from Barbecues and Picnics by Clare Ferguson, photography by David Munns; Colston Bassett Stilton from Cheese by Patricia Michelson, photography by Lisa Linder.

Author's acknowledgments

A special and rather large thanks goes to all of the following:
Mum for her unwavering love, kindness and support; Dad and family for generous guidance and encouragement; Barnaby for being a brilliant big brother and for providing invaluable musical inspiration; Tom, Hattie, and Ned Deards for even more lovely spreads and all-round greatness; the splendid Catherine Hutton for putting up with a humdrum housemate; Matthew, Sonya, and Sophia Dallat for their support; Tom Sandham and Claire Jagot—many thanks for "running" the business in my absence; Eddie and Zoe Gapper; Tessa, Jacques, Alison, and Louis le Bars; James and Diane Amos; James "left side magic" Wheatley; Toby Dormer, Tom Innes; Lovely Lisa; Matt and Debbie Hartley-Fisher; Adam Slate; Dave Curson; whoever invented caffeine; QPR FC; all who play for Nottsborough FC, and, last but not least, Terry and Monkey.

Before I salute the hordes of people who have helped put this book together, I must firstly give my heartfelt thanks to the wonderful Jo Copestick for being a terrific editor. Constantly reducing mountains to molehills, she's been a model of calm, reassurance and unfaltering organization without whom this book would never have been finished and without whom I would no doubt be wearing one of those coats with the arms at the back.
Special thanks must also go to design guru Robin Rout who, despite provocation from an often shambolic writer, kept his patience and humor through all of this.
Hats off to Lesley Felce for keeping hundreds of plates spinning;
Jacqui Small for her encouragement and advice, and photographer Simon Murrell for making beer look beautiful.
I also owe an enormous thanks to the exceptional work undertaken by Catherine Ball, Melissa Smith, and Mona Mahmoud —thank you so much for chasing images all over the world, it's hugely appreciated.

In compiling and writing this book, the sage advice, knowledge, assistance, passion, and guidance of other writers and journalists, beer lovers, bloggers, and brewers was both invaluable and an inspiration. I am indebted to the following for their help, advice, and editorial contributions:
Eddie Baines, Stephen Beaumont, Will Beckett, Fiona Beckett, Jeff "Stonch" Bell, Mikkel Borg Bjergsø, Lew Bryson, Ferrán Centelles at El Bulli, Scott Collins, Emma Currin, Tom Dalldorf, Richard Dinwoodie and Mike Hill from Utobeer, Sean Franklin, Eddie Gershon, Bryan Harrell, Peter Haydon, Alastair Hook, Aubrey Johnson, Julie Johnson, Tony Johnson, Greg Koch, Laurent Mousson, Des Mulcahy, Maryanne Nasiatka, Robert Newland, Garrett Oliver (I promise to stop bothering you now), Ron Pattinson, Rupert Ponsonby and everyone at R&R Teamwork, Evan Rail, Martyn Railton at Euroboozer, Simon Russell, Paul Ruschmann, David Seijas, Rick Stein, Vivienne Taylor, Ted Thomas, Sally Toms, Tim Webb, the online beer blogging community at ratebeer.com and beeradvocate.com… and every brewery in the world that kindly donated beers, glassware, photography, and more.
The first casualty of this book has been my liver, swiftly followed by my short-term memory, so sincere apologies if somehow I have failed to mention you when I should have done.

"There was an Old Man with an owl,
Who continued to bother and howl;
He sat on a rail, and imbibed bitter ale,
Which refreshed that Old Man and his owl."
EDWARD LEAR
ENGLISH ARTIST, WRITER 1812–1888

"Beauty is in the eye
of the beer holder."

ANONYMOUS

288